The Ice Dream Cookbook:

Dairy-free Ice Cream Alternatives
with
Gluten-Free Cookies, Compotes & Sauces

Rachel Albert-Matesz

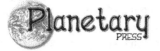

Planetary Press, Phoenix, AZ

The information and suggestions contained in this book are not intended to substitute for appropriate care of a licensed health practitioner. The author and publisher assume no responsibility for your actions or for any unintended effects that may arise.

For information about permission for excerpts, articles, or bulk discounts write to:
Planetary Press, P.O. Box 97040, Phoenix, AZ 85060-7040
Or, call (602) 840-4556, or email: PlanetaryPress@earthlink.net
www.PlanetaryPress.net

ISBN: 978-0-9641267-2-5
Library of Congress Catalog Number: 2008927728

Albert-Matesz, Rachel, 1965-
    The ice dream cookbook : dairy-free ice cream
    alternatives with gluten-free cookies, compotes & sauces
    : 80 delicious & healthy recipes with more than 100
    variations / Rachel Albert-Matesz. -- 1st Planetary
    Press ed.
        p. cm.
        Includes index.
        LCCN 2008927728
        ISBN-13: 978-0-9641267-2-5
        ISBN-10: 0-9641267-2-9

    1. Non-dairy frozen desserts. 2. Milk-free diet--
Recipes. 3. Gluten-free diet--Recipes.   I. Title.

    RM234.5.A43 2008   641.5'63
                                QBI08-858

Editor: Marilyn Glidewell: Bothell, WA, mglidewell2@gmail.com
Cover, interior design, layout: Brenda Weishaar, Aberdeen, SD, dakkid@nvc.net Interior images from clipart.com, all rights reserved
Food styling for cover: Chef J Whiting, Phoenix, AZ, chefj@safe-mail.net
Cover photos: Reed Hamel, RTH Photo, Phoenix, AZ, vashvip9082@yahoo.com
Nutrition Analysis: Linda Redfield, NC, Arcata, CA, linda@holisticselfhealing.org
Indexing: Janet Perlman, Southwest Indexing, jperlman@aol.com

First Planetary Press Edition: October 2008

10 9 8 7 6 5 4 3 2 1

CONTENTS

Also by Rachel Albert-Matesz

The Garden of Eating
Cooking with Rachel

Acknowledgements

I would like to acknowledge and thank everyone who has helped bring this book to life. I have had a wonderful time working on this project, and my joy was enhanced by the resounding support and encouragement I have received from so many people:

To my dear friend, nutrition buddy, and husband for 17 years, Don Matesz, who has inspired me to read, study, learn, and grow personally and professionally.

To Patricia Poggi, Jennifer Vaughan, Heather Crimson, Heather Wolcott, Marsha Tilley, Judy Genova, and JoAnn Brown for their unconditional support and faith in me and my project.

To my recipe testers, who tirelessly tested and sometimes retested recipes until we got them right: Heather Wolcott, Kelli Meechem, Jennifer Dailey, Karlene Blair, Julie Anne Elefante, Andrea Murschel, Heather Crimson, Anita Richesson, Mary Matthews, Stacy Conkle, and LuAnn Brentlinger.

To my team of enthusiastic tasters: Shauna Halawith, The Fishhugger Family (Kenny, Brenna, Zane, and Kaleb Aschbacher), Dana and Kim Blankenship, cooking students too numerous to mention, and of course, Don Matesz.

To Marilyn Glidewell, one of my earliest cooking students who has become a dear friend, and, now, my editor, for her countless hours of work and attention to detail.

To my graphic designer, Brenda Weishaar, for her skillful design and layout of the text and cover, as well as for proofreading and catching typos.

To my food stylist, Chef J Whiting, who taught me cool tricks for making ice cream look fabulous under the lights.

To my photographer, Reed Hamel, for his patience and steadiness, and knowing where to shine the light.

To Linda Redfield for her skill and enthusiasm in calculating the nutritional values for each of the recipes.

To Shauna Halawith of Kitchen Classics, for hosting so many of my cooking classes and allowing me to use her ice cream makers and freezers when my freezer would hold no more.

Finally, many thanks to my indexer, Janet Perlman, for ensuring that we can easily find what we're searching for.

I am deeply grateful to you, dear reader, for supporting me in doing what I love to do: play with food, read, write, and teach.

Acknowledgments

Introduction

The Accidental Ice Cream Maker

I didn't set out to write a frozen dessert book, or any dessert book for that matter. Ten years ago, my friends and cooking students would have nominated me as the most unlikely candidate for writing an ice cream cookbook. I rarely ate ice cream, I certainly didn't own an ice cream maker, and everyone knew I didn't have sugar or other such dessert ingredients in my cupboards. Instead of the usual cookies, cakes, pies, and pastries, my desserts were usually some manner of cooked fruit. I rarely consumed milk products or frozen desserts. That was 1997.

Health Quest

As health guru Bill Phillips (father of the Body for Life Challenge) said in his movie, *Body of Work* (1998), "Half of getting what you want is knowing what you have to give up to get it." In my quest for greater health and relief from the sugar blues, I gave up a lot of things.

I grew up eating a typical American diet of refined and overly-processed foods. On many days, I didn't eat any vegetables at all, unless you count French fries or ketchup. I drank soda pop and artificially-flavored fruit drinks instead of water, ate candy and chewed gum incessantly, and usually ate sugary foods three times a day. This nutritionally deficient diet led to health problems such as cavities, brittle nails, painful constipation, hypoglycemic episodes, acne, PMS, depression, mood swings, painful menstrual periods, and a weight problem.

Betty Baker

My mother never gave me a nickname because she didn't like her own. But if she had, I think Betty (as in Betty Crocker) would have been fitting. As a child prodigy baker, I logged many hours making desserts. I first helped my mother make Toll House Chocolate Chip and Quaker Oatmeal Cookies in first grade. I liked the dough as much as the cookies.

By sixth grade, my mother allowed me to bake anytime I wanted—I didn't need permission or supervision. I started with cookies, cakes, and bars from mixes, and later graduated to back-of-the-box variations, apple crisp, and bundt cakes, and then to baking from scratch. *The Betty Crocker Cookie Book* was my culinary bible. I didn't know a thing about cooking fish, poultry, meat, vegetables, fruits, or whole grains back then.

When my mother had company, it was my job to make dessert. On rainy days, or when I was bored or lonely (we lived 30 minutes outside the city limits in a small town in New Mexico, so I didn't have many playmates nearby), I pulled out the cookbooks and baked. When I had friends over I would often teach them how to bake cookies. Neither of us foresaw my future career in the culinary arts.

I still remember the first and last names of my mother's friends who taught me how to make desserts. I remember which recipes each person showed me how to make, from Rice Krispy Marshmallow Treats, Snickerdoodles, and Brownies to Mississippi Mud Pie, Fudge Marble Cake, Pineapple Poppy Seed Bundt Cake, and French Apple Pie—dishes I've not made in decades.

I remember the name of my seventh and eighth grade French teacher who taught me how to make crepes, beignets (French doughnuts), Peach Melba, and cream puffs, recipes I practiced making at home. In my mid teens, I baked banana and zucchini bread from *The Fannie Farmer Cookbook*, by Marion Cunningham, and made half whole wheat versions of many goodies.

In ninth grade, my dentist, Dr. Harnick, urged me to read *Sugar Blues*, by William Dufty, and *Lick the Sugar Habit*, by Nancy Appleton. He could see that I had a problem with sugar. He had improved his own diet and said he felt much better (he looked better, too), and he wanted to help me do the same. I wanted to give up refined flour, white sugar, and fast food, but I didn't know what else to eat. My recipe repertoire consisted of hard boiled and scrambled eggs, grilled cheese sandwiches, pizza, macaroni and cheese from a box, pancakes from a mix, and a litany of desserts. So, I continued eating a high-fat, low-fiber, dessert-centered diet.

In college, I set about to improve my diet and health. I began to eat regularly scheduled meals and to develop a healthier

Your Sense of Taste

Have you ever eaten something that tasted bland to you, but seemed just right to someone else? Have you ever liked a dish that someone else thought was too spicy or too sweet?

You're not alone. People think the taste is in the food. That's only half right. How a food tastes to you depends on what you're accustomed to eating. Taste is relative.

If you regularly drink soda or other sugared or artificially sweetened beverages, plain water might seem dull and uninteresting. If you eat white bread and white rice, you might find 100% whole wheat bread and brown rice to be heavy, dry, and bland. If you eat conventional sweets, you may find that fresh fruit or baked sweet potatoes don't satisfy your sweet tooth.

Why? If you eat very salty or intensely sweet foods on a daily basis, your taste receptors will down-regulate. Your body shuts off some of your taste receptors because it no longer needs them. Then, if you eat more plain and simple foods, the flavors don't register. The tastes are there, but you can't sense them because your taste receptors have a higher threshold. You need more stimulation—more salt, more sugar, more spice—to notice the flavors.

Let me give you an analogy. If you regularly drink alcohol, you'll have a higher tolerance for it than someone who rarely or never drinks. It takes more booze for you to get a buzz than it does for a nondrinker. We each experience the alcohol differently depending on whether or how much we normally drink. It's the same with foods and flavors. If you decide to reduce or eliminate sugar, it can take 30 to 90 days for your taste receptors to up-regulate so they have greater sensitivity. If you persist, you can reset your taste receptors. I've done it, and I've watched other people do it.

If you want to achieve better health, you have to make choices that meet your body's nutritional needs first, and then have patience while your taste buds catch up. Your body will gradually begin to respond in noticeable ways. In the meantime, you have to use the power of positive intention to retrain your body and mind.

relationship with food and my body. I developed an intense aversion to junk foods and a great fondness (call it a craving) for nourishing whole foods. I finally succeeded in toning down my sweet tooth while satisfying my palate in healthier ways.

Halfway through my freshman year of college, I gave up soda pop and chewing gum. They gave me indigestion, and I'd read about the ill effects of both sugar and artificial sweeteners.

The next year I gave up fast food, including fried food and ice cream, and later, dairy products and refined white flour. I remember trying Tofutti and Ice Bean in college and I enjoyed them as a treat. I tried Rice Dream when it first came out, but I didn't care for the aftertaste.

During my twenties, adherence to a macrobiotic diet and lifestyle relegated even these dairy-free frozen desserts to infrequent use: birthdays, 4th of July, or some other special occasion. After that, I experimented with a Zone-style diet and then a hunter-gatherer (or paleo) diet, which excluded such treats.

I once went three months without eating any fruit or concentrated sweeteners—no sugar, rice syrup, barley malt, honey, molasses, or maple syrup. This really helped tone down my sweet tooth. After that, a juicy peach was a satisfying treat. I now have less of a sweet tooth than during my childhood and young adult years, and I derive far more pleasure from simple treats such as sweet vegetables, fruit, nuts, and occasional low-sugar desserts. I enjoy eating as much as ever, but I now prefer foods that nourish my body on a daily and meal-by-meal basis even when I want a treat. If you would like to read the whole story of how I got into natural foods, you can visit my blog at TheHealthyCookingCoach.com.

I changed my tastes, and you can change yours, too. It's a matter of choice. Each of us can, at any time, choose good health; we can choose not to let junk foods undermine our health. Our thoughts become our habits, so each time we choose healthy foods, we are changing our habits for the better. In time, the mental picture of what we want to eat will change. Tune out the advertisements and false promises for instant gratification with the latest food or drink. Trust that only whole foods can bring lasting good health

and the happiness that goes along with it. Eventually, all those overly-processed, health-robbing treats you thought you couldn't live without will become a thing of the past—you will no longer care about them. Wholesome, natural foods will take their place in your mind, in your home, and on your plate.

The Path to Health

During my late teens, I became interested in the macrobiotic approach to diet and health. After graduating from college with a liberal arts degree, I packed my bags and flew off to London, England to study special cooking techniques at the Kushi Institute of Great Britain. Armed with new skills and inspiration, I then began my career as a nutrition educator and cooking instructor. Although I had very little experience in this area, I had enthusiasm, and a keen desire to help others.

I hosted weekly dinners and cooking classes and monthly potlucks in my little apartment. I taught cooking classes for a local chain of health foods co-ops and ran a small macrobiotic take-out service. I wrote two cookbooks, and self published one of them. I opened and operated Rachel's Natural Foods Café in Seattle, Washington. Through all of these activities, I taught the principles of balance as I shared my passion for beautifully prepared whole foods.

After 12 years, nearly nine of them as a vegan (dairy-free vegetarian), I began to feel that I had stalled, and perhaps even reversed, my journey to health. It was during this period that I met and fell in love with Don. We eventually married, and I now had a partner who shared my interest in whole foods and my commitment to better health.

Dissatisfied with the macrobiotic approach, together, Don and I adopted a dairy-free, omnivorous whole foods diet. Don's ongoing studies led him to become a nutritionist, an herbalist, and finally, an acupuncturist. In more than 20 years together, Don and I have rarely eaten commercial ice cream. On a few—and I mean *rare*—special occasions, we carefully sought out the best quality ice cream that was available. Writing a book about frozen desserts was hardly on my radar screen at that time.

How to Change Your Tastes & Preferences

Occasionally, someone will say that they don't like the taste of some of the natural foods I recommend. Realize that your tastes are not engraved in stone for eternity, but are habits that will often change when you establish new habits. In fact, although your taste buds might appear to prefer processed foods, your body certainly does not. Your body prefers foods that have real flavors that come with high nutrient content.

The problem is that due to the influence of advertising, the conditioning and habits of families, and possibly misinformation, your taste buds have fallen out of harmony with your body. So, remember, it's your taste buds and your brain that must be trained to accept natural foods. If you practice eating natural foods, you will grow to like them so much that you may never want anything else.

Unfamiliar foods are like strangers. You don't know them, and, unless you're an adventurous eater, you may feel suspicious of them. When you or your family tries a new food for the first time, try at least three mouthfuls. Do this for at least three days in a row and then try at least three different recipes using the same food. If that seems too difficult, then every time you try a new food, eat at least three mouthfuls, try the food at least three days in a row, and then try the food again in at least two more recipes, eaten at least three times.

Yes, I did just repeat myself! The only way to change your habits is through repetition. If you want better health, you have to make choices that meet your body's nutritional needs. Some things will be unfamiliar at first, but your body will eventually thank you for making the change.

A Fork (or was it a Spoon?) in the Road

I would have continued to abstain from ice cream and I might never have come up with the recipes for this book had it not been for an acquaintance named Tracy. She suffered from hypoglycemia and she was trying to lick (I mean kick) the sugar—and ice cream—habit. Whoever gave her an ice cream maker for Christmas knew how much she and her husband loved frosty, frozen desserts. That was January of 1999.

I assured Tracy that I could come up with a delicious, nutritious, lower-sugar, preservative-free, and even protein-rich ice cream. Don and I had many years of recipe development under our belts. Since we'd experimented with various whole foods diets, including vegan, vegetarian, macrobiotic, low-fat, no-fat, dairy-free, gluten-free, and omnivorous diets, we were both adept at modifying and writing up new recipes that came out great the first time—without endless testing! I welcomed the challenge of creating healthier ice cream recipes that she and my cooking students would enjoy.

I borrowed Tracy's instruction manual, checked out some books from the library, and then set to work drafting a couple of recipes. The first two, chocolate and vanilla, were made with real cream. (It was Tracy's choice and Tracy's ice cream maker.) I added vanilla whey protein and an herbal supplement called stevia that has a strong sweet taste. (You'll learn more about stevia in Chapter 1.) The idea was to create a blood sugar- and hormone-balancing, immune-boosting dish that would make a healthy between-meal snack.

New recipe in hand, Tracy and I whipped up the first two prototypes. Hard at work in our home laboratory, we tasted, adjusted the mix, and jotted down our notes before freezing. The results were rich, creamy, delightful, and mouth-watering. We used no refined sugar, additives, preservatives, trans fats, or artificial flavorings. Later, when I borrowed Tracy's ice cream maker, I replaced the cream with coconut milk—it contains half the fat and calories and it's dairy-free. I had already been using coconut milk in smoothies, frosty fruit whips, and puddings. Since Don and I weren't using dairy products at that time, I was curious to see how well the coconut would fill in for cream.

Once I got Tracy started, I shared the two frozen dessert recipes with a few friends who were inspired enough to rush out and buy ice cream makers and were ready to give up their conventional ice cream. Yay! Later, I borrowed an ice cream maker from one of these early converts. I replaced the whey protein with egg white protein to create a completely dairy-free frozen dessert. Later, I reformulated the mix to exclude the egg white protein because I wasn't satisfied with the amount of processing these products went through and because they unnecessarily increased the cost of the recipes.

An American Obsession

According to a report by the international market analyst, Euromonitor, Americans lead the world in ice cream consumption, eating six times as much ice cream as any other nation in the world. In 1990, per capita ice cream consumption in America was 23 quarts, almost six gallons per person per year. Figures for ice milk consumption are similar. Frozen yogurt, sorbet, and sherbet have always been the caboose of the frozen dessert market, although they have risen in recent years as a result of the low fat craze. If you don't eat ice cream, or rarely indulge in it, you may be wondering who's been eating yours.

Baskin-Robbins reportedly develops one new flavor per month. At last count, they had concocted more than 1,000 flavors.

http://www.baskinrobbins.com/About/OurHistory.aspx.

What's On Your Shopping List?

Because ice cream had not been on our shopping list or in our freezer for more than a decade (and more than 20 years at the time of this writing), I was out of touch with just how much and how often most Americans were eating ice cream. So, I was surprised to learn how excited my friends and cooking students were when I told them about the recipes I had created. I knew I was onto something when they practically begged me for the recipes.

I relented. A year and a half after creating the first two flavors of what I called Better Balanced Ice Cream, I ordered several ice cream makers. A few weeks later, one hand-crank and two electric ice cream makers appeared on our doorstep. Later, I acquired two more.

Over the next few months, I wrote and tested a dozen recipes and used them in a series of cooking classes. I sketched out ideas for the first couple of chapters for a new book. Meanwhile, Don and I enjoyed the treats that summer as they provided welcome relief from the humid Midwestern summer in a house with no air conditioning. (It was hot enough in our kitchen to turn my raisins alcoholic!) Still, I did not yet see the full potential for my discovery.

Well, actually I did see the potential. It's just that my teaching had been

How Much Ice Cream Are We Eating?

U.S. per capita consumption of ice cream reached an all-time high of 23 pounds (more than 20 quarts or 5 gallons per person) in 1946 as America celebrated its World War II victory and sugar rationing was lifted. From 1949 through 1987, per capita ice cream consumption remained relatively constant in the U.S. As more prepackaged ice cream was sold through supermarkets, traditional ice cream parlors and soda fountains started to disappear. Also, during this period, average consumption of other frozen dairy products, such as sherbet and reduced-fat ice cream, increased. Since 1988, Americans, on average, have been eating a little less ice cream overall, but consumption of the higher priced, higher milk fat, premium and super premium ice creams, as well as frozen yogurt and other frozen dairy products, has increased.

Source: U.S. Department of Agriculture (USDA).

centered around helping people get the essential whole foods into their diets, and I had mixed feelings about encouraging the consumption of frozen desserts. Because of Don's involvement in Traditional Chinese Medicine, I was regularly reminded that cold foods could be detrimental to health (see What's Wrong with Frozen Foods, page xv), and I was reluctant to promote them. I shelved my idea. However, as I continued to work with my students, it became increasingly clear to me that people were not going to give up their frozen desserts--they were here to stay. Finally, I could no longer contain my excitement. I had something to offer that was far better than the commercial frozen desserts that most people were eating. I knew it was time to dust off the recipes and rev up the ice cream makers.

On the Move

In December of 2003, Don and I moved from Toledo, Ohio, to Phoenix, Arizona, a city that could easily be the ice cream capital of the United States. I made my chocolate and vanilla frozen desserts in a few cooking classes and people loved them. By then I was busy finishing and, then later, promoting our book, *The Garden of Eating: A Produce-Dominated Diet and Cookbook*. I didn't have the time and energy to develop enough recipes for a frozen dessert book.

Dessert or Desert?

During our first and second summers in Arizona, I put more thought into turning my ideas into a book. As Don was getting closer to completing his master's degree in acupuncture and herbal medicine, I was thinking about frozen desserts. How could I not when the temperature was hitting 100, 105, and 116 degrees outside and I was surrounded by people who had ice cream on their minds and in their freezers.

Chilling Out

Many of my clients and students consumed ice cream or dairy-free alternatives throughout the year. Many of them were trying to get their family members to warm up to the idea of eating healthy foods and to wean themselves off of overly processed, packaged, and artificial foods.

I wanted to help my students and their families ease the transition, and I figured they'd be much better off eating my lower-sugar, lower-fat, immune-enhancing coconut frozen desserts than conventional ice cream made from hormone-laced milk, sweetened with high-fructose corn syrup, and modified with hydrogenated fats. Finally, during the summer of 2007, I transferred my book idea from the freezer to the front burner. I pulled out the files and recipes I'd previously created. I began collecting ice cream cookbooks. Then I began writing, testing, and tweaking recipes and sharing them with my cooking students, clients, assistants, and acquaintances.

The Birth of The Ice Dream Cookbook

Since my recipes don't contain cream, the term "ice cream" seemed out of place. The

According to some estimates, **more than 90%** of households in the United States consume ice cream and related frozen desserts.

"Total U.S. production of ice cream and related frozen desserts in 2004 amounted to about **1.6 billion gallons**, translating to about 21.5 quarts [a little more than 5 gallons] per person."

Source: *U.S. Department of Agriculture (USDA).*

"Americans are consuming about 6 gallons of ice cream per person — roughly **19,200 calories**, for those who are counting," says Gordon T. Anderson, CNN/ Money staff writer (July 29, 2005: 9:44 AM EDT, CNN.com).

market already had Rice Dream, Ice Bean, and Soy Dream. I met people who were dissatisfied with the flavor or the ingredients in these dairy-free options. They dreamed of something better. I finally settled on calling my creation Ice Dream.

Reading ice cream books helped me dream up more flavors and further affirmed the name I had chosen. Next, I came up with ideas for accompaniments: cookies, ice cream sandwiches, sauces, and ice cream-like pies. I had eaten my share of ice cream as a child. I celebrated many birthdays in ice cream parlors with ice cream and cake. I worked in an ice cream parlor during my sophomore year of high school. I knew ice cream. All I needed was a nudge, and I became Betty Baker once again. But this time, I had added a healthier twist to my recipes, and I had helpers.

Kitchen Help

Forward to the summer of 2007. To get my Ice Dream Cookbook ready for publication by the next summer, I knew I would need help. I enlisted the aid of some of my cooking students and assistants who were eager to help test and taste my new recipes. They agreed to follow my recipes to the letter, take notes, and share the finished products (but not the recipes) with their families, friends, and co-workers. We'd get instant feedback. The Ice Dream testing went smoothly. Most of the recipes required only one run-through—two at most. Some, I repeated for cooking classes.

Recipe Makeovers

The cookie recipes were tested and retested—often 3 or 4 times each—and numerous revisions were made along the way. Not only was I making them free of refined sugar and lower in fat and overall sugar than conventional recipes, I was making them wheat-free and gluten-free. Many of my students and clients, or their children, suffer from food intolerances, including celiac sprue (CD), a severe gluten-intolerance, or from gluten-sensitivity, an earlier progression of the same disorder. It took a lot of trial and error to finally come up with these delicious, kid-tested and kid-approved recipes.

While I don't suffer from celiac disease myself, I sympathize with people who do. In

What's Wrong With Frozen Foods?

According to the view taken by ancient and modern practitioners of traditional Chinese medicine, your digestive system works like a fire. A fire functions best and burns more cleanly when fed with warm, dry wood. Put too much wood or cold, wet logs on a fire and you will dampen or extinguish it. Ditto for your digestive system.

Cold, iced, or frozen foods interfere with digestion by lowering the temperature of the digestive tract to levels where enzymes do not function efficiently. They also reduce blood flow to the intestines, cause blood to coagulate, and steal heat, a form of vital energy, from the whole body which you may not notice if the environment is very hot or you have a hot condition or constitution.

Chinese medical guidelines for enhancing digestion suggest that we eat mostly foods that are neutral to slightly warm in nature and cooked, as this helps to maintain the body's naturally tropical temperature of 98.6 degrees Fahrenheit, or 37 degrees Centigrade. From this perspective, the occasional frozen treat taken in warm weather usually has no serious consequences.

However, excessive consumption of cold foods, especially in cold weather, along with a nutritionally inadequate diet, could injure the digestive organs, depress metabolism, aggravate stiffness, and promote menstrual disorders. Obesity, formation of abdominal clots, cysts, and even tumors could also result from too much cold food. Use this information and awareness of your own condition to guide to you in how much to indulge in frozen desserts.

my mid-twenties, I went through a period when eating wheat or corn would make my face and ears flush red. I often felt sleepy and sluggish, and I experienced other side effects as well. So, for a period of time, I had to avoid these and certain other offending foods so that I could heal. Fortunately, I

Do You Have Undiagnosed Gluten Sensitivity?

We may have an epidemic of undiagnosed gluten sensitivity. Although celiac disease was once assumed to be rare, 21st century studies show that the combined rates of full-blown and silent celiac disease may exceed 1% in Western countries and around the world.

According to transcripts of a lecture given by Kenneth Fine, M.D., to the Greater Louisville Celiac Sprue Support Group, June 2003, 42 percent of Americans have genes for gluten sensitivity. The combined rates of delayed allergies to wheat gliadin range from very mild to very severe and may afflict as many as 29 percent of people in the United States. Gluten sensitivity may also be a factor in at least 77 percent of all cases of autoimmune disease.

42% of Americans have genes for gluten sensitivity

The article, *Just How Common is Celiac Disease and Gluten Intolerance, Anyway?* (found at http://members.cox.net/hal.kraus/gluten/prevalence.htm at 3 pm on March 1st of 2008) discusses Dr. Fine's findings:

"Dr. Fine developed a test program based on the idea that t h e highest concentrations of gliadin anti-bodies should be found where the body had the greatest exposure to gliadin, that is, inside the intestines. Rather than testing in the blood where 'only' 11% of Americans have anti-gliadin antibodies (AGA), he tests the stool where he has learned that actually 29% of Americans have anti-gliadin antibodies. This means that three decades of research missed most of the cases of gluten sensitivity in their screenings! This also means more than 1 in 4 Americans have some delayed allergic reaction to wheat, barley, and rye! Yes, a large portion of those people will have only mild reactions for most of their lives, but this still suggests that tens of millions of Americans will slowly develop many unnecessary chronic illnesses over the years and will consume expensive medical treatments and large quantities of immunosuppressant drugs unless they consider removing the allergen from their diet.

"If you or relatives have chronic or nagging symptoms, and no cause for them except 'genetics' or 'irritable bowel,' or you are told 'it's just stress,' get your stools tested or try a two to three week gluten-free holiday, or both. If you can, find any doctor or friend to support you and not try to tell you 'it's just your imagination.' Study up – the more you know about the Gluten Free Diet *before* you start, the better your chances are of having a good result."

Here is a place to get tested: http://www.enterolab.com/

For a copy of the transcript mentioned above visit:
http://www.finerhealth.com/Essay/

did recover, but I know what it feels like to have to cut out some of my favorite familiar foods.

Avoiding gluten is not easy. Wheat and wheat products are common ingredients in many packaged and processed foods, and they are used in the preparation of a wide variety of dishes. Wheat and gluten can be hard to spot because they are hidden under many aliases. For more on this, refer to the Appendix.

When I set out to write this book, I wanted to make recipes that would suit people with food allergies and intolerances, yet taste so good that their family and friends would also want to eat and enjoy them.

Formula for Success

Once we got the cookies down to a science, the rest was easy. Ice Dream pies, cakes, and silky-smooth sauces—the more we shared, the more excitement we generated. People I knew, and some I didn't, started asking how and when they could order copies of the book. When they found out that it hadn't yet been finished or published, they wanted their names on a list. I began to demonstrate some of the recipes in my cooking classes. I found that even those uninitiated in the ways of healthy eating, seemed to love the cookies,

What is Celiac Sprue? The short answer

Celiac sprue (also called celiac disease or CD) is an inherited food intolerance characterized by sensitivity to gluten, a protein found in wheat, barley, rye, and triticale. The disease affects both children and adults with symptoms precipitated by eating gluten-containing foods.

Symptoms of CD can vary but may include one or more of the following:
Gas
Recurring abdominal bloating and pain
Chronic diarrhea
Constipation
Pale, foul-smelling, or fatty stool
Weight loss/weight gain
Fatigue
Unexplained anemia (a low count of red blood cells causing fatigue)
Bone or joint pain
Osteoporosis, osteopenia
Behavioral changes
Tingling numbness in the legs (from nerve damage)
Muscle cramps
Seizures
Missed menstrual periods (often because of excessive weight loss)
Infertility, recurrent miscarriage
Delayed growth
Failure to thrive in infants
Pale sores inside the mouth, called aphthous ulcers
Tooth discoloration or loss of enamel
Itchy skin rash called dermatitis herpetiformis

Source for symptoms above: The National Digestive Diseases Information Clearinghouse (NDDIC) found online at the following address:
http://digestive.niddk.nih.gov/ddiseases/pubs/celiac/#1

Note: Some people with celiac disease have no symptoms. These people are still at risk for complications which could include malnutrition, osteoporosis, seizures, cancer, and other disorders. The longer someone goes undiagnosed and untreated, the greater the risk of developing malnutrition and other complications.

Celiac disease may be one of the most underdiagnosed disorders, in part because its symptoms are easily and frequently attributed to other health problems. Very few doctors and health practitioners know much about celiac, and very few laboratories in the U. S. have experience and skill in testing for the disease. To further complicate matters, many doctors pooh-pooh their patients' requests to be tested for celiac disease because they think it is so rare and unlikely.

To find out more about gluten sensitivity and celiac disease and to request the right tests, see Appendix C.

especially the soft cake-like texture, as much as the health enthusiasts. The frozen desserts were a big hit everywhere I went. Almost everyone loved them; the exceptions were a rare few who said they didn't like the taste of coconut or who were set on eating only the sweetest of sweets.

Sweet Success

I was relieved to find that people who previously didn't think they liked stevia (because they'd used too much and experienced a bitter aftertaste), said they couldn't taste stevia in my recipes. (I'll teach you how to use this sweet herb skillfully when we get to the Ingredients and Techniques sections.) A few super-tasters detected stevia in some of the recipes, but most did not. Minor detection didn't bother me, and it probably won't bother you once you learn more about stevia's benefits and sugar's ill effects. They loved the desserts and were amazed to learn that they were low in sugar and fat and could still taste so good. It seemed the dream had come true.

Dessert Delivery

My friends would show up with batches of cookies, brownies, or Ice Dream they had tested for me. I'd give them samples of what I'd made that week. Over an eight month period, Don and I ate more frozen desserts, cookies, and sweet sauces than we'd eaten over the previous 15 years. But we didn't eat the treats every day and we didn't gain weight. Our secret to staying slim was that we always gave away more than we ate. Sometimes we had six different flavors in the freezer at one time and some of them sat for four, five, six, or even eight weeks at a time, which was actually a good thing because it allowed me to see how well they withstood the test of time in the freezer.

Whenever we went to our friends' homes for dinner, I brought dessert. When they came to our house, I served what I had on hand. When my girlfriends took me out for my birthday, we went back to my house for—you guessed it—Ice Dream and cookies. I made Ice Dream deliveries to a few friends and sampled them out in cooking classes even when I didn't have them on the menu. I watched for the smiles, oohs, ahhs, and requests for the recipes. I knew it was time for the dream to come true.

Warming Up to Ice Dream

When Don told people he felt tired of having to taste some of every Ice Dream flavor my assistants and I made, they didn't get it. They thought he was lucky. He thought he was doing his digestive system a disservice. When the weather turned cold, we both noticed that our frequent Ice Dream indulgences had dampened our digestive fires. I figured it was for a good cause, all in the line of service. With a Chinese medicine balancing act, we were able to ameliorate the effects with some warming ginger and cinnamon tea and a temporary break from eating Ice Dream.

Although I don't eat Ice Dream every day, or even every week, I enjoy it immensely and I can't think of any commercial frozen dessert that can compare with my homemade Ice Dream. I encourage you to enjoy the Ice Dream recipes in moderation and, especially, to limit consumption during cold weather if you suffer from weak digestion or if you are recovering from a serious health problem. The fruit compotes, poached pears, and fruit sauces, taste great when warmed. We enjoy them throughout the year. And the cookies make a wonderful treat served with a cup of Teeccino or my Roasted Chicory & Dandelion Root Coffee Alternative.

Bon appetite and good health,

Chef Rachel

Chef Rachel

About the Recipes and Nutrition Analysis

Ingredients are listed in the order in which they are called for in recipes. Ingredients within a group, e.g., sweeteners, milk alternatives, and fats and oils, are listed in order of preference in terms of nutritional value, taste, or texture with the author's favorite item listed first, such as honey or agave nectar with honey being the first choice.

The nutritional analysis following each recipe is calculated using the master recipe without optional ingredients. Where you see a range for the amount of an ingredient, such as 1/4 to 1/3 cup honey, nutrition breakdowns have been calculated for the smallest amount. Where there is a range for the number of servings a recipe yields, such as 8 to 10 servings, calculations were made on the smallest number.

The analyses were performed using the computer program Recipe Calc.v4.0 by Mark Muller, 2000. Additional data came from Nutrition Facts searches on the net, The Daily Plate.com, and Nutrition Data.com, Nutritive Value of American Foods USDA Handbook no. 456, 1975, The Complete Book of Food Counts by Corinne T. Netzer, and from product manufacturers (see Appendix A for Resources).

OVEN TEMPERATURE CONVERSIONS & METRIC CONVERSIONS

Farenheit (°F)	Celcius (°C)
32°F	0°C
40°F	4°C
140°F	60°C
150°F	65°C
160°F	70°C
170°F	75°C
212°F	100°C
275°F	135°C
300°F	150°C
325°F	165°C
350°F	175°C
400°F	200°C
425°F	205°C
450°F	230°C
500°F	260°C

U.S. Customary	Approximate Metric Conversion (ml)
1/8 teaspoon	0.5 ml
1/4 teaspoon	1.0 ml
1/2 teaspoon	2.5 ml
1 teaspoon	5.0 ml
1 tablespoon (3 teaspoons)	15.0 ml
1/4 cup (4 tablespoons)	60.0 ml
1/3 cup (5 1/3 teaspoons)	79.0 ml
1/2 cup (8 tablespoons)	118.0 ml
3/4 cup (12 tablespoons)	177.0 ml
1 cup (16 tablespoons)	237.0 ml

chapter 1

Essential Ingredients & Shopping Tips

Y ou may be wondering why anyone would devote an entire book to promoting the use of coconut, coconut milk, coconut oil, and recipes that are free of wheat and refined sugar. Maybe you've been drinking milk and eating ice cream, sugar, and wheat all your life and you wonder why you should stop now.

There are many compelling arguments for weaning yourself from cow's milk, even high quality dairy products. Equally strong evidence supports reduction or elimination of refined sugar, wheat, and other gluten-containing grains from your diet. Whether you eliminate these foods entirely or simply cut back on them, will depend upon your particular health condition, whether you have food allergies or intolerances, and the particular path to health you choose.

I'll hit on some highlights and then show you the wonderful alternatives I've discovered for making healthier versions of popular desserts. To learn more about the ideas presented in this chapter, refer to *The Garden of Eating: A Produce-Dominated Diet & Cookbook,* my previously published book, which I co-authored with my husband, Don Matesz, an herbalist, licensed acupuncturist, and nutrition instructor. It is available at www.TheGardenOfEatingDiet.com. For additional reading, please consult the recommended reading list in the Appendix for books and web sites.

Allergies by the Dozen

Cow's milk protein contains more than 25 different peptides that may induce allergic reactions in humans. Cow's milk is the most common cause of allergies among infants, and research indicates that cow's milk protein can act as a diabetogen (inducer of diabetes) if given to infants. Consumption of cow's milk has also been linked to lymphoma and, via autoimmune reactions, to rheumatoid arthritis and irritable bowel syndrome (IBS).

Dairy linked disorders most commonly appear in the digestive, respiratory, circulatory, nervous, and immune systems. Pasteurized cow's milk has been linked to sudden infant death syndrome, intestinal bleeding, infant anemia, allergies, asthma, heart disease, several cancers (breast, ovarian, prostate), Type I diabetes, criminal behavior, multiple sclerosis, rheumatoid arthritis, schizophrenia, and osteoporosis.

Modern Milk Production Gone Awry

Modern milk production is a world apart from traditional herding. You might have an image of contented cows grazing freely on a family farm, but in fact, most modern dairy cows stand around on concrete pads in corporate owned confinement dairies where they are implanted with synthetic hormones, dosed with antibiotics, and fed an artificial grain diet.

Hormones are used to force these confined cows to produce abnormal amounts of milk. In the 1940s, a cow was productive if she gave 4500 pounds of milk per lactation. Today's force-fed and drugged cows produce a whopping 17,000 pounds of milk each, 20 times more than is needed to feed a calf. When a cow is forced to produce this volume, her milk has fewer nutrients, so each cup you drink is less nutritious.

Pastured Cows, Pastured Milk

The milk used by healthy primitive groups came from animals raised entirely on pasture and hay, with no grain or hormones. That kind of milk is much healthier than mass-marketed milk, which is sorely deficient in several good fats.

Milk from exclusively grass-fed cows has three times more omega-3 essential fatty acids, which are beneficial for the vascular and nervous systems. Such milk also contains five times more conjugated linoleic acid (CLA), a fat that may help humans burn body fat, build muscle, and prevent cancer. Milk from completely grass-fed cows is also much higher in vitamin A, carotenes, vitamin E, and other antioxidants—all because grass provides nutrients not found in grains.

Modern milk processing has more side effects. Pasteurization involves heating milk to only 145° F (62° C) for 30 minutes or 161° F (72° C) for 15 seconds. This fails to destroy all microbes and only partially denatures the milk's protein. When this altered protein contacts stomach acid, it forms a gluey mass that is very difficult to digest.

If you choose to use animal milk, cheese, yogurt, or butter, seek out raw milk products from pasture-fed cows purchased from as close to home as possible. Local is logical. Supporting small, local dairies will provide a safer, more nutritious, and more ecological food supply. Seek out products labeled rBGH free (the cows were not fed recombinant bovine growth hormone).

Top 10 Most Common Food Allergens

1. Nuts
2. Eggs
3. Milk
4. Soybeans
5. Wheat
6. Peanuts
7. Chicken
8. Fish
9. Shellfish
10. Mollusks

91% percent of adverse reactions in children are triggered by four major foods:

1. Nuts (43%)
2. Eggs (21%)
3. Milk (18%)
4. Soy (9%)

Source: *Life Span Nutrition—Conception Through Life* by Sharon Rady Rolfes, Linda Kelly DeBruyne, and Eleanor Noss Whitney. St. Paul: West Publishing Company, 1990.

What about Sucanat and Raw Sugar?

Nutritionally speaking, sucanat (evaporated cane juice), turbinado sugar, and raw cane sugar don't differ much from refined white sugar. Yes, some versions contain more minerals and trace elements than table sugar, but the amount is so minimal that it doesn't contribute a significant amount to your nutritional bank account.

I don't buy these products and I rarely consume them. Although I do buy bittersweet dark chocolate with a high cocoa content and a lower sugar content than other chocolates, I don't make this a daily indulgence. I prefer to use a smaller amount of honey, agave nectar, maple syrup, or rice syrup paired with dried dates, raisins, bananas, and/or stevia. This reduces the total amount of sugar and calories and the stress on my immune system.

More Dangers in the Dairy

Homogenization reduces the size of the milk's fat globules, rendering them more readily absorbed, which then facilitates absorption of an enzyme, xanthine oxidase (XO), suspected of damaging arteries. Why do processors do this? They want to even out the consistency of milk, preventing separation of the fat. This process doesn't make it healthier. Removing fat from milk (fractionation) also removes its fat-soluble vitamins and co-factors required for assimilation of its minerals, making the milk less healthful.

Most people have at least some difficulty digesting unmodified (non-fermented) milk. This is especially true of people who were not breast fed for at least 12 months or were given unmodified cow's milk as infants. In cultures where milk is used as a primary food, it is almost invariably prepared by fermentation to make products such as yogurt, kefir, and koumiss. The fermentation predigests milk proteins and milk sugars, so they are less likely to cause discomfort or disease.

Many people have difficulty digesting even the best quality raw, grass-fed, and fermented milk products. Others who may not suffer digestive problems from consuming milk may still experience sinus congestion, skin rashes, allergies, asthma, arthritis, or other immune system disorders associated with milk products.

Don't worry if you can't tolerate any animal milk products. Humans don't require non-human milk to be healthy. You can get everything you need from other foods.

For full references and to read more on this subject, refer to **The Garden of Eating: A Produce-Dominated Diet & Cookbook** (**www.TheGardenOfEatingDiet.com**).

THE SCARY SIDE OF SUGAR

Sugar Blues

There are many good reasons to reduce your sugar consumption. When you want a boost of sweetness beyond what you'd get from fresh or dried fruit and sweet vegetables, using higher quality sweeteners makes sense for a lot of reasons.

Isolated sugar, whatever the form—sucrose, fructose, honey, corn syrup, high fructose barley malt, rice syrup, maple syrup, or any other—provides empty calories, meaning calories that provide virtually no vitamins, minerals, or other essential nutrients in any significant amount. Why does this matter? Because careful studies have shown that when lab animals are fed sugar-rich foods, especially sugar-rich fluids such as soda, they develop voracious appetites and become extremely obese. Studies also show a direct link between increased sugar consumption and increased rates of disease.

Suicide by Sugar

Prior to the industrial revolution, people regularly obtained sugar in the natural whole food forms of vegetables and fruits, and infrequently had small amounts of raw honey. They didn't have the abundant sources of isolated sugar available today.

Nowadays, half of all carbohydrate calories consumed by the average American come from simple sugars. Compare this to 200 years ago when the per capita sugar consumption was less than 10 pounds per year.

But isn't sugar natural? Don't we need it? Carbohydrates from whole foods provide essential nutrients. Sugar does not. We have absolutely no physiological requirement for sugar. All our nutritional needs can be met

3

The Scary Side of Soda

Soft drinks may seem innocuous. Most people drink them without thinking about the consequences. That's what marketers want. That's what pads their pockets.

Less than five percent of the world's population lives in the United States, yet we lead the world in soda consumption. In 1999 the U.S. accounted for one-third of the world's total soda consumption. Soda is the most popular drink among Americans, who drank an average of 211 liters (1 liter is approximately 1 quart) of it in 1999, compared to only 109 liters (or quarts) of tap water.

U.S. soda consumption doubled between 1970 and 1999. Teenagers today consume more soft drinks than any previous generation. They also drink 40% less milk and less fruit juice than previous generations.

The average 12-ounce can of soda contains a whopping 10 teaspoons of sugar (usually in the form of high fructose corn syrup). The average 20-ounce bottle of soda contains 17 teaspoons of sugar—5 teaspoons more than the USDA's recommended daily upper limit for sugar consumption for the average person.

Unlike juice, which contains vitamins and minerals, soda consists of carbonated water, sweeteners, flavoring, and in many cases, caffeine. Consumption of these calorie-laden, nutritionally devoid drinks displaces healthier foods and contributes to dietary deficiencies and disease.

Have you wondered why one-third of Americans are now clinically obese? Obesity among children in the U.S. increased by 100% between 1980 and 1994. Obesity increases your risk of developing diabetes, heart disease, and certain cancers.

Research published in the Lancet showed that one soda pop or sugared fruit drink per day could more than double your child's chances of becoming obese. Researchers at Boston's Children's Hospital found that every sugared soft drink consumed daily increased a child's Body Mass Index (BMI) regardless of how much the child exercised. Calculating BMI is a way to measure for obesity.

A Harvard School of Public Health study linked soda consumption with obesity in adults. Looking at tens of thousands of female nurses over eight years, researchers found that women who increased their consumption of soft drinks from less than one a week to one a day *gained* an average of 18 pounds. Researchers also that found women who consumed soft drinks daily had twice the risk of diabetes as those who drank little or no soda.

in full without taking a single spoonful of white, brown, raw, or powdered sugar, corn syrup, or other concentrated sweeteners.

What's Wrong with Sugar?

Researchers have found that ingesting sugar increases the rate at which we excrete calcium, while it upsets the body's calcium to phosphorus ratio. While some people point the finger at protein as the villain that puts us at risk for osteoporosis, sugar may be the real culprit.

Sugar disarms the phagocytes, or Pac-Man-like white blood cells of the immune system, decreasing their ability to engulf bacteria and fight off invaders.

Cancer cells and tumors also feed on sugar. So the more sugar you eat, the more fuel you have to feed the growth of cancer, as wall as pathogenic bacteria, viruses, and microbes. A high sugar diet also increases insulin output, which triggers the production of a series of prostaglandins (prohormone-like substances) that incite the growth of cancer cells. Tumors do not and cannot feed on fat or protein.

Excessive consumption of refined sugar has been linked to dental decay, heart disease, Type II diabetes, lung and stomach cancers, several female cancers, hyperactivity, osteoporosis, premenstrual disorder, immune suppression, digestive disorders, and many other ailments.

Pseudonyms for Sugar

A large portion of the sugar we eat is hidden. Many canned, bottled, frozen, packaged and processed foods contain sugar as the third most plentiful ingredient. Ingredient lists on packages are required to list ingredients in the order in which they appear in products, so the higher up on the label you see sugar, the more the product contains. However, manufacturers can get around this by using two, three, or four different kinds of sugar.

Most people are unaware of the names behind which sugar masquerades: agave nectar or syrup, barley malt, beet sugar, brown sugar, cane juice, confectioner's sugar, corn syrup, date sugar, date syrup, dextrose, fructose, fruit concentrate, fruit juice concentrate, glucose, high fructose corn syrup, honey, lactose, maltose, maple syrup, molasses, Rapadura, raw sugar, rice malt syrup, rice syrup, sorghum, Sucanat, and sucrose.

The Good News

You can avoid the hazards of refined sugar and potentially dangerous synthetic sugar substitutes and still satisfy your sweet tooth. I'll show you how to use fresh and dried fruits supplemented with smaller than usual amounts of honey, agave nectar (cactus syrup), maple syrup, and even smaller amounts of a sweet herb called stevia. By using this herb in combination with a concentrated sweetener, you'll be able to achieve a satisfying level of sweetness with one-third to one-half the customary amount of sugar, honey, agave nectar, or maple syrup. You'll be able to enjoy some special treats and still reduce the impact of these indulgences.

Caution: If you attempt to reconstruct your favorite cookies, cakes, pies, and pastries by exclusively using honey, agave nectar, sorghum syrup, brown rice syrup, or maple syrup to replace refined sugars, you may still suffer from the sugar blues. Although these sweeteners are better than white sugar in some respects, they are still refined carbohydrates, and will impact your body in much the same way. Consumed excessively, they can still crowd out other more nutritious foods and promote all the disorders related to excess sugar consumption. So, use them in small amounts and learn how to tame your sweet tooth.

⸻One Sweet Nation⸻

Here are some facts about Americans' infatuation with sugar and syrup:

In 1967, Americans ate 114 pounds of sugar and sweeteners per capita, nearly all of it as either raw or refined sugar. In 2003, each person consumed about 142 pounds of sugar.

Since high fructose corn syrup was developed more than 30 years ago, consumption of the sweetener, which flavors everything from soda pop to ranch dressing, has skyrocketed. Americans currently down about 61 pounds of it each year.

Since 1950, soft drink consumption per capita has quadrupled, from about 11 gallons per year to about 46 gallons in 2003—nearly a gallon a week per person.

With all that sugar eating, it's no wonder people don't have much room for their vegetables. In 2003, Americans consumed, on average, a dismal 8.3 pounds of broccoli and just over 25 pounds of dark lettuce—the kind that is so good for you.

Source: March 28, 2005, print edition of *U.S. News & World Report*.

WHEAT: TO EAT OR NOT TO EAT?

Troublesome Grains

Among the grains, wheat and related grains (spelt, kamut, rye, barley, oats, and triticale) are perhaps the most allergenic. They contain gluten, a protein that causes celiac sprue and has been linked to at least 20 autoimmune diseases, including alopecia areata, arthritis, atresia, autoimmune thyroid disease, biliary sclerosis, Crohn's disease, diabetes mellitus, oral cankers, fibromyalgia, hypoparathyroidism, idiopathic thrombocytopenic purpura, microscopic colitis, cirrhosis, multiple sclerosis, optic neuritis, nephropathy, sarcoidosis, systemic lupus erythematosus, trigeminal neuritis, and vasculitis.

Gluten has also been linked to various cancers (esophageal, mouth, pharynx, breast, and small intestinal lymphoma), osteoporosis, schizophrenia, infertility, recurrent miscarriage, amenorrhea, and low birth weight.

For full references and to read more on this subject, refer to *The Garden of Eating: A Produce-Dominated Diet & Cookbook* (**www.TheGardenOfEatingDiet.com**).

GOT COCONUT?

Friendly Plant Fats

You will find healthier alternatives to vegetable oils in this chapter as well as in the recipes and the Resource section of this book. Most vegetable oils contain excessive amounts of omega-6 fatty acids that contribute to fatty acid imbalances and disease. Worse yet, are the refined, hydrogenated, and partially hydrogenated vegetable oils.

Go Nuts

You can nix nuts and seeds from your "no-no" list. Recent research has affirmed

Wheat-Free is Not Gluten-Free

Celiacs are not the only people living without wheat––one of the top 10 foods involved in food-based reactions.

"Wheat can cause immediate, very serious anaphylactic reactions associated with food allergies (IgE-based). Wheat is also a factor in food intolerances (IgG-based) where reactions are delayed and comparably milder, but certainly annoying––such as headaches, respiratory congestion, stomachaches, gastrointestinal distress, rashes, and joint aches, to name a few.

"Wheat is also implicated in chronic sinus and ear infections, migraine headaches, and osteoarthritis. Avoiding wheat is often a part of the treatment of autism, fibromyalgia, and certain autoimmune conditions such as lupus, multiple sclerosis, and rheumatoid arthritis.

"Fortunately, the wheat family of grains can be replaced with a variety of nutritious substitutes such as amaranth, buckwheat, corn, millet, quinoa, tapioca, teff, sago, sorghum, rice, potato, and sweet potato."

Source: Carol Fenster, Ph.D., nationally recognized author of award-winning gluten-free cookbooks, including *Wheat-Free Recipes & Menus*. Centennial, Colorado: Savory Palate Press, 2002; reprinted with permission from *What? No Wheat?* by LynnRae Reis. Phoenix: What? No Wheat? Publishing Company, 2003

Wheat as a Top Food Allergen

"A wheat-free label indicates that a food contains no wheat. But it *could* contain related grains (such as barley, rye, spelt, triticale, or kamut) that belong to the wheat family––much like oranges, lemons and limes are part of the citrus family.

"A gluten-free label, on the other hand, indicates that a food contains *no* wheat or wheat-related grains––nor do any of its other ingredients.

"Some people avoid wheat, but eat wheat-related grains. Celiacs, however, must avoid *all* forms of wheat because they *all* contain the offending gluten."

Source: Carol Fenster, Ph.D., nationally recognized author of award-winning gluten-free cookbooks, including *Wheat-Free Recipes & Menus*. Centennial, Colorado: Savory Palate Press, 2002; reprinted with permission from *What? No Wheat?* by LynnRae Reis. Phoenix: What? No Wheat? Publishing Company, 2003.

what your taste buds already knew: nuts are great for your health. Findings from five epidemiological studies conducted between 1996 and 2001 concluded that consumption of one ounce of nuts at least five times a week may significantly reduce your risk of developing coronary artery disease.

That amounts to 1/4 cupful of nuts or 2 tablespoons of nut butter five times a week—not a difficult amount to get down. Although peanuts were included in these studies, they're actually a legume, not a nut, but we won't split shells over that. Just know that whole nuts and nut butters are better for you than extracted nut, seed, and vegetable oils.

Tropical Fats: Friend or Foe?

Have you heard that coconut, coconut milk, and coconut oil are harmful to your health and will cause elevated cholesterol levels, atherosclerosis, and heart disease? Because these fats are largely composed of saturated fatty acids, they've been blacklisted by many doctors, dieticians, and health organizations.

The truth is that unrefined, natural coconut and palm oil products do not raise cholesterol levels and they do not promote atherosclerosis or heart disease unless they've been refined or hydrogenated. How do we know this?

People in traditional cultures who liberally use naturally saturated vegetable fats, such as coconut and palm oil, don't have the health problems we Americans suffer from. Studies of primitive Polynesians have absolved coconut oil as a cause of heart disease. The Tokelauans obtain about 57 percent of their daily calories from fat, most of it from coconut. They average130 grams of saturated fat and only 6 grams of unsaturated fat per day. And yet the Tokelauans and other Polynesians who consume coconut are practically immune to heart disease.

Heart disease is rampant among Americans, and, in baffling defiance of common sense, conventional nutritionists have blamed coconut and palm oils as well as butter and egg yolks. Yet, coconut and palm oils make up an insignificant portion of the typical American diet, and whole egg and butter consumption has plummeted since 1910. Most Americans get the bulk of their fat calories from refined polyunsaturated vegetable oils made from corn, canola, cottonseed, soy, safflower, sunflower, and other oils—not from coconut or palm oil.

For full references and to read more on this subject, refer to **The Garden of Eating: A Produce-Dominated Diet & Cookbook (www.TheGardenOfEatingDiet.com)**.

WHAT'S RIGHT ABOUT STEVIA?
The Sweet Leaf

Stevia is a non-caloric herbal sweetener extracted from the leaf of a South American plant—*Stevia Rebaudiana*—a small perennial shrub that produces incredibly small, sweet leaves that taste 50 times sweeter than table sugar.

Europeans have known about it since the 16th century when the Spanish conquistadors discovered the natives of South America using the leaves of the stevia plant to sweeten maté, their traditional herbal beverage. Researchers were amazed to discover that it took only one leaf to sweeten an entire jar of their bitter tea. The leaves have also been used therapeutically by indigenous people as an antiseptic and aid to healing wounds.

The stevia plant was first studied by Antonio Bertoni, a Botanist from Paraguay, in 1887. He wrote the first research articles about stevia at the beginning of the 20th century. In 1931 researchers identified the molecules that give the plant its sweetness. They found eight photo-chemicals, called glycosides, and found stevioside the sweetest of them.

What Makes the Leaf So Sweet?

Stevia contains sweet glycosides (molecules) that are created by photosynthesis and stored by the plant in the leaves. The three main constituents that have been identified are steviosides, rebaudiosides, and dulcosides. Modern stevia products contain varying concentrations of these constituents, with steviosides being the most common.

A Sweet Record of Safety

Stevia has been used widely as a sweetener in Paraguay, Brazil, Korea, Thailand, China, Japan, and several other countries, with no reported adverse affects. In Japan, stevia

The Big SATURATED FAT Scare

The deceitful propaganda campaign against coconut oil and other naturally saturated fats, such as palm oil and butter, was initiated by manufacturers of hydrogenated oil products such as vegetable shortening and margarine. They set out to discredit harmless natural saturated fats so they could increase sales of processed polyunsaturated vegetable oils, shortening, and margarine.

Source: Mary Enig, Ph.D. *Know Your Fats: The Complete Primer for Understanding The Nutrition of Fats, Oils, and Cholesterol.* Silver Springs: Bethesda Press, 2000: 178-179.)

"Dr. C. Everett Koop, former surgeon general of the United States, called the tropical oil scare 'foolishness.' and added commercial interests either trying to divert blame to others or ignorantly following the saturated fat hysteria were 'terrorizing the public about nothing.' "

"Dr. David Klurfeld, chairman of the Department of Nutrition at Wayne State University, called the anti-tropical oils campaign 'public relations mumbo jumbo.' He pointed out that tropical oils amounted to only about 2 percent of the American diet and that even if they were as bad as the ASA claimed, they wouldn't have much of an effect on health: 'The amount of tropical oils in the U.S. diet is so low that there is no reason to worry about it. The countries with the highest palm oil intakes in the world are Costa Rica and Malaysia. Their heart disease rates and serum cholesterol levels are much lower than in Western nations. This [tropical oils scare] never was a real health issue.' "

Source: Fife, Bruce, C.N., N.D., *The Coconut Oil Miracle.* New York: Avery Publishing, 2004: 13.

This was a case of the kettle calling the pot black. Over the past 60 years, research has consistently shown that refined and hydrogenated polyunsaturated vegetable oils, shortening, and margarine are strong promoters of both cancer and heart disease. During the last 100 years in America, animal fat intake has remained virtually constant, while consumption of processed, unsaturated vegetable oil products has increased four-fold, parallel with the rate of major degenerative diseases--obesity, heart disease, cancer, and diabetes. (Marieb EN. *Human Anatomy and Physiology,* Fifth Edition. New York: Benjamin Cummings, 2001: 673).

In contrast to vegetable oils, natural coconut and palm products have numerous health benefits. They differ from other oils in several ways. Palm oil has been used as food for centuries in Africa and Asia. Because it is about 50 percent saturated, it is more resistant to heat damage than other vegetable oils, making it a good cooking oil. Did you know the other half of its fatty acid profile is mostly monounsaturated like olive oil?

Dr. Mary Enig PhD, a well known lipid scientist, has studied and written extensively on the unique properties of coconut oil. She explains how coconut fat differs from other fats and oils. First, 65 percent of coconut fat consists of short- and medium-chain saturated fats (caprylic, capric, and lauric acids), which are easily assimilated, rapidly converted to energy in the liver, and can increase metabolic rate. Second, 40 percent of coconut fat is lauric acid, a fat that has antimicrobial, antifungal, and antiviral actions that naturally occur in human mothers' milk and is included in infant formulas. Finally, coconut fat has fewer calories per unit weight than the predominant saturated fats in conventional animal fats.

·· The Mother of All Milk ·······

Dr. Mary Enig, PhD, author of *Eat Fat, Lose Fat* and *Know Your Fats*, and foremost researchers of fats and oils, writes, "In fact lauric acid may prove to be a conditionally essential saturated fatty acid, and the research to establish this fact around the world needs to be vigorously promoted." Lauric acid has been shown in various scientific studies to contain bacterial and anti-viral properties, making it especially important for immune-suppressed individuals. A form of lauric acid is found naturally in human milk and helps to keep infants from being infected by viruses and bacteria.

(**Source:** *www.omeganutrition.com/products-gourmet-coconut.php*)

What a great reason to eat your Ice Dream

is allegedly the sugar substitute of choice, capturing up to 47 percent of the sweetener market. Toxicity tests and more than 30 years of continuous use in Asia attest to the safety of this sweetener.

Top Secret Sweetener

Stevia was first introduced to the United States in 1918, yet very few Americans have heard of it. Why? Stevia is an unpatentable product of nature; it threatens the multi-billion dollar a year artificial sweetener industry, which has lobbied heavily to keep the sweet leaf off the market.

In the 1980s stevia was used in several commercial herbal teas in the United States. In 1991, the Food and Drug Administration (FDA) labeled the leaf an "unsafe food additive," blocked importation into the United States, and demanded that manufacturers remove it from their products, despite having no legitimate indication that stevia could be harmful to humans.

Retailers and consumers lobbied to have stevia added to the GRAS (generally recognized as safe) list of foods, herbs, and nutrients because of its historical use, but permission was denied. Products with shorter and less honorable track records, such as saccharin, remained on the market.

Book Banning and Burning?

In 1996, FDA officials ordered the Stevita Company of Arlington, Texas, to destroy all copies of *Stevia Rebaudiana: Nature's Sweet Secret* by David Richard, *The Stevia Story*

by Donna Gates and Linda and Bill Bonvie, and *Cooking with Stevia* by James Kirkland. The feds considered the books to be product labeling for Stevita, the stevia product they sold, an act they deemed illegal. Products containing stevia were suddenly considered adulterated food products.

Since the passage of the Dietary Supplement Health and Education Act in 1994 (DSHEA), consumers once again have access to stevia, but manufacturers may not label it as a *sweetener;* they can only call it a dietary *supplement.* Commercially, stevia cannot be added to teas or other food products, with the exception of protein powders, which are classified as "dietary supplements."

A Cut Above

Unlike caloric sweeteners, stevia is non-cariogenic, which means it doesn't promote tooth decay, and it has no effect on blood glucose levels, which makes it safe for diabetics, people who suffer from reactive hypoglycemia, and anyone who wants to avoid the adverse effects of sugar and artificial sweeteners. Individuals following ketogenic, low-carbohydrate, anti-fungal, and candida diets can also use stevia. Unlike artificial sweeteners, stevia is safe at high temperatures, which means you can bake with it and it won't break down. You can also combine it with acid fruits and it won't degrade.

Unlike artificial sweeteners, stevia is non-toxic and has a record of safe and continuous use for hundreds of years. At this time, no adverse affects have been attributed to the herb or its extracts. The only downside is a bitter taste if you use too much of it. This can be avoided by precisely measuring stevia and by adding it in very small amounts, usually tiny pinches of the purified powder or several drops of the clear liquid, at a time.

Shopping for Stevia

Stevia comes in several forms and concentrations.

Green Stevia Leaves and Powder:

Made from the leaves, this represents the least concentrated form of the herb. It possesses the most therapeutic value (great for facial masks and poultices). This form can have a strong licorice-like flavor. Still you can add it to foods and beverages. You'll notice less aftertaste if you combine it with fresh or dried fruits. I don't use this form in the recipes in this book.

White Stevia Extract Powder:

This form of stevia is extracted from the leaves of the plant and has a smoother flavor than the unrefined green powder. It possesses approximately 200 to 300 times the sweetening power of sugar by weight. Its higher concentration of steviosides

and rebaudiosides means higher quality and less chance of an aftertaste. Many consumers prefer these products even though they lack the therapeutic properties of the whole green leaf.

Stevia is sold straight as well as diluted with maltodextrin (a bland carbohydrate), erythritol (a granulated filler from fruits, vegetables, and grains), or FOS (fructo-oligo-saccharides) to create a more diluted product sold in single serving packets, like sugar or artificial sweeteners. I recommend against buying it in a diluted form because brands vary in concentration, because they don't easily translate into my recipes, and because some of the fillers used, such as FOS (fructo-oligo-saccharides)—a pesky indigestible carbohydrate—can cause painful gas and intestinal bloating for many individuals. Instead, I prefer to use pure (undiluted) white stevia extract powder and clear stevia extract liquid, which range from 100 to 300 times the sweetness of sugar.

Green Stevia Liquid:

Liquid is made from whole stevia leaves.

Clear Stevia Extract Liquid:

This is made from the concentrated steviosides. You can buy it plain or flavored, in an alcohol base or a non-alcoholic

Looking for Food in All the Wrong Places

When you change your diet, whether you go gluten-free or simply improve the kinds of fats, oils, sweeteners, flour, and other ingredients you use, you will most likely need to start shopping in different places.

Although some of the ingredients I use can be found in the health foods section of supermarkets, many of the dry goods are difficult (if not impossible) to find in supermarkets, but are readily available in natural foods stores, health food co-operatives, catalogs for co-op buying clubs, and online. If you have trouble locating any of the items I recommend, please refer to the resource section in the Appendix.

If you go to a supermarket, shop the periphery for fresh produce, nuts, and seeds and the freezer section for frozen fruit. Check the health foods section, and make only a brief foray into the inner aisles for cocoa or baking chocolate and dried fruits. Some supermarkets sell omega-3 rich eggs, but your best bet will be to seek these out from local farmers, farmers' markets, or natural foods stores.

Always read labels. Do not assume that every item sold in natural foods stores is healthy; there, too, you will find vegetable oils, hydrogenated fats, refined sugars, artificial flavors and colors, and other adulterants lurking in many of the products. Look for products with the simplest and fewest ingredients, as close to their natural state as possible. Eat foods that spoil, but eat them before they do.

The Gluten-Free Pantry

If everyone in your house decides to adopt a gluten-free diet, your job will be easier. If not, you will need to take special precautions to avoid cross contamination. In mixed households with gluten-eaters and gluten-free individuals, some people find that it works best to keep separate tools and cutting boards and to maintain some gluten-free cupboards and refrigerator spaces. Regardless of how you deal with this, you will want to label everything.

Celiac cookbooks and resource books offer additional suggestions in this department.

glycerin base. Both are interchangeable, but some people prefer the flavor of one over the other. These colorless liquids are easy to use and ideal for enhancing the sweetness of many foods and beverages.

Using Stevia

While stevia is not perfect—it doesn't taste or function exactly like sugar— and it may take some time for you to get familiar with using it, I think it is worth the effort. With it, you can come close enough to producing the sweet tastes you enjoy without the ill effects of sugar. If you follow the recipes, and adjust the sweeteners to suit your needs, you can have your sweets and improve your health.

The biggest problem people have with using stevia is knowing how much to use. You can't remove a cup of sugar, add stevia, and have it turn out the same.

Sugar serves multiple functions in most recipes. In beverages it adds a sweet taste, but in baked goods it provides volume, texture, and mouth feel. When you replace sugar and syrups with stevia, particularly in baked goods, you have to adjust the amount of liquid and dry ingredients up or down to compensate for the sweetener you're adding or subtracting. If you reduce granulated sugar by 1/2 cup, you have to reduce the liquids or increase the dry ingredients by the same amount or close to it. If you reduce a liquid sweetener by 1/2 cup, you have to add 1/3 to 1/2 cup of extra liquid—juice or water—or omit 1/3 to 1/2 cup of dry ingredients. Sounds complicated, but it's not once you get the hang of it.

Sugar contributes to the texture and browning of baked goods while stevia does not. Sugar also encourages carmelization and browning, which stevia doesn't do. Sugar also provides a depth of flavor that you can't get from using stevia alone. For this reason, I like to use stevia to supplement the flavor and sweetness of other sweeteners in most recipes. In this way, I cut the amount of sugar but maintain a similarly satisfying level of sweetness.

While I can't give you a hard and fast formula for exactly how much stevia to use to replace sugar, honey, or maple syrup, I can offer some ideas and guidelines. The charts in Chapter 3 and the recipes in this book will help you learn to use stevia skillfully.

Stevia: More is Not Always Better

Just remember that stevia is so concentrated that only a miniscule amount is needed to produce a sweet taste. In fact, too much will produce an unpleasant bitter aftertaste. If a recipe offers a range for the amount of stevia, always start with the smaller amount, stir or blend well, then taste, and work your way up slowly if you want a sweeter taste.

Glossary of Ingredients & Shopping Tips
Start Next Page

Glossary of Ingredients
Shopping Tips

ALCOHOL

FYI: A little alcohol works like antifreeze, making ice cream softer and smoother, even after weeks in the freezer. Too much alcohol prevents freezing, so don't go wild with the bottle. You don't need to have a liquor cabinet or a large supply of alcoholic beverages on hand for making the recipes in this book, but keeping a few products on hand can help improve the texture and keeping quality of your homemade frozen desserts.

Flavored liqueurs

About: A liqueur is a sweet alcoholic beverage that is usually flavored with fruits, nuts, herbs, spices, flowers, seeds, roots, plants, or barks. Some contain cream. The word *liqueur* comes from the Latin word *liquifacere*, meaning "to dissolve," a reference to the process of dissolving flavorings into alcohol to make liqueur. These products are aged for a short period of time, just long enough to allow their flavors to marry.

The words cordial and liqueur are often used interchangeably. Technically, liqueurs are flavored with herbs, and cordials are prepared with fruit pulp or juices. Both are highly sweetened. My recipes call for them in small amounts, usually 1 or 2 tablespoons at a time. Be sure to add these before you add additional sweetener to the recipes, because you may not need as much honey or agave nectar if you include a liqueur.

You can find a wide assortment of flavored liqueurs on the market, from banana to orange, cherry to mint, almond to chocolate, and coffee to butterscotch. Buy the smallest bottle you can find.

Where to find: In liquor stores and supermarkets.

How to store: At room temperature.

Rum: light, dark, or coconut

About: Rum is made by fermenting and distilling sugarcane byproducts such as molasses and sugarcane juice. The clear liquid that results is usually aged in oak or other barrels. You'll find different varieties and grades of rum. In general, lighter rums have very little flavor, aside from a slight sweetness, and darker rums have a stronger flavor. You'll also find spiced rum and rum infused with the flavors of fruit such as mango, orange, citrus, coconut, or lime. Recipes in this book call for very small quantities of rum and other spirits, so you may want to buy small bottles.

Where to find: In liquor stores and supermarkets.

How to store: At room temperature.

White wine, dry or sweet

About: The natural chemical constituents of grapes allow grape juice to be fermented without the addition of sugars, acids, enzymes, or other nutrients. Wines are usually named after the kind of grapes they contain or their place of production. Only one recipe in this book calls for wine, which is simmered with dried fruit for flavor and to keep the Ice Dream from icing up and freezing hard.

Where to find: Look for a dry or sweet white wine, such as Chardonnay, Fumé Blanc, Sauvignon Blanc, Pinot Grigio, Moscato, Riesling, or dry Riesling in liquor stores and supermarkets. You don't need something expensive for cooking; a $3 or $4 bottle will do.

How to store: Refrigerate after opening. For a few dollars, you can buy a bulb-top stopper that allows you to reseal a bottle of wine and place it on its side in the refrigerator so it doesn't leak. If you're using it only for cooking, it's not a problem if it sits in the fridge for several months.

CAROB

About: Carob comes from a leguminous evergreen tree native to the Mediterranean, Northern Africa, and Western Asia. It also grows in some parts of the United Sates. Ancient Egyptians used carob pods as a sweetener and digestive aid, and they used the seeds to make a gummy adhesive for mummy wraps.

Nowadays, carob pods are ground to produce carob powder. The seeds are ground to make carob bean gum (also known as locust bean gum), which is used commercially as a thickener, emulsifier, and stabilizer in beverages, candies, ice cream, and salad dressings and in many other processed foods, and in ink, cosmetics, toothpaste, and adhesives. Carob seeds are also processed to make carob powder, carob chips, and carob candies.

Unprocessed carob powder has a naturally sweet taste. Whereas cocoa powder is bitter and 23% of its calories are from fat and only 5% from natural sugar, carob powder contains only 2% fat and up to 48% natural sugar. When processed to make commercial confections, candy, or chips, the differences between carob and cocoa often disappear because both products are mixed with additional fat and sugar. Carob candy bars usually contain as much fat and sugar as chocolate bars; however, if you're allergic to chocolate or it gives you migraines, switching to carob may allow you to enjoy similar versions of your favorite treats.

Carob powder is often used as a replacement for unsweetened cocoa, while carob chips and candies are often used to replace chocolate chips and candy bars. While it bears some resemblance, carob lacks the bitter kick of cocoa. However, you can make carob desserts taste more like chocolate if you combine carob with roasted nuts or nut butters and coffee or an herbal-coffee alternative (see Almost Chocolate Ice Dream).

Where to find: Look for unsweetened carob powder on the baking aisle of natural foods stores, in the health foods section of supermarkets, or order online.

Note: I have only found carob powder that is processed on equipment that is shared with wheat and other gluten-containing products, making it off limits for those on gluten-free diets.

How to store: In a cool, dry place at room temperature.

Carob chips

Where to find: Carob chips come both sweetened and unsweetened. Some brands contain milk solids; others are dairy-free.

Where to find: Look for unsweetened carob chips with the simplest and fewest ingredients on the baking aisle of natural foods stores, in the health foods section of supermarkets, or online.

Note: I have found only carob chips that are processed on equipment that is shared with wheat and other gluten-containing products, making them off limits for those on gluten-free diets.

How to store: In a cool, dry place at room temperature.

About Carob Candy Bars: When I was a child, carob candy bars were readily available in natural foods stores. I recall eating and enjoying them. I thought they would make the perfect substitute for bittersweet chocolate bars in some of the sauces and frozen desserts in this book, particularly for people who avoid chocolate; unfortunately, I couldn't find any in my local natural foods stores, although I did find half a dozen brands online. Look for products with the simplest and fewest ingredients that are low in sugar, and avoid carob candies that contain anything hydrogenated.

CHOCOLATE PRODUCTS
Bittersweet dark chocolate

About: Different kinds of chocolate—bittersweet, semisweet, extra-bittersweet, and sweet chocolate—vary in the amount of cocoa butter, sugar, vanilla, and chocolate liquor they contain. Semisweet and sweet contain 15 to 30% cocoa solids; bittersweet contains at least 35% cocoa solids; and premium brands of dark or bittersweet dark chocolate contain a much higher percentage of cocoa solids.

I recommend and prefer bittersweet dark chocolate bars that contain 70 to 73% cocoa solids, which means they contain more cocoa solids and less sugar. The label may or may not contain the word *bittersweet*, but will usually say *dark*. Buy organic and Fair Trade chocolate products if your budget permits.

Where to find: The baking aisle, the candy section, or by the cash register in specialty and natural foods stores and supermarkets. **Note:** Some chocolates are processed on machinery shared with wheat products. See Appendix for a list of gluten-free chocolates.

Fair Trade

What Does it Mean?

The Fair Trade Certified™ Label guarantees consumers that strict economic, social and environmental criteria were met in the production and trade of an agricultural product. For more information about how this affects farmers, the environment, and you, see the following website: http://transfairusa.org/

How to store: In a cool, dry place such as a cupboard.

Chocolate chips

About: Most chocolate chips are formulated with less cocoa butter than chocolate bars so they'll retain their shape when heated. For this reason, they don't work well as a replacement for chocolate bars in recipes that call for melting. Chocolate chips also contain more sugar than bittersweet dark chocolate bars.

In recipes that call for chocolate chips, you can substitute a bittersweet dark chocolate bar (with 70 to 73% cocoa content) if you chop it coarsely. Bittersweet chocolate chips contain significantly less cocoa and more sugar, so I don't use them as often. Buy organic and Fair Trade chocolate products if your budget permits.

Where to find: In the baking aisle, the candy section, or by the cash register in specialty and natural foods stores and supermarkets. **Note:** Some chocolate chips are processed on machinery shared with wheat products. See Appendix for a list of gluten-free chocolates.

How to store: In a cool, dry place, such as a cupboard.

Cocoa nibs (cacao nibs)

About: Cocoa nibs (also spelled cacao nibs) are roasted cocoa beans separated from their husks and broken into small bits. They can be used in place of nuts in cookies or as a garnish for ice cream.

Where to find: Gourmet and natural foods stores and online. See Appendix for gluten-free brands.

How to store: In a cool, dry place, such as a cupboard or refrigerator.

Unsweetened cocoa powder

About: All recipes that call for cocoa powder use unsweetened cocoa powder. Do not use or confuse this with cocoa drink mixes or products labeled "powdered chocolate," which contain sugar and other ingredients. You want a product that contains only cocoa powder.

Buy organic and Fair Trade chocolate products if your budget permits.

Where to find: On the baking aisle of gourmet and natural foods stores, in the health foods section of supermarkets, and online. **Note:** Some cocoa powders are processed on machinery shared with wheat products. See Appendix for a list of gluten-free chocolates.

How to store: In a cool, dry place, such as a cupboard or refrigerator.

Unsweetened baker's chocolate:

About: Unsweetened chocolate, also sold as bitter or baking chocolate, is simply unadulterated chocolate. It contains no sugar or flavorings. It comes in bars or individually wrapped 1-ounce squares in boxes. Buy organic and Fair Trade chocolate products if your budget permits.

Where to find: The baking aisle of supermarkets, specialty and natural foods stores, and online. **Note:** Some chocolates are processed on machinery shared with wheat products. See Appendix for a list of gluten-free chocolates.

What is Dutched or Dutch-Process Cocoa Powder?

Many cocoa powder products are treated with alkaline solutions to raise the pH level, which makes it easier to control the color and flavor. This is called Dutching. It has a darker color than natural cocoa powder. You can use either version in my recipes.

How to store: In a cool, dry place, such as a cupboard.

COCONUT PRODUCTS

Coconut butter

About: Unlike coconut oil, coconut butter is not an extracted product. Just as almond butter is made from puréed almonds and peanut butter is made from puréed peanuts, coconut butter comes from puréed coconut meat. It has a thick, fibrous, and dense texture and a slightly sweet flavor.

It looks a lot like white icing. I like to drizzle it over fresh fruit, poached pears, or apple compote. To make a frosting brownies or a filling for sandwich cooki you can mix it with a small amount of honey or agave nectar, vanilla extract, and a pinch of salt; add a few drops of clear stevia extract liquid for a sweeter taste.

Where to find: The refrigerator case of natural foods stores or online.

How to store: Store at room temperature. If it's too hard to stir, run the bottle under hot water or empty the contents into a stainless steel bowl and place that bowl inside a larger bowl of hot water to melt it enough to stir and emulsify.

Coconut milk

About: This non-dairy product forms the base of the frozen dessert recipes in this book. It effectively replaces cream and milk. Premium (full-fat) coconut milk provides a rich taste and texture with roughly half the fat and calories of cream.

Not to be confused with the liquid inside a coconut, which is actually coconut water, coconut milk is made by blending coconut meat with water to produce a creamy liquid. You can make it from scratch with fresh, whole coconuts, using an ice pick, hammer, and a food processor or Vita-Mix, but it's quite time-consuming and potentially dangerous unless you find young coconuts with soft meat you can easily scoop out with a spoon.

For convenience and consistency in texture, flavor, and calorie counts, I recommend purchasing coconut milk by the can or the case. Look for a brand that contains no added sugar, preservatives, or additives such as sulfites (potassium metabisulfite or sodium metabisulfite). Sulfites can trigger allergic reactions or migraine headaches in susceptible individuals. The addition of guar gum or xanthan gum is not a problem; these vegetable gums help ensure a more even texture.

My favorite brands, in order of preference, include Thai Kitchen, Whole Food, Wild Oats, and Native Forest.

Most of the recipes in this book call for premium (full-fat) coconut milk. Most of the recipes that call for lite coconut milk use it in combination with melted chocolate or diluted nut butter. Although you will cut the fat and calories if you use lite coconut milk,

---

Don't Like Coconut?

If you've never tried unsweetened coconut milk, you're in for a treat. It doesn't taste like the sugary sweetened coconut commonly sold in supermarkets and used in conventional cookies, cakes, pies, and candies. It has a milder coconut flavor and it takes on the flavor of whatever you mix it with, so it can be used to make an almost endless variety of flavors. With the exception of Vanilla Ice Dream and other flavors that use Vanilla Ice Dream as a base, in many cases, people won't guess that you've used coconut milk.

The recipes that use Vanilla Ice Dream have the strongest coconut flavor. If you plan to serve Ice Dream to someone who isn't wild about coconut, make it with lite (reduced fat) or a combination of regular and lite coconut milk. Better yet, start with one of the Ice Dream flavors that contains added fruit or chocolate, which will mute the coconut taste.

Note: If you use 100% lite coconut milk, plan to use the batch immediately or within 24 hours before it becomes hard and icy. With a lower fat content, frozen desserts made from lite coconut milk freeze harder and quickly develop ice crystals.

your frozen desserts will become hard and icy if not consumed immediately, or within a couple of days, after churning.

Where to find: Look for canned, unsweetened, sulfite-free coconut milk on the ethnic aisle of supermarkets and natural foods stores. **Caution:** Do not substitute sweetened Coco Lopez or products labeled "cream of coconut."

How to store: After opening the can and stirring or blending the contents, pour into an impeccably clean, wide mouth 16-ounce jar; cover and refrigerate the unused portion. Coconut milk will thicken within several hours and will rarely separate again. Use within 5 days or freeze in ice cube trays for longer storage. Frozen cubes will last almost indefinitely.

Tips for Opening a New Can of Coconut Milk

Shake the can well before completely removing the lid. In warm weather, canned coconut milk will be liquid at room temperature. During cool or cold weather, the contents may appear thick or chunky on top and watery on the bottom. This is normal. Don't toss it out unless it smells like spoiled milk, which is rare! If it's too thick to blend by hand, purée it in a blender, Vita-Mix, or food processor before using or storing.

Coconut oil

About: Coconut oil is one of nature's most valuable and most misunderstood foods. The same heat stable properties of natural saturation that make it an ideal cooking oil are also the source of much of the misunderstanding about it. Non-hydrogenated, naturally saturated coconut oil does not contain trans-fatty acids.

Many commercial grade coconut oils are made from copra, the dried kernel (or meat) of the coconut. These inferior products must be refined and purified to make them sanitary for consumption. Avoid refined coconut oil because it is processed with high heat extraction methods; it is often treated with chemicals, and is then bleached and deodorized. Also avoid hydrogenated or partially-hydrogenated coconut oil.

Virgin or extra virgin coconut oil is made from fresh coconut meat. Chemicals and high heating are not used in processing, since the natural, pure coconut oil is very stable with a shelf life of several years.

Organic and virgin coconut oils have a pleasantly pronounced coconut flavor and fragrance, whereas the refining process leaves the copra-based coconut oils with a bland taste.

Seek out unrefined, virgin-pressed coconut oil packaged in glass or at least heavy, rather than soft, plastic containers. Use coconut oil to replace vegetable oils, margarine, shortening, and/or butter in cooking, baking, or at the table. Refer to the Index and Appendix for sources. Some of my favorites include Tropical Traditions, Omega Nutrition, Nutiva, and Garden of Life.

Where to find: Look for organic virgin-pressed or extra virgin coconut oil in natural foods stores, the health foods section of some supermarkets, and online.

How to store: At room temperature. Do not refrigerate or it will be impossible to get a spoon in to use the product. It is stable at room temperature for several years.

Note: Coconut oil will liquefy in hot weather (above 70° F) and solidify in colder weather. Do not be alarmed when this happens. It has not spoiled.

Shredded, unsweetened, sulfite-free coconut

About: Look for shredded, dried coconut that has not been treated with sulfites (bleaching agents). Avoid the sweetened angel flake coconut sold in supermarkets. Natural unsweetened coconut has a different taste and texture. The label should say "sulfite-free, unsweetened coconut," and nothing else.

Some companies sell this product in large flakes; others sell medium or finely flaked macaroon-style coconut cut into smaller pieces. Large flaked pieces are great for trail mix; smaller flakes are best for garnishing fruit salads or making macaroons. You can turn large flakes into small flakes in a blender, Vita-Mix, or food processor by pulsing the machine on and off.

What if I'm Allergic to Coconut Milk?

You can still make the recipes in this book—with a few modifications. You can replace the coconut milk with a combination of cow's milk and heavy cream, using equal parts milk and cream or 2 parts cream to 1 part milk. To improve the keeping quality of the ice cream if you don't plan to serve it immediately, include the gelatin or agar agar listed in the recipes, dissolving and heating it in a portion of the milk.

If you use milk, cream, or other dairy products, I recommend that you seek out products that have been raised and labeled organic, preferably raw, grass-fed (also called pasture-raised) from a small, local dairy. At the very minimum, the products should be labeled rBGH-free or rBST-free so you have no added growth hormones.

• •

CAUTION

Confined Cows on Drugs

Modern milk production is a world apart from traditional herding. You might have an image of contented cows grazing freely on a family farm, but in fact most modern dairy cows stand around on concrete pads in corporate-owned confinement dairies where they are implanted with synthetic hormones, dosed with antibiotics, and fed an artificial diet of grain.

These hormones and antibiotics can migrate into the dairy products you buy. Antibiotic residues in modern milk are sufficient to trigger allergies to antibiotics. Recently, dairy farmers have been using rBGH (bovine growth hormone) to increase milk output in cows. Research indicates that milk from cows treated with this drug contains levels of IGF (insulin like growth factors) that may promote cancer growth in humans who consume the milk. So, that's what's wrong with modern milk.

Where to find: The bulk foods, produce, or baking aisle of natural foods stores, or online. Shredded coconut in airtight packages will be fresher than similar products sold in bulk bins, which can become rancid from over-exposure to air, or contaminated with wheat if other shoppers have inadvertently used the wrong scoops.

How to store: Refrigerate or freeze in an airtight container.

COFFEE & TEA

Coffee

About: How well your coffee-flavored frozen dessert turns out depends upon the quality and strength of the coffee or espresso you use. Use strong, freshly brewed coffee or espresso in the Coffee Ice Dream recipe.

Where to find: Supermarkets, gourmet shops, natural foods stores, and online.

How to store: Refrigerate or freeze coffee beans or grinds to prolong their shelf life.

Instant coffee or espresso granules

About: Instant coffee is regular brewed coffee that's been freeze-dried to remove the water. It offers the convenience of dissolving instantly in hot water, but lacks the depth of flavor of traditionally brewed coffee, and it is often made from the lowest grade coffee beans. If you use this product, look for an organic brand to avoid herbicide and pesticide residues.

Where to find: Specialty and natural foods stores, supermarkets, and online.

How to store: In a cool dry place or the refrigerator.

Roasted chicory and dandelion root

About: If you're cutting back on coffee or simply searching for a full-bodied alternative to black, green, or herbal teas, try roasted chicory and dandelion root to make a satisfying brew with a more robust flavor. You can brew them individually, or in combination, for a caffeine-free coffee extender or substitute. In the Deep South, roasted chicory root has been blended with coffee for decades to make gourmet French Market Coffee.

Use of chicory and dandelion roots dates from the time of the Egyptian pharaohs. These roots have been used to detoxify the liver and to remedy acne, age spots, anemia, arthritis, asthma, diabetes, jaundice, spleen problems, gout, gallstones, hepatitis, hypoglycemia, high blood pressure, loss of appetite (in the underweight person), liver disorders, rheumatism, eczema, elevated cholesterol, and constipation.

Bitter flavors stimulate peristalsis and elimination. These roots contain substances that increase the flow of bile which is necessary for proper liver function and metabolism of fat and cholesterol. Herbalists have also used chicory and dandelion root to reduce symptoms of PMS. By improving liver function these herbs help the body maintain hormonal balance. So, you can actually benefit from using these herbal coffee-like grinds.

Where to find: Although some natural foods and health foods co-ops sell these products, many do not. You can mail order or buy them online.

How to store: At room temperature in the original packaging. Refrigerate leftover brewed beverage in glass jars.

Chai tea

About: Chai (rhymes with pie), the word for tea in many parts of the world, is a centuries-old beverage that usually consists of rich black tea, heavy milk, a combination of various spices, and a sweetener. The spices vary from region to region and among households throughout India. The spices commonly used include cardamom, cinnamon, ginger, cloves, and pepper.

Where to find: Supermarkets, gourmet shops, natural foods stores, tea and herb shops, and online.

How to store: In an airtight container in a cool, dry place. Refrigerate leftover tea after brewing.

Green tea powder (matcha)

About: Matcha, powdered green tea from Japan, can be made as a tea or used as an ingredient in recipes. Premium-grade matcha is made in limited amounts in Japan and is usually labeled "thin" (usucha) or "thick" (koicha) and is used to make tea. Ingredient-grade matcha is more abundant and is used in cooking and drink making.

What makes matcha so green? Farmers cover the tea plants with bamboo mats several weeks prior to harvest. This increases the chlorophyll content and turns the leaves dark green. After harvest, the leaves are steamed, dried and de-spined (stems are removed), and then stone ground into a powder.

Where to find: In Asian grocery stores, natural foods markets, and online. Green tea leaves do not work as a substitute.

⋅ ⋅Why Not Just Drink Decaf? ⋅ ⋅ ⋅ ⋅ ⋅ ⋅ ⋅ ⋅ ⋅ ⋅ ⋅ ⋅

Even decaffeinated coffee contains at least 7 to 10 milligrams of caffeine per 6-ounce cup. Decaf from coffee bars can contain twice as much caffeine because it is typically brewed stronger than with standard brewing methods. So, if you are drinking a 16-ounce cup of decaf, you may be getting as much as 20 to 30 milligrams of caffeine. Studies have shown a higher incidence of rheumatoid arthritis among decaf drinkers.

Most decaf has been extracted with methylene chloride, a carcinogen, which leaves behind small but significant residues. Decaf is even harder on the gastrointestinal tract than regular coffee because it is made from a variety of coffee beans called robusta that have stronger acids. If you have gastrointestinal problems or suffer from acid indigestion, you may find that eliminating coffee from your diet, whether decaf or regular, will help with your recovery process.

Source: Compiled from information found at http://www.teeccino.comFAQs.aspx#gluten

How to store: In a cool dry place in a closed container, preferably a tea canister or jar.

Teeccino Caffeine-Free Herbal Coffee

About: Teecino, a caffeine-free coffee alternative, looks like coffee, but is made from herbs, grains, fruits, and nuts that are roasted and ground. It looks and cooks like coffee but contains no coffee beans or caffeine. It contains 3 grams of carbohydrate and 1 gram of fiber per cup for a total of 15 calories. It provides 65 milligrams of potassium to give your body a natural energy lift, and 365 milligrams of inulin to enhance your digestion and improve elimination.

Some people use this product to wean themselves off of coffee. The Teeccino web site offers a painless method to help you kick the coffee habit: blend Teeccino with your regular coffee and gradually increase the amount over a period of two to three weeks while reducing the amount of coffee grinds (www.teeccino.com). I have recommended something similar for many years using roasted chicory root and dandelion root.

Where to find: Look for it on the coffee and tea aisles of natural foods stores, the health foods section of supermarkets, and online. It comes in 8.5 once and 1 pound cans, 1 pound bags, and a sample-size envelope in a variety of flavors: Original, Vanilla Nut, Hazelnut, Almond Amaretto, Java, Mocha and Chocolate Mint.

How to store: Store at room temperature. Teeccino won't go stale at room temperature like coffee because it doesn't contain coffee oils. Just replace the plastic cap on the can after using it, and it will last for at least 2 years. **Note:** Brewed Teeccino can last up to five days in the refrigerator making it easy to drink iced Teeccino in the summer.

DRIED FRUIT

Dried dates
About: Dates are Mother Nature's candy; they're exceedingly sweet. Botanists recognize more than 1,500 varieties of dates worldwide; yet, most Americans are familiar with only one or two varieties—Medjools and Deglet Noors—commonly used in cookies, ice cream, hot and cold cereal, fruit cakes, quick breads, and puddings.

Is Teeccino Really Gluten Free?

The label says "Brewed Teeccino is Gluten free," even though it contains barley. I wrote to the company thinking they'd made an error. Here's what I discovered:

The company's dietician assured me that gluten does not extract from barley during the process of brewing it in water. They regularly have the product tested at the University of Nebraska's Allergy Testing lab where Teeccino has had no detectable levels of gluten found at 10PPM. You can view these test results on their website: http://www.teeccino.com/FAQs.aspx#gluten.

The registered dietician who answered my questions said that she has never had anybody come back to her saying that they've had a reaction. In fact, this has been a topic on their discussion forum on their website, and they have had good feedback from consumers who have celiac who have stated that they regularly consume Teeccino without problems.

What are the natural flavors in Teeccino?

Natural flavors are made from flavoring constituents that are extracted from natural ingredients like fruits, spices, herbs and even coffee. Teeccino flavors do not contain any constituents from meat, seafood, poultry, eggs, or edible yeast. Teeccino does not allow any monosodium glutamate, propylene glycol, or preservatives in its flavors.

Source: www.teeccino.com/FAQs.aspx#cans

If you live in one of the date-growing regions of the world, you can experiment with different varieties of dates, such as Barhee (Barhi), Black Sphinx, and Honey Dates, as well as Halawy, Hayani, and even Khadrawy and Zahadi. Each has a slightly different flavor and texture. I find Medjools the most uniformly sweet, moist, and soft.

Look for whole unpitted dates; they'll be fresher, moister, and they'll last longer. You can easily pit them yourself. They should feel soft and look plump. Their slightly shiny, smooth (only slightly wrinkled) skin should be free of dry, cracked, or shriveled sections and crystallization. They should not have a fermented smell. You can substitute coconut date rolls for dates in most recipes.

Where to find: Look for dried dates in bulk bins, bags, packages, or refrigerated coolers in the produce department of natural foods markets, on the baking aisle of supermarkets, and online. For the best flavor and freshness, buy locally grown varieties at farmers' markets and natural foods stores.

How to store: Store at room temperature in wide mouth canning jars. Refrigerate in humid or extremely hot weather to extend the shelf life. They easily absorb odors, so avoid storing near strong smelling foods.

Coconut date rolls

About: Coconut date rolls are made from dried, pitted dates put through a grinder twice, rolled in sulfite-free, unsweetened coconut flakes, and shaped into logs. You can buy them already made. They make a great sweetener for cookies, brownies, and

bars, and the perfect filling for the Dark Chocolate-Dipped Date Nut Truffles in Chapter 9. Different brands vary in their size, sweetness, and moisture content. Experiment to find your favorite source.

To make your own coconut date rolls: Pulverize soft pitted dates in a food processor, adding warm water a tablespoon at a time as needed to create a stiff cookie dough texture. Add 1/2 cup unsweetened, sulfite-free coconut per half pound of pitted dates. Coconut can be left out if allergy is a concern. Form into 1-ounce logs.

Where to find: In the bulk foods or produce department of natural foods and specialty foods stores, or online.

How to store: Room temperature in wide mouth canning jars. Refrigerate in humid or extremely hot weather to extend shelf life. Avoid storing near strong smelling foods. They will last at least three years at room temperature and at least five years in the freezer. **Note:** Some date brands recommend refrigeration, usually for very moist dates that have not been dried as long.

Dried apricots

About: Dried apricots vary in flavor, color, and texture. Generally, those with a pale or bright orange color have been treated with sulfites (sulphur dioxide, a bleaching agent and preservative), to which many people

---

What's so **Great** *about* **Dates?**

Nature's original candy beats bananas as one of the best sources of potassium, an essential mineral we require in abundance. Dates are virtually fat free, sodium free, and a significant source of B-complex vitamins, magnesium, iron, and fiber. A 100 gram portion (5 to 6 medium dates) provides, 248 milligrams of potassium (7% of the Daily Value), 31 grams of carbohydrate (10% of DV), 3 grams of fiber (14% of DV), 4% of the DV for magnesium, and 2% of the DV for calcium, iron, riboflavin, niacin, folate, phosphorus, pantothenic acid, and vitamin B-6. They provide all of this in only 248 calories.

DATE YIELDS: 1 POUND UNPITTED DATES = 2 1/2 CUPS PITTED AND CHOPPED
8 OUNCE PACKAGE PITTED DATES = 1 1/4 CUPS CHOPPED

How to Pit a Date: Cut a slit down the top of each date, pull the sides apart, remove seed, and then press the date together again.

Can I Use Date Sugar in Your Recipes?

The highest quality date sugar is made from dried, powdered dates. It makes a great alternative to brown sugar in baked goods; however, it doesn't dissolve as readily as sugar. Although I've used it in some recipes, I decided not to include it in this book because date sugar is not readily available, even in natural foods stores. Date sugar costs significantly more than dried dates and other sweeteners.

To complicate matters, some companies add oat flour to reduce the stickiness of dates when grinding them. This dilutes the sweetness and throws off the amount you need to add to recipes. It also makes this sweetener off limits for people on gluten-free diets. I know of one oat-free brand, Chattfield's, but their product label says that the items are often processed on the same machinery that is used for wheat and other common allergenic foods. For these reasons, I use the more affordable and more readily available dried dates in my recipes as a replacement for brown sugar in the cookies, brownies, and bars

are allergic. I prefer the darker, unbleached varieties, particularly Turkish dried apricots, which are smaller, softer, more moist, and much sweeter than American-grown apricots.

Where to find: Look for sulfite-free dried apricots in natural foods stores, gourmet shops, the health foods section of supermarkets, or online.

How to store: Store at room temperature in wide mouth canning jars. Refrigerate in humid or extremely hot weather to extend the shelf life. They will last for at least three years at room temperature and at least five years in the freezer.

Dried bananas

About: Most dried bananas sold in the U.S. are made from sliced, sugared, and deep fried bananas. Look for dried (not fried), unsweetened banana slices. They look like strips of leather and have nothing added, not even sulfites. They make a great addition to frozen desserts as you will soon discover.

Where to find: Check specialty natural foods stores for these slightly beige to brownish colored dried banana slices. You may need to order them online.

How to store: Store at room temperature in wide mouth canning jars. Refrigerate in humid or extremely hot weather to extend shelf life. Avoid storing near strong smelling foods. They will last for at least three years at room temperature and at least five years in the freezer.

Dried cherries

About: Many of the dried fruits sold in supermarkets and natural foods stores have been sweetened with sugar and treated with sulfites to brighten their color. Look for unsweetened or fruit-sweetened dried fruits and, whenever possible, avoid products that contain sulfites (sulphur dioxide), which can trigger migraines or respiratory distress in susceptible individuals.

Where to find: Look for sulfite-free, dried, fruit-sweetened, or unsweetened (sweet) cherries in natural foods stores, gourmet shops, and the health foods section of supermarkets, or online.

How to store: At room temperature in wide mouth canning jars. Refrigerate in humid or extremely hot weather to extend the shelf life. Avoid storing dried fruits near strong smelling foods as they easily absorb odors. They will last for at least three years at room temperature and at least five years in the freezer.

Raisins

About: Did you know that 1 tablespoon of raisins is the condensed version of 1/2 cup of fresh grapes? It's true. That means they're almost as calorie dense as nuts. To get more flavor for your money, use them as a mix-in for desserts (see Rum Raisin Ice Dream, Apple Apricot Compote, Cranberry Apple Compote, Poached Pears, and Banana Oatmeal Raisin Ice Dream Sandwich Cookies) or fruit salad to make a little bit go a long way.

find: Look for the unbleached ...s sold in supermarkets, natural ..., and specialty foods stores.

...ote: Light colored raisins are usually treated with sulfites, a bleaching agent.

How to store: At room temperature in wide mouth canning jars. Refrigerate in humid or extremely hot weather to extend the shelf life.

EGGS & EGG REPLACERS
Ener-G Foods Egg Replacer

About: For people who cannot eat eggs, this product can be substituted in some recipes.

This product contains potato starch, tapioca starch flour, leavening (calcium lactate from dairy-free sources, calcium carbonate, and citric acid), cellulose gum, and carbohydrate gum.

It doesn't work in all cases because eggs perform different functions depending upon what you're making. It doesn't work in recipes where eggs serve as a main ingredient or provide a specific flavor, texture, or structure—scrambles, omelets, quiches, meringues, macaroons, mayonnaise, or angel food cake.

You can use this egg replacer in recipes such as cakes where eggs act as a leavener and add a lighter, fluffier texture, and in cookies, brownies, and muffins where eggs add moisture, act as a binder, and add additional leavening. The package instructions won't tell you this, but I find it helpful to add a few tablespoons of applesauce, or other liquid, for each egg you omit to roughly equal an egg's volume.

How to use: To replace one whole egg or one egg white, combine 1 1/2 teaspoons Ener-G Egg Replacer with 2 tablespoons warm water. Mix thoroughly just before adding this to a recipe. To replace one egg yolk, mix 1 to 1 1/2 teaspoons Egg Replacer into 1 tablespoon warm water.
Note: For more moisture, add an additional 2 tablespoons of water, nut milk, or applesauce for each egg you omit; 1 egg = 3 to 4 tablespoons in volume.

Where to find: On the baking aisle of natural foods stores, in the health foods section of supermarkets, or online.

How to store: At room temperature in a cool dry place.

That Golden Yolk

Have you been throwing out egg yolks thinking that they're bad for your health? Many important nutrients are concentrated in egg yolks. All the vitamin A and D, 84 % of the vitamin B12, 87 % of the pantothenic acid, 81 % of the folic acid, 92 % of the calcium, 45 % of the protein, and 23 % of the potassium in an egg, are concentrated in the yolk! All the vitamin E and omega-3 essential fatty acids in pasture-raised or wild bird eggs are in the yolk.

Egg yolks supply choline, lecithin, and other phospholipids that are vital to cell membranes throughout your body. They are especially important to nerve cells. Phospholipids emulsify other fats, keeping them suspended in blood and body fluids, allowing fat soluble substances, such as vitamins and hormones, to pass easily into and out of cells.

The functioning of all your cells and the integrity of your cell membranes can only be maintained if you eat foods rich in natural phospholipids. Some evidence suggests a link between age-related cognitive decline and a lack of dietary phospholipids, which are abundant in egg yolks, a food many people avoid. So, don't toss those golden yolks, they're the most nutritious part of the egg.

Liquid egg whites

About: Liquid egg whites are convenient to use when you plan to make a lot of macaroons or angel food cake. There's no waste and they are easy to measure. If you buy them, look for a product that contains only 100% liquid egg whites and nothing else. Otherwise, use the same high quality farmers' market fresh eggs you'd normally buy, then use the extra yolks to bind meatballs or meatloaves, or feed 1 or 2 yolks per day to your dog or cat with meals.

Where to find: Supermarkets and natural foods stores.

How to store: Refrigerate and check the "sell by" date.

Whole eggs

About: Recipes in this book call for medium to large eggs. A large egg in the shell weighs approximately 2 to 2 1/2 ounces and measures between 3 tablespoons and 1/4 cup. One yolk equals 1 tablespoon and one white equals about 2 tablespoons. The Ice Dream recipes do not call for eggs, but most of the baked goods do. While you can use a powdered egg replacer (see notes above) in cookies and bars, it will not work in macaroons or angel food cake. Skip those recipes altogether if you have an egg allergy.

The best eggs come from local farms where the chickens are allowed to run in open pastures or gardens where they eat bugs, worms, grubs, and vegetable scraps (they like this stuff). These eggs have more flavor and are packed with more vitamins and antioxidants than eggs from cooped up, factory-farmed birds fed antibiotic-laced chicken chow.

Note: Eggs from pasture-fed chickens have firm, golden orange, well-rounded yolks rich in flavor. Once you become accustomed to eating them, you may find conventional supermarket eggs to be disappointing.

Where to find: Check your local farmers' market, with friends or neighbors who raise eggs or know people who do, or buy omega-3 or DHA-rich eggs in specially marked cartons in natural foods stores and supermarkets.

How to store: Refrigerate and use within 1 month. Check "sell by" dates when buying commercial eggs from a store.

FATS & OILS

Almond oil

About: Pressed from almonds, this delicate oil is best in applications that do not require heat, such as salad dressings, to replace butter on vegetables at the table,

or in Karli's Carob or Chocol[...]
Like other nut, seed, and veget[...]
contains an abundance of omega-6 [...]
acids, and could contribute to fatty acid imbalances. Modern people already get too much omega-6, so use this sparingly, not as a major source of fat or oil in your diet.

Where to find: Look for extra virgin almond oil sold in dark bottles in specialty and natural foods stores and online. Avoid refined versions.

How to store: Store in the refrigerator. Do not heat.

Avocado oil

About: An edible oil pressed from the flesh of the avocado, it can be used to replace other oils in salad dressings, in cooking, and in Karli's Carob or Chocolate Sauce. It has a light, nutty, buttery taste and a vibrant deep green color. Like olive oil, it contains an abundance of monounsaturated fats, as well as vitamin E. It is more heat stable and shelf stable than other vegetable, nut, and seed oils.

Where to find: Look for extra virgin avocado oil sold in dark bottles in specialty and natural foods stores and online.

How to store: Store in the refrigerator; can be used in cooking at moderate heat.

Coconut oil, see listing under Coconut

Palm shortening

About: Palm shortening is extracted from palm fruit, just as olive oil is extracted from olives and avocado oil is extracted from avocadoes. It doesn't require refining, only filtering. In its natural state, palm oil contains a mixture of 45% saturated and 55% unsaturated fat; most of the unsaturated fat is monounsaturated.

Palm shortening is palm oil that has some of its unsaturated fats removed, giving it a very firm texture and high melting point (97° F), it is highly stable for long-term storage. Processors combine the palm olein and palm stearine into a whipped shortening that behaves like, and has a similar consistency to, butter or margarine, making it a popular choice in vegan desserts. This product is not hydrogenated, and it contains no trans fats. Because palm shortening has been separated from some of the unsaturated portion of the oil, it is colorless and odorless

Can I Use Butter in Your Recipes?

In some cases, yes. In recipes for cookies, brownies, bars and sauces, you can replace palm shortening or coconut oil with unsalted, real creamery butter. This will reduce the fat and calories. One tablespoon of butter contains 10 grams of fat and 100 calories, whereas one tablespoon of oil contains 13 grams of fat and approximately 125 calories.

If you use butter, buy organic, preferably from pasture-raised cows, to avoid hormone and antibiotic residues. If you can find some that is locally produced, all the better.

Note: For greasing baking pans, you will be better off using palm shortening, ghee, or clarified butter. These products will not burn the way butter can when used for this purpose. (Ghee and clarified butter are made from butter that has been simmered to evaporate moisture and strained to remove the milk solids.)

and will not affect the taste of foods the same way that virgin palm oil does.

Note: Do not confuse palm shortening with palm kernel oil, two very different products. Palm kernel oil is one of the fattiest oils and is extracted from a nut (not a fruit); it is usually extracted with solvents and refined. Do not substitute red palm oil in recipes in this book; it has a very pronounced flavor and fragrance that easily overpowers other foods.

How to use palm shortening: Use palm shortening to replace butter, margarine, conventional shortening, and vegetable oils in baked goods in equal amounts.

Where to find: In natural foods stores, health foods section of some supermarkets, and online. I recommend Spectrum Shortening and Tropical Traditions Organic Palm Shortening.

How to store: At room temperature.

FLAVORINGS & EXTRACTS

About: Good quality extracts and flavorings cost more than artificially flavored products, but they're worth the extra expense. I keep a wide variety of flavorings on hand, including almond, butterscotch, caramel, coffee, lemon, orange, maple, peppermint and vanilla.

Look for products in an alcohol base, or if you follow a gluten-free diet and avoid products that might contain grain alcohol, buy flavorings in a non-alcoholic glycerine

base. My favorite brands include Frontier, Spicery Shoppe, and Flavorganics. As I understand it, the term *extract* refers to the nut, seed, spice, or fruit essence in an alcohol base, whereas the same product in a glycerine base must be labeled *flavor*.

Avoid products that say artificial or synthetic on the label, and limit or avoid those that contain propylene glycol, artificial flavorings, artificial colorings, sugar, and corn syrup.

Where to find: Specialty and natural foods stores and online.

How to store: In a cool dry place.

Sea salt: unrefined and mineral-rich

About: Conventional table salt is refined to 99% sodium chloride (39% sodium and 60% chloride). It has been stripped of trace minerals and trace elements and has a sharp, salty taste. Most of the sea salt on the market, including what you find in the bulk bins of natural foods stores, is refined to 97% sodium chloride and is virtually identical to table salt with the exclusion of added sugar and anti-caking agents found in table salt. These salts have been kiln dried at high temperatures.

In contrast, sun-dried, mineral-rich, unrefined sea salt contains a wide range of trace minerals. The Celtic Sea Salt I have used for more than 25 years has the highest mineral content of any unrefined sea salt I have found. It contains more than 80 different trace minerals; it is 83% sodium chloride (31% sodium and 52% chloride) and 17% moisture and trace minerals. It tastes better than ordinary table salt.

Salt is a catalyst. When cooked with food, it neutralizes bitter flavors, balances the acid quality of fruits, and brings out a subtle richness and sweetness in food that you don't get when you add it at the table. Even desserts profit from the addition of a pinch or two of unrefined sea salt.

Celtic Sea Salt is harvested off the coast of Brittany, the northwestern region of France. This light grey sea salt is available in a coarse and a fine grade. Use finely ground sea salt in recipes that require little or no cooking or contain very little liquid, such as cookies and other baked goods. The coarse grade should only be used in recipes where there is sufficient time, heat, and liquid to dissolve it, such as cooked fruit compotes or simmered fruit sauces.

High quality unrefined sea salt costs more than lower quality, refined sea salt. Once you begin cooking with it, you'll find it worth the investment. However, if budget is an issue, or you want a product from closer to home, use Redmond Real Salt, which is harvested from a huge rock salt deposit near Redmond, Utah, halfway between Provo and St. George in the southwestern part of the state. This light pink sea salt does not contain any additives or chemicals, and it does not undergo heat processing. It is extracted from deep within the earth, and then crushed, screened, and packaged. It contains 50 natural trace minerals essential to human health, including natural iodine.

You can use unrefined sea salt in equal amounts to replace table salt and refined sea salt in any recipe. Although it contains slightly less sodium per teaspoon, you do not need to use more of it.

Where to find: Natural foods stores and online.

How to store: Store indefinitely at room temperature in its original packaging or a sealed glass jar.

FLOUR & GRAIN PRODUCTS

Arrowroot
About: This flavorless white flour is ground from the root of a tropical root vegetable. You can use arrowroot in place of cornstarch, measure for measure, if you are allergic to corn genetically modified food. organic, most corn and corn. now genetically modified.)

Where to find: In bottles in section of supermarkets and natu stores. You will save a small fortun you buy it in 1-pound bags on the baking aisle of natural foods stores, the health foods section of supermarkets, through a buying club, or online.

How to store: This keeps indefinitely at room temperature in an airtight jar.

Brown rice flakes
About: This product is made from short grain brown rice that has been fire roasted and rolled into quick cooking flakes, or steamed and rolled into thicker flakes. You can use it to replace quick cooking or old-fashioned rolled oats (oatmeal) in recipes.

Where to find: In natural foods stores and online. It's more readily available in Europe, the UK, and Australia than the U.S.

How to store: At room temperature in an airtight container in cool weather. Refrigerate or freeze in warm weather.

Brown rice flour
About: This flour, made from unpolished brown rice, contains the nutritious bran and germ. You can use it in baked goods combined with other flours.

Where to find: Although you can find it on the baking aisle of many natural foods stores, on the health foods aisle of some supermarkets, or online, it will be fresher if you grind it yourself. For this you will need a Vita-Mix or grain mill.

How to store: Made from the whole grain, it requires refrigeration or freezing to keep from going rancid. Store in a sealed container, like a wide-mouth canning jar.

White rice flour
About: This flour, made from polished white rice, has had the bran and germ removed, making it less nutritious than the whole grain. Use it in baked goods combined with other flours.

Where to find: In natural foods stores, supermarkets, in Asian markets, or online. You can also make your own flour by grinding short or medium grain white rice in a Vita-Mix or grain mill.

Oats and the Gluten-free Diet

According to dietitian Shelly Case, author of *Gluten-Free Diet: A Comprehensive Resource Guide*, "Historically, the avenin prolamin in oats was thought to be toxic based on the early work of Dr. W.K. Dicke and his colleagues in 1953; however, the safety of oats has been widely debated since then. Many studies in Europe and the USA over the past 10 years in both children and adults with celiac disease have revealed that consumption of moderate amounts of oats is safe for most people."

Case emphasizes that "the majority of studies showing oats safe for celiacs used pure, uncontaminated oats. Unfortunately, the majority of commercial oat products on the market are contaminated with wheat, barley, and/or rye during harvesting, transportation, storage, milling, and processing." Testing of various commercially available oats has revealed varying levels of gluten contamination.

Case believes that "Cross-contamination has been the major reason why most health professionals and celiac groups have not allowed oats on a gluten-free diet." A small number of companies in Europe and North America currently offer pure, uncontaminated oats. If you suffer from celiac sprue, seek out oats that have been certified gluten-free.

Whether or not a particular celiac patient can tolerate oats is an individual matter. Some individuals with celiac disease may not tolerate even pure, uncontaminated oats. The Celiac Sprue Association and many other celiac experts advise excluding oats until it can be determined whether the responses that occur arise from cross-contamination of commercially-processed oats, to the protein structure of the grain itself, or to individual differences among people.

Source: Shelly, Case. *The Gluten-Free Diet.* 2006. Saskatchewan, Canada: Centax Books, 2001 and 2006.

How to store: Because it is made from polished (white) rice, it keeps well at room temperature in an airtight jar. It lasts indefinitely, so don't worry about spoilage.

Sweet brown rice flour

About: This flour, made from whole grain sweet brown rice, has a sticky, glutinous texture not found in other varieties of rice. Despite the description, it does not contain gluten. It adds moisture and a cake-like texture to gluten-free baked goods. Use it in combination with other flours. Traditionally, this grain was used in Asia to make mochi (sweet rice cakes).

Where to find: On baking aisle of many natural foods stores, on the health foods aisle of some supermarkets, or online. It will be fresher if you grind it yourself using a Vita-Mix or grain mill.

How to store: Because it is made from the whole grain, it requires refrigeration or freezing to keep it from going rancid. Store in a sealed container, such as a wide-mouth canning jar.

Sweet white rice flour

About: This flour, made from refined (white) sweet rice, has a sticky, glutinous texture not found in other varieties of rice. It does not contain gluten. The word glutinous refers to the grain's sticky texture. It makes an excellent thickener or addition to gluten-free baked goods, where it adds moisture and a cake-like texture.

You must use it in combination with other kinds of flour. Traditionally, this grain was used in Asia to make mochi (sweet rice cakes).

Where to find: In natural foods stores, supermarkets, online, and in Asian markets under the name Mochikko Sweet Rice Flour.

Make your own flour by grinding polished sweet white rice in a Vita-Mix or grain mill. Polished sweet white rice can be found in natural foods stores and Asian markets.

How to store: Because it is made from polished (white) sweet rice, it keeps well at room temperature in an airtight jar. It lasts indefinitely, so don't worry about spoilage.

26

Chestnuts

About: Technically, the chestnut is not a grain, but for our purposes we'll lump it into this category. Chestnuts come from a species of deciduous trees and shrubs that belong to the beech family, which is native to temperate regions of the northern hemisphere. They produce an edible sweet-tasting nut that is high in carbohydrate and low in fat.

Look for fresh chestnuts in the shell in the fall and winter; dried and peeled chestnuts are available year round.

Cut an "X" in the shell of fresh chestnuts, and roast, boil, or pressure cook until tender (usually 30 to 60 minutes); then peel away the shells and the inner skin. Dried chestnuts require soaking and boiling or pressure cooking. See Chapter 6 for detailed instructions.

Where to find: Farmers' markets, some specialty and natural foods stores, and online.

How to store: Keep fresh chestnuts in the shell in a cool dry place or in the refrigerator. Keep dried chestnuts in a cool dry place, preferably in the refrigerator or freezer to prevent bug infestation. Refrigerate after cooking.

Chestnut flour

About: A century ago chestnut flour was more common than wheat flour in the Italian Alps. It's widely used in Italy and France, but relatively unknown in the U.S.

Not to be confused with water chestnuts, a different species altogether, chestnut flour is made from dried chestnuts. It makes a great addition to gluten-free cakes, bars, breads, muffins, pancakes, and more. Use it in combination with other flours.

Where to find: Some Italian and specialty foods stores sell this flour, but in most cases you will need to order it online. I like to order it from small American producers rather than the imported varieties all the way from Europe. (See Appendix for sources.)

How to store: Because it is made from a whole food, it requires refrigeration or freezing to keep it from going rancid. Store in a sealed container, such as a wide-mouth canning jar.

Millet flour/meal

About: A staple for millions in northern China and Africa, millet is t... grain that has a slightly alkaline in baked goods, millet flour or meal... a taste and texture almost indistinguis... from corn. Use it in combination v... another kind of flour.

Where to find: Although you can find it on the baking aisle of many natural foods stores, it will be fresher if you grind it yourself. You can make your own flour by grinding whole grain millet (sold in natural foods stores) in a spice-dedicated coffee grinder (a coffee-grinder used only for herbs and spices), Vita-Mix, or grain mill.

How to store: Because it is made from whole grain, it requires refrigeration or freezing to keep it from going rancid. Store in a sealed container, such as a wide-mouth canning jar.

Potato starch (unmodified)

About: Made from potatoes, this fine white flour adds lightness to gluten-free baked goods. It must be used in combination with other flours. Do not confuse this with potato flour; it is not the same and will not produce the same results in recipes.

Where to find: Look for it in natural foods stores, supermarkets, or by mail order. It is most readily available in chain grocery stores during Passover.

How to store: This keeps indefinitely at room temperature in an airtight jar.

Quinoa flakes

About: This product is made from partially cooked quinoa (see Quinoa flour) that has been rolled into quick cooking flakes. You can use it to replace quick cooking oatmeal in recipes. It has a slightly nutty, earthy flavor. It won't taste exactly like oats, but it will do the job.

Where to find: In natural foods stores and online.

How to store: At room temperature in an airtight container or in the refrigerator.

Quinoa flour

About: Pronounced (Keen-wa), this whole grain has a higher protein and mineral profile than most other grains. It is native to South America. The ancient Incas referred to it as the Mother Grain. It has a slightly bitter flavor and is best used with larger volumes of other flours.

Where to find: Although you can find quinoa flour on the baking aisle of many natural foods stores and on the health foods aisle of some supermarkets, it will be fresher if you grind it yourself. Because it has a soft shell, you can grind whole grain quinoa into a fine flour in a spice-dedicated coffee grinder if you don't own a Vita-Mix or grain mill.

How to store: Made from the whole grain, it requires refrigeration or freezing to keep from going rancid. Store in a sealed container, like a wide-mouth canning jar.

Rolled oats or oatmeal

About: A traditional standby, oats contain 50 percent more protein than wheat and twice as much as brown rice. While most of the fiber in other grains is the insoluble type, half of the fiber in oats is the soluble variety also predominant in fruits and vegetables, which has a cholesterol-reducing effect.

Rolled oats are what most Americans know of as oatmeal (old-fashioned, quick-cooking, or instant). This is the whole oat kernel or oat groat put through a steamroller that transforms them into flakes.

Where to find: Natural foods stores, health foods section supermarkets, or online.

How to store: Oatmeal (aka rolled oats) is more shelf stable than oat flour, but rolled oats can still become bitter if left too long at room temperature. Store in a cool dry place, refrigerate, or freeze if space permits.

Sorghum flour

About: This new flour, ground from specially bred sorghum, a grain grown in the Midwest region of the United States, contains more protein than rice and most other gluten-free grains. It makes a suitable replacement for wheat flour in recipes, although it produces the best results when combined with another kind of flour.

Where to find: Look for it in natural foods stores, the health foods section of supermarkets, or online. You can make your own sorghum flour by grinding whole grain sorghum in a Vita-Mix or grain mill.

How to store: Because it is made from the whole grain, it requires refrigeration or freezing to keep it from going rancid. Store in a sealed container, such as a wide-mouth canning jar.

FRESH FRUITS & CITRUS

About: The quality of fruit-based Ice Dream depends largely on the quality of the fruit you start with. If a recipe calls for fresh fruit, try to use only fruits that are in season so they will be at their peak of flavor and freshness.

Choose fruits grown as close to home as possible. For example, buy American-grown apples rather than New Zealand apples if you live in the U.S., and purchase apples from your state or region rather than from farther away, whenever possible. Fresh, locally grown produce will generally contain more vitamins and antioxidants than food picked long ago and far away. Locally grown and marketed food will also leave a lighter ecological footprint on the earth.

Some varieties of fruit will continue to ripen at room temperature after you bring them home, such as avocado, pineapple, pears, melons, and stone fruits such as apricots, peaches, plums, nectarines, and mangoes.

Note: If fruit is unripe and hard, place it in a bowl or paper bag at room temperature next to one or more ripe apples or bananas. The natural ethylene gas in the ripe fruit will speed up the ripening process of the unripe fruit. Once ripe, fragrant, and tender, refrigerate what you don't plan to consume within a few days.

With other fruits, such as berries, cherries, and apples, what you see is what you get. They won't get any riper than when you buy them, although they will get soft and mealy or mushy if left to sit too long.

Note: Lemons, limes, oranges, and other citrus fruits will soften and ripen a bit after picking, but not much. Rinse fruit before slicing, even if you plan to peel it. Wash the outside of melons with soapy water to remove any potential surface bacteria.

Where to find: Local farmers' markets, natural foods stores, and supermarkets.

How to store: Store unripe fruit in open bowls or baskets at room temperature. Store ripe fruit, as well as all berries, cherries, grapes, kiwifruit, and all sliced fruits, in the refrigerator. Apples, oranges, lemons, and limes can be kept at room temperature or in the refrigerator, depending upon available space.

Note: Citrus should be refrigerated at 42° F to extend shelf life. Unrefrigerated citrus will keep well for 7 to 10 days. Refrigerated citrus has a 21 to 30 day shelf life.

FRUIT JUICE

Fruit juice

About: While fruit is a whole food, fruit juice is not. Juice is a refined food, a highly concentrated substance extracted from whole fruits. Although it does not contain as many nutrients as whole fruits, it does serve a purpose in cooking, where it can sweeten while adding more vitamins and antioxidants than sugar or syrups.

Some of the recipes in this book call for fruit juices. Citrus juice can be easily squeezed or pressed from fresh fruit; the others should be purchased in glass bottles. Avoid juice packaged in plastic; chemicals can leach from the plastic into the juice and increase your risk of developing endocrine disorders. The softer the plastic, the more its chemicals interact with the juice.

Look for 100 percent real fruit juice or fruit juice concentrate. Buy organic whenever possible to avoid herbicide and pesticide residues.

Where to find: Supermarkets, natural foods stores, and farmers' markets. You'll find frozen fruit juice concentrates in the freezer section of markets.

How to store: Keep frozen concentrates frozen until ready to use. Store bottled juice at room temperature until you've broken the seal, and then refrigerate.

FRUIT PRESERVES

Fruit preserves

About: In recipes that call for fruit preserves or fruit-sweetened jam, look for products with the simplest and fewest ingredients. Look for a fruit-sweetened brand. Fruit, not juice, should be the first ingredient listed, with fruit juice concentrate as the sweetener instead of sugar, sucanat, fructose, or artificial sweeteners. I prefer St. Dalfours brand; you can find it in natural foods stores and many chain supermarkets. Unfortunately, most of the small, locally-made preserves in the U.S. contain sugar, which doesn't provide any antioxidants.

Where to find: The jam and jelly section of supermarkets, specialty, and natural foods stores.

How to store: Refrigerate after opening.

LEAVENERS

Baking soda

About: This white crystalline powder, also known as sodium bicarbonate, has a slight alkaline taste. It is a component of the mineral natron and is found dissolved in many mineral springs. The natural mineral form is known as nahcolite.

It is used to leaven baked goods. When combined with acidic ingredients and moisture, the acid-alkali combination creates carbon dioxide and makes baked goods rise. You don't need to buy a special kind—baking soda is baking soda.

Where to find: Supermarkets, drugstores, the baking aisle of natural foods stores, and online.

How to store: In an airtight container at room temperature.

Non-aluminum baking powder

About: This dry powdery substance is used in cooking, mainly for baking. Traditional baking powder was composed of a mixture of tartaric acid and bicarbonate of soda (baking soda), with a small amount of flour to reduce the strength. When dissolved in water, the acid and bicarbonate react and release carbon dioxide gas, which expands, producing bubbles to leaven the batter.

Most modern baking powders are double acting—they contain two acid salts, one that reacts at room temperature, producing a rise as soon as it is mixed into the dough or batter, and another that reacts at a higher temperature, causing a further rise during baking. This is the kind I prefer.

Baking powders that contain only the low-temperature acid salts are called single acting. They may work in conventional recipes that call for creaming the butter and sugar to introduce tiny seed bubbles that the leavening gas will further expand. Common low-temperature acid salts include cream of tartar, calcium phosphate, and citrate.

Because excess aluminum in the diet has been linked to Alzheimer's disease, I recommend that you find a brand of aluminum-free baking powder such as Rumford's or Bob's Red Mill; both are widely available. Read labels carefully because some brands may contain wheat.

Where to find: The baking aisle of natural foods stores, supermarkets, and online.

How to store: In an airtight container at room temperature.

NUT MILKS
Almond, hazelnut, and hemp milk

About: Nut milks are made from raw nuts which may or may not be soaked or blanched before they are blended with water and strained. Nut milks have a more watery consistency than cow or goat milk, but they make an adequate replacement for milk in cooking and baking. Homemade nut milk has a thicker consistency and a fresher and richer flavor; it's also lower in sugar.

Look for the brand with the lowest sugar content. Some companies now sell unsweetened almond milk. **Note:** The starch-splitting cereal enzymes used to make commercial almond and rice milks may interfere with the thickening in some recipes. This may present problems in recipes for puddings (especially rice pudding), custards, and pastries. I have not had problems using small amounts of nut milks in the recipes in this book, but you may encounter difficulties if you use larger amounts of these milks in recipes. To avoid this problem you can make your own nut milk and sweeten it with honey or agave.

To read more about this, refer to *The Garden of Eating: A Produce-Dominated Diet & Cookbook* (www.TheGardenOfEatingDiet.com), or search for one of the many recipes available online.

Where to find: Natural foods stores, the health foods section of supermarkets, and online.

How to store: Refrigerate after opening and use within 2 to 3 weeks.

NUTS & SEEDS

About: Nuts add a delightful crunch to so many recipes. Because of their high oil content (70 to 80% of calories from fat in most nuts), they go rancid quickly, but will keep well if stored in the refrigerator or freezer. Your best bet nutritionally, is to pick or buy nuts and seeds in the shell. You'll have to invest time in cracking them open. If this doesn't appeal to you, look for raw, shelled whole nuts and seeds.

Where to find: Farmers' markets, natural foods stores, produce or health foods section of supermarkets, or online.

Can Soy, Rice, or Nut Milk Replace Animal Milk?

Most milk alternatives, including soy, oat, rice, almond, and hazelnut milks, contain large amounts of sugar and very little protein. They are not suitable as replacements for milk for children or adults. Soy milk is the alternative that contains the most protein and has the best protein, carbohydrate, and fat profile if it's an unsweetened brand. However, controversy exists about the effects of soy phytoestrogens on human health. To read more about this, visit http://soyonlineservices.com or read *The Whole Soy Story* by Kaayla Daniel, Ph.D., CCN.

Most of the calories in rice milk beverages come from sugars formed from fermented rice. They contain low quality oil and too little protein or fat to nourish growing children. The sugar in one cup of rice milk is the equivalent of *two tablespoons* of white sugar. Many nut milks contain a tablespoon of sugar per cup.

These milks present similar problems for both children and adults when used in large amounts. They are better used for cooking, baking, or flavoring tea or coffee. Although unsweetened coconut milk does not contain sugar, it is too high in fat and calories to be used as a beverage. Instead, it works well as a replacement for cream or half-and-half in cooking, baking, tea, or coffee.

When Shopping for Nuts & Seeds

Look for

1) **Whole raw nuts and nut halves:** Whole nuts are higher in nutrients than chopped or broken nut pieces. Buy whole almonds, cashews, hazelnuts (filberts), and pine nuts. Buy walnut and pecan halves.

2) **Whole raw seeds:** Look for raw, unhulled brown or black sesame seeds, green pumpkin seeds (aka pepitas), and sunflower seeds.

3) **Refrigerated nuts and seeds:** Whenever possible, buy from a store that keeps these items in the refrigerator case; they'll be fresher than products at room temperature. If this is not possible, buy from a store that has a rapid turnover of product.

4) **As local as possible:** Choose nuts and seeds grown as close to home as possible—from your city, state, region, or bioregion—in preference to something from farther away.

5) **Fresh food:** If they taste or smell bitter or bad, return them to the store where you bought them and ask for a refund or exchange.

Avoid

1) **Crushed or slivered nut pieces:** When cut into smaller pieces they go rancid more quickly.

2) **Roasted nuts or seeds:** You can toast them at home at a lower temperature and without adding oil or salt.

3) **Candied nuts and seeds:** You can do this at home with less fat and sugar.

4) **Nuts and seeds treated with preservatives:** Nuts don't need sulfur dioxide (sulfites), dyes, maltodextrin and other starches, or MSG, and neither do you.

5) **Irradiated nuts and seeds:** These have a long shelf life but a lower nutrient content.

How to store: In the refrigerator or freezer, even after toasting or roasting. The longer they sit at room temperature, the greater the risk of their natural oils going rancid.

NUT BUTTERS

About: Nut butters are made from raw or roasted nuts that have been puréed into a thick creamy paste. Although peanut butter is the most well known, many other varieties exist. In fact, you can make your own nut butter if you own a food processor or Vita-Mix machine. If you want to make your own, you'll find a recipe in my book, ***The Garden of Eating: A Produce-Dominated Diet & Cookbook*** (www.TheGardenOfEatingDiet.com).

Look for natural nut butters free of hydrogenated oil, sugar, and preservatives. Some newer peanut butter brands contain honey, but I prefer unsweetened. If you can't afford to buy organic nut butters, make sure to buy only organic peanut butter. Conventional peanuts and peanut butter can have high concentrations of herbicide, pesticide, and insecticide residues.

Raw or roasted? Most of the time, I prefer the richness and depth of flavor of roasted nut butters over the raw varieties. Roasting breaks down some of the phytates and enzyme inhibitors in raw nuts that can cause gas and bloating. Still, you'll want to go easy on nuts and nut butters; they are very concentrated sources of calories.

Note: When you open a new jar, don't try to stir it until you transfer the contents to a bowl or food processor. Stir with a sturdy spoon or process until smooth; measure out what you need and return the rest to the jar, then cover and refrigerate. Now, the nut butter will have a more even consistency. It will never separate again, and you'll avoid making an oily mess.

Where to find: Natural foods stores, health foods section of supermarkets, and online.

How to store: Refrigerate after opening a sealed jar. Immediately refrigerate nut butters packaged in plastic tubs. Better yet, avoid buying nut butters in plastic containers.

OTHER
Applesauce, unsweetened

About: Made from cooked, puréed apples, it is one of the easiest sauces to make. Although you can buy this in stores, you

.. Know Your Nut Butters, ...

Most natural foods stores sell a wide assortment of raw and roasted nut butters. You can make your own from any kind of nut using a food processor fitted with a metal blade or a Vita-Mix machine. Pulverize warm, lightly roasted (or toasted) nuts, adding oil a little at a time if needed, to make a thick and creamy paste. This usually takes 2 to 3 minutes. If using a Vita-Mix, you will definitely need to add oil.

Note: Raw nuts are harder to blend and require more oil. They are also more likely to cause digestive distress because they contain more phytates, substances that can interfere with the action of your digestive enzymes. Toasting breaks down some of these substances.

FYI: If you or your family members suffer from a nut or soy allergy, you may need to make your own nut butters because some companies use the same equipment to make peanut butter as they do for tree nuts or soy.

Almond butter: Made from puréed raw or roasted almonds.

Cashew butter: Made from puréed raw or roasted cashews.

Peanut butter: Made from puréed roasted peanuts. These are legumes; don't eat them raw.

Hazelnut butter: Made from puréed raw or roasted hazelnuts. Rub off the bitter outer skins with a towel before pulverizing to reduce bitterness.

Macadamia nut butter: Made from puréed raw or roasted macadamia nuts.

Pecan butter: Made from puréed raw or roasted pecans.

Pistachio butter: Made from puréed raw or roasted pistachios.

Walnut butter: Made from puréed raw or roasted walnuts. Walnuts have very bitter skins that can give an off taste. Roast or dry toast walnuts; to reduce bitterness, rub off the outer skins with a towel, and then purée.

will find homemade applesauce infinitely more delicious. Once you have tried it, you will probably find store bought varieties watery and unsatisfying.

If you do buy it, look for a brand made from organic apples (commercial apples are heavily sprayed with pesticides) that contains no sweetener or is sweetened only with fruit juice.

Where to find: Supermarkets, natural foods stores, and online.

How to store: Refrigerate if homemade, or after opening; freeze to extend shelf life

SPICES

Apple pie spice

About: Look for non-irradiated, preferably organic herbs and spices free of added salt, MSG, sugar, corn syrup, FD & C dyes, artificial flavorings and colorings, hydrogenated or partially hydrogenated oils, and chemical names and numbers.

To economize, buy herbs and spices from the bulk section of a natural foods store or co-op. You needn't buy a lot. You can purchase whatever amount you want, from a tablespoon to a cup—more if you like, although you probably won't want more than that at one time. Buying small amounts allows you to experiment with new seasonings without committing to an entire bottle. Once you know what you like, you can purchase amounts to fill your own spice jars (usually about 1/2 cupful per jar).

Dried herbs and spices don't last forever. They begin to lose flavor and fragrance after about one year. Buy them from a store with a rapid turnover for the freshest product. Some of my favorite brands include Frontier Herbs, Spicery Shoppe, The Spice Hunter, and Simply Organic.

Whole spices will keep for 2 or 3 years in a cool dry place. If you buy these, you can grind them in small amounts in a spice-dedicated coffee grinder. Examples include whole coriander, cardamom, anise, fennel seeds, and cinnamon twigs.

Where to find: Natural foods stores, the health foods section of supermarkets, specialty kitchen shops, ethnic markets, and online.

How to store: In a cool, dry place in sealed bottles or jars at room temperature, away from heat and bright, sunny windows.

Do not store herbs and spices over or close to the stove, and avoid opening and measuring them out over hot pots.

Ginger (fresh gingerroot)

About: Gingerroot has been prized as a food and medicine by people all around the world for centuries. Many of the world's great cuisines rely on it and more than 100 species have been identified. This root, or underground stem, contains vitamins, minerals, antioxidants, and enzymes that benefit health. It adds a pungent, warm, and slightly spicy flavor to foods.

Where to find: Look for fresh gingerroot in natural foods stores and the produce section of supermarkets. The skin should be firm, smooth, and unblemished, and should be free of pink, black, or moldy spots. If possible, avoid buying ginger wrapped in plastic, which makes it hard to examine the quality and check for mold.

How to store: Store at room temperature (not in the refrigerator) in a basket or open bowl. Cut off slices as needed. The exposed portion will become dry; slice it off the next time you use it. Discard the gingerroot if it appears wilted, soft, mushy, or moldy.

Ginger juice

About: Fresh raw ginger is a popular ingredient in marinades, salad dressings, and Asian-inspired soups. It contains enzymes that help tenderize meat by breaking down its proteins, and that aid digestion. While some recipes call for minced or grated ginger, others call for freshly squeezed ginger juice without the fibrous pulp.

To make ginger juice, begin by peeling and finely grating a piece of fresh gingerroot. A microplane grater or flat Japanese-style grater works best. Pick up a handful of the grated mass and squeeze it in your fist over a small bowl to catch the juices. If you find this awkward, you can wrap the gratings in cheesecloth. Squeeze the juice through the fine mesh cloth. Either way, as long as the ginger is fresh, there should be no problem squeezing out enough juice.

If you use ginger on rare occasions only, you may not have any fresh on hand when needed. Some chefs recommend wrapping ginger tightly in a plastic bag and storing it in the freezer. To make juice, grate the frozen ginger and squeeze out the juice. Don't thaw it first—it is easier to grate when still frozen. I'm not a fan of this method.

Where to find: If you don't want to make it yourself, you can buy bottled organic ginger juice on the ethnic aisle of some natural foods stores. Read labels carefully to find a brand with nothing added except citric acid. The Ginger People make a very pure product.

How to store: If you squeeze more ginger juice than you need for immediate use, store it in a small jar in the refrigerator and use within a few days. Commercial bottled ginger juice will last for months in the refrigerator.

STABILIZERS

Cream of tartar

About: This white crystalline powder is a byproduct of the wine-making industry. It is used by bakers to stabilize and add volume to beaten egg whites. It is the acidic ingredient in some brands of baking powder.

Where to find: The baking aisle of supermarkets and natural foods stores.

How to store: At room temperature in an airtight container. It keeps indefinitely.

Guar gum

About: This powder is made from the seed of the plant *Cyamopsis tetragoncelloba*. You can use it to replace xanthan gum in gluten-free baked goods, where its fibers help to make up for the structure normally provided by gluten from wheat flour. Think of it as the scaffolding that will make gluten-free baked goods rise well and crumble less. It can usually be used interchangeably with xanthan gum.

Note: You don't need much of this; 1/4 to 1/2 teaspoon per cup of flour in cookies, quick breads, and muffins will usually suffice. Gluten-free baked goods that require kneading, such as yeast breads (which this book does not contain), require 1 to 2 teaspoons per cup of flour. Too much guar gum can cause gas, bloating, or loose stools in people with sensitive digestive systems.

Where to find: In natural foods stores, the health foods section of supermarkets, and online.

How to store: This keeps indefinitely at room temperature in an airtight container.

Xanthan gum

About: This powder is made from the dried cell coat of a microorganism called *Xanthomonas campestris*, grown under laboratory conditions. It is used in gluten-free baking to replace the gluten found in wheat. It makes up for the structure lost when you omit wheat. Think of it as the scaffolding that will make gluten-free baked goods rise well and crumble less. It can usually be used interchangeably with guar gum.

Note: You don't need much of this; 1/4 to 1/2 teaspoon per cup of flour in cookies, quick breads, and muffins will usually suffice. Gluten-free baked goods

Shopping for Healthy Cookies & Brownies

If you don't make your own brownies (or cookies), look for the brand that is lowest in sugar in natural foods stores or the health foods section of supermarkets.

The product should not contain any vegetable oils (corn, safflower, sunflower, canola, or soy oil), hydrogenated oil, fructose, or high fructose corn syrup. The healthiest fats for baked goods include butter, palm oil, palm shortening, and coconut oil.

If you follow a gluten-free diet, the cookies should not contain wheat, barley, rye, unbleached flour, enriched flour, cake flour, or all-purpose flour.

I recommend the following brands: Pamela's gluten-free baked goods, Mi-Del, Kinnikinnick, Jennies Macaroons, and Trader Joe's Gluten-Free Ginger Snaps. All have gotten good reviews.

Note: Read labels carefully; not all Trader Joe's cookies are gluten-free.

that require kneading, such as yeast breads (which this book does not contain), require 1 to 2 teaspoons per cup of flour. Too much xanthan gum can cause gas, bloating, or loose stools in people with sensitive digestive systems.

Where to find: In natural foods stores, the health foods section of supermarkets, and online.

How to store: This keeps indefinitely at room temperature in an airtight container.

SWEETENERS
Agave nectar (cactus honey)

About: Agave syrup, or nectar, is a sweetener commercially produced in Mexico from several species of agave plants, including agave tequilana (also called blue agave or tequila agave), and the salmiana, green, grey, thorny, and rainbow varieties. This sweetener has a thinner consistency and a slightly sweeter taste than honey.

To produce agave nectar, juice is expressed from the core (the piña) of the agave plant. It is filtered and then heated to hydrolyze (break down) the carbohydrates into sugars. The main carbohydrate is a complex form of fructose called inulin or fructosan.

Advantages of Agave

Agave nectar's main selling point is its low glycemic index (GI), which comes from its high fructose and low glucose content. Different sources vary in the exact percentage of fructose relative to glucose. According to Wikipedia, the free encyclopedia online, accessed February 1, 2008, "One source gives 92% fructose and 8% glucose; another gives 56% fructose and 20% glucose. These differences presumably reflect variation from one vendor of agave syrup to another."

The glycemic rating of agave nectar varies with the brand and depends on whether a particular chart uses white bread or pure glucose as the standard. With white bread as the standard (GI = 100), some varieties of agave nectar have a GI of 27, compared to 83 for honey. With glucose as the standard, I have seen the GI of agave syrup listed at 11, 19, and 32 verses 58 for honey.

For more on the glycemic index visit: http://www.mendosa.com/gilists.htm

Or read: *The New Glucose Revolution: The Authoritative Guide to the Glycemic Index - the Dietary Solution for Lifelong Health* by Dr. Jennie Brand-Miller, Thomas M.S. Wolever, Kaye Foster-Powell, and Stephen Colagiuri. New York: Marlowe & Co, 2003.

Syrup as Sweet as Honey

Agave nectar has the same caloric value as sucrose. Like honey, it is 25 to 50 percent sweeter than sugar, so it doesn't take as much to achieve the same level of sweetness. I use the same conversion formula for honey as I do for agave nectar, which you will find on page 65.

Note: I rarely make a one-to-one substitution. Instead, I prefer to replace 1/3 to 1/2 of the sugar, honey, or agave nectar in a recipe with stevia, dates, or some combination.

When baking, if you replace 1 cup of sugar with 3/4 cup of agave, you must reduce the liquids by 1/3 and reduce the oven temperature by 25° F, because honey and agave nectar brown more quickly than sugar. In salad dressings, sauces, smoothies, or Popsicles, where only a small amount of sweetener is called for, agave syrup may be used interchangeably with table sugar or liquid sweeteners without adjusting liquid or dry ingredients.

Shopping for Agave nectar

Whereas the color and flavor of honey can vary widely from one variety and source to the next, agave syrup has a milder and more consistent flavor. Light agave syrup is the most subtle. Dark amber agave syrup has a slight maple-like flavor. It dissolves readily in both hot and cold liquids. It has a long shelf life stored at room temperature. Unlike honey, it doesn't crystallize, so it's always easy to pour and measure.

Where to find: Natural foods stores and online. Some companies provide both organic and kosher certification.

How to store: At room temperature.

Brown rice syrup

About: In the Orient, people have been using rice malt as a sweetener for centuries. The traditional product, called "brown rice malt syrup" was made from cooked brown rice mixed with sprouted barley, which digests the carbohydrates in the grain, reducing them to simpler forms: maltose (grain-malt sugar), glucose, and water. Next they evaporate most of the water. Proponents of this sweetener claim that its high maltose content slows the release of the carbohydrates into the blood stream.

Most modern manufacturers use enzymes, rather than sprouted barley, to reduce the starches in the grain into simpler sugars; this makes their product gluten-free and safe for more consumers. Read labels carefully and seek out a brand, such as Lundberg Family Farms, that specifically says gluten-free.

You can use brown rice syrup measure for measure to replace honey, corn syrup, or maple syrup. **Note:** I rarely use rice syrup, except when I want a caramel-like taste. I prefer the flavor, economy, versatility (see notes below), and ecology of buying locally produced honey.

Important note about rice syrup: When used in recipes that contain thickening or leavening agents, enzyme-treated syrups may liquefy batters and doughs. The starch-splitting enzymes that turn whole grain brown rice into maltose-rich syrup can turn your cookies, cakes, pie fillings, and puddings into mush. This is more likely to happen in recipes that don't contain eggs.

Where to find: Natural foods stores, the health foods section of supermarkets, and online.

How to store: At room temperature.

Honey

About: A relatively unrefined and viscous sweetener produced by honey bees and derived from the nectar of flowers, honey tastes significantly sweeter than table sugar (3/4 cup of honey has the sweetening power of 1 cup of sugar).

The calories in honey come primarily from fructose (about 38.5%) and glucose (about 31.0%); the remaining carbohydrates include maltose, sucrose, and other complex carbohydrates. Although honey contains trace amounts of several vitamins and minerals, it is not enough to make a significant contribution of micronutrients to the diet. Honey also contains trace amounts of several antioxidant compounds, but not the quantity you'd get from eating fresh fruits and vegetables.

Because honey provides relatively empty calories, I rarely use it as the sole sweetener in recipes. Instead, I usually combine it with fresh or dried fruit, or trace amounts of stevia, so I don't need to use as much of it.

The distinctive colors, flavors, and textures of honey vary with the nectar the bees have access to. Some people complain that honey overpowers the flavor of recipes they use it in. The problem may be in the type of honey used. I recommend a light colored honey for a mild flavor and darker for a stronger flavor. The darkest varieties sometimes taste similar to molasses. You'll find many variations in between.

If you buy honey from small bee keepers in your state or region, or from stores that support them, you can find higher quality, more flavorful and fragrant varieties than what most supermarkets stock.

Where to find: Farmers' markets, specialty and natural foods stores, and supermarkets.

How to store: Store in an airtight jar at room temperature. If the honey crystallizes (mine rarely does), you can open the jar and set it in a bowl of hot water until it softens and liquefies.

Maple syrup

About: Maple syrup is made from the sap of maple trees. The traditional process of harvesting involved tapping a maple tree through the bark, into the wood phloem, and letting the sap run into a bucket, which required daily collections. Less labor-intensive modern methods use continuous plastic pipelines in all but cottage-scale production.

A mature sugar maple produces about 10 gallons of sap during the 4-6 week sugaring season. To make 1 gallon of pure maple syrup, approximately 40 gallons of clear, barely sweet maple sap must be boiled down. That means 39 gallons of water must be boiled away. That's why it costs more than other sweeteners.

Don't use maple-flavored pancake syrup. Look for pure maple syrup in one of three varieties or grades. Grade A maple syrup comes in amber, medium amber, and dark amber. Grade B comes later in the season and has a pronounced caramel flavor. The darker the syrup, the stronger the maple flavor. I recommend grade B or Grade A, medium or dark amber maple syrup.

Because maple syrup provides relatively empty calories, I rarely use it as the sole sweetener in recipes. Instead, I usually combine it with fresh or dried fruit, or trace amounts of stevia, so I don't need to use as much of it.

Where to find: Farmers' markets, specialty and natural foods stores, supermarkets, and online.

How to store: Refrigerate after opening.

Sorghum syrup

About: Sorghum syrup is a natural sweetener made by processing juice squeezed from the stalks of certain types of sorghum (*Sorghum bicolor*), also called sweet sorghum or sorgo. Sweet sorghum is grown for syrup or forage, whereas most other varieties of sorghum, commonly referred to as milos or kafirs, are grown for grain. Sweet sorghums resemble grain sorghum at maturity, except that the former grows three times taller, reaching a height of 12 feet or more.

Specialized milling equipment is used to extract the juice from the stalks, and evaporative pans with heating units are used to steam off excess water, leaving syrup. It takes 8 to 12 gallons of sorghum juice to make 1 gallon of finished syrup. Sorghum syrup has a light amber color like honey. If you live in a region where this is plentiful, you may use it to replace honey in recipes; however, don't confuse "sorghum" with "sorghum molasses."

The correct label for sorghum syrup is "sorghum syrup" or "pure sorghum." Molasses, unsulphured molasses, cane molasses, and cane syrup are byproducts of sugarcane processing and sugar crystallization. "Sorghum molasses" is a blend of sorghum syrup and sugarcane molasses.

Where to find: Some natural foods stores, health foods co-ops, farmers markets, or online.

How to store: In sealed jars in a cool, dry place.

Stevia extract powder

About: See pages 7, 9-11 for more on stevia. Look for *pure* stevia extract powder with nothing added. Sometimes the same company will produce 100% pure stevia extract powder as well as products that contain vegetable or grain starches, FOS, or other fillers; the latter will not work in my recipes.

My favorite brands include SweetLeaf

made by Wisdom Natural Herbs, NuNaturals, and Trader Joe's.

Where to find: Natural foods stores, supplement stores, and online.

How to store: At room temperature. It will not spoil.

Stevia extract liquid

About: See pages 7, 9-11. It's sold in an alcohol base and an alcohol-free glycerine base. My favorite brands of liquid stevia include SweetLeaf made by Wisdom Natural Herbs, NuNaturals, and Trader Joe's.

Where to find: Look for *clear* stevia extract liquid, plain or flavored, in natural foods stores, supplement stores, and online.

How to store: At room temperature. It will not spoil.

THICKENERS

Arrowroot (see Flour)

Agar agar powder

About: Although I usually use unflavored gelatin to thicken and stabilize fruit gels and Ice Dream, I offer the option of using agar agar powder for vegetarians and

---

What is agar agar?

Agar (a-gar') or agar agar is a gelatinous substance obtained from the cell membranes of some species of red algae (also known as seaweed). Agar agar has been used in the Orient for centuries. It is a unique and completely natural vegetarian substitute for gelatin. You can use it to thicken jellies, custards, ice cream, and other frozen desserts, as well as Japanese desserts called kanten. The word *agar* comes from the Malay word *agar-agar* (meaning jelly).

White, semi-translucent, and flavorless, it is sold in packages as washed and dried strips, or in powdered form. It naturally contains iodine and trace minerals. Its setting properties are stronger than unflavored gelatin, and it will set at room temperature after an hour.

vegans. In my recipes, it acts, like gelatin, as a stabilizer, improving the texture of the frozen custards; it adds loft (height and levity) normally provided by egg whites, and reduces icing during storage.

When shopping, look for agar agar *powder,* not agar agar flakes. The flakes cost more than the powder, and they have a different concentration—you need six times more agar agar flakes than powder, and the flakes require longer cooking to dissolve. If you were to use the flakes in my recipes, you would need to increase the water used for simmering, which would take 10 to 15 minutes instead of the 2 to 3 minutes for the powder. You may have to mail order agar agar powder or ask someone at your local natural foods store to special order it for you, because few natural foods stores keep it in stock. Agar agar powder is light in weight and very concentrated, so you don't need to buy a large quantity. Recipes in this book generally call for 3/4 teaspoon at a time, so a 2-ounce bottle will go a long way.

Where to find: Natural foods stores in the bulk foods or Asian/Macrobiotic section, in Asian markets, or online. Make sure it doesn't contain added sugar.

How to store: In a sealed jar in a cool, dry place.

Unflavored gelatin

About: Gelatin comes from the French word gélatine. It is a translucent, colorless, and nearly tasteless solid substance that historically has been extracted from the collagen inside the bones and connective tissue of animals. Some companies, such as Great Lakes Gelatin, now make it exclusively from pork skin or beef hide (not bones), giving consumers a choice of which variety they want, depending upon their dietary leanings. Although gelatin has many commercial non-food uses, we will concern ourselves here with its culinary applications.

Gelatin melts when heated and solidifies when cooled. It is best known for its role in making gelatin desserts, such as Jell-O, although it is also used to make jelly, trifles, aspic, marshmallows, and some candies, such as gummy bears. Gelatin also serves as a stabilizer, thickener, or texturizer in foods such as ice cream, jams, yogurt, cream cheese, and margarine; it is used in fat-reduced foods to simulate the texture of fat and to create volume without adding calories.

In the absence of heavy whipping cream, milk proteins, egg yolks and whites, or commercial stabilizers, homemade frozen desserts, particularly non-dairy versions, lack the light, lofty texture of premium ice cream. When made with very little sugar, honey, or maple syrup, frozen desserts freeze to a harder consistency and become difficult, if not impossible, to scoop directly from the freezer. (See more on this, and solutions, in Chapter 3.)

Unless stored in small, airtight containers, homemade frozen desserts develop ice crystals when frozen for more than a week or two. These problems can be minimized by adding unflavored beef- or pork-based gelatin to the custard or ice cream base. Gelatin helps to stabilize the dessert as it freezes, adding loft, improving the whipping quality, and yielding a smooth texture after freezing. It also helps frozen desserts withstand the rigors of repeated freezing and thawing.

Gelatin to Agar Agar Conversions

The following gelling agents may be used interchangeably; although they require different cooking times. For example, agar agar flakes need to be simmered for 10 to 15 minutes to dissolve.

2 tsp. agar agar powder = 1/4 cup agar agar flakes = 2 Tbsp. unflavored gelatin
1 tsp. agar agar powder = 2 Tbsp. agar agar flakes = 1 Tbsp. unflavored gelatin
3/4 tsp. agar agar powder = 4 tsp. agar agar flakes = 2 tsp. unflavored gelatin

Food grade gelatin comes in the form of sheets, granules, or powder. Recipes in this book call for unflavored, granulated gelatin sold in individual envelopes and boxes in supermarkets, and in canisters in natural foods stores. I usually use Great Lakes Gelatin, but have also used Knox brand with good results.

Where to find: On the baking aisle of supermarkets, in natural foods stores, in supplement stores, and online.

How to store: In a sealed container, in a cool dry place.

ZEST

About: Zest is the oil-rich outer skin of a lemon, lime, orange or other citrus fruit. It contains the flavorful and volatile oils of the fruit. Some recipes call for it in addition to the juice of the fruit. The process of removing citrus zest is known as zesting. Most kitchen supply stores sell tools specifically designed to remove the zest from citrus fruits.

Anatomy of a citrus fruit: The peel of a citrus fruit contains two top layers. The zest is the shiny, brightly colored, and textured part found on the outer surface of the fruit. The pith is the white fibrous membrane located below the zest; it protects the fruit inside. The pith has a bitter flavor so you don't want to add it to recipes.

There's more than one way to zest citrus fruit. Some zesters work like graters, delicately shredding the zest into tiny flakes. Others take the zest off in long strips, which make great decorations for desserts. Skilled cooks can remove lemon zest with a paring knife or vegetable peeler; it requires a light hand to take the zest and leave the pith behind.

The easiest way to grate the zest of a lemon, lime, orange, or other citrus fruit

How to Dry Zest

If you grate off more citrus zest than you need immediately (sometimes I do this on purpose), don't throw it away. You can spread it on a saucer, or thinly in a shallow bowl, and set it on a windowsill to dry at room temperature for 3 to 5 days. When crisp and no traces of moisture remain, transfer the dried zest to a small jar; label and date. You can use this in cooking or baking to add a zesty citrus flavor to salad dressings, sauces, puddings, compotes, cookies, cakes, chutneys, custards, and other dishes. You can replace 1 tablespoon of fresh citrus zest with 1 teaspoon of dried zest.

is to rinse or lightly wash the fruit with a biodegradable, non-toxic dish soap or produce wash; pat it dry, and then rub it along the smallest holes of a cheese grater or a microplane grater. Keep turning the fruit to grate off only the colored part (remember the white part tastes bitter). Use a spatula—not your fingers—to scrape the zest from the back of the microplane, which is razor sharp. Store the naked orange in a covered container in the refrigerator to keep it from drying out.

In baked goods, citrus zest can be used to add a burst of lemon, orange, lime, or tangerine flavor to the finished food product that you won't get from citrus juice alone. In simmered sauces or custards, long strips of citrus zest permeate the cooking liquid, intensifying the flavors of other foods and adding citrus overtones. Either way, the natural oils in the zest will infuse the food with flavor while also aiding digestion.

Shopping Checklist

ALCOHOL

- ❑ Brandy
- ❑ Banana liqueur
- ❑ Cognac
- ❑ Creme de cacao
- ❑ Creme de menthe
- ❑ Cherry liqueur
- ❑ Kahlua or other coffee liqueur
- ❑ Orange liqueur
- ❑ Rum: light, dark, or coconut
- ❑ White wine, dry
- ❑ Whiskey

CAROB

- ❑ Carob candy bars
- ❑ Carob chips
- ❑ Carob powder

CHOCOLATE PRODUCTS

- ❑ 70 to 73% dark chocolate
- ❑ Chocolate chips
- ❑ Cocoa nibs (cacao nibs)
- ❑ Unsweetened baker's chocolate
- ❑ Unsweetened cocoa powder

COCONUT PRODUCTS

- ❑ Coconut butter
- ❑ Coconut milk
- ❑ Coconut oil
- ❑ Shredded, unsweetened, sulfite-free coconut

COFFEE & TEA

- ❑ Coffee beans
- ❑ Coffee grounds
- ❑ Chai tea
- ❑ Green tea powder (matcha)
- ❑ Instant coffee or espresso granules
- ❑ Instant grain coffee
- ❑ Roasted chicory root granules
- ❑ Roasted dandelion root granules
- ❑ Teeccino

DRIED FRUIT

- ❑ Dates
- ❑ Dried apricots
- ❑ Dried bananas
- ❑ Dried cherries
- ❑ Dried strawberries
- ❑ Raisins

EGGS & EGG REPLACERS

- ❑ Ener-G Foods® Egg Replacer
- ❑ Liquid egg whites
- ❑ Whole eggs

FATS & OILS

- ❑ Almond oil
- ❑ Avocado oil
- ❑ Butter
- ❑ Coconut oil
- ❑ Palm oil
- ❑ Palm shortening

FLAVORINGS & EXTRACTS

- ❑ Almond extract/flavoring
- ❑ Butterscotch flavoring
- ❑ Caramel flavoring
- ❑ Coffee extract/flavoring
- ❑ Lemon extract/flavoring
- ❑ Maple flavoring
- ❑ Orange extract/flavoring
- ❑ Peppermint extract/ flavoring
- ❑ Vanilla extract/flavoring
- ❑ Yellow food color, natural
- ❑ Sea salt, unrefined, mineral-rich

FLOUR & GRAIN PRODUCTS

- ❑ Arrowroot
- ❑ Brown rice flakes
- ❑ Brown rice flour
- ❑ Chestnut flour
- ❑ White rice flour
- ❑ Sweet brown rice flour
- ❑ Sweet white rice flour
- ❑ Millet flour/meal
- ❑ Potato starch (unmodified)
- ❑ Quinoa flakes
- ❑ Quinoa flour
- ❑ Rolled oats/oatmeal
- ❑ Sorghum flour

FRESH FRUITS & CITRUS

- ❑ Apples
- ❑ Apricots
- ❑ Bananas
- ❑ Blueberries
- ❑ Blackberries
- ❑ Cherries

✓ CONTINUES NEXT PAGE

Shopping Checklist

☐ Blueberries
☐ Blackberries
☐ Kiwi fruit
☐ Lemons
☐ Limes
☐ Mango
☐ Melon
☐ Nectarines
☐ Oranges
☐ Peaches
☐ Pears
☐ Raspberries
☐ Strawberries
☐ Tangerines
☐ Tangelos

FRUIT JUICE

☐ Apple juice, apple cider
☐ Apricot juice/nectar
☐ Black cherry juice concentrate
☐ Blueberry juice blend
☐ Lemon juice
☐ Lime juice
☐ Peach juice/nectar
☐ Pear juice/nectar
☐ Orange juice
☐ Pineapple juice
☐ White grape juice

FRUIT PRESERVES

☐ Apricot fruit preserves
☐ Blueberry fruit preserves
☐ Peach fruit preserves
☐ Raspberry fruit preserves
☐ Strawberry fruit preserves

LEAVENERS

☐ Baking soda
☐ Non-aluminum baking powder

NUT MILKS

☐ Almond milk
☐ Cashew milk
☐ Hazelnut milk
☐ Hemp milk

NUTS & SEEDS

☐ Almonds
☐ Cashews
☐ Coconut (see coconut)
☐ Hazelnuts (filberts)
☐ Pecans
☐ Pumpkin seeds
☐ Walnuts
☐ Sesame seeds

NUT BUTTERS

☐ Almond butter
☐ Cashew butter
☐ Peanut butter
☐ Hazelnut butter
☐ Macadamia nut butter

OTHER

☐ Apple sauce, unsweetened
☐ Chestnuts, fresh or dried
☐ Chestnut purée, unsweetened

SPICES

☐ Apple pie spice
☐ Basil, fresh
☐ Cinnamon
☐ Cardamom, ground
☐ Nutmeg
☐ Pumpkin pie spice
☐ Ginger (fresh gingerroot)
☐ Ginger juice
☐ Ginger, dried, ground

STABILIZERS

☐ Cream of tartar
☐ Guar gum
☐ Xanthan gum

SWEETENERS

☐ Agave nectar (cactus honey)
☐ Brown rice syrup
☐ Honey
☐ Maple syrup
☐ Sorghum syrup
☐ Stevia extract powder
☐ Stevia extract liquid

THICKENERS

☐ Arrowroot
☐ Agar agar powder
☐ Unflavored gelatin

ZEST

☐ Dried lemon peel
☐ Dried orange peel

2

Equipment

H aving the right equipment can, in some cases, make or break your success in the kitchen. Although you may not need every item I've listed on the following pages, having a wide assortment of kitchen tools will help you turn out consistently delicious and nutritious dishes more easily and efficiently. To help you decide what you need now and what can wait, I've compiled a list of essential and optional equipment. Be assured that everything on this list will have multiple uses beyond the requirements of the recipes in this book.

You don't have to invest a small fortune to outfit your kitchen. If you can't afford new equipment, search online for special offers, shop for bargains at thrift stores or garage and estate sales, or buy used goods online at eBay or Craig's List. **Note:** Some chain kitchen and housewares stores accept coupons, their own or competitors, even after they've expired. Some allow you to use two coupons at once.

APPLIANCES
Ice Cream Maker (essential):

An ice cream maker is the most important piece of equipment you will need for making the recipes in this book. Machines for home use can run as little as $35 or as much as $2,000 new. Before you rush out and buy the least expensive model, read through this section to learn more about the pros and cons of each kind of machine.

How Does it Work?

Ice cream freezes by giving up its warmth to the ice or frozen coolant surrounding it. In some units, the canister rotates and the dasher stays put. In others, the canister stays put while the dasher circulates, scraping ice crystals from the sides back into the mix as they form.

Ice and Rock Salt Machines

These have been around for a long time and they're still the most economical. Models with plastic buckets start at $35. Models with wooden buckets sell for about $150. They come in 3-, 4-, and 6-quart models. You can get an electric or hand-crank version. Cranking usually takes 20 to 45 minutes.

Pros: You can have fun hand churning your own ice cream and get some exercise in the process. You can control the dasher speed and rate of freezing, and you can make large batches—double or triple the recipes I've provided. You don't need to prefreeze the canister, so you can make ice cream with less planning. If you have a hand-crank model you can do this outdoors. You can also make two consecutive batches of ice cream, provided you have enough ice and rock salt.

Cons: These machines require large amounts of crushed ice and rock salt. (Don't waste your good quality sea salt here.) For best results, you will need to at least double my Ice Dream recipes when using a 3- to 6-quart model. Motorized versions make a lot of noise and their large ice buckets can be unwieldy. You'll need to place the bucket in a sink or on the porch to allow drainage as the ice melts, and use a heavy-duty extension cord outdoors. Setup and cleanup is more involved with these units compared to sealed-in-coolant or self-refrigerating ice cream makers. You can't open the top to add mix-ins while churning. Models with wooden buckets also require presoaking, sometimes overnight, to prevent leaking. Do you still want one of these?

Sealed-in-Coolant Machines with Prechill Canisters

This is the newest, and my favorite, type of ice cream maker on the market. I think it's the most practical for home use, especially for busy people. These machines

---

⌐Anatomy of an Ice Cream Maker⌐

An ice cream maker has four basic parts: 1) a power source—that's you in the case of a hand-crank model, or electricity for electric-powered models; 2) a covered canister; 3) a dasher with scraper blades; and 4) a container of coolant or a container to hold the coolant (ice and rock salt for some machines).

Some models mount the motor above the ice cream canister. Others mount it below so you can lift the lid without removing the motor. Most units have an opening in the lid that allows you to monitor the freezing and add mix-ins (e.g., chopped nuts, chocolate bits, or berries) when your ice cream (or Ice Dream) is almost done.

The size and shape of the canister affects the freezing. Small machines work great for making small batches, and large machines work best for large batches. Ice cream makers work best when filled at least half full, although they should never be filled beyond the recommended capacity. So, you don't want to buy a 3- or 4-quart model if you live alone or prepare food for only two or three people. You'd do best with a 1- to 1 1/2-quart capacity.

are inexpensive and durable, and they perform well. They rely on a special coolant permanently sealed inside a hollow metal or plastic canister. Before you make ice cream (or Ice Dream), freeze the canister for at least 24 hours (some smaller manual units may require only 12 hours). Some units have a temperature indicator on the exterior to show when the chill chamber is thoroughly frozen; most do not. Follow the manufacturer's recommended pre-freezing time before churning ice cream; otherwise, your dessert won't freeze and you'll have to start over.

To churn ice cream, combine the dasher and lid with the prechill canister. If your unit is electric, place the canister on the base, plug it in, and turn it on so the dasher is moving, then pour in the chilled custard. The crank rotates until the mixture freezes, about 20 to 30 minutes. If your unit is not electric, simply turn a small crank 5 or 6 times every minute or two until the mixture appears thick and fluffy, usually 15 minutes.

Pros: These are easy to operate and cost $35 to $60. They don't require ice or salt. They don't take up a lot of cupboard or counter space. Children can use them with a little help from an adult. Clean up is easy. Electric units produce marvelously smooth and fluffy-textured frozen desserts that are lighter than ice cream churned in an old style motorized or hand-crank machine.

Cons: They require advance planning (but then so does making and chilling the custard for Ice Dream or ice cream). You have to clear away enough space to stash the canister in the freezer for at least 24 hours prior to making ice cream. You can't make two batches of ice cream in a row or on the same day unless you have two prechill canisters,* which you can buy in stores or order online.

* Note: You can get around this and still prepare a variety of flavors by making two or three batches of custard on one day and then churning one batch of Ice Dream a day, several days in a row, or over the course of a week, dividing each of the finished batches between several smaller containers so you have a selection of flavors on hand.

In very hot weather, if you don't have an air conditioner, the ambient temperature may thaw the coolant before the ice cream is completely frozen. If this happens, harden the soft ice cream (or Ice Dream) in the freezer for 1 to 3 hours before serving. During the summer months, churn the ice cream first thing in the morning.

Freezer with Self-Contained Refrigeration

These high-end models, most of them made in Italy, provide the ultimate in luxury. Like standard home freezers, they have a built-in compressor, which means the freezing element is built into the machine. Imagine freezer coils wrapped around an ice cream canister. A motorized dasher mixes the ice cream as it freezes. All you have to do is pour in the chilled custard, press a button, and wait. They work fast, incorporate very little air into the custard, and turn out dense premium ice cream in 30 to 45 minutes.

Note: If you decide to buy one of these, make sure it has a removable chilling container to make clean up easy and sanitary.

Pros: These are the most effortless and quiet to operate: no ice, no salt, and no canister to prefreeze. They freeze at lower temperatures than most ice cream makers and turn out better quality low-fat ice creams, sorbets, and gelatos. As long as you have chilled custard, you can make frozen desserts on demand and freeze several batches consecutively. The constant beating of the dasher produces velvety smooth, commercial-quality ice cream. After one batch is done, you can freeze another one almost immediately.

Cons: They don't call them the Rolls-Royce of ice cream makers for no reason. These models run from $160 to $1,500. They take up more counter or cabinet space than smaller machines, and range from 9 ½ to 20 inches wide by 10 to 13 ½ inches deep, and 12 to 13 ½ inches across. Some cannot be moved without waiting 12 hours before use, because moving the unit upsets the coolant in its freezing system. This is not a problem if you keep it permanently positioned on the counter for ready use, but impractical in a smaller kitchen. Some weigh as much as 60 to 75 pounds; others weigh in at 20 to 30 pounds.

That said, I have a friend who has owned one of these machines for 30 years. She uses it regularly, often making many batches one after the other for parties. It has endured several cross-country moves and survived the eager hands of grandkids. Her machine can turn out several batches of ice cream in 15 to 20 minutes. She is one happy user.

Note: If you lose the instruction manual for your ice cream maker, you can find a copy online at http://www.pickyourown.org/icecreammakermanuals.htm

Blender or Vita-Mix: Aside from your ice cream maker, and possibly a food processor, this will be your next most important piece of equipment for making recipes in this book. You'll need one of these tools for blending the base (custard) for the Ice Dream recipes, for puréeing dried fruits for the cookies and brownies, and for some of the sauces. Immersion or stick blenders will not work for these purposes.

Replace the blade and/or motor on your blender if it's old and doesn't mix well. Look in the phone book or online for an authorized repair center in your city. The parts are often very inexpensive. If you've burned out blenders, as I have, consider getting a Vita-Mix. **Note:** You can save $25 on a Vita-Mix if you use author Chef Rachel's affiliate code 06-001266.

Food processor: While it's not absolutely necessary to have this, you'll find it makes blending dates and mixing cookie dough infinitely faster and easier than mixing in a blender. They come equipped with a metal slicing blade that can thinly slice

My Favorite Ice Cream Makers

I've tried at least half a dozen ice cream makers. The one I use the most is my Cuisinart.

Cuisinart: I get the most mileage from this sealed-in-coolant style Cuisinart Ice Cream Maker (1 1/2 quart). It's durable, easy to assemble and operate, and easy to clean up. Similar models include the Cuisinart Classic Ice Cream & Sorbet Maker and the Pure Indulgence 2 Quart Automatic Frozen Yogurt, Sorbet, and Ice Cream Maker. To make two batches of ice cream (or Ice Dream) simultaneously, get the Cuisinart Duo Frozen Yogurt 1 Quart Ice Cream Maker. It has two canisters and space for both to run at the same time.

I've used the Cuisinart Mix-It-In Soft Serve Ice Cream Maker, but I don't use it often because it takes more time to assemble and is much harder to clean up than their standard models. It gets very messy if you don't let the canister freeze solidly before you try to churn the custard.

Krups La Glacière: A good sealed-in-coolant style machine that's easy to operate; however, mine didn't hold up well. The sides came apart and leaked coolant. I also found that the top-mounted motor made clean up messier. The company is coming out with a new model that will probably overcome these weaknesses.

Rival 1- and 1 1/2-quart Ice Cream Makers: This sealed-in-coolant style machine makes great ice cream and operates smoothly; however, it takes some fiddling to assemble and disassemble the top-mounted motor onto the lid. I broke one lid trying to snap apart the pieces for clean up.

Nordic Ware Non-Electric Ice Cream Maker: This hand-crank, virtually silent model requires no electricity to operate. It makes only 1 ½ pints (3 cups) worth of ice cream at a time, though. If you have custard that won't fit in the machine, you can pour it into Popsicle molds.

Machines to Try

I have not tried these machines:

Camper's Dream Mega Ice Cream Maker: What a novel idea. This ball-shaped ice cream maker requires no electricity. You just add ice and rock salt to one end and ingredients to the other, then roll or throw the ball around for 20 minutes (no kicking), and—voila—homemade ice cream.

KitchenAid Ice Cream Maker Attachment: Perfect for anyone who owns a KitchenAid mixer. The rotating dasher and insulated freezer bowl attach to your mixer, whipping up two quarts of your favorite frozen dessert in just 20 to 30 minutes. Mixing action blends ice cream to a velvety smooth consistency, while a specially formulated liquid inside the double-walled bowl ensures uniform freezing.

Deni Soft Serve Ice Cream Maker: This sealed-in-coolant style machine has a 1 1/2 quart capacity and dispenses soft-serve ice cream.

Rival Gel Canister Electric Ice Cream Maker: This newer model of sealed-in-coolant style machine has a space-saving freezer bowl and ring that nest together for compact freezer storage, so it takes up less space than other prechill canisters. Online reviews suggest easy cleanup with this 1 1/2 quart model.

Villaware Electric Ice Cream Maker: This sealed-in-coolant style machine has a 1 1/2 quart capacity and two speed selection for different consistencies. It resembles the Cuisinart Ice Cream Maker.

Euro Pro Triple Canister Ice Cream Maker: You can whip up three different kinds of ice cream at once with this unique triple-canister appliance made of stainless steel. How cool is that?

Cuisinart ICE Supreme Commercial Quality Ice Cream Maker: Has a built-in compressor freezer, so there's no bowl to pre-freeze. This self-contained refrigerant style machine will process batch after batch of scrumptious ice cream, fruity sorbet, and frozen yogurt. Just add the ingredients and turn it on.

Gelato by Lello and Lello Gelataio: A self-contained refrigerant style ice cream maker. Just add the ingredients and turn it on.

Stainless Steel Lussino Ice Cream Maker by Musso (1 quart); Musso Stainless Steel Pola Ice Cream Maker (2 quart): self-contained refrigerant style ice cream makers. Just add the ingredients and turn it on.

several pounds of cored and halved apples in record time. You'll find many other uses for this machine. I love the versatility of my 14-cup capacity Cuisinart food processor. If you can't buy one that large, get one with at least a 7-cup capacity.

Spice-dedicated coffee-grinder: Even if you don't drink coffee, you'll want to have one of these to grind whole spice seeds for the freshest flavor and best fragrance. If other family members use one for coffee, buy a second grinder dedicated to spices. You can get them for as little as $15.

Note: To clean the inside of the container between spices, add 1/4 cup of baking soda, cornstarch, or 2 tablespoons of white rice; cover and grind to pull away spice residues, and then empty. Do not use water or a damp cloth to clean.

Can I Make Ice Cream in My Vita-Mix?

You may have seen advertisements in magazines with eye-popping pictures of strawberry frozen yogurt or other concoctions made in a Vita-Mix. I've made these desserts and they taste great, but the machine does not freeze anything. You freeze the ingredients first, and then blend them in the machine using approximately one part liquid to four parts frozen material to produce an icy mixture with a texture similar to sorbet or frozen yogurt. In this case, the mix is the coolant. You freeze the ingredients and the high-powered, high-speed machine purées them.

Don't get me wrong. I love my Vita-Mix and I get a lot of use out of it. It's an amazing machine that performs many tasks very well, but it won't work for turning out the frozen dessert recipes in this book.

Electric mixer (essential if you plan to make macaroons or angel food cake): You don't have to spend a lot for this. If you need one only for beating egg whites and an occasional cake batter, buy a $15 handheld mixer instead that comes with 2 beaters. If you already have a stand mixer, you're set.

Toaster oven: I use my Cuisinart Convection Oven Toaster Broiler daily, not only for toasting nuts and cooking, but also for reheating leftovers, including some of the desserts from this book. A toaster oven with a convection mode takes less time to preheat and uses less energy than a conventional full size oven. Surrounding food with evenly heated airflow saves energy, retains more of the natural flavors than a microwave, and eliminates the risk of radiation leakage imposed by microwave ovens. Look for one that's large enough to bake a 9-inch pie or 9x9x2-inch fruit crisp.

BAKING PANS & TOOLS

Baking mats/baking liners: Silpat, Cook-eze, Exopat, and similar rubber-like baking mats turn any baking pan into a nonstick surface. They come in a variety of sizes to line cookie sheets, roasting pans, and cake pans. Place cookies, cake batter, or other raw material directly on the mat and bake. The pan won't need greasing and the food won't stick. Made from food grade silicone, they can be used 2,000 to 3,000 times and they are safe up to 600° F.

Baking pans (essential): Look for sturdy stainless steel or tempered glass baking pans. You'll need an 8x8x2-inch square or 9-inch round baking pan for brownies and blondies. You'll need a 9x9x2-inch square or 12-inch oval gratin pan for fruit crisps. For a double batch, you'll need two of these or an 11x17x2-inch square baking pan. For stainless steel pans without the usual non-stick finish, contact Natural Lifestyle online at http://www.natural-lifestyle.com/

Baking sheets & cookie sheets: You'll want at least two sturdy stainless steel cookie sheets or baking pans with shallow rims to keep food from falling off, especially when toasting nuts. Don't substitute oblong pans with 1 1/2- to 2-inch sides—your cookies won't bake evenly.

It's difficult to find baking sheets that don't have nonstick coatings; however, Natural Lifestyle still sells them and so do other online vendors. Standard sizes include 12x5 1/2 and 11x7-inch.

Note: If you use aluminum pans, line them with parchment paper or a Silpat bake liner.

Pie plates: I use these for pies, fruit crisps, and baked custards. Look for a deep-dish 9- or 10-inch Pyrex pie plate.

Springform pan: This is a two piece pan that has sides that can be removed and a bottom that comes out. It has a round base and an interlocking band, usually 2 to 3 inches high, that forms the sides, opening and closing with the flick of a latch. Assemble the pan pieces for baking or making an ice cream cake; once the contents have cooked and cooled (or frozen, for recipes in this book), open the band to remove the sides.

Springform pans come in a variety of sizes with 8, 9, and 10 inches in diameter being the most common. It doesn't matter whether you buy one with a smooth or dimpled bottom because you'll be greasing and lining it with parchment paper.

Cooling racks (essential): You'll use these to cool baked goods still in the pan or after they're removed from baking sheets. These should be metal and of sturdy construction. Buy stacking racks if you don't have much counter space.

Muffin tins: Look for heavy-duty stainless steel muffin tins. I usually avoid pans with nonstick coating because of the potential health hazard and environmental harm. Very few stores sell uncoated stainless steel tins. Check online for sources. I've had great success with the ones I purchased from Natural Lifestyle http://www.natural-lifestyle.com almost 20 years ago.

Oven mittens: Get heavy-duty mitts for serious protection against heat, steam, and splatters. Don't waste your money on cheap cotton or polyester mitts. I prefer mitts rated to 450° F that work well even when wet. Keep two on hooks near the stove.

Trivets: Have at least 6 heavy-duty wood, cork, ceramic, tile, or quilted cloth trivets to keep hot pots and baking pans from burning counters, table tops, and tablecloths.

Unbleached parchment paper (essential): Use this paper to line baking trays for easy clean up, to roll out cookie dough without having to flour the dough or the cutting board, and for lining aluminum foil so it doesn't come in contact with food. Avoid carcinogenic dioxin bleaches by choosing unbleached brown colored parchment sold in kitchen shops and natural foods stores.

Unbleached muffin liners: Use to line muffin tins. Look for unbleached (brown colored) liners; the muffins won't stick like they do to bleached and colored papers, and you'll avoid toxic dyes and bleaches.

BOWLS

Mixing bowls (essential): You can't have too many mixing bowls. You'll need them for chopping, premeasuring, and mixing multiple dishes. They serve double duty for food storage in the refrigerator, where you can cover them with a small saucer or 9-inch dinner plate, and stack as needed.

I prefer nested stainless steel bowls because they are lightweight, easy to lift, and they do not break. Invest in one or two sets. You may be able to find the odd piece at a thrift store or garage sale. Heatproof glass bowls also work, but they are heavier.

Get at least one 4-, 8-, 12-, 16-, 24-, and 32-ounce bowl. Lids are a plus but not essential. Invest in 6-, 8-, and 12-quart stainless steel bowls for washing a lot of fruit at once.

Prep bowls and custard cups (essential): Small stainless steel or glass preparation bowls allow you to measure out all of the ingredients for a recipe (or multiple recipes) before you start cooking. You'll find pinch bowls (starting at 1/8 cup or 2 tablespoons) handy for portioning out salt, spices, and many other ingredients, and slightly larger sizes for oil, nuts, nut butter, syrup, and other essentials. These small bowls make a large contribution to organization and efficiency in your work space.

KNIVES & BOARDS

Wood or bamboo cutting boards: Get one large, thick, sturdy wood cutting board—preferably 12x18x1-inch—to leave on the counter for daily chopping of fruits, vegetables, and nuts. Wood boards are more attractive and durable, and they won't dull your knives as quickly as plastic boards.

But aren't plastic boards more sanitary? Although they have been touted as being more sanitary, plastic cutting boards trap bacteria, according to a study conducted by microbiologists at the University of Wisconsin's Food Research Institute (Madison). "Tests proved that wood cutting boards are actually so inhospitable to contaminants like poultry and meat juices that bacteria disappeared from wood surfaces within minutes. On the other hand, bacteria from the plastic boards multiplied at room temperature." (Source: *The Food*

Lovers Tiptionary: An A to Z Culinary Guide with more than 4,500 Food and Drink Tips, Secrets, Shortcuts, and Other Things Cookbooks Never Tell You by Sharon Tyler Herbst, Hearst Books 1994).

Note: Do not soak wood boards or put them in the dishwasher. Clean with a sponge or dishcloth and citrus-based dish soap or all-purpose cleaner and water, then wipe with a towel. Every few months, saturate the board with olive or coconut oil, and allow the oil to soak in overnight to moisten and prevent warping and cracking.

Chef's knife (essential): You don't need a fancy set of knives. You do need one or two high quality chef's knives or Japanese-style vegetable knives. You'll enjoy chopping and you'll work more efficiently if you have a good, sharp knife (and you keep it that way). You can use this knife for most things: fruit, nuts, meat, and awkward items, like

You Have to Sharpen Them?

Quality knives help you cut food faster, more easily, attractively, and safely. But you have to keep them sharp. Unfortunately, many people neglect sharpening even first-rate knives, making kitchen prep more difficult, tiring, and potentially dangerous. Before you rush out to buy a knife sharpener, you need to understand the difference between sharpening and honing. Although you need to do both regularly, these tasks require different tools.

Sharpening

This involves regrinding the edge of a dull knife once it has "brittled off." A knife sharpening expert can do this for you using machinery too large and costly to keep in your home. Check the yellow pages in your area for a shop that sells knives and offers this service. Call gourmet kitchen and cutlery shops in your area. If they don't sharpen knives, they can refer you to a skilled machinist who does. Fees for sharpening often run $1 to $2 a knife.

For best results, have your knives professionally sharpened once every six months. At home, hone your knives at least once a week. For heavy use, you'll need to hone and sharpen them more frequently. If you regularly use your knives to cut through fibrous and hard produce, you'll need to sharpen them even more often, in which case you might as well buy a manual or electric knife sharpener. Prices start at about $20.

Honing

Using a sharpening steel requires a great deal of precision. You have to keep the knife at a constant 15 to 25 degree angle, depending on the type of knife, as you move it from one side to the other across the steel in an arching motion. Many home cooks have difficulty getting the angle right. As a result, they can inadvertently dull or damage their knives or fail to create a consistently sharp edge.

For ease and simplicity, you can buy a device that holds your knife at the precise angle while you stroke it across tension-mounted miniature steel rods in the device's frame. It hones the blade in half the time required by conventional steeling. These easy-to-use tools require no special skills. They eliminate the uncertainty and inconsistency of using an unguided steel. They take up very little space on the counter or in a drawer, and allow you to fine tune knife blades within minutes. You can get a good one for less than $45.

hard winter squash. They're durable and lightweight.

Look for a knife with a comfortable handle and full-tang construction. This means the blade is one solid piece that extends through the handle to prevent the knife from coming apart. Still, don't put a good knife in the dishwasher.

I recommend hollow ground Santoku-style knives (a combination lightweight cleaver and all-purpose chef's knife) made by Mac, Messermeister, Cuisinart, and others. I also like the Japanese-style vegetable knives with a squared-off blade from Mac, NHS Professional, and Caddie Vegetable Knives. I find 6- to 7-inch blades the most versatile. You can get a good knife in this category for $30 to $120. Ceramic versions run more.

Note: Do not put knives in the dishwasher and don't drop them into a sink or pan of dishwater. Wipe with a sponge, wet rag, or bottle brush; rinse and dry with a towel and return the knife to the cutting board, a knife block, or a knife case or guard.

Note: You're more likely to cut yourself with a dull knife. Sharpen once a week with a rod, stone, machine, or other appropriate device. Some meat or kitchen shops will sharpen your knives free or for a small fee.

Paring knives: Along with a chef's knife, get a smaller version of one or two of the knives above—something with a 3- to 4-inch blade—and you can make any recipe in this book and perform most kitchen tasks. Mac paring knives start at $14. Santoku-style paring knives run slightly higher. Ceramic versions run even higher.

Serrated knife (great for chocolate): While not essential, a serrated knife works quite well for chopping chocolate bars into small pieces. Consider a long bread knife or a smaller tomato knife for this job. Prices run the gamut, but you can get a decent one for $15 to $20. You'll find countless uses for it.

Honing tool (essential): These non-electric tools are inexpensive and easy to operate. You run the knife between 2 tension-mounted sharpening steels that simultaneously hone both sides of the blade at the correct angle. I have a Chef's Choice Steel Pro and a Chantry by Messermeister.

Knife sharpener: Many people have difficulty using sharpening rods and standard sharpening steels without dulling or damaging their knives. Sharpening with a machine is an easier option. If you buy an electric sharpener, check out Chef's Choice manual and electric, 1-, 2-, and 3-stage knife sharpeners.

Knife guards: Also called edge guards, these hard plastic tools slip over the blade of your knife, protecting your fingers and the blade when in storage. Get one for each of your sharp knives if you don't have a knife block.

MEASURING TOOLS

Measuring spoons (essential): Buy sturdy heavy-gauge stainless steel measuring spoons that go from 1/8 teaspoon up to 1 tablespoon. I have four sets, and I think every kitchen should have at least two. One set should be narrow enough to reach into spice jars, allowing you to measure wet and dry ingredients without having to stop to wash and dry in between ingredients. Hang the sets on hooks near the blender, stove, and cutting board.

Measuring cups (essential): Get at least one set of sturdy heavy-gauge stainless steel dry nesting measuring cups that includes 1/4-, 1/3-, 1/2-, and 1-cup measures (some sets include 1/8 cup, which is 2 tablespoons). I prefer metal over plastic because the latter can absorb odors, hold oil residues, and leach toxins into your food.

Liquid measuring cups (essential): I think every kitchen should have 1-, 2-, and 4-cup heatproof liquid measuring cups. Although you can use clear plastic, I prefer Pyrex for reasons noted above. The larger sizes also work for mixing some batters.

Food scale (essential): Accurate measurements are crucial to many recipes which often require precision that can only be expressed in weight. If a recipe calls for 3 1/2 pounds of apples, it's hard to estimate the weight because apples vary so much in size. Placing the apples on a scale will tell you how much you need for a given amount of spices and other ingredients, increasing the likelihood that your dish will turn out good.

For recipes in this book, you'll need a scale for weighing fruit and chocolate. I use one daily for vegetables and meats as well. **Note:** Digital scales are usually more accurate than spring-loaded models, particularly for lightweight foods.

Look for a scale that weighs from 1 ounce to several pounds. I have a compact stainless steel digital scale from Ikea that cost about $24. It weighs in both ounces and grams up to 6 1/2 pounds of food. I also have a larger Cuisinart scale for bulkier and heavier items. It holds up to 22 pounds of food. I use it a lot for weighing out 3 or 4 pounds of apples or bulky vegetables. I keep both on the counter all the time.

MIXING TOOLS

Mixing spoons (essential): Buy assorted sizes and shapes of wood and metal spoons for mixing, mashing, and serving. They're more durable and safer than plastic spoons, particularly when used to stir hot food.

Bamboo rice paddle: This is the perfect tool for removing ice cream or Ice Dream that has frozen solidly on the side of your ice cream canister. It won't damage the canister the way metal spoons and spatulas can.

Wire whisk (essential): This ball- or teardrop-shaped mass of wires extends from a handle, allowing you to stir, mix, and aerate batters or easily incorporate ingredients such as melted chocolate into other liquids. Look for a stainless steel whisk. You might want a couple of sizes. Flexible whisks work best for thin batters and liquids; stiff ones for thick batters.

Flexible spatulas (essential): Multiple sizes come in handy for scraping ingredients off the sides of bowls during mixing and out of pots, saucepans, bowls, and jars. I prefer heatproof silicone spatulas because they won't melt when they contact hot pots or ingredients.

OTHER TOOLS

Aluminum foil: When you use this to cover a baking pan, cut a piece of unbleached parchment to just cover the pan's contents; use a larger piece to cover the pan with enough overhang to crimp the foil to make a tight seal. When wrapping leftovers in foil, cut a piece of parchment slightly smaller than the foil and place this between the food and the foil to insulate the food and keep it from absorbing aluminum.

Colander (essential): Use to wash and drain vegetables and fruits. Stainless steel lasts longer than plastic; it won't absorb odors or leach chemicals into your food.

Cotton or linen napkins: You'll want to have a few cotton or linen napkins to wrap up dry baked goods to revive them with steam before serving. Thick towels won't work for this purpose.

Flour sifter (essential): Look for a stainless steel sifter; you'll use it to aerate flour for baked goods.

Funnel (essential): A narrow funnel helps pour dried herbs and spices into bottles and soups, stocks, and sauces into jars without mess. A wide mouth funnel will prove useful for transferring cooked fruit compote, sauce, and liquid Ice Dream custard to wide mouth glass jars for storage without spilling the contents. I prefer stainless steel.

Kitchen shears (essential): These are an important tool for a working kitchen. You can use them to cut parchment paper, open packages (don't use a knife for this—it's dangerous and it dulls your knife), cut string, and slice dried fruit. I prefer to use a small pair for slicing dried fruit, leaving the larger, sharper shears for cutting chicken.

Popsicle molds: You'll need these to make Ice Dream Pops. They come in a wide array of shapes and sizes, including flat, rectangular, rocket, 3-tier, shooting star, and sailboat shapes. Look for them in kitchen shops, department stores, and online at www.amazon.com, www.alphamom.com, www.williams-sonoma.com, www.target.com, and other websites.

Metal spatula (essential): You'll need this versatile tool for removing cookies and fruit crisp from baking pans. The sharper the edge, the better it works. Look for one made of stainless steel. I prefer a mini-spatula for removing brownies from the pan.

Timers: Even if you think you can multi-task, get two of these to keep track of cooking times. Keep them on the counter and discipline yourself to use them. If the timer on your oven works well, you may need to buy only one.

Thermometers (essential): To make sure your oven, refrigerator, and freezer are operating at the proper temperatures, invest in special thermometers designed for each of these spaces. You will prevent premature food spoilage, be able to monitor the accuracy of your oven, and prevent over or under baking (provided you also use a kitchen timer). See Chapter 3 for more.

Tea towels or dish towels (essential): Have at least 12 sturdy cotton dish towels and change them daily. A good supply can eliminate the need for paper towels.

Tongs or slotted spoons (essential): You'll need at least one of these for lifting and turning poached fruit or removing it from liquid. A slotted metal spatula will sometimes work.

Ruler and measuring tape (essential): Keep these in a kitchen drawer for measuring the size of pots, pans, and parchment paper and to score cookie dough to insure that you're using the right size pan for your recipes to bake evenly.

Strainers (essential): Use to drain just-washed berries and other fruit and to strain out whole herbs and spices from simmered liquid. A small tea strainer with a long wooden handle and wire mesh basket that fits into a tea cup will come in handy for straining out gingerroot or tea.

Marking pens: A colorful assortment will come in handy for writing on masking tape to mark the contents and dates of foods.

Wide masking tape (essential): Keep a roll in the kitchen for labeling jars and other food storage containers that you plan to place in the refrigerator or freezer. Indicate the date and contents of the container.

SAUCE POTS & PANS

Saucepans and skillets (essential): Look for heavy-gauge stainless steel pots and pans, the thicker the better, to reduce burning and facilitate cleanup. Insulated handles and a warranty are a plus. My essentials include a 1-cup and a 2-cup, two 1 1/2-quart, one 2 1/2-quart, and one 3-quart saucepans for steaming, simmering, boiling, stewing, and other tasks. A 3 1/2- to 4-quart enamel-lined cast iron or stainless steel Dutch oven will work for applesauce and fruit compotes, but it's not essential. You'll need a tight fitting lid for each pan.

Heavy-duty stainless steel skillets are just as handy. I recommend 8- to 9-inch, 10-inch, and 12- to 13-inch sauté pans with tight fitting lids for each.

My favorites: Cuisinart, All-Clad, Multi-Clad, and Neova. All but the Neova are sold in kitchen shops. Neova waterless cookware is sold through Vita-Mix Corporation. These pots and pans cost more, but they come with a 25 year warranty.

Stacking steamer trays, bamboo or metal: Look for a set of 2 stacking bamboo steamer trays with a lid. They should have a tight weave and sturdy construction and measure at least 8, and preferably 10 inches, from inside edge to inside edge for maximum versatility.

To use the steamer, rest it inside the rim of a wok or over a pot that has a matching diameter. Fill the pot with 1 to 3 inches of water. In addition to bamboo, Asian markets sell stainless steel sets that include a pot that holds the water and steamer trays; these are especially convenient.

You can use these trays to cook, reheat leftovers, such as fruit compotes and sauces, and revive dry cookies and bars (as well as bread, muffins, and other baked goods) wrapped in a cotton or linen napkin. The stainless steel trays are easier to clean, but the bamboo also works well and isn't hard to clean since you'll put most foods (except for fresh vegetables) in bowls rather than directly on the bamboo.

Wok or pot to hold steamer: If you buy bamboo or metal steamer trays that don't come with a matching pot, you'll need a heavy-duty flat bottom stainless steel or carbon steel wok to hold the steamers. I suggest getting a wok without a nonstick finish to avoid the off-gassing of harmful chemicals.

Steamer insert: A stainless steel accordion-style basket with overlapping petals will expand to fill a pot and collapse for storage. It turns any covered pot or saucepan into a steamer. Look for 1-inch legs and a central handle that unscrews so you can place heatproof bowls or dishes on the metal platform to warm leftovers. You can also use a pot with 1 or 2 steamer-style pasta inserts that rest on the pot's rim several inches above boiling water. You can get a 9-inch collapsible vegetable steamer for as little as $6 and an 11-inch for $8.

STORAGE CONTAINERS

Heatproof and freezer-safe custard cups and storage containers (essential): Get at least a dozen assorted clear heatproof bowls or cups with lids. You'll need more as you begin to get rid of plastic food storage containers. They can be round or square. I like 4-, 8-, 12-, 16-, 24-, and 32-ounce freezer and heatproof Pyrex or Corningware bowls for storing, serving, reheating, and/or freezing single, double, or larger portions of leftovers. Heatproof square and oblong Pyrex baking pans with snap-on lids work for storing, freezing, and even reheating foods, including fruit crisp, baked fruit, cookies, and bars.

Use the smaller sizes for storing meal size portions of sauces you plan to reheat, and for freezing Ice Dream in amounts you'll use up quickly.

Don't use larger containers for storing frozen desserts unless you're serving a lot of people; they take longer to soften, and repeated freezing and thawing will damage the texture of the frozen desserts.

Note: The lids are not heatproof; you'll reheat the contents uncovered or topped with parchment paper secured with twine or covered with foil.

Wide mouth jars: Even if you don't can, you'll want to stock up on pint and quart size canning jars. Get at least 1 dozen pint and 1 or 2 dozen quart Mason jars for storing Ice Dream custard (before churning), raw and toasted nuts, dried fruit, fruit sauce, cooked fruit compote, countless other dry and perishable foods, and assorted leftovers. Half pint (1 cup) and 4-ounce jam jars also

What's so great about jars?

1 Wide mouth glass jars are inert, non-toxic, and won't have off-gassing of chemical fumes or hold residual flavors or odors from previously stored foods.

2 They're easy to line up in the side door and shelf of the refrigerator and cupboards.

3 Contents are easily and quickly identified.

4 The vibrant colored vegetables, fruits, and nuts will invite you to eat more wholesome foods.

5 They're inexpensive.

You can also save jars from nut butter, mustard, fruit preserves, and other foods. Watch out for pickle and olive jars; their strong odors can linger for a long time. Soak the labels off in a sink full of water with a generous splash of cheap vinegar.

work well for storing and steam heating a small amount of sauce.

You can freeze food in jars as long as you leave at least 1 inch of space at the top (below the rim) and cool the contents to refrigerator temperature before transferring them to the freezer. Freeze liquids in wide mouth jars only; narrow mouth jars will crack when liquids expand.

Cardboard ice cream containers: Look for food grade pint and half pint containers with lids. They resemble the pint-size ice cream containers you see in the freezer section of supermarkets and health foods stores without the labels. Restaurant supply and outlet stores sell them in packs of 25 with a pack of lids. They're inexpensive, unbreakable, 100% biodegradable, and you can write on the outside (do this before you fill with Ice Dream). They're less fragile than glass jars, which can tumble out of the freezer and break if you're not careful about where you place them.

USEFUL UTENSILS

Apple corer: Quickly core apples for baking, simmering, stewing, making compotes, baked or dried apple chips, and more. Look for the kind that removes only the core, which is not the same as an apple wedger. It should have a thick ergonomic handle.

Bench scraper: This tool portions out dough, chops nuts, scoops up sliced fruit, nuts, and other foods for transfer from the cutting board to a pot or bowl. It has a straight handle constructed of wood or metal and a flat rectangular-shaped dull metal blade.

Cherry pitter: This small handheld spring-loaded tool will make short work of removing pits from fresh cherries. They don't cost much, so it's worth buying even if you use it only during the height of cherry season. It's safer than using a paring knife. Buy a stainless steel model.

Citrus reamer: Save 20 seconds every time you juice with a wooden reamer. Halve citrus fruit, pick out seeds, and use this tool to quickly squeeze the juice into a bowl. You can also use a handheld citrus press that comes in different sizes for lemons, limes, and oranges. They're sold in kitchen shops.

Coffee maker: This is not just for coffee. It's also useful for making herbal coffee alternatives, for which you'll find recipes in this book. You don't have to invest in a fancy machine. I find a stainless steel percolator produces a stronger, more flavorful brew than a drip coffee maker. It has no plastic parts, cleans up easily, and will last for years. Look for a stovetop or an electric model, or use a drip coffee maker if you already own one.

Graters (essential): These come in many varieties, each with its own benefits.

Box grater: This has four sides with different sized openings and shapes on each side. The smallest holes work well for grating gingerroot. The slicing side works for making citrus zest.

Microplane or rasp-type grater: This is a long handheld grater available in several sizes. Most are long and narrow. It will finely grate ginger and citrus zest and requires less effort than a box grater. Use caution—the razor-sharp teeth can shred your skin. Don't run your finger down the back to remove the grated food; instead, rap the tool on the counter or run a butter knife or small flexible spatula down the back. Clean with a bottle brush and running water, and slip the tool back into its protective sheath to avoid cutting yourself.

Ginger grater: This flat porcelain grater has a nubby ridged surface that's perfect for finely grating gingerroot so you can easily squeeze out the maximum amount of juice. You can buy small compact graters measuring 2 or 3 inches across or larger ones in most Asian markets.

Ice cream scoops (essential): You'll find two main types: spring-loaded or trigger scoops and solid scoops. Whichever kind you buy, look for something sturdy, and buy a couple of sizes so you can have fun making small and standard size scoops. Look for something with the most metal and least amount of plastic.

Spring loaded scoop: The most common, it requires a little more effort when scooping; however, it has the benefit of a thin metal arc that helps release the ice cream and creates perfectly rounded scoops. Cheaper versions stick and break easily.

Solid one piece scoop: This has no moving parts to break. It has a smooth design and a handle that is usually filled with antifreeze, which allows it to easily scoop through even the firmest ice cream.

Note: Don't run this through the dishwasher—it can damage the finish and the effectiveness of the coolant inside.

Melon baller: This stainless steel kitchen utensil comes in various sized scoops. Insert into the flesh of a melon and twist to form the shape of a ball. This makes pretty shaped pieces of fruit or fruit salad to serve under scoops of ice cream or as a garnish.

Pressure cooker: If you have a stainless steel pressure cooker it will come in handy for cooking dried chestnuts and applesauce in 1/3 to 1/2 the time required for boiling. If you're buying one new, look for a simple 3- to 4-quart model without a nonstick coating. Presto is usually the least expensive.

Rolling pin: Get a wooden or straight stainless steel pin if you plan to make graham crackers, which require rolling out; otherwise, you won't need this.

Vegetable peeler: Buy one with a thick handle for speed and ease of use for peeling apples, pears, and veggies. If you have one that has become dull or has a thin metal handle, it should be replaced.

Zester: A zester removes the flavorful colored part of citrus fruits without cutting into the white bitter pith. The head resembles a small metal hand with small, sharp-edged rings in place of fingers. This tool cuts the zest into thin strips as it scrapes along the surface. This is not essential for my recipes.

Equipment Checklist

APPLIANCES

- ❑ Blender or Vita Mix
- ❑ Coffee-grinder, spice dedicated
- ❑ Electric mixer (handheld or stand)
- ❑ Food processor (7 cup or larger)
- ❑ Ice cream maker (1- to 2-quart)
- ❑ Toaster oven

BAKING PANS & TOOLS

- ❑ Baking mats/liners (Silpat or Cook/eze)
- ❑ Baking pan, 8x8x2-inch square
- ❑ Baking pan, 9x9x2-inch square
- ❑ 12-inch oval gratin pan
- ❑ Baking pan, 11x17x2-inch square
- ❑ Baking sheets, rimmed
- ❑ Cake pan, 8x2-inch round
- ❑ Cake pan, 9x2-inch round
- ❑ Cookie sheets or half sheet pans
- ❑ Pie plate, deep dish 9- or 10-inch
- ❑ Springform pan, 8-, 9-, or 10-inch
- ❑ Cooling racks
- ❑ Muffin tins
- ❑ Oven mittens, heavy duty
- ❑ Trivets
- ❑ Unbleached parchment paper
- ❑ Unbleached muffin liners

BOWLS

- ❑ Mixing bowls, assorted
- ❑ Prep bowls, assorted
- ❑ Custard cups, assorted

KNIVES & BOARDS

- ❑ Wood or bamboo cutting boards
- ❑ Chef knife: 8- or 9-inch
- ❑ Paring knife
- ❑ Bread or tomato knife (for chocolate)
- ❑ Honing tool
- ❑ Electric sharpener
- ❑ Knife guards

MEASURING TOOLS

- ❑ Measuring spoons, 1/8 teaspoon to 1 tablespoon (2 sets)
- ❑ Liquid measuring cups, 1-, 2-, and 4-cup
- ❑ Dry measuring cups, 1/4 cup to 1 cup, (2 sets)
- ❑ Electronic scale

✓ CONTINUES NEXT PAGE

Equipment Checklist

MIXING TOOLS

☐ Wooden spoons (2 or more)
☐ Bamboo rice paddle
☐ Wire whisk
☐ Flexible spatulas (2 or more)

OTHER TOOLS

☐ Aluminum foil
☐ Colander, stainless steel
☐ Flour sifter
☐ Funnel, wide and narrow, metal
☐ Kitchen shears
☐ Marking pens, Colorful assortment
☐ Masking tape, 2-inch wide
☐ Metal spatula
☐ Heat proof flexible spatulas
☐ Timers
☐ Thermometers: oven-,
   refrigerator-, and freezer-type
☐ Tea towels/dish towels
☐ Tongs
☐ Ruler and measuring tape
☐ Slotted spoons
☐ Strainers, fine and coarse, metal

SAUCE POTS & PANS

☐ Saucepans with lids, 1/2- to 4-
   quart
☐ Skillets with lids, 8- or 9-inch

☐ Stacking steamer trays, bamboo
   or metal
☐ Wok or pot to hold steamer
☐ Steamer insert, accordian type

STORAGE CONTAINERS

☐ Custard cups, assorted heat proof
   w/lids
☐ Containers, heat proof w/lids,
   assorted 4- to 16-ounce
☐ Pint containers, round pints w/lids
☐ Wide mouth canning jars w/lids:
   half-pint-, pint-, and quart-size

USEFUL UTENSILS

☐ Apple corer
☐ Bench scraper
☐ Citrus reamer
☐ Cherry pitter
☐ Grater, cheese type
☐ Grater, microplane
☐ Grater, porcelain ginger grater
☐ Ice cream scoops, large and small
☐ Lemon, lime, and orange press
☐ Melon baler
☐ Popsicle molds
☐ Rolling pin
☐ Vegetable peeler
☐ Zester or rasp

Essential Techniques

Cooking is both an art and a science. It involves chemistry, mathematics, and biology, and if one is to cook with health in mind, a cursory understanding of physiology as well.

I know some people think cooking is something to be gotten through as quickly as possible, avoided, or farmed out to someone else. But, what could be more important than providing good nourishment for your family, your friends, and yourself.

We have grown accustomed to buying much of our food pre-made and preserved. Our culture values activities that produce money or goods and places a high value on hard science more than arts and self cultivation. Many of us get the message from the media and the peddlers of processed foods that we have better and more important things to do, out in the work world, than to take the time to cook our own meals at home.

As a result, many young people grow up not knowing how to cook or knowing only how to prepare food from cans, boxes, and freezer packages. They know little or nothing about how to cook from scratch using fresh, whole, unrefined or minimally processed foods. Changing how they shop, cook, and eat can seem mysterious, even daunting. I know this because I frequently encounter people in my cooking classes, usually women, who have never cooked, don't have basic knife skills, don't own basic equipment, and don't know where to start.

Whether you live alone or cook for a family, whether you've been cooking all your life or are just starting, and whether you already cook with whole foods or you're making the transition, my goal is to provide you with a foundation of recipes and skills that will allow you to consistently turn out predictably delicious foods.

You don't need the skills of a chef to create mouth-watering desserts. You do need to pay special attention to detail, particularly when working with unfamiliar ingredients. You'll need to pare away careless habits and cultivate more mindfulness in the kitchen. Put more attention into planning, gathering the ingredients and tools needed, measuring, and following instructions. This won't take the fun out of cooking; rather, it will make the process less stressful and, hopefully, a lot more enjoyable.

SECRETS FOR SUCCESS IN THE

KITCHEN

Work from Recipes

Practice using recipes. Build a repertoire of recipes you know and love. Follow them to the letter, at least initially. With practice, you will learn the format of the recipes you use most, and you'll become familiar enough with the ingredients and techniques so that you can successfully modify or even create your own recipes.

Read and Reread

Read a new recipe a couple of times until you can visualize what you need to do and what the final product will look like. If you're still unsure, ask an experienced cook or baker for tips, or search online for pictures or streaming videos of tools and techniques with which you are unfamiliar.

Survey the Recipe

Make sure you have all of the ingredients and equipment you need. When baking, use the size and type of pan specified in a recipe. This can make the difference between success and disappointment. If you don't have the correct size and type of pan, look for a substitute as close to what the recipe calls for or borrow one from a friend. For some recipes, pan size matters a lot; for others, only a little.

WHY Measure WHY Bother?

If you've never made it a habit to measure and follow recipes, I encourage you to start now. Good cooks, like good carpenters and draftsmen, use the tools of their trade. Measuring cups, measuring spoons, scales, and appropriate pots, pans, and knives are just some of the tools a good cook can use to his or her advantage.

You cannot expect to build a solid or attractive house without an idea of what you want to create. A skilled craftsman starts with a plan. He measures, follows step-by-step procedures, draws on his knowledge of basic proportions, and works methodically carrying out each step in the proper order. The same approach will serve you well in cooking.

If you start without a plan, or you don't use recipes or basic proportions (which you can eventually memorize) in your assembly and preparation, it's likely that your results will be erratic. Imagine what our nation's highways, bridges, and buildings would look like if the engineers and draftsmen decided to just wing it—if they didn't measure and didn't follow a recipe or blueprint.

If a recipe comes out too watery, oily, or dry, or too sweet, sour, bitter, salty, or spicy, how will you know how to avoid the same mistake? How will you know what to do differently next time? If it comes out great, how will you be able to repeat that, or share the recipe with an admiring guest?

The difference between a good cook and one who has disappointing results, is one of accuracy and practice. Sure, some people can turn out tasty food by pouring in a lot of oil or sugar, or smothering food in cheese or cream sauce, but to turn out great food, moderate in fat, that supports health, takes some attention to detail.

Make Your Lists and Check Them Twice

Note what you don't have that you need to buy or borrow. Although some substitutions will work, deviating more than 20 percent from a recipe, particularly when working with low-sugar preparations or gluten-free flours, can yield unsatisfactory results. It's worth searching for the ingredients called for in the recipes, even if you have to order them by phone or online.

Get Ready, Get Set

Set out all ingredients and equipment in the recipe. This will reduce the risk of leaving out anything that's essential. It often helps to group wet ingredients and dry ingredients on separate areas of the counter.

Prep

Measure out all the ingredients before you start mixing. The French call this *mise en place*, meaning everything in its place. Measure and place each ingredient in a separate bowl or custard cup. If you watch cooking shows, you will notice that this is a common practice. If you are interrupted by the phone or someone at the door, when you return, you won't have to wonder if you've already added the salt or baking soda. If you have it measured out, it's either in the batter or pot or on the tray.

No Strays with Trays

If you're making more than one recipe in a single cooking session, you can organize your space efficiently by placing ingredients for each recipe on a separate tray. Mark each tray with masking tape and write the name of the recipe on it, or place a copy of the recipe on each tray. Cooking instructors do this and you can too. Look for trays at restaurant supply stores or estate sales.

Write it Down

If you plan to cut a recipe in half or to double it, write in the margin on a copy of the recipe, or on a clean piece of paper, the halved or doubled amounts for each ingredient. Otherwise, it's too easy to lose track and get part way through a recipe only to find that you've just added the entire amount when you meant to cut everything in half, or worse, that you've cut some ingredients in half, but not others.

Similarly, if you plan to make additions or substitutions in a recipe, write them down; if the recipe comes out great, you'll know how to repeat it, and if not, you'll know what not to do.

Know Your Oven

Take its temperature. Invest in an oven thermometer, the kind you leave in the oven on the middle or lower shelf, to monitor the temperature for accuracy. Over time, your oven can lose calibration, making it run hotter or colder than the temperature you set. This can lead to costly mistakes. Preheat the oven for 20 minutes and check it before and during baking several times. If it runs higher or lower than what you wanted, adjust the temperature accordingly, or have a serviceman recalibrate it so the oven temperature matches what's on the dial.

Keep it Cold

Keep thermometers in your refrigerator and freezer to make sure they maintain the proper temperatures. If too warm, your food will spoil prematurely. If too cold, your food will freeze, even in the refrigerator. Keep refrigerator between 36 and 41° F. The freezer temperature should be 0° F or lower. Do not put steaming hot food in the refrigerator or freezer; it will raise the temperature inside the unit, causing it to overwork, and possibly spoiling other food.

Cool it

Cool foods properly before refrigerating. This is particularly important for foods with a high moisture content. Transfer a hot pot or pan of food to a cooling rack or divide it between several smaller heatproof containers and leave the lid off to allow air to circulate. Do not put hot food in plastic containers. For faster cooling, place the hot pot in an ice bath and stir frequently to dissipate heat. Aim to cool hot foods within 90 minutes, and then get them into the refrigerator.

Start on the Low End

When a recipe lists a range for the cooking time, such as 15 to 20 minutes, always check after the first amount of time, then stay nearby and check often to avoid overcooking. Similarly, when you see a range for the amount of a particular ingredient, such as 1/4 to 1/3 cup of honey

How You Measure Matters

How you measure ingredients, particularly for desserts, can significantly alter the outcome. People can end up with widely varying results from the same recipe because of the way they measure.

1 **Use heatproof glass measuring cups to measure liquid ingredients.** This includes water, coffee, tea, milk, egg whites, and oil in amounts at or above 1/4 cup; use measuring spoons for less than 1/4 cup unless you have a 1/8 cup measure. I use 1-, 4-, and 8-cup liquid measures; the larger ones double as mixing bowls.

Note: Use nested dry measuring cups (1/4-, 1/3-, 1/2-, and 1- cup sizes; some sets include 1/8 cup) to measure liquid sweeteners such as honey, agave nectar, and maple syrup, so you can fill to the rim for accuracy. Although they are liquid, they are harder to measure accurately in many liquid measuring containers.

Place the measuring container on a level surface and pour into the cup to the level required. Bend down so you can view the markings on the cup at eye level.

2 **Use nested, dry measuring cups to measure dry ingredients.** This includes all flour, cocoa powder, flaked coconut, dried fruit, and nuts, as well as solid fat, peanut butter, honey, molasses, and other syrups. Use standard measuring spoons for amounts less than 1/4 cup.

Note: Most of the cookie recipes in this book call for using a 1/3 cup measure to divide the dough. This is important not only for making Ice Dream Sandwiches where you want matching cookies, but also for uniformity in texture and baking time.

3 **Use standard measuring spoons for small amounts of wet and dry ingredients.** It helps to have a set that measures as little as 1/8 teaspoon in addition to the usual 1/4, 1/2, and 1 teaspoon and 1 tablespoon. Unfortunately, not all measuring spoons are calibrated equally. You will find some variation from one set to another. I have also found differences between plastic and stainless steel measuring tools.

Note: Don't try to measure ingredients for recipes with spoons designed for table use.

4 **Keep a ruler and tape measure on hand.** I keep these in my kitchen drawer and use them to measure the size of pots, pans, and parchment paper and to score cookie dough. When scoring dough, place the ruler on the dough and use it as a guide for marking with your knife. Your recipes will bake more evenly if you divide the dough evenly.

5 **Do not confuse fluid ounces with ounces by weight.** People often confuse weight and volume measures when the unit of measure is listed in ounces. Although weight can be measured in ounces, volume is measured in fluid ounces––they're different.

• *Continued next page* •

• How You Measure Continued •

A standard liquid measuring cup holds 8 fluid ounces; however, the contents of the cup will not always weigh 8 ounces. One cup (8 fluid ounces) of cornflakes weighs only 1 ounce, whereas 1 cup (8 fluid ounces) of nut butter weighs 9 ounces.

Federal regulations require that manufacturers label thick and viscous products by weight. However, recipes usually specify a quantity by volume (i.e., tablespoons or cups). The weight of products heavier or denser than water will always be more than their volume in fluid ounces. For example, a 16-ounce jar of cashew butter contains 1 3/4 cups of nut butter (not 2 cups). When purchasing products, keep in mind that canned and bottled liquid products will contain fewer fluid ounces than the number of ounces by weight that appears on the label.

Cocoa powder and chocolate chips are measured by volume (e.g., 1/4 cup, 1/2 cup, or 1 cup). Recipes that use chocolate bars, whether sweetened or unsweetened, call for the amount by weight.

Many recipes call for fruit by weight (such as apples, pears, or peaches) rather than offering a specific number of apples (or other fruit) because fruits can vary widely in weight. Although you can weigh ingredients in a supermarket, you cannot easily do this at a farmers' market, and you will probably want to buy more fruit than you need for a single recipe. You will produce more consistent results and yields if you purchase and regularly use a food scale.

⑥ Measure flour using the spoon and sweep method. Flour packs down during storage. You need to fluff it up in its container with a fork and spoon it into the appropriate size measuring cup or measuring spoon, filling it completely. Then, using the long straight edge of a spatula or the back of a butter knife, level the top. Wipe away the excess to make it even with the top edge of the measuring cup or spoon. If you reach into the bag of flour or cocoa with the measuring cup and scrape it along the side of the bag, you will pack the ingredients and invariably end up with more flour than called for, which will make heavy, dry brick-like baked goods.

⑦ Learn measuring equivalents. Know how many teaspoons are in a tablespoon, how many tablespoons in 1/4, 1/3, 1/2, 2/3, 3/4 cup and 1 cup, how many cups in a pint, pints in a quart, and quarts in a gallon. This will make it easier for you to shop for ingredients and know how much to buy. It will also make it easier for you to halve or double recipes and accurately assess what size pot, pan, jar, or storage container to use for whatever you are working with. You will find a table of equivalents and conversions in the Appendix.

or 1/4 to 1/2 teaspoon of stevia, start with the smaller amount, stir, taste, and then add more only if needed.

MASTERING MASTER RECIPES

People often wonder how I create such delicious recipes. Some people imagine me in my kitchen testing every recipe five or six times to get it right. Not so. I have a secret that I'll share with you. I'm a theme-and-variation kind of cook. I like to find, fiddle with, and then follow a master recipe to its logical conclusion—multiple variations.

Calories in Common Sweeteners

	per tablespoon	per cupful
Powdered sugar	29	466
Xylitol	30	480
Turbinado sugar	46	736
Granulated sugar	46	736
Brown sugar	52	829
Maple syrup	52	832
Corn syrup	58	928
Molasses	60	960
Agave nectar	60	960
Sorghum syrup	60	960
Honey	64	1024
Brown rice syrup	75	1200

Source: *Understanding Nutrition* by Ellie Whitney & Sharon Rady Rolfes. St. Paul: Thomas Learning Inc., 2005)

The master recipe provides a framework for success. Think of it as a template or an outline. Once you have the basic structure down, you can confidently tinker with the details— different herbs, spices, flavoring extracts, nuts, seeds, nut butters, fruits, vegetable purées, and so on. If you have familiarity with what flavors go well together or you look at other ice cream recipes, you can get a lot of great ideas, as I have, and translate them into delicious new recipes.

By following a master recipe, whether I create it myself or model it on someone else's recipe, I can cook with the confidence of knowing that my seemingly new creations will turn out good, and maybe even exceptional, almost every time, because I'm not creating them out of thin air. I'm following a recipe. I'm measuring. I'm following a set of steps that I know will work. Throwing ingredients together and hoping they'll magically transform into something good is a recipe for trouble, weight gain, or expensive garbage that I don't recommend.

One of the most crucial steps that allowed me to dramatically improve my cooking was taking on the discipline of measuring, following recipes, and learning and following basic techniques and procedures. I still measure and follow recipes to this day, even

if I've made a particular one 10, 20, 30, or more times. It saves me from constantly having to taste at the stove or kitchen counter, and thus prevents unwanted weight gain and digestive distress. It also allows me to thoroughly enjoy what I've made when I finally sit down to a consciously chosen meal or an intentional snack.

After making the same recipes many times, I memorize the ones I use most. They become etched in my brain like the phone numbers I dial most often. You can do the same thing with practice and careful attention to details. When you cook, pay attention to the ingredients, the proportions, the basic steps, and the techniques.

I often recommend that my cooking students take a recipe for soup, stew, fruit compote, roasted vegetables, or something else they like, and make it every week for a month, changing one element each time. Try a new variation each time, if present, or change an herb or spice, the kind of nut, seed, dried fruit, fresh fruit, (the variety of apple or pear or the type of fruit altogether), the vegetable or combination of vegetables, the flavoring, fat, oil, grain, or flour. Do this often and you will recall more parts of the recipe each time you make it. Do it with more recipes and you will build your recipe repertoire. Each time you make a familiar recipe, you will be able to assemble it more quickly, easily, and confidently. As a bonus, you will enjoy great tasting food more often. Eventually, you may look like you're winging it, while you're actually following recipes that are in your head.

Modifying Made Easy

When I set out to modify a recipe (my own or someone else's), I write down what I plan to do *before* I enter the kitchen. If I make additional changes as I work, I write these down, too. If I make minor changes to an otherwise time-tested recipe, I'm not straying so far that I risk creating something inedible or loaded with excess fat or sugar calories. Keep in mind that fats, oils, and sugars are very calorie dense and easy to overeat. If we use them unconsciously, without measuring, as many chefs and home cooks do, we can easily consume more energy than we burn up in a day, leading to unwanted weight gain and health problems.

How I Substitute for Sugar

Step #1: Replace sugar with a liquid sweetener, such as honey or agave nectar.

Use these exchange rates as a starting point. You may need to adjust the amounts as you work with a particular recipe. Have pencil and paper ready so you can write down what you add or omit, so you'll know what to repeat next time for the results you want. As you memorize the table of equivalents on page 264, you will find it easier to halve, double, and otherwise modify recipes confidently and with greater speed.

Sugar amount in cups	=	Sugar amount in tablespoons	Replace with this amount of honey or agave nectar
1 cup	=	16 tablespoons	3/4 cup
3/4 cup	=	12 tablespoons	1/2 cup + 1 tablespoon
2/3 cup	=	10-2/3 tablespoons	7-1/2 tablespoons (scant 1/2 cup)
1/2 cup	=	8 tablespoons	1/4 cup + 2 tablespoons
1/3 cup	=	5-1/3 tablespoons	1/4 cup
1/4 cup	=	4 tablespoons	3 tablespoons
1/16 cup	=	1 tablespoon	2-1/4 teaspoons

Step #2: Supplement with Stevia

Once I've converted the sugar in a recipe to a less refined liquid sweetener such as honey or agave nectar, I usually cut the amount of syrup in half. To make up the difference in sweetness, I then add stevia, but not just any stevia. I use specific kinds in specific amounts.

Note: This chart contains approximations only. Some recipes may require more stevia or more of other sweeteners for balance. The amounts listed below apply only to *pure* stevia extract powder with nothing added. Powdered stevia products diluted with fillers, such as FOS, erythritol, maltodextrin, or lactose, do not work well in my recipes or with the ratios below. Expect some variation in sweetness and flavor from one brand to another.

Sugar amount	Replace with this amount of *pure* stevia extract powder	Replace with this amount of *clear* stevia extract liquid
1 cup	1 teaspoon	2 teaspoons
3/4 cup	3/4 teaspoon	1-1/2 teaspoon
2/3 cup	2/3 teaspoon	1-1/3 teaspoon
1/2 cup	1/2 teaspoon	1 teaspoon
1/3 cup	1/3 teaspoon	2/3 teaspoon
1/4 cup	1/4 teaspoon	1/2 teaspoon
1 tablespoon	1/16 teaspoon	1/8 teaspoon
1 teaspoon	toothpick-size pinch	2 to 4 drops

For tips on how to sweeten drinks, see next page

How I Create Recipes

To create the frozen dessert recipes for this book, I studied dozens of ice cream recipes; I looked for their similarities and differences. I noted what volume of total ingredients and custard were required to make a quart or a quart and a half of ice cream, as well as how much cream, sugar, and flavorings they called for. I then began my work of upgrading the ingredients: coconut milk to fill in for cream or cream and milk; honey, agave, or maple syrup plus stevia for the sugar; unflavored gelatin or agar agar powder for the eggs; and natural flavorings in place of the synthetic flavors.

How did I know coconut milk would work? I'd already used it one-for-one to replace cream in creamy vegetable soups and I had diluted it with water to replace milk or yogurt in fruit smoothies.

How did I know that gelatin and agar agar powder would help to achieve a silky smooth texture, lightness, and loft while improving the keeping quality of my Ice Dreams?

I had experience using these gelling agents to make healthier fruit and fruit juice based versions of Jell-O and puddings. I knew, from repeatedly measuring and following recipes, how much I needed to lightly gel a quart of liquid. I also knew that my earlier versions of non-dairy frozen desserts iced up more quickly and attained a grainy texture when stored for more than a few days.

How did I know I could cut the amount of sweetener by at least half using a combination of honey, agave nectar, or maple syrup with stevia? How did I know how much to use? Again, years of working with these ingredients, measuring, and writing down what I was going to make, and keeping track of any changes I made in the kitchen, taught me how much of each ingredients was needed to achieve the desired sweetness. I created formulas that I applied to recipes that contained larger volumes of concentrated sweetener than I wanted to use.

The Price of Stevia

The price of stevia may seem high until you realize that a $10 (2-ounce bottle) of the liquid provides 350 to 400 servings. Stevia is non-perishable, so you don't need to toss it out if it's been in your kitchen for a year or more. Like arrowroot and most other dried foods, stevia is shelf stable for years.

Using Stevia to Sweeten Drinks

To sweeten 1 cup of your favorite beverage (coffee, tea, or sparkling mineral water):

* **Add** 2 to 4 drops of *clear* stevia extract liquid, plain or flavored,

* **or** the amount of *pure* stevia extract powder that fits on the end of a toothpick,

* **or** 1 or 2 stevia tablets,

* **or** 1 drop of stevia extract liquid for every 2 ounces.

To sweeten 1 quart of lemon- or lime-flavored water or mineral water

* **Add** 1/8 to 1/4 teaspoon stevia extract powder,

* **or** 1/4 to 1/2 teaspoon, or approximately 8 to 12 drops, of *clear* stevia extract liquid

MAKING THE PERFECT ICE DREAM CUSTARD

I modeled my Ice Dream recipes on custard-based, French-style ice cream, which has a thick, smooth texture due to the emulsifying properties of egg yolks and the volumizing effect of egg whites. Eggs, cream, milk, and sugar, in varying proportions, are cooked on the stovetop until they come together as a thick, satiny sauce. In contrast, Philadelphia-style ice creams are usually made by mixing milk or cream, sugar, and other ingredients.

Don't worry if you've never made French-style ice cream custard. I used that as a

Replacing Brown Sugar

When recipes call for brown sugar, I usually substitute soft, pitted dates. Although date sugar could work, particularly if supplemented with a little bit of molasses for moisture, most of the brands of date sugar on the market contain oats. Manufacturers often add oat flour to reduce the stickiness of the dates; however, this dilutes the sweetness, and for celiacs who cannot tolerate oats, makes date sugar an unacceptable ingredient.

starting point only. I don't use eggs, so you don't have to worry about accidental curdling and turning your custard into liquid scrambled eggs. I've changed the ingredients and simplified the process, which I'll walk you through, step by step.

While some of the recipes vary slightly, all rest on this basic set of steps.

1. Softening the gelatin or agar agar: Add 1/3 cup of cool or cold filtered water (in some recipes you'll use tea) to a small saucepan. Slowly sprinkle the gelatin or agar agar powder over the water. You don't want the granules to clump up. Let the mixture stand for 2 to 5 minutes to allow the granules to soften and swell. Sometimes dry spots will disappear immediately; other times they will settle on the surface. If you get distracted and have to let it stand longer, no harm done.

2. Melting the gelatin or agar agar: Warm the mixture over medium-low heat, without stirring, until gelatin or agar agar dissolves. Do not stir as that can cause the granules to lump up and fail to dissolve. Don't use high heat or the gelatin may toughen, or worse, boil over.

How do you know if the gelatin has dissolved? Dip a metal spoon into the mixture and allow the liquid to run off. If the spoon appears covered in a completely clear glaze, it's done. If the coating liquid is opaque (whitish), simmer another 30 seconds or so. As long as the gelatin has softened and the liquid is steaming hot, the gelatin is virtually guaranteed to melt.

3. Blending the gelatin or agar agar: Pour the hot or warm gelatin mixture into a blender, Vita-Mix, or food processor. Be sure to scrape out every last bit of goodness (the liquid and gelatin). Some of the dissolved gelatin will invariably settle on the bottom of the saucepan, particularly if you leave it sitting for a few minutes while you measure out other ingredients. Run a heatproof rubber or silicone (my favorite) spatula over the bottom of the pan to remove it. Failing to do this will lessen the loft of your frozen dessert and cause it to melt and develop ice crystals more quickly. Once you have this mixture in the machine, cover and process until smooth and frothy, about 20 seconds.

4. Adding the other ingredients: Most of the recipes call for adding honey, agave nectar, or maple syrup and salt next. This is important because unprocessed raw

Making Time to Make Ice Dream

The idea of making your own ice cream may sound unrealistic or unnecessary. However, if you want to maintain or improve your health and that of your family and still enjoy eating frozen desserts more than once or twice a year, you and your family will benefit from making your own at home. It's not difficult or time consuming. Set aside some time to whip up a batch of custard, which is the first step in making Ice Dream. Hands-on prep time is 20 to 30 minutes for most of my recipes if you use an ice cream maker with a prechilled canister (also called a sealed-in-coolant machine), which I highly recommend for ease of use and cleanup. The old fashioned ice and rock salt machines require more hands-on time and make a mess.

When to make the custard or base

You can assemble the custard in the morning and churn it later in the day or the next day, or assemble it at night and churn it in the morning or later the next day. When you churn will depend upon whether you want to eat it straight from the machine or freeze it in containers and eat it at another time.

honey can be thick, and salt dissolves best in warm or hot liquid. By blending these ingredients together while the mixture is still warm, you will ensure that they spread evenly throughout the custard.

From here, you will usually add the coconut milk, flavoring extracts or fruit in some cases, and stevia (which we'll get to in a minute). Blend and then scrape the sides of the container with a spatula to make sure you've incorporated the ingredients well and that nothing remains stuck to the side of the blender or food processor.

5. Adding the stevia: Remember, stevia is very concentrated at 100 to 300 times the sweetness of sugar. The biggest mistake people make with stevia, is adding too much; this leaves a bitter aftertaste. Measure the stevia carefully, filling the appropriate sized measuring spoon and leveling with your finger or a butter knife.

Measure—do not guess. It makes a difference. If you measure and you're happy with the results, you'll know how to repeat your success. If it's not sweet enough, or if it's too sweet, you'll know how to adjust next time. If you don't measure, you will likely repeat the mistakes. You don't want to notice the stevia; it should sweeten silently without calling attention to it.

Whenever you see a range for the amount of sweetener, start with the smallest amount. Once you've blended all of the ingredients into the custard, taste and adjust in tiny increments.

If the mixture doesn't taste as sweet as you would like, add an additional 1/8 teaspoon pure stevia extract powder or 1/4 teaspoon clear stevia extract liquid and/or 1 tablespoon honey. Blend, taste, and repeat if needed. Go slowly to avoid over sweetening the custard. You want a pleasant taste while using the smallest amount of sweetener you can. If I need to add more sweetener than the starting amount, I usually start with

stevia because it adds no calories and no carbohydrates.

6. Containing the custard: Pour the blended liquid into one or more wide-mouth jars. You should have between 4 and 4-1/2 cups of liquid custard. You may have started with 4 cups before blending, but because the blender incorporates some air into the mix, it will rarely fit into a quart jar. Use a wide-mouth quart mason jar and a wide funnel to get the mixture into the jar without spilling. Pour the remainder into a smaller 4- to 6-ounce jar.

I stick a strip of wide masking tape on each jar and write the name of the flavor and the date with a

Go by the Book

If you're like most of my students, you're busy. When you get a new kitchen gadget or appliance, you want to use it––immediately. You don't want to read the instructions. I urge you to take the time now to prevent problems later. Each machine has specific requirements and you need to be familiar with your product before you use it.

If you skip this step, you might end up with a batch of dessert that overflows the machine, fails to freeze, or, worse, damages the machine. So stop, take a few minutes, and read through the manual so you know the names of the parts, how they work, how to clean them, which parts are dishwasher safe, and what kinds of utensils to use or avoid using when removing ice cream or Ice Dream from the machine.

labeling your creations

Label your containers using wide masking tape and a marking pen. (The tape can be removed more easily than sticky labels.) Write the name of the flavor and the date on the top and sides of the container. It works best to apply the tape/label to containers *before* you fill them with frozen dessert. Cold foods can prevent the tape from sticking. If you use disposable cardboard pint and half pint containers, you can write directly on them, provided you do this before filling the containers.

It also makes sense to label and date homemade sauces, compotes, and other foods. Although chocolate and caramel sauces will usually keep for a month or more in the refrigerator without spoiling, in the absence of preservatives and a high sugar content, cooked fruit dishes will spoil faster and can harbor bacteria if kept too long. Dating food will help you decide what to use up first.

colorful marking pen. I write "1 of 2" on one jar and "2 of 2" on the other so I'll know how many jars I need to pull out of the fridge when I churn the custard. This step insures that I won't overlook a second jar.

7. Chilling the custard: Cover and refrigerate the mixture for at least 6 hours before churning. This is essential. A warm or hot liquid will cause the ice cream canister to melt before the custard turns into ice cream. You don't want that! During chilling, the custard will get thicker. Some flavors will look like soft Jell-O; others will look like ready-to-eat pudding. The thickness of the custard will help add loft (height) and lightness to the Ice Dream and improve the keeping quality.

Now you need to know how to churn the custard, the final step in making Ice Dream.

CHURNING & SERVING ICE DREAM IN A SEALED-IN-COOLANT STYLE MACHINE

While similarities exist among various makes and models of ice cream makers, they vary in some ways. The instructions that follow will guide you through the preparatory steps for using most ice cream makers that feature a canister with a sealed-in coolant, such as the Cuisinart 1 to 1 1/2-quart Automatic Ice Cream, Frozen Yogurt, and Sorbet Maker, Rival 1-quart

and 1 1/2-quart Gel Canister Ice Cream Makers, and Krups La Glacier.

Note: The same company often makes and markets different kinds of machines, some of which require different operating instructions. For example, Cuisinart also makes a soft-serve machine and Rival also makes a machine with a bucket that requires several pounds of ice and rock salt. So, you will benefit by reading the operating instructions that come with your particular machine.

1. Freezing the canister: Wrap the ice cream canister in a plastic bag. Why? To prevent freezer burn and keep water from ice cube trays from spilling into the canister and freezing. This could prevent the dasher from fitting properly when you're ready to churn the chilled custard. Store it in the freezer, preferably in the middle or back, away from the door, for at least 24 hours, or longer if desired.

Some people keep a canister in the freezer at all times so it's ready for churning on short notice. Keep two canisters in the freezer if you want the option of making two batches in a row.

2. Checking the canister: Shake it before using to make sure it has frozen solid. If you hear a sloshing sound, return the canister to the freezer and check it again in 6 to 12 hours. Do not attempt to use the canister before it has frozen; the custard won't freeze and you'll be disappointed.

The Perfect Storage Containers

Choose the smallest container possible when storing Ice Dream. You don't want a container that leaves a lot of air space in which ice crystals can form. Multiple small containers work better than one large container. The reason? Repeatedly thawing and refreezing your dessert will alter its texture, unpleasantly. I prefer to store Ice Dream in 4-, 6-, 8-, 12-, or 16-ounce containers.

I abhor plastic and use as little as possible in my kitchen. I store most foods in glass, Pyrex, CorningWare, and stainless steel containers because they are non-toxic, heatproof, freezer-safe, and durable. Plus, they don't absorb odors or emit toxic chemicals. I have many sizes and shapes, some for 20 years.

Storing Ice Dream

My favorite Ice Dream storage containers are made of food grade cardboard. They're called Double Poly Paper Food Containers and are made by SOLO. They resemble the pint-size ice cream containers you see in the freezer section of supermarkets and health foods stores, but without the fancy labels. I buy them in packs of 25 with a pack of lids at Smart & Final. Other outlet, warehouse, discount, and restaurant supply stores also sell them. They're inexpensive. The white exterior allows me to write directly on the container with colorful pens. You or your children can decorate them if you like. They're 100% non-toxic and biodegradable. Some stores also sell the half-pint size (8-ounce). They're less fragile than glass, which can tumble out of the freezer and break if you're not careful about where you place it.

Look for them online. You could ask stores in your area to special order them or keep them in stock. They may be called 16-ounce paper food containers or double poly food containers with lids. (My containers have item# H4165 2050 16 OZ DSP Food Container and the lids have item# CH16A4000 16 OZ Vented Paper Lid).

Try these online sources:
www.solocup.com
www.diamondpaperltd.com
www.Reliablepaper.com
www.cupdepot.com

Clear, round, and tempered glass containers with tight fitting lids also work. Just make sure to choose several smaller containers rather than one large container so you won't have to thaw and freeze the same portions of Ice Dream repeatedly. Ice Dream stored in round cardboard containers (mentioned above) softens more quickly than if stored in glass, which freezes harder and stays cold longer.

Storing Sauces

For storing sauces, I prefer to use baby food jars, small jam jars, and empty mustard jars for small portions, and 6-, 8-, 12-, and 16-ounce wide-mouth nut butter or canning jars for larger amounts. I label these with wide masking tape as well, and freeze whatever sauces I don't plan to use within 2 or 3 weeks. **Note:** Chocolate and caramel sauces will keep longer in the fridge than fruit-based sauces and compotes.

Storing Cooked Fruit

I store fruit compotes, poached fruit, and fruit crisps in wide-mouth pint and quart canning jars or heatproof and freezer-safe containers with lids. If stored in heatproof

• *Continued next page* •

• The Perfect Storage Containers Continued •

containers, you can transfer cold apple crisp or compote to the toaster oven for easy reheating, and then take the same container to the table. You can also freeze food in these containers if you chill the food to refrigerator temperature beforehand. If you skip this step, your containers may shatter. You will want to leave 1 inch of space at the top of containers, and 2 inches for jars, or the contents can swell and shatter the glass.

Storing Cookies & Bars

I like to store these in clear, round, or oblong tempered glass containers with tight fitting lids, metal cookie tins, wide-mouth jars, or stainless steel containers with lids, called tiffens, which you'll find in Asian markets or Indian grocery stores.

Note: For tips on reheating leftover dessert sauces without a microwave oven, see page 73.

---

3. Assembling the Machine: The machines I use that have canisters with sealed-in coolant require inserting the dasher, attaching the lid, plugging in the machine and turning on the machine before adding the custard. Since machines vary, read the instructions before you start.

4. Adding the Custard: Scrape the chilled custard into the canister of your ice cream maker, and then use a flexible rubber or silicone spatula to add *all* the custard from the sides of the jar or jars into the canister.
Note: The machine will work best when it is at least half full. So, make a full or a half batch, but no less.
5. Churning Custard: Churn according to manufacturer's instructions. My machines take 20 to 25 minutes to turn out thick, fluffy, and voluminous Ice Dream.
Note: Stay close by while the Ice Dream churns. When the mixture thickens maximally, turn it off. Running it beyond this point will not make the custard freeze more. It can strain the motor and cause it to overheat, and the sealed-in coolant will eventually start to melt along with your Ice Dream.

6. Removing the Frozen Custard: To avoid damaging the canister, use a firm silicone spatula, wood spoon, or bamboo rice paddle to remove the Ice Dream from the machine. If you wish to use an ice cream scoop, use it to scoop out only the soft dessert from

the center of the canister. Do not allow any sharp or metal utensils to touch or scrape the walls of the container.

7. Serving & Storing Your Frozen Desserts: Do not leave the custard in the machine. Do not store frozen desserts in the canister. Serve immediately or spoon into several 8- to 16-ounce freezer-safe containers with lids, leaving 1-inch of space in the top of the container for possible expansion in freezing.

Smaller containers are preferable to large containers. Repeated freezing and thawing of homemade frozen desserts will cause them to ice up, so you want to minimize this. Large containers that leave a lot of air space also invite the formation of ice crystals. Cover and freeze your freshly churned frozen dessert for 3 or more hours for a firmer texture.

8. Preparing for Your Next Batch: Hand wash and dry your ice cream canister, top, and dasher. Allow the parts to air dry or towel dry. Rewrap the canister in an airtight bag to prevent freezer burn. Refreeze if desired. Wait at least 24 hours before using the canister again. It takes that long for most canisters to solidly re-freeze. **Note:** There are some exceptions. Read your instruction manual for details.

9. Serving Solidly Frozen Dessert: Ice Dream freezes more solidly than commercial

Why Does My Ice Dream Freeze Harder Than Store Bought Brands?

Commercial ice cream is made in high-speed machines that whip extra air (called overrun) into the ice cream. Adding more air to each pint, quart, or gallon of ice cream increases their profit while improving the texture of the product. A denser, less airy product will freeze more solidly. Commercial frozen desserts also contain more sugar and a long list of often unpronounceable preservatives, additives, stabilizers, and emulsifiers that make their products more shelf stable and more scoopable right from the freezer.

Ice cream makers for home use don't churn as fast or have as much power as commercial machines, so your homemade frozen desserts won't have as much air; they'll be denser but all the more delicious. By adding unflavored gelatin or agar agar, you can counter this problem to some degree, but not completely.

To make matters more challenging, most home freezers are colder than the ideal serving temperature. So, you'll need to remove them from the freezer 15 to 45 minutes before serving to allow them to soften enough to scoop. You can reduce this time by adding some alcohol to the custard (see side bar for more on this), but don't go overboard. Follow the recipes—at least until you are familiar enough with them to create your own.

ice cream. Some flavors will be scoopable straight from the freezer (particularly if they contain liqueur), but most will not be. Soften solidly frozen dessert by placing it in the refrigerator for 30 to 45 minutes or on the counter for 15 to 30 minutes before serving. The sides of the container will

The Proof is in the Ice Cream

Alcohol works like anti-freeze for ice cream (or Ice Dream). It prevents homemade frozen desserts from freezing too hard (alcohol doesn't freeze). This reduces tempering time in some cases, allowing you to remove a container from the freezer, scoop, and serve your treat right away. Alcohol also adds flavor.

You'll find rum, cognac, white wine, kirsch, Cointreau, and other flavored liqueurs listed as an optional ingredient in many recipes and as an essential ingredient in others. In some cases the alcohol contributes considerably to the flavor, such as in Rum Raisin or Date Rum Pecan Ice Dream. In others, you may not notice its presence or absence, except for a change in texture, which you will notice if you don't serve all of the Ice Dream right away and it is stashed in the freezer for several days or weeks. Omit the alcohol if you'll be serving children or anyone who avoids it. In recipes that call for cooking, such as simmering dried fruit in rum or wine, some of the alcohol will dissipate. Some recipes provide tips for substitutions that add a similar flavor, such as white grape juice in place of white wine. However, the juice won't give it the softening effect that many people like.

Note: While a little alcohol improves the texture, too much can prevent the mixture from freezing at all. As a general rule, you can add up to 3 tablespoons of 40% (80 proof) liquor, such as rum or whiskey, to 1 quart of custard mixture without any problem, or as much as 1/2 to 3/4 cup rum or wine if you will be cooking the fruit in this liquid before combining it with other ingredients. In this case, the cooking will dissipate most of the alcohol.

soften before the center portion, so scoop from the outside first.

Note: If you use an ice and rock salt style ice cream maker or a self-refrigerating machine, be sure to read the instruction manual. Assembly and operating procedures vary from those presented above.

HOW TO WARM UP LEFTOVERS WITHOUT USING A MICROWAVE

Here, I will list a few simple techniques for heating leftovers without having to rely on a microwave oven. Any of these techniques will ensure that your food will have more flavor, better texture, and will retain more nutrients. They require little attention—no stirring, very little pot watching, and minimal clean up—because they allow you to refrigerate, heat, and serve leftovers in the same container. You will avoid the use of toxic plastic containers, which release even more chemicals when heated.

Toaster Oven

This is a useful tool for heating leftovers. It's even easier if your leftovers are stored in heatproof Pyrex, CorningWare, or stainless steel bowls or rectangular containers.

Use: To reheat leftover baked, poached, or stewed fruit or sauces made from fruit, chocolate, or caramel. It also works for other leftovers, such as poultry, meat, roasted vegetables, and casseroles. (Do not place food in jars in the oven or toaster oven; they can shatter.)

1. Preheat the toaster oven to 250° to 350° F. Position rack to allow room for heatproof container of food and place on rack. Leftover fruit crisp should be covered if it begins to darken.

2. Close oven, heat for 10 to 15 minutes until food is warmed through.

3. Remove container with oven mittens and serve.

Steamer

This works for reheating leftovers, large or small. It's even easier if your leftover food items have been stored in heatproof Pyrex, CorningWare, or stainless steel bowls or rectangular containers. Unlike the oven, a steamer will work for gently heating food in tempered glass jars if you keep the heating time brief. You'll find several variations on the steamer technique below.

Use this technique to reheat leftover baked, poached, or stewed fruit and chocolate, fruit, or other sauces. It works for other leftovers such as rice, hot cereal, poultry, meat, roasted vegetables, and casseroles. You will need to modify the technique according to the ingredients and the type of container used.

Covered bowl-within-a-pot method

Use this when heating foods in a stainless steel mixing bowl.

1. Place food in a stainless steel bowl (perhaps the same container used for storage).

2. Place the bowl in a 1 1/2- to 5-quart pot. Do not use this technique for glass or other breakable containers.

3. Add enough water to the pot to surround the bowl with water that rises to no more than 1/4 to 1/3 the height of the bowl. If you've added too much water, remove some of it.

4. Cover the bowl with a heatproof saucer* (perhaps the same one you used to cover it in the refrigerator). If this is not possible, cover the container with unbleached parchment paper and secure with kitchen twine or a rubber band.

5. Bring the pot of water to a boil over high heat. Reduce heat to medium and steam until heated through, 4 to 15 minutes depending upon the size and contents.

6. Uncover and remove with oven mittens.

* Note: You can find heatproof saucers in thrift stores and garage sales. The bottom of the saucer will usually say "oven to table" or something similar.

Covered bowl-on-a-trivet method

Use this when heating foods in Pyrex,

CorningWare, or other tempered glass containers.

Follow the procedure outlined above with one exception: place a small trivet in the bottom of pot, and rest the bowl directly on top of the trivet. Proceed as directed above.

Covered bowl-on-a-rack or steamer tray method

Use this technique to heat food in a shallow stainless steel, heatproof glass, Pyrex, or CorningWare container or one or more custard cups, small canning jars, or baby food jars.

1. Place food in a shallow tempered glass, Pyrex, CorningWare, or stainless steel bowl or food tin (perhaps the same container used for storage).

2. Place an accordion-style steamer insert into a 1 1/2- to 4-quart pot, or rest a bamboo steamer tray inside a wok or directly on the rim of a pot with a matching diameter, or place a metal steamer insert inside the pot that goes with it.

3. Add 1 to 2 inches of water to the bottom of the pot. The water should not touch the bottom of the steamer rack, tray, or insert.

4. Place the heatproof container directly on the rack or tray elevated above the water. Cover it with a metal lid, a heatproof saucer*, or parchment paper secured with twine or a rubber band. **Note:** If using a jar, leave the lid ajar.

5. Bring the pot of water to a boil over high heat. Reduce heat to medium and steam until heated through. **Note:** If using a jar, steam for only 1 or 2 minutes, turn off heat, and let stand for several minutes. Repeat if needed.

6. Uncover and remove with oven mittens.

* **Note:** You can find heatproof saucers in thrift stores and garage sales. The bottom of the saucer will usually say "oven to table" or something similar.

Napkin on-a-steamer tray method

Use this technique to freshen and remoisten dry cookies, brownies, muffins, or bread. This is a great way to revive foods that you thought were stale.

1. Place the baked goods in a dry white or beige cotton or linen (not paper) napkin, fanning them out across the cloth. Fold the cloth over the food to cover.

2. Place an accordion-style steamer insert in a 1 1/2- to 4-quart pot, or rest a bamboo steamer tray inside a wok or directly on the rim of a pot with a matching diameter, or place a metal steamer insert inside the pot that goes with it.

3. Add 1 or 2 inches of water to the bottom of the pot. The water should not touch the bottom of the steamer rack, tray, or insert.

4. Place the bundle of food on the steamer tray or rack elevated above the water. Cover the pot and bring to a boil over high heat. Reduce the heat to medium and steam for 2 to 4 minutes until moistened but not soggy.

5. Remove the bundle with oven mittens and serve. Refrigerate any leftover baked goods to prevent the formation of mold.

How to Expertly Toast Nuts

Toasting nuts takes only a few minutes of hands-on time. It enhances the flavor and inactivates substances in raw nuts that can inhibit digestion. You don't need to add oil; 70 to 80% of the calories in nuts come from fat. One handful packs 350 to 400 calories. This technique makes them taste richer, which makes it easier for you to use them judiciously as a garnish.

Why shouldn't you buy them already roasted? Many companies roast nuts in refined or hydrogenated vegetable oils at high temperatures. Some brands contain added salt or sugar, which add more fat, sodium, and calories. I suggest starting with whole raw nuts or nut halves. Avoid buying slivered or crushed nuts and nut pieces, because more of their oils spoil in storage. Buy them refrigerated if possible. Once home, store all nuts (and seeds) in the refrigerator or freezer.

1. Remove shelled, raw nuts from the refrigerator or freezer. Allow them to stand at room temperature for at least 1 hour for uniform toasting.

2. Position an oven rack in the center of the oven. Preheat the oven to 350° F. Reduce heat to 325° F in a toaster oven.

3. Spread the nuts in a single layer in a shallow-rimmed baking pan. If toasting more than one kind of nut, use a separate pan for each variety. Place the pan in the oven and toast until the nuts become lightly golden and aromatic. This should take 10 to 15 minutes for large nuts and 5 to 7 minutes for small nuts such as pine nuts. Because the nuts on the outside of the pan will toast faster than the nuts on the inside, shake the pan or stir 2 or 3 times during cooking.

4. To check for doneness, remove a nut from the oven after about 10 minutes and cut it open. Check every few minutes until they turn a light golden brown all the way through. Watch closely so they don't burn.

5. Wrap walnuts or hazelnuts in a clean kitchen towel; rub to loosen the skins, and then remove the nuts and discard the skins. Allow the nuts to cool before chopping or pulsing in a food processor or a mini-chopper.

6. Transfer cooled nuts to wide-mouth jars, label and date, then cover and refrigerate. Use within 2 to 4 months for the best flavor.

chapter 4

The Basic Flavors

Best Bites

Vanilla Ice Dream

HANDS-ON: 20 MINUTES • **CHURNING:** 20 TO 25 MINUTES • **YIELD:** 5 TO 6 CUPS; 8 SERVINGS

INGREDIENTS

1/3 cup cool or cold filtered water

2 teaspoons unflavored gelatin **or** 3/4 teaspoon agar agar powder (not flakes)

1/4 cup honey **or** agave nectar; additional 1 to 2 tablespoons as needed

1/4 to 1/2 teaspoon *pure* stevia extract powder **or** 1/2 to 1 teaspoon *clear* stevia extract liquid (start with less; add more only if needed)

1/8 teaspoon finely ground, unrefined sea salt

3 1/2 cups (two 14-ounce cans) unsweetened, preservative-free coconut milk (regular, not lite)

1 tablespoon pure vanilla extract **or** alcohol-free vanilla flavoring

Like conventional vanilla ice cream, this dairy-free alternative goes well with almost everything. I like to serve it over fresh fruit, a mixed fruit salad, with Poached Pears, Apple Compote, or a fruit sauce. For a fancier presentation, it can be served with Chocolate, Fudge, or Caramel Sauce (see index for recipes).

1 SERVING (REGULAR):
230 calories
2.2 grams protein
15.9 grams carbohydrate
17.5 grams fat
77 milligrams sodium

1 SERVING (HALF LITE):
170 calories
1.4 grams protein
13.3 grams carbohydrate
12.4 grams fat
61 milligrams sodium

DIRECTIONS

1. Add 1/3 cup water to a small saucepan. Slowly sprinkle with gelatin or agar agar powder. Let stand for 2 to 5 minutes to soften. Warm over medium-low heat, without stirring, until gelatin or agar agar dissolves. Scrape the mixture into a blender, Vita-Mix, or food processor. Cover and process until smooth.

2. Add honey, stevia, and sea salt. Blend. Add the coconut milk and vanilla, and blend until smooth, stopping to scrape the sides with a spatula. For a sweeter taste, add an additional 1/8 teaspoon stevia and/or 1 tablespoon honey. Blend, taste, and repeat if needed.

3. Pour into one or more wide-mouth jars. Cover and refrigerate for at least 6 hours before churning.

4. Scrape the chilled custard into the canister of your ice cream maker. Churn according to the manufacturer's instructions.

5. Serve immediately or spoon into several 8- to 16-ounce freezer-safe containers. Cover and freeze for 3 or more hours for a firmer texture.

6. Soften solidly frozen dessert by placing it in the refrigerator for 30 to 45 minutes or on the counter for 15 to 30 minutes before serving.

~Continued next page~

Vanilla Ice Dream ~ continued

VARIATIONS

* **Maple Vanilla Ice Dream:** Replace honey or agave nectar with 1/4 cup + 2 tablespoons pure maple syrup. Use darker maple syrup for a stronger flavor. Use a total of 1/2 teaspoon stevia extract powder and replace vanilla with 1 to 1 1/2 teaspoons maple extract or alcohol-free maple flavoring. For a sweeter taste, add 1 or 2 more tablespoons maple syrup.

* **Lite Vanilla Ice Dream:** Replace half of the coconut milk with lite (reduced fat) coconut milk. Alternatively, use 100% lite coconut milk, but plan to use the batch immediately or within 24 hours before it becomes hard and icy.

Of all the Ice Dream flavors, this one has the strongest coconut flavor. If you plan to share this with someone who isn't wild about coconut, make it with lite or a combination of regular and lite coconut milk. Better yet, start with one of the Ice Dream flavors that contains added fruit or chocolate, which will mute or hide the strong flavor.

Chocolate Chip Ice Dream

ASSEMBLY: 20 MINUTES • **CHURNING:** 20 TO 25 MINUTES • **YIELD:** 6 CUPS; 8 SERVINGS

INGREDIENTS

1 recipe Vanilla **or** Maple Vanilla Ice Dream (Page 78)

1 cup organic, malt-sweetened, fruit-sweetened, or dairy-free chocolate chips **or** bittersweet chocolate, coarsely chopped into 1/4-inch pieces

DIRECTIONS

1. Prepare Vanilla or Maple Vanilla Ice Dream through step #4, but don't remove it from the machine. When the mixture reaches the soft-serve stage, add the chocolate chips or bits to the machine. Run the machine for 1 or 2 more minutes.

2. Serve immediately or spoon into several 8- to 16-ounce freezer-safe containers. Cover and freeze for 3 or more hours for a firmer texture.

3. Soften solidly frozen dessert in the refrigerator for 30 to 45 minutes or on the counter for 15 to 30 minutes before serving.

Once frozen, chocolate chips become difficult to chew. The solution: chop the chips and refrigerate for 2 or more hours before adding them to freshly churned Ice Dream. Better yet, coarsely chop a bar of bittersweet chocolate, using one with 70 to 73% cocoa content. It contains less sugar and more antioxidants than bittersweet or semi-sweet chocolate chips.

Note: If you avoid chocolate, see the variation below.

1 SERVING (REGULAR):
306 calories
3.2 grams protein
24.9 grams carbohydrate
21.5 grams fat
77 milligrams sodium

1 SERVING (HALF LITE):
246 calories
2.4 grams protein
22.3 grams carbohydrate
16.2 grams fat
61 milligrams sodium

VARIATIONS

* **Chocolate Chocolate Chip Ice Dream:** Replace Vanilla Ice Dream with Cocoa Ice Dream or Dark Chocolate Ice Dream (Page 86 or 88).

* **Lite Chocolate Chip Ice Dream:** Replace half of the coconut milk with lite (reduced fat) coconut milk. Alternatively, use 100% lite coconut milk, but plan to use the batch immediately or within 24 hours before it becomes hard and icy.

* **Carob Chip Ice Dream:** Replace chocolate chips with carob chips. You may have to try several brands to find one you like. If you follow a gluten-free diet, read labels because some carob products are processed on machines that are used to package gluten-containing products.

* **Cocoa Nib Crunch Ice Dream:** Replace chocolate chips with cocoa nibs (also called cacao nibs). They're made from crushed cacao beans with nothing added. They are not sweet like chocolate chips.

Maple Pecan Ice Dream

ASSEMBLY: 15 MINUTES • CHURNING: 20 TO 30 MINUTES • YIELD: 6 CUPS; 8 SERVINGS

INGREDIENTS

1 recipe Maple Vanilla Ice Dream (Page 78)

3/4 cup shelled, toasted pecans (Page 75), **or**
Pralined Pecans (Page 214) coarsely chopped

DIRECTIONS

1. Prepare Honey Vanilla or Maple Vanilla Ice Dream through step #4, but don't take it out of the machine. When it reaches the soft-serve stage, add the chopped nuts to the machine. Run the machine for 1 or 2 more minutes.

2. Serve immediately or spoon into several 8- to 16-ounce freezer-safe containers. Cover and freeze for 3 or more hours for a firmer texture.

3. Soften solidly frozen dessert in the refrigerator for 30 to 45 minutes or on the counter for 15 to 30 minutes before serving.

VARIATIONS

* **Maple Walnut Ice Dream:** Replace pecans with toasted walnuts or Walnut Pralines above.

* **Vanilla Pecan Ice Dream:** Replace Maple Vanilla with Vanilla Ice Dream above.

* **Lite Maple Pecan Ice Dream:** Use Lite Maple Vanilla Ice Dream above.

Top this tasty dessert with Blueberry, Apricot, Peach, Cherry, or Nectarine Sauce, or one of the Chocolate, Fudge, or Caramel Sauces in Chapter 8. For an elegant dessert, serve it over Poached Pears with Raisins & Dried Apricots, or Cranberry Apple Compote with a drizzle of Chocolate, Fudge, or Caramel Sauce. For a decadent treat, serve it over Better Brownies with a sauce on top (see index for recipes).

1 SERVING (REGULAR):
315 calories
3.1 grams protein
19.1 grams carbohydrate
25 grams fat
78 milligrams sodium

1 SERVING (HALF LITE):
218 calories
2.2 grams protein
15.6 grams carbohydrate
16.2 grams fat
52 milligrams sodium

Cinnamon Ice Dream

HANDS-ON: 30 MINUTES • **CHURNING:** 20 TO 25 MINUTES • **YIELD:** 4 TO 5 CUPS; 8 SERVINGS

INGREDIENTS

3 1/2 cups (two 14-ounce cans) unsweetened, preservative-free coconut milk (regular, not lite), divided

2 (3-inch) cinnamon sticks, broken in half

3 (2-inch by 1/2-inch) strips of lemon peel or zest, removed with a vegetable peeler

1/3 cup cool or cold filtered water

2 teaspoons unflavored gelatin **or** 3/4 teaspoon agar agar powder (not the flakes)

1/4 cup honey **or** agave nectar; additional 1 to 3 tablespoons as needed

1/4 to 1/2 teaspoon *pure* stevia extract powder **or** 1/2 to 1 teaspoon *clear* stevia extract liquid (start with less; add more only if needed)

1/8 teaspoon finely ground, unrefined sea salt

1 1/2 teaspoons ground cinnamon

1 teaspoon pure vanilla extract **or** alcohol-free vanilla flavoring

Spicy cinnamon sticks add a warm contrast to this cold dessert and a more complex flavor than you'd get from ground cinnamon alone. This is a perfect alternative to whipped cream. Serve it over apple crisp; baked, poached, or stewed fruit; or your favorite chocolate dessert.

1 SERVING (REGULAR):
232 calories
2.3 grams protein
16.2 grams carbohydrate
17.5 grams fat
77 milligrams sodium

1 SERVING (HALF LITE):
171 calories
1.4 grams protein
13.6 grams carbohydrate
12.2 grams fat
61 milligrams sodium

DIRECTIONS

1. Combine 2 cups of coconut milk with the cinnamon sticks and lemon zest in a medium saucepan. Bring to boil over medium heat. Cover, reduce heat, and simmer for 10 minutes. Remove from heat and let steep at room temperature for 1 hour.

2. Add 1/3 cup water to a small saucepan. Slowly sprinkle with gelatin or agar agar powder. Let stand for 2 to 5 minutes to soften. Warm over medium-low heat, without stirring, until gelatin or agar agar dissolves. Scrape the mixture into a blender, Vita-Mix, or food processor. Cover and process until smooth. Add the honey, sea salt, stevia, ground cinnamon, and vanilla. Blend.

3. Reheat the cinnamon-infused coconut milk. Remove the cinnamon sticks with a slotted spoon and discard. Add the cinnamon-infused coconut milk to a blender with the gelatin mixture. Cover and process until smooth. Add the reserved 1 1/2 cups coconut milk. Blend. For a sweeter taste, add an additional 1/8 teaspoon stevia and/or 1 tablespoon honey.

~Continued next page~

> **FYI:** To zest a lemon, wash and pat dry an organic lemon. With a paring knife or vegetable peeler, shave off the colored part of the skin. Add the amount indicated below. Refrigerate the naked lemon in a covered container to keep it from drying out.

Cinnamon Ice Dream ~ continued

4. Pour into one or more wide-mouth jars. Cover and refrigerate for at least 6 hours before churning.

5. Scrape the chilled custard into the canister of your ice cream maker. Churn according to the manufacturer's instructions. Serve immediately or spoon into several 8- to 16-ounce freezer-safe containers. Cover and freeze for 3 or more hours for a firmer texture.

6. Soften solidly frozen dessert in the refrigerator for 45 minutes or on the counter for 20 to 30 minutes before serving.

VARIATIONS

* **Lite Cinnamon Ice Dream:** Replace half of the coconut milk with lite (reduced fat) coconut milk. Alternatively, use 100% lite coconut milk, but plan to use the batch immediately or within 24 hours before it becomes hard and icy.

* **Cinnamon Chocolate Chunk Ice Dream:** Add 1/2 cup coarsely chopped bittersweet chocolate (a bar with 70 to 73% cocoa solids) when Ice Dream reaches the soft serve stage. Run the machine for 1 or 2 more minutes.

* **Cinnamon Cookie Crumble Ice Dream:** When Ice Dream reaches the soft-serve stage, add 1 to 1 ½ cups coarsely crumbled Gluten-Free Graham Crackers (Page 230), commercial gluten-free honey Graham crackers, or crumbled gluten-free ginger snaps. Run the machine for 1 or 2 more minutes.

Nutmeg Ice Dream

HANDS-ON: 20 MINUTES • **CHURNING:** 20 TO 25 MINUTES • **YIELD:** 4 1/2 TO 5 CUPS; 8 SERVINGS

INGREDIENTS

3 1/2 cups (two 14-ounce cans) unsweetened, preservative-free coconut milk (regular, not lite), divided

3 (2-inch by 1/2-inch) strips of lemon peel or zest, removed with a vegetable peeler

1/3 cup cool or cold filtered water

2 teaspoons unflavored gelatin **or** 3/4 teaspoon agar agar powder (not the flakes)

1/4 cup honey **or** agave nectar; additional 1 to 3 tablespoons as needed

1/4 to 1/2 teaspoon *pure* stevia extract powder **or** 1/2 to 1 teaspoon *clear* stevia extract liquid (start with less; add more only if needed)

1/8 teaspoon finely ground, unrefined sea salt

1 teaspoon ground nutmeg (freshly ground tastes best)

Nutmeg usually shows up in sweet and spicy dishes, particularly desserts such as pies, puddings, custards, spice cakes, and eggnog. In most dishes, it plays back-up for cinnamon and ginger. However, in Nutmeg Ice Dream, it is the star. Served over Apple Compote, Apple Crisp, Poached Pears, or Squash Pudding Pie, this dish is the perfect alternative to whipped cream, especially during the chilly months of fall and winter.

1 SERVING (REGULAR):
232 calories
2.2 grams protein
16 grams carbohydrate
17.6 grams fat
77 milligrams sodium

1 SERVING (HALF LITE):
171 calories
1.4 grams protein
13.4 grams carbohydrate
12.3 grams fat
61 milligrams sodium

DIRECTIONS

1. Combine 1 cup of coconut milk with the lemon zest in a medium saucepan. Bring to boil over medium heat. Cover, reduce heat, and simmer for 10 minutes. Remove from heat. Let steep at room temperature for 1 hour.

2. Add 1/3 cup water to a small saucepan. Slowly sprinkle with gelatin or agar agar powder. Let stand for 2 to 5 minutes to soften. Warm over medium-low heat, without stirring, until gelatin or agar agar dissolves. Scrape the mixture into a blender, Vita-Mix, or food processor. Add the honey, sea salt, stevia, and ground nutmeg. Cover and process until smooth.

3. Remove the lemon zest from the coconut milk. Discard the zest. Add the lemon-infused coconut milk to the blender with the gelatin mixture and the reserved 2 1/2 cups coconut milk. Blend until smooth, stopping to scrape the sides with a spatula. For a sweeter taste, add an additional 1/8 teaspoon stevia and/or 1 tablespoon honey. Blend, taste, and repeat if needed.

~Continued next page~

> **FYI:** To zest a lemon, wash and pat dry an organic lemon. With a paring knife or vegetable peeler, shave off the colored part of the skin. Add the amount indicated below. Refrigerate the naked lemon in a covered container to keep it from drying out.

Nutmeg Ice Dream ~ continued

4. Pour into one or more wide-mouth jars. Cover and refrigerate for at least 6 hours before churning.

5. Scrape the chilled custard into the canister of your ice cream maker. Churn according to the manufacturer's instructions. Serve immediately or spoon into several 8- to 16-ounce freezer-safe containers. Cover and freeze for 3 or more hours for a firmer texture.

6. Soften solidly frozen dessert by placing it in the refrigerator for 30 to 45 minutes or on the counter for 15 to 30 minutes before serving.

VARIATIONS

* **Lite Nutmeg Ice Dream:** Replace half of the coconut milk with lite (reduced fat) coconut milk. Alternatively, use 100% lite coconut milk, but plan to use the batch immediately or within 24 hours before it becomes hard and icy.

* **Nutmeg Chocolate Chunk Ice Dream:** Add 1/2 cup coarsely chopped bittersweet chocolate (a bar with 70 to 73% cocoa solids) when Ice Dream reaches the soft-serve stage. Run the machine for 1 or 2 more minutes.

* **Nutmeg Cookie Crumble Ice Dream:** When Ice Dream reaches the soft-serve stage, add 1 to 1-1/2 cups coarsely crumbled Gluten-Free Graham Crackers (Page 230), commercial gluten-free honey Graham crackers, or crumbled gluten-free ginger snaps. Run the machine for 1 or 2 more minutes.

* **Nutty Nutmeg Ice Dream:** When Ice Dream reaches the soft-serve stage, add 1 cup chopped toasted almonds, walnuts, or pecans (see Page 75 for toasting tips), or Pralined Pecans (Page 214). Run the machine for 1 or 2 more minutes.

In small doses, nutmeg aids digestion and improves the appetite. Used to excess, it imparts a bitter flavor.

Cocoa Ice Dream

HANDS-ON: 20 MINUTES • **CHURNING:** 20 TO 25 MINUTES • **YIELD:** 5 TO 6 CUPS; 8 SERVINGS

INGREDIENTS

1/3 cup cool or cold filtered water

2 teaspoons unflavored gelatin **or** 3/4 teaspoon agar agar powder (not the flakes)

1/4 cup honey **or** agave nectar; additional 1 to 3 tablespoons as needed

1/4 to 1/2 teaspoon *pure* stevia extract powder **or** 1/2 to 1 teaspoon *clear* stevia extract liquid (start with less; add more only if needed)

1/8 teaspoon finely ground, unrefined sea salt

3 1/2 cups (two 14-ounce cans) unsweetened, preservative-free coconut milk (regular, not lite)

1/2 cup unsweetened cocoa powder (natural **or** Dutch-process)

2 teaspoons pure vanilla extract **or** alcohol-free vanilla flavoring

1 to 2 tablespoons coconut rum or light or dark rum, optional

Unsweetened cocoa powder adds a light chocolatey taste to this dairy-free frozen dessert with a fraction of the fat found in bittersweet or semisweet chocolate. If you prefer a stronger chocolate taste, try the Dark Chocolate Ice Dream (Page 88). Either way, I usually serve this with fresh fruit or a cooked fruit sauce. This provides extra antioxidants, and may help you feel more satisfied on less Ice Dream.

1 SERVING (REGULAR):
253 calories
3.3 grams protein
18.7 grams carbohydrate
18.2 grams fat
78 milligrams sodium

1 SERVING (HALF LITE):
192 calories
2.4 grams protein
16.1 grams carbohydrate
12.9 grams fat
62 milligrams sodium

DIRECTIONS

1. Add 1/3 cup water to a small saucepan. Slowly sprinkle with gelatin or agar agar powder. Let stand for 2 to 5 minutes to soften. Warm over medium-low heat, without stirring, until gelatin or agar agar dissolves. Scrape the mixture into a blender, Vita-Mix, or food processor. Cover and process until smooth.

2. Add honey, stevia, and sea salt. Blend. Add coconut milk, cocoa powder, and vanilla. Blend until smooth, stopping to scrape the sides with a spatula. For a sweeter taste, add an additional 1/8 teaspoon stevia and/ or 1 tablespoon honey. Blend, taste, and repeat if needed.

3. Pour into one or more wide-mouth jars. Cover and refrigerate for at least 6 hours before churning.

4. Scrape the chilled custard into the canister of your ice cream maker. Add the optional rum. Churn according to the manufacturer's instructions.

~Continued next page~

Cocoa Ice Dream ~ continued

5.   Serve immediately or spoon into several 8- to 16-ounce freezer-safe containers. Cover and freeze for 3 or more hours for a firmer texture.

6.   Soften solidly frozen dessert in the refrigerator for 45 minutes or on the counter for 20 to 30 minutes before serving.

VARIATIONS

* **Lite Cocoa Ice Dream:** Replace half of the coconut milk with lite (reduced fat) coconut milk. Alternatively, use 100% lite coconut milk, but plan to use the batch immediately or within 24 hours before it becomes hard and icy.

* **Maple Cocoa Ice Dream:** Replace honey with 1/4 cup + 2 to 4 tablespoons maple syrup in the master recipe above.

* **Cocoa Crunch Ice Dream:** Add 3/4 cup cocoa nibs (aka cacao nibs) when Ice Dream reaches the soft-serve stage. Run the machine for 1 or 2 more minutes.

* **Cocoa Mint Ice Dream:** Add 1 1/2 teaspoons peppermint extract or alcohol-free peppermint flavoring along with the vanilla in step #2. Add an extra ½ teaspoon if a stronger mint flavor is desired.

Dark Chocolate Ice Dream

HANDS-ON: 30 MINUTES • **CHURNING:** 20 TO 25 MINUTES • **YIELD:** 4 1/2 TO 5 CUPS; 8 SERVINGS

INGREDIENTS

1/3 cup cool or cold filtered water

2 teaspoons unflavored gelatin **or** 3/4 teaspoon agar agar powder (not the flakes)

1/4 cup honey **or** agave nectar; additional 1 to 3 tablespoons as needed

1/2 teaspoon *pure* stevia extract powder **or** 1 teaspoon *clear* stevia extract liquid

1/8 teaspoon finely ground, unrefined sea salt

3 cups unsweetened, preservative-free lite (reduced fat) coconut milk, divided

4 ounces bittersweet dark chocolate (70 to 73%), coarsely chopped

1 teaspoon pure vanilla extract **or** alcohol-free vanilla flavoring

2 tablespoons light or dark rum, optional

DIRECTIONS

1. Add 1/3 cup water to a small saucepan. Slowly sprinkle with gelatin or agar agar powder. Let stand for 2 to 5 minutes to soften. Warm over medium-low heat, without stirring, until gelatin or agar agar dissolves. Scrape the mixture into a blender, Vita-Mix, or food processor. Cover and blend until smooth. Add the honey, stevia, and sea salt. Blend.

2. Bring 1 cup of coconut milk to a boil in a small saucepan. Remove from heat. Add chocolate and stir until smooth. Add this to the gelatin mixture. Blend until smooth. Add the remaining 2 cups coconut milk and vanilla. Blend. For a sweeter taste, add an additional 1/8 teaspoon stevia and/or 1 tablespoon honey. Blend, taste, and repeat if needed.

3. Pour into one or more wide-mouth jars. Cover and refrigerate for at least 6 hours before churning.

Bittersweet chocolate adds a rich flavor and silky smooth texture that you don't get with unsweetened cocoa powder. To counter the higher fat content of the chocolate bar, I use lite (reduced fat) coconut milk. The result is a velvety rich chocolate flavor so smooth that your guests will never suspect that you used coconut milk for the base.

I like to serve this over a fresh fruit salad or topped with a fruit sauce. Caramel Sauce would also taste great here (see index for recipes). For a more chocolatey flavor and crunch, garnish with roasted cocoa nibs (aka cacao nibs) or mix them in near the end of churning.

1 SERVING (LITE):
191 calories
2 grams protein
14.4 grams carbohydrate
13.7 grams fat
45 milligrams sodium

1 SERVING
(LITE W/CACAO NIBS):
235 calories
2.8 grams protein
16.1 grams carbohydrate
17.4 grams fat
45 milligrams sodium

~Continued next page~

Dark Chocolate Ice Dream ~ continued

4. Scrape the chilled custard into the canister of your ice cream maker. Add the optional rum. Churn according to the manufacturer's instructions.

5. Serve immediately or spoon into several 8- to 16-ounce freezer-safe containers. Cover and freeze for 3 or more hours for a firmer texture.

6. Soften solidly frozen dessert by placing it in the refrigerator for 30 to 45 minutes or on the counter for 15 to 30 minutes before serving.

VARIATIONS

*   **Maple Dark Chocolate Ice Dream:** Replace honey with 1/4 cup + 2 to 3 tablespoons maple syrup above.

*   **Cocoa Nib Crunch Ice Dream:** Add 1/2 cup cocoa nibs (aka cacao nibs) when Ice Dream reaches the soft-serve stage. Run the machine for 1 or 2 more minutes.

*   **Dark Chocolate Espresso Ice Dream:** Replace bittersweet chocolate with an espresso-flavored bittersweet dark chocolate bar, or in step #1, add 2 teaspoons instant espresso powder or instant coffee powder. If desired, add 1/2 cup cocoa nibs during the last 2 minutes of churning.

*   **Dark Chocolate Orange Ice Dream:** Replace bittersweet chocolate with an orange-flavored bittersweet dark chocolate bar or add 1 teaspoon pure orange extract or natural orange flavoring in step #2.

*   **Dark Chocolate Mint Ice Dream:** Replace bittersweet chocolate with a mint-flavored bittersweet dark chocolate bar or, in step #2, add 1 teaspoon pure peppermint extract or alcohol-free peppermint flavoring. Taste, and add an additional 1/4 teaspoon peppermint flavoring if needed.

*   **Dark Chocolate Ginger Ice Dream:** Replace bittersweet chocolate with a ginger-flavored bittersweet dark chocolate bar or, when the mixture reaches the soft-serve stage, add 3 to 4 tablespoons minced candied (crystallized) ginger to the machine. Run the machine for 1 or 2 more minutes.

Almost Chocolate Ice Dream

HANDS-ON: 30 MINUTES • **CHURNING:** 20 TO 25 MINUTES • **YIELD:** 5 TO 6 CUPS; 8 SERVINGS

INGREDIENTS

1/3 cup cool or cold filtered water

2 teaspoons unflavored gelatin **or** 3/4 teaspoon agar agar powder (not the flakes)

1/2 cup strong brewed Roasted Chicory Root Coffee, Roasted Dandelion Root Coffee, Roasted Chicory & Dandelion Root Coffee, (Page 248), **or** double strength Teeccino Caffeine-Free Herbal Coffee (Page 249)

1/4 cup honey **or** agave nectar; additional 1 to 3 tablespoons as needed

1/4 to 1/2 teaspoon *pure* stevia extract powder **or** 1/2 to 1 teaspoon *clear* stevia extract liquid (start with less; add more only if needed)

1/8 to 1/4 teaspoon finely ground, unrefined sea salt

2 1/4 cups unsweetened, preservative-free coconut milk (regular, not lite)

1/4 cup unsweetened, roasted almond butter **or** hazelnut butter, thoroughly mixed

1/4 cup roasted carob powder

2 teaspoons pure vanilla extract **or** alcohol-free vanilla flavoring

My husband and I lived without chocolate for many years, but, as much as we enjoy it, we didn't feel deprived. We developed a surprisingly similar flavor by combining carob (which lacks the bitter kick of cocoa) with roasted almond or hazelnut butter and an herbal beverage made from roasted chicory and dandelion root. For a healthy alternative to chocolate, give this recipe a try.

Note: Look for roasted chicory and dandelion root grinds in the bulk herb/ spice section or in tea bags in natural foods stores and Teeccino, another herbal coffee alternative, in cans and bags on the coffee aisle of natural foods stores. You can also order these products online (see Resources, Page 253).

DIRECTIONS

1. Add 1/3 cup water to a small saucepan. Slowly sprinkle with gelatin or agar agar powder. Let stand for 2 to 5 minutes to soften. Warm over medium-low heat, without stirring, until gelatin or agar agar dissolves. Scrape the mixture into a blender, Vita-Mix, or food processor. Cover and process until smooth.

2. Add honey, stevia, and sea salt. Blend. Add brewed Chicory & Dandelion Root Coffee or Teeccino, coconut milk, almond or hazelnut butter, carob, and vanilla. Blend until smooth, stopping to scrape the sides with a spatula. For a sweeter taste,

1 SERVING (REGULAR):
226 calories
2.7 grams protein
18 grams carbohydrate
15.8 grams fat
62 milligrams sodium

1 SERVING (HALF LITE):
187 calories
2.2 grams protein
16.4 grams carbohydrate
12.4 grams fat
52 milligrams sodium

~Continued next page~

FYI: Although Teeccino contains barley, an independent laboratory at the University of Nebraska that specializes in gluten testing found no detectable levels of gluten in Teeccino. Although gluten is present in barley, it most likely does not extract out of the barley using conventional coffee brewing techniques. Gluten is not extracted by boiling water although it can be extracted using ethanol alcohol, which of course is not present in Teeccino. The company regularly has Teeccino tested at the University of Nebraska's Allergy Testing lab where it has had no detectable levels of gluten found at 10PPM.

To view the lab report visit: http://www.teeccino.com/FAQs.aspx#gluten

---

Almost Chocolate Ice Dream ~ continued

add an additional 1/8 teaspoon stevia and/or 1 tablespoon honey. Blend, taste, and repeat if needed.

3. Pour into one or more wide-mouth jars. Cover and refrigerate for at least 6 hours before churning.

4. Scrape the chilled custard into the canister of your ice cream maker. Churn according to the manufacturer's instructions. Serve immediately or spoon into several 8- to 16-ounce freezer-safe containers. Cover and freeze for 3 or more hours for a firmer texture.

5. Soften solidly frozen dessert by placing it in the refrigerator for 30 to 45 minutes or on the counter for 15 to 30 minutes before serving.

VARIATION

* **Lite Almost Chocolate Ice Dream:** Replace half of the coconut milk with lite (reduced fat) coconut milk. Alternatively, use 100% lite coconut milk, but plan to use the batch immediately or within 24 hours before it becomes hard and icy.

Pumpkin Ice Dream

HANDS-ON: 20 MINUTES • **CHURNING:** 20 TO 25 MINUTES • **YIELD:** 3 1/2 TO 4 CUPS; 8 SERVINGS

INGREDIENTS

1/3 cup cool or cold filtered water

2 teaspoons unflavored gelatin **or** 3/4 teaspoon agar agar powder (not the flakes)

1/4 cup honey or agave nectar, **or** 1/4 cup + 2 tablespoons maple syrup; additional 2 tablespoons as needed

1/4 to 1/2 teaspoon *pure* stevia extract powder **or** 1/2 to 1 teaspoon *clear* stevia extract liquid (start with less; add more only if needed)

1/8 teaspoon finely ground, unrefined sea salt

1 1/2 teaspoons apple pie spice **or** pumpkin pie spice (see note above)

2 1/4 cups unsweetened, preservative-free coconut milk (regular, not lite) thoroughly blended

1 cup frozen or canned pumpkin, **or** baked or simmered and mashed winter squash (See *Shopping for winter squash* on next page)

2 teaspoons pure vanilla extract **or** alcohol-free vanilla flavoring

2 tablespoons coconut rum **or** dark rum, optional

DIRECTIONS

1. Add 1/3 cup water to a small saucepan. Slowly sprinkle with gelatin or agar agar powder. Let stand for 2 to 5 minutes to soften. Warm over medium-low heat, without stirring, until gelatin or agar agar dissolves. Scrape the mixture into a blender, Vita-Mix, or food processor. Cover and process until smooth.

2. Add honey, stevia, spice, and sea salt. Blend. Add coconut milk, pumpkin or squash, and vanilla. Blend. For a sweeter taste, add an additional 1/8 teaspoon stevia and/or 1 tablespoon honey. Blend, taste, and repeat if needed.

3. Pour into one or more wide-mouth jars. Cover and refrigerate for at least 6 hours before churning.

For best results, use sweet winter squash. Frozen squash or canned pumpkin (which often contains some squash) will work well, too. Read labels to ensure that you're buying solid-pack pumpkin rather than pumpkin pie mix; it should be free of added sweeteners and spices.

For a holiday meal, serve Pumpkin Ice Dream over poached pears. This flavor pairs well with Avocado, Vanilla, Ginger, Cocoa, or Dark Chocolate Ice Dream, or it can be served with a drizzle of Chocolate, Fudge, or Caramel Sauce (see index for recipes).

Note: If apple or pumpkin pie spice is not available, substitute 3/4 teaspoon ground cinnamon, 1/2 teaspoon dried ginger powder, 1/4 teaspoon ground nutmeg, 1/4 teaspoon dried orange zest, and 1/8 teaspoon ground cloves.

1 SERVING (REGULAR):
174 calories
1.7 grams protein
16.1 grams carbohydrate
11.4 grams fat
61 milligrams sodium

1 SERVING (HALF LITE):
134 calories
1.2 grams protein
14.4 grams carbohydrate
7.9 grams fat
51 milligrams sodium

~Continued next page~

> **How to shop for winter squash:** Choose Hokkaido pumpkin, kabocha, buttercup, honey delight, or butternut squash that feels heavy in relation to its size. Kabocha, Hokkaido, and buttercup squash should have dark green skins; any spots should be bright orange, not pale or yellow. A ripe butternut squash will be orange all over with no hint of green. Store all hard winter squashes at room temperature.
>
> **How to cut and cook hard winter squash:** Cut off the stem. Place a folded dish towel on a cutting board (this will keep the squash from slipping). Lay the squash on the towel. Cut in half from top to bottom, rocking the knife back and forth. Scoop out and discard the seeds. Bake squash halves cut side down on a rimmed baking sheet, uncovered, in a 400° F oven for 35 to 50 minutes until fork tender and juicy. Scoop out the flesh and discard the skin. Purée the flesh in a food processor, or force it through a medium mesh sieve or the medium disk of a food mill. Freeze what you don't plan to use within 3 days.

Pumpkin Ice Dream ~ continued

4. Scrape the chilled custard into the canister of your ice cream maker. Add the optional rum. Churn according to the manufacturer's instructions.

5. Serve immediately or spoon into several 8- to 16-ounce containers. Cover and freeze for 3 or more hours for a firmer texture.

6. Soften solidly frozen dessert in the refrigerator for 45 minutes or on the counter for 20 to 30 minutes before serving.

VARIATIONS

*   **Lite Pumpkin Ice Dream:** Replace half of the coconut milk with lite (reduced fat) coconut milk. Alternatively, use 100% lite coconut milk, but plan to use the batch immediately or within 24 hours before it becomes hard and icy.

*   **Pumpkin Orange Ice Dream:** Zest 1 medium orange (colored part only) and set aside. In step #1, replace 1/3 cup water with fresh orange juice. After sweetener has been added to taste (step #2), stir in orange zest. Proceed as directed above.

*   **Chocolate Pumpkin Ice Dream:** Add 1/3 cup unsweetened cocoa powder in step #2. Taste and adjust with an additional 1/4 teaspoon stevia extract powder or 1 to 2 tablespoons honey or maple syrup as needed.

*   **Pumpkin Nut Ice Dream:** Add 1/2 cup toasted, coarsely chopped almonds, pecans, or macadamia nuts (see Page 75) when Ice Dream reaches the soft-serve stage. Run the machine for 1 or 2 more minutes. **Note:** Every 1/2 cup of nuts adds 400 calories, 14 grams protein, 4 grams carbohydrate + 3 to 8 grams fiber, and 36 grams fat. The calorie count will be slightly higher if Pralined Pecans (Page 214) are used.

*   **Pumpkin Ice Dream with Hazelnuts & Chocolate:** Add 1/2 cup chopped, toasted hazelnuts (skins removed as described on Page 75) to the machine when Ice Dream reaches the soft-serve stage. Run the machine for 1 or 2 more minutes.

*   **Pumpkin Pie Ice Dream:** Fold 1 to 1 1/2 cups coarsely crumbled Gluten-Free Graham crackers (Page 230), commercial gluten-free honey Graham crackers, or crumbled gluten-free ginger snaps into the Ice Dream before removing it from the machine.

Orange Cream Ice Dream

HANDS-ON: 20 MINUTES • **CHURNING:** 20 TO 25 MINUTES • **YIELD:** 5 TO 6 CUPS; 8 SERVINGS

INGREDIENTS

1/3 cup cool or cold filtered water

2 teaspoons unflavored gelatin **or** 3/4 teaspoon agar agar powder (not flakes)

1/4 cup light-colored honey **or** agave nectar; additional 1 to 2 tablespoons as needed

1/4 to 1/2 teaspoon *pure* stevia extract powder **or** 1/2 to 1 teaspoon *clear* stevia extract liquid (start with less; add more only if needed)

1/8 teaspoon finely ground, unrefined sea salt

2/3 cup frozen orange juice concentrate, defrosted

Zest of 1 orange, finely grated (colored part only)

1 teaspoon natural orange flavoring **or** orange extract, optional

3 cups unsweetened, preservative-free coconut milk (regular, not lite)

2 teaspoons pure vanilla extract **or** alcohol-free vanilla flavoring

DIRECTIONS

1. Add 1/3 cup water to a small saucepan. Slowly sprinkle with gelatin or agar agar powder. Let stand for 2 to 5 minutes to soften. Warm over medium-low heat, without stirring, until dissolved. Scrape the mixture into a blender, Vita-Mix, or food processor. Cover and process until smooth.

2. Add honey, stevia, and sea salt. Blend. Add the orange juice concentrate and coconut milk. Blend until smooth, stopping to scrape the sides with a spatula. Add orange zest and optional orange flavoring. For a sweeter taste, add an additional 1/8 teaspoon stevia and/or 1 tablespoon honey. Blend, taste, and repeat if needed.

I spent most of my growing-up years in rural towns in New Mexico where we didn't have ice cream trucks. Only when I visited friends in the city and during the year I lived in Norman, Oklahoma, did the ice cream man peddle his summertime treats in my neighborhood. I had three favorite flavors: orange creamsicle push-up pops, ice cream sandwiches, and chocolate coated vanilla ice cream bars on a stick.

Recently, while trying to use up some frozen orange juice concentrate, I hit on this flavor and learned that my husband loved it, too. After trying more than 30 different Ice Dreams, he deemed this one his favorite. Serve it alone or top it off with a chocolate or fudge sauce, chopped bittersweet chocolate, or serve with another fruit- or chocolate-flavored Ice Dream. See index for recipes.

1 SERVING (REGULAR):
240 calories
2.4 grams protein
23.9 grams carbohydrate
15 grams fat
71 milligrams sodium

1 SERVING (HALF LITE):
188 calories
1.6 grams protein
21.6 grams carbohydrate
10.5 grams fat
57 milligrams sodium

~Continued next page~

Orange Cream Ice Dream ~ continued

3. Pour into one or more wide-mouth jars. Cover and chill for at least 6 hours before churning.

4. Scrape the chilled custard into the canister of your ice cream maker. Churn according to the manufacturer's instructions.

5. Serve immediately or spoon into several 8- to 16-ounce freezer-safe containers. Cover and freeze for 3 or more hours for a firmer texture.

6. Soften solidly frozen dessert by placing it in the refrigerator for 30 to 45 minutes or on the counter for 15 to 30 minutes before serving.

VARIATIONS

*   To prevent or reduce icing up during storage, add 2 tablespoons orange liqueur before churning the Ice Dream.

*   **Lite Orange Cream Ice Dream:** Replace half of the coconut milk with lite (reduced fat) coconut milk. Alternatively, use 100% lite coconut milk, but plan to use the batch immediately or within 24 hours before it becomes hard and icy.

*   **Maple Orange Cream Ice Dream:** Replace honey or agave nectar with 1/4 cup + 2 tablespoons pure maple syrup. Use darker syrup for a stronger maple flavor.

Beyond
The Basic Flavors

Best Bites

Avocado Ice Dream

HANDS-ON: 20 MINUTES • **CHURNING:** 20 TO 25 MINUTES • **YIELD:** 5 TO 6 CUPS; 8 SERVINGS

INGREDIENTS

1/3 cup cool or cold filtered water

2 teaspoons unflavored gelatin **or** 3/4 teaspoon agar agar powder (not the flakes)

1/3 cup honey **or** agave nectar; additional 1 to 2 tablespoons as needed

1/8 teaspoon finely ground, unrefined sea salt

2 1/2 cups unsweetened, preservative-free coconut milk (regular, not lite)

2 small to medium-size ripe avocados, rinsed, halved, pitted, pulp scooped out

2 tablespoons fresh lemon juice **or** lime juice

2 teaspoons pure vanilla extract **or** natural vanilla flavoring

1/4 to 1/2 teaspoon *pure* stevia extract powder **or** 1/2 to 1 teaspoon *clear* stevia extract liquid (start with less; add more only if needed)

DIRECTIONS

1. Add 1/3 cup water to a small saucepan. Slowly sprinkle with gelatin or agar agar powder. Let stand for 2 to 5 minutes to soften. Warm over medium-low heat, without stirring, until gelatin or agar agar dissolves. Scrape the mixture into a blender, Vita-Mix, or food processor. Cover and blend until smooth.

2. Add honey, stevia, and sea salt. Blend. Add the coconut milk, avocado, lemon or lime juice, vanilla, and stevia. Blend until smooth, stopping to scrape the sides with a spatula. For a sweeter taste, add an additional 1/8 teaspoon stevia and/or 1 tablespoon honey. Blend, taste, and repeat if needed.

3. Pour into one or more wide-mouth jars. Cover and refrigerate for at least 6 hours before churning.

Avocados in ice cream? The monounsaturated fats in avocado give this frozen dessert a silky smooth texture, and the natural antioxidants give it a pale green color. This is a perfect compliment to sliced fresh fruit, cooked fruit compote, poached pears, or fruit sauce for a healthy snack or the finale to a great meal. For a fancy touch, sprinkle with grated, bittersweet dark chocolate, or drizzle with chocolate sauce (see index for recipes).

FYI: The base for this Ice Dream thickens enough when refrigerated that it can be served as a pudding, unfrozen, spooned into parfait or wine glasses, layered with sliced strawberries, bananas, and kiwi fruit. Of course, it also tastes great frozen.

1 SERVING (REGULAR):
298 calories
2.8 grams protein
21.1 grams carbohydrate
22.5 grams fat
71 milligrams sodium

1 SERVING (HALF LITE):
253 calories
2.1 grams protein
19.2 grams carbohydrate
18.7 grams fat
60 milligrams sodium

~Continued next page~

How to buy avocadoes: Buy them up to a week in advance (if they feel rock hard) to give them time to ripen. Buy 2 more than you need in case one turns out overripe and black inside. You can always turn extras into guacamole or add them to a salad.

How to store avocadoes: If hard, keep them at room temperature in a bowl or basket. Use them when their skins darken and they yield to gentle pressure. When a toothpick inserts easily into the fat end with no resistance, they're ready to use. If not, leave them out and try again in a day or two. Once ripe, you need to refrigerate them to prevent spoilage.

Note: To easily open an avocado, cut it in half with a paring knife around the outside from stem to base. Then twist the sides in opposite directions, as if to unscrew. Squeeze the bottom half that holds the pit to release it. Now it's ready to scoop from the skin.

Avocado Ice Dream ~ continued

4. Scrape the chilled custard into the canister of your ice cream maker. Churn according to the manufacturer's instructions.

5. Serve immediately or spoon into several 8- to 16-ounce containers. Cover and freeze for 3 or more hours for a firmer texture.

6. Soften solidly frozen dessert by placing it in the refrigerator for 30 to 45 minutes or on the counter for 15 to 30 minutes before serving.

VARIATIONS

* **Avocado Chocolate Chunk Ice Dream:** When the mixture reaches the soft-serve stage, add 3/4 to 1 cup malt-sweetened, fruit-sweetened, dairy-free, or bittersweet chocolate chips **or** a bittersweet dark chocolate bar (70 to 73%), coarsely chopped into 1/4-inch pieces. Run the machine for 1 or 2 more minutes.

* **Cocoa Avocado Ice Dream:** In step #2, add 1/3 to 1/2 cup unsweetened cocoa powder. Taste, and add additional sweetener (1/8 to 1/4 teaspoon stevia extract powder or 1 to 2 tablespoons honey at a time) to achieve the desired sweetness.

* **Lite Avocado Ice Dream:** Replace half of the coconut milk with lite (reduced fat) coconut milk. Alternatively, use 100% lite coconut milk, but plan to use the batch immediately or within 24 hours before it becomes hard and icy.

Basil Ice Dream

HANDS-ON: 30 MINUTES • **CHURNING:** 20 TO 25 MINUTES • **YIELD:** 5 TO 6 CUPS; 8 SERVINGS

INGREDIENTS

3 1/2 cups (two 14-ounce cans) unsweetened, preservative-free coconut milk (regular, not lite), divided

1/8 teaspoon finely ground, unrefined sea salt

1 cup packed fresh basil leaves

1/3 cup cool or cold filtered water

2 teaspoons unflavored gelatin **or** 3/4 teaspoon agar agar powder (not the flakes)

1/3 cup honey **or** agave nectar; additional 1 to 2 tablespoons as needed

1/4 to 1/2 teaspoon *pure* stevia extract powder **or** 1/2 to 1 teaspoon *clear* stevia extract liquid (start with less; add more only if needed)

Zest of 1 lemon, preferably unsprayed, rinsed and patted dry, optional

When you have tired of making and eating pesto, try adding some fresh basil to ice cream or to this dairy-free Ice Dream. Experiment with different kinds of basil. For instance, Italian basil imparts a slight anise-like scent; lemon basil has a citrus flavor; cinnamon basil and anise basil add a slightly spicy flavor; then there's Genovese basil...

This recipe pairs well with sliced strawberries, blueberries, peaches, apricots, nectarines, or a sauce made from any of these fruits. Also try it with Chocolate or Hot Fudge Sauce (see index for recipes).

DIRECTIONS

1. Combine 1 cup coconut milk with the sea salt in a heavy, medium-size saucepan. Cook over medium heat until bubbly. Stir in the basil leaves and remove from heat. Cover and let stand at room temperature for 20 minutes.

2. Meanwhile, add 1/3 cup water to a small saucepan. Slowly sprinkle with gelatin or agar agar powder. Let stand for 2 to 5 minutes to soften. Warm over medium-low heat, without stirring, until gelatin or agar agar dissolves. Add honey and stevia and set aside.

1 SERVING (REGULAR):
243 calories
2.2 grams protein
19 grams carbohydrate
17.5 grams fat
78 milligrams sodium

1 SERVING (HALF LITE):
182 calories
1.4 grams protein
16.4 grams carbohydrate
12.3 grams fat
62 milligrams sodium

3. Process the basil coconut milk mixture in a blender or Vita-Mix until smooth, stopping to scrape the sides with a spatula. Pour the milky mixture through a fine mesh strainer into a bowl. Discard the bits of basil).

4. Return the strained milk mixture to the blender with the gelatin-

~Continued next page~

Basil Ice Dream ~ continued

sweetened mixture. Add the remaining 2-1/2 cups of coconut milk. Process until smooth. For a sweeter taste, add an additional 1/8 teaspoon stevia and/or 1 tablespoon honey. Blend, taste, and repeat if needed. For a lemon flavor, stir in the zest of 1 lemon. (Refrigerate the unused lemon in a covered container and use within 3 days.)

5. Pour into one or more wide-mouth jars. Cover and refrigerate for at least 6 hours before churning.

6. Scrape the chilled custard into the canister of your ice cream maker. Churn according to the manufacturer's instructions.

7. Serve immediately or spoon into several 8- or 16-ounce containers. Cover and freeze for 3 or more hours for a firmer texture.

8. Soften solidly frozen dessert in the refrigerator for 45 minutes or on the counter for 20 to 30 minutes before serving.

VARIATIONS

* **Lite Basil Ice Dream:** Replace half of the coconut milk with lite (reduced fat) coconut milk. Alternatively, use 100% lite coconut milk, but plan to use the batch immediately or within 24 hours before it becomes hard and icy.

* **Chocolate Chip Basil Ice Dream:** When Ice Dream reaches the soft-serve stage, add 1/2 to 3/4 cup bittersweet chocolate chips or dark chocolate (70 to 73%), grated or coarsely chopped into 1/4-inch pieces. Run the machine for 1 or 2 more minutes.

One of my friends and recipe testers, Heather Wolcott, served this flavor over my Squash Pudding Pie for Thanksgiving. Two young children licked their dessert plates clean.

Ginger Ice Dream

HANDS-ON: 30 MINUTES • **CHURNING:** 20 TO 25 MINUTES • **YIELD:** 5 TO 6 CUPS; 8 SERVINGS

INGREDIENTS

1 cup filtered water

1/2 cup peeled and grated fresh gingerroot (from a 3-ounce chunk)

2 teaspoons unflavored gelatin **or** 3/4 teaspoon agar agar powder (not the flakes)

1/4 cup honey **or** agave nectar; additional 1 to 2 tablespoons as needed

1/8 teaspoon finely ground, unrefined sea salt

1/4 to 1/2 teaspoon *pure* stevia extract powder **or** 1/2 to 1 teaspoon *clear* stevia extract liquid (start with less; add more only if needed)

3 1/2 cups (two 14-ounce cans) unsweetened, preservative-free coconut milk (regular, not lite)

2 teaspoons pure vanilla extract **or** alcohol-free vanilla flavoring

1/4 cup candied ginger, minced

Ginger adds a spicy sweet flavor and warm contrast to the coolness of Vanilla Ice Dream. Fresh ginger simmered in the coconut milk adds the first layer of flavor, while candied fresh ginger, added near the end of freezing, provides a crunchy texture with an extra burst of spice.

This recipe pairs nicely with sliced fresh fruit, fresh fruit salad, Poached Pears, Apple Apricot Compote, or cooked fruit sauce. Add a drizzle of Hot Chocolate Sauce or Hot Fudge Sauce for a festive touch (see index for recipes).

Note: If you don't care for candied ginger, leave it out, and add 1 teaspoon dried powdered ginger with the vanilla.

DIRECTIONS

1. Combine the water and ginger in a medium saucepan. Or, place the ginger in a small muslin or cheesecloth bag, or wrap it in a square of cheesecloth and secure with twine. Bring the mixture to a boil. Cover, reduce heat, and simmer for 15 minutes. Remove from heat. Let steep with the lid on for 20 more minutes.

2. Squeeze the cheesecloth or muslin bag to extract as much ginger tea as possible, or pour the tea through a fine mesh strainer into a heat-proof measuring container, pressing on the solids to release more juices. You should have 1/2 cup ginger tea. If you have more, simmer to reduce. If less, add warm water to make 1/2 cupful.

3. Return the tea to the saucepan and slowly sprinkle with gelatin or agar agar powder. Let stand for 2 to 5 minutes to soften. Warm over medium-

1 SERVING (REGULAR):
261 calories
2.2 grams protein
23.5 grams carbohydrate
17.6 grams fat
91 milligrams sodium

1 SERVING (HALF LITE):
200 calories
1.4 grams protein
20.9 grams carbohydrate
12.3 grams fat
65 milligrams sodium

~Continued next page~

> **FYI:** Look for fresh gingerroot with firm, smooth and unblemished skin that is free of wrinkles and pink, black, or moldy spots, in the produce section of supermarkets and natural foods stores. Store at room temperature (not in the fridge) in a basket or open bowl. Cut off slices as needed. Look for candied ginger on the baking aisle of supermarkets or gourmet and natural foods stores.

Ginger Ice Dream ~ continued

low heat, without stirring, until gelatin or agar agar dissolves. Scrape the mixture into a blender, Vita-Mix, or food processor. Cover and process until smooth.

4. Add the honey, stevia, and sea salt. Blend. Add the coconut milk, stevia, and vanilla. Blend until smooth, stopping to scrape the sides with a spatula. For a sweeter taste, add an additional 1/8 teaspoon stevia and/or 1 tablespoon honey. Don't add too much sweetener; the candied ginger will add more sugar to the mix later. Blend, taste, and repeat as needed.

5. Pour into one or more wide-mouth jars. Cover and refrigerate for at least 6 hours before churning.

6. Scrape the chilled custard into the canister of your ice cream maker. Churn according to the manufacturer's instructions. When the mixture reaches the soft-serve stage, add the chopped candied ginger to the machine. Run the machine for 1 or 2 more minutes.

7. Serve immediately or spoon into several 8- or 16-ounce containers. Cover and freeze for 3 or more hours for a firmer texture.

8. Soften solidly frozen dessert in the refrigerator for 45 minutes or on the counter for 20 to 30 minutes before serving.

VARIATIONS

* **Lite Ginger Ice Dream:** Replace half of the coconut milk with lite (reduced fat) coconut milk. Alternatively, use 100% lite coconut milk, but plan to use the batch immediately or within 24 hours before it becomes hard and icy.

* **Ginger Chocolate Chunk Ice Dream:** Add 1/2 to 3/4 cup coarsely chopped and chilled bittersweet dark chocolate (70 to 73%) with the candied ginger. Run the machine for 1 or 2 more minutes.

* **Ginger Cookie Crumble Ice Dream:** Leave out the candied ginger. Fold 1 to 2 cups coarsely crumbled Gluten-Free Graham Crackers (Page 230), commercial gluten-free honey graham crackers, or crumbled gluten-free ginger snaps into the Ice Dream before removing it from the machine.

* **Ginger Nut Ice Dream:** Add 1/2 to 3/4 cup toasted, coarsely chopped walnuts or pecans, or Pralined Pecans (Page 75 or 214) when Ice Dream reaches the soft-serve stage. Run the machine for 1 or 2 more minutes.

Lemon Cookie Crumble Ice Dream

HANDS-ON: 20 MINUTES • **CHURNING:** 20 TO 25 MINUTES • **YIELD:** 6 TO 7 CUPS; 8 TO 12 SERVINGS

INGREDIENTS

1/3 cup fresh lemon juice

2 teaspoons unflavored gelatin **or** 3/4 teaspoon agar agar powder (not the flakes)

1/4 cup + 2 tablespoons maple syrup **or** 1/3 cup honey or agave nectar; additional 1 tablespoon as needed

1/4 + 1/8 teaspoon *pure* stevia extract powder; additional 1/8 teaspoon as needed **or** 1/2 to 1 teaspoon *clear* stevia extract liquid

1/8 teaspoon finely ground, unrefined sea salt

3 1/2 cups (two 14-ounce cans) unsweetened, preservative-free coconut milk (regular, not lite)

1 teaspoon pure vanilla extract **or** alcohol-free vanilla flavoring

1 teaspoon pure lemon extract **or** alcohol-free lemon flavoring

1 teaspoon 100% natural yellow food coloring, such as Seelect, optional

1 to 2 cups coarsely chopped or crumbled gluten-free lemon shortbread cookies, crunchy lemon cookies, **or** Lemon Graham Crackers (Page 230)

Lemon juice, lemon extract, and lemon-flavored shortbread cookies add layers of lemon flavor to this delicate frozen dessert created by my cooking student and assistant, Andrea Murschel. Look for cookies with the simplest and fewest ingredients in natural foods stores or the health foods section of supermarkets. Look for a gluten-free brand, such as Pamela's, Kinniknnick, or Nana's, that doesn't contain hydrogenated or partially hydrogenated oil, high fructose corn sweetener, or artificial ingredients.

1 SERVING (REGULAR):
312 calories
2.6 grams protein
27.2 grams carbohydrate
21.3 grams fat
111 milligrams sodium

1 SERVING (HALF LITE):
256 calories
1.7 grams protein
24.4 grams carbohydrate
15.9 grams fat
96 milligrams sodium

DIRECTIONS

1. Add 1/3 cup lemon juice to a small saucepan. Slowly sprinkle with gelatin or agar agar powder. Let stand for 2 to 5 minutes to soften. Warm over medium-low heat, without stirring, until gelatin or agar agar dissolves. Scrape the mixture into a blender, Vita-Mix, or food processor. Cover and blend until smooth.

2. Add honey, stevia, and sea salt. Blend. Add the coconut milk, vanilla, lemon extract, and optional yellow food coloring. Blend until smooth, stopping to scrape the sides with a spatula. For a sweeter taste, add an additional 1/8 teaspoon stevia and/or 1 tablespoon maple syrup or honey. Blend, taste, and repeat if needed.

~Continued next page~

Note: If using bottled lemon juice, taste it before you use it; if left to sit too long in the refrigerator, lemon juice can develop an unpleasant harsh and bitter flavor. For a more lemony look, I like to add natural yellow food coloring made from turmeric that colors, but doesn't flavor recipes. You have to use more of this product than conventional food coloring. Health foods stores stock it on the baking aisle along with flavoring extracts.

Lemon Cookie Crumble Ice Dream ~ continued

3. Pour into one or more wide-mouth jars. Cover and refrigerate for at least 6 hours before churning.

4. Scrape the chilled custard into the canister of your ice cream maker. Churn according to the manufacturer's instructions. When Ice Dream reaches the soft-serve stage, add 1 cup of the crumbled cookies. Run the machine for 1 or 2 more minutes. If your machine appears very full or you want more cookies, fold the cookies into the Ice Dream before removing it from the machine.

5. Serve immediately or spoon into several 8- to 16-ounce containers. Cover and freeze for 3 or more hours for a firmer texture.

6. Soften solidly frozen dessert by placing it in the refrigerator for 30 to 45 minutes or on the counter for 15 to 30 minutes before serving.

VARIATIONS

*   **Lite Lemon Cookie Crumble Ice Dream:** Replace half of the coconut milk with lite (reduced fat) coconut milk. Alternatively, use 100% lite coconut milk, but plan to use the batch immediately or within 24 hours before it becomes hard and icy.

*   **Lemon Ginger Cookie Crumble Ice Dream:** Replace lemon cookies with gluten-free ginger snaps or Gingerbread Ice Dream Sandwich Cookies (Page 226)

Macaroon Madness Ice Dream

ASSEMBLY: 20 MINUTES • **CHURNING:** 20 TO 25 MINUTES • **YIELD:** 8 TO 9 CUPS; 10 SERVINGS

INGREDIENTS

1 recipe Vanilla or Maple Vanilla Ice Dream (Page 78)

1 1/2 cups Hot Chocolate Sauce (Page 168), Hot Fudge Sauce (Page 166), **or** Almond Buttery Hot Chocolate Sauce (Page 170),

1 1/2 to 2 cups My Favorite Macaroons (Page 202) **or** Jennies Macaroons, chopped in 1/4- to 1/2-inch pieces

DIRECTIONS

1. Prepare the base for Vanilla Ice Dream as directed.

2. Prepare the chocolate or fudge sauce as directed. Set aside and let cool to room temperature.

3. Prepare Vanilla or Maple Vanilla Ice Dream as directed. Spoon about one-fourth of the frozen dessert into 4 (16-ounce) freezer-safe containers. Spoon a layer of chocolate or fudge sauce evenly over the Ice Dream (about 6 tablespoons total). Spoon about one-fourth of the macaroon pieces (about 6 tablespoons) over the sauce. Top with another layer of Ice Dream. Add another layer of sauce and macaroon pieces. Repeat two more times until you've used up the ingredients.

4. Cover and freeze for at least 3 hours, until firm, before serving.

5. Soften solidly frozen dessert by placing it in the refrigerator for 30 to 45 minutes or on the counter for 15 to 30 minutes before serving.

VARIATIONS

* Replace Vanilla Ice Dream with Cocoa or Dark Chocolate Ice Dream, or replace coconut macaroons with cocoa macaroons.

* **Caramel Macaroon Madness Ice Dream:** Use cocoa macaroons above, and then replace Chocolate or Fudge Sauce with Caramel Sauce (Page 176).

If you're short on time, buy Jennies Coconut or Almond Macaroons in natural foods stores. They come in 8-ounce round tins, and they're made with simple and pure ingredients, including unsweetened, sulfite-free coconut, honey, and egg whites. They're moist, sweet, and delicious. They are free of artificial flavorings, colorings, or trans fats. I actually modeled my recipe after theirs, but I reduced the amount of honey and added stevia for part of the sweetness.

Note: You can make the fudge sauce several days ahead, and then gently warm it in a saucepan over very low heat, or in a heatproof bowl in a toaster oven, or in a bowl-on-a-rack (Page 74). Allow it to cool to room temperature before you layer it with freshly churned Ice Dream.

1 SERVING (REGULAR):
369 calories
3.5 grams protein
33.5 grams carbohydrate
24.5 grams fat
89 milligrams sodium

1 SERVING (HALF LITE):
320 calories
2.8 grams protein
31.4 grams carbohydrate
20.3 grams fat
76 milligrams sodium

Peppermint Wafer Ice Dream

ASSEMBLY: 20 MINUTES • **CHURNING:** 20 TO 15 MINUTES • **YIELD:** 6 TO 7 CUPS; 9 TO 12 SERVINGS

INGREDIENTS

1 recipe Vanilla Ice Dream (Page 78), Cocoa Ice Dream (Page 86), **or** Dark Chocolate Ice Dream (Page 88)

2 cups honey-sweetened peppermint patty candies (see notes), cut into 1/2-inch chunks

DIRECTIONS

1. Prepare Vanilla, Cocoa, or Dark Chocolate Ice Dream as directed. Fold the chopped peppermint patty candies into the Ice Dream before removing it from the machine.

2. Serve the Ice Dream immediately or spoon into several 8- to 16-ounce freezer-safe containers. Cover and freeze for 3 or more hours for a firmer texture.

3. Soften solidly frozen dessert by placing it in the refrigerator for 30 to 45 minutes or on the counter for 15 to 30 minutes before serving.

VARIATION

* **Lite Peppermint Wafer Ice Dream:** Replace half of the coconut milk with lite (reduced fat) coconut milk. Alternatively, use 100% lite coconut milk, but plan to use the batch immediately or within 24 hours before it becomes hard and icy.

If you're a fan of chocolate-covered peppermint patties, you're in for a treat with this flavor and the wholesome candies that go into it. SunRidge Farms uses only honey, unsweetened chocolate, and oil of peppermint to make a more natural version of the commercial peppermint patty candies.

Look for SunRidge Farms Chocolate Honey Mints in the bulk foods or candy section of natural foods stores or buy them over the Internet. Three of these candies (about 32 grams) contain 110 calories, 5 grams fat, 21 grams of carbohydrate, 1 gram of fiber, and 18 grams of sugar), no sodium, and no trans fats.

1 SERVING (REGULAR):
367 calories
2 grams protein
45.2 grams carbohydrate
23.1 grams fat
69 milligrams sodium

1 SERVING (HALF LITE):
348 calories
1.2 grams protein
42.8 grams carbohydrate
18.3 grams fat
58 milligrams sodium

Rum Raisin Ice Dream

HANDS-ON: 30 MINUTES • **CHURNING:** 20 TO 25 MINUTES • **YIELD:** 5 TO 6 CUPS; 8 SERVINGS

INGREDIENTS

2/3 cup raisins

1/2 cup dark rum, premium golden rum, **or** coconut rum

1-inch by 2-inch strip of orange or lemon zest (colored part only)

1/3 cup cool or cold water

2 teaspoons unflavored gelatin **or** 3/4 teaspoon agar agar powder (not the flakes)

1/4 cup honey **or** agave nectar, additional tablespoon as needed

1/2 teaspoon *pure* stevia extract powder **or** 1 teaspoon *clear* stevia extract liquid

1/8 teaspoon finely ground, unrefined sea salt

3 cups unsweetened, preservative-free coconut milk (regular, not lite)

During my sophomore year of high school, I worked in a family-owned ice cream parlor run by an ex-New Yorker named Davey Ricks. He named a lot of flavors after mixed drinks—Amaretto, Brandy Alexander, Pink Squirrel, Kahlua and Cream. For Bacardi Rum Raisin, he soaked the raisins in rum for 2 weeks. For the version below, I decided to simmer the raisins to reduce the alcohol content.

1 SERVING (REGULAR):
248 calories
2.4 grams protein
25.6 grams carbohydrate
15.1 grams fat
72 milligrams sodium

1 SERVING (HALF LITE):
169 calories
1.6 grams protein
22.6 grams carbohydrate
7.8 grams fat
50 milligrams sodium

DIRECTIONS

1. Heat the raisins, rum, and orange or lemon zest in a small saucepan over medium heat. Reduce heat and simmer for 2 minutes, then remove from heat. Cover and let stand for a few hours. Transfer to a glass bowl or jar. Cover and refrigerate for up to 1 day.

2. Add 1/3 cup water to a small saucepan. Slowly sprinkle with gelatin or agar agar powder. Let stand for 2 to 5 minutes to soften. Warm over medium-low heat, without stirring, until gelatin or agar agar dissolves. Pour into a blender, Vita-Mix, or food processor. Cover and process until smooth.

3. Add the honey, stevia, and sea salt. Blend. Add the coconut milk. Cover and blend until smooth, stopping to scrape the sides with a spatula. For a sweeter taste, add 1 more tablespoon honey.

4. Pour into one or more wide-mouth jars. Cover and refrigerate for at least 6 hours before churning.

5. Drain raisins over a bowl, reserving the rum. Discard the orange zest.

~Continued next page~

> **FYI:** A little alcohol works like anti-freeze, making ice cream softer and smoother, even after weeks in the freezer. Too much alcohol prevents freezing, so don't go overboard.

Rum Raisin Ice Dream ~ continued

Measure the reserved rum, adding more, if necessary, so you have a total of 3 tablespoons. Stir the rum into the chilled Ice Dream custard. Scrape the custard into the canister of your ice cream maker. Churn according to the manufacturer's instructions. When it reaches the soft-serve stage, add the rum-soaked raisins. Run the machine for 1 or 2 more minutes to mix.

6. Serve immediately or spoon into several 8- to 16-ounce freezer-safe containers. Cover and freeze for 3 or more hours for a firmer texture.

7. Soften briefly in the refrigerator or on the counter before serving if desired.

VARIATIONS

* **Lite Rum Raisin Ice Dream:** Replace half of the coconut milk with lite (reduced fat) coconut milk. Alternatively, use 100% lite coconut milk, but plan to use the batch immediately or within 24 hours before it becomes hard and icy.

* **Rum Cherry Ice Dream:** Replace raisins with dried, unsweetened or fruit-sweetened cherries. Make sure to use sweet rather than sour cherries.

* **Italian Rum Raisin Ice Dream:** Replace rum with grappa and proceed with the recipe as directed.

* **Rum Raisin Crunch Ice Dream:** Add 3/4 cup crumbled gluten-free biscotti to the machine when the mixture reaches the soft-serve stage. Run the machine for 2 more minutes to mix in the cookies.

Serve this flavor with sliced fresh fruit, particularly kiwi, peaches, apricots, or berries. Layer over a gluten-free brownie, or combine with other fruit-flavored Ice Dreams.

Vanilla Brownie Crumble Ice Dream

ASSEMBLY: 20 MINUTES • **CHURNING:** 20 TO 25 MINUTES • **YIELD:** 6 TO 7 CUPS; 8 SERVINGS

INGREDIENTS

1 recipe Vanilla or Maple Vanilla Ice Dream (Page 78)

1 1/2 cups coarsely chopped or crumbled Better Brownies (Page 216), **or** Chocolate Ice Dream Sandwich Cookies (Page 222), **or** store bought brownies, such as Pamela's Gluten-Free Brownies

DIRECTIONS

1. Prepare Vanilla or Maple Vanilla Ice Dream as directed. Fold the chopped or crumbled brownies into the Ice Dream before removing it from the machine.

2. Serve immediately or spoon into several 8- to 16-ounce freezer-safe containers. Cover and freeze for 3 or more hours for a firmer texture.

3. Soften solidly frozen dessert in the refrigerator for 30 to 45 minutes or on the counter for 15 to 30 minutes before serving.

It took me several attempts to create a moist, gluten-free, reduced-fat, reduced-sugar brownie. Immediately, I knew what to do with it: crumble and add it to Vanilla Ice Dream for a healthier twist on the Cookies-n-Cream Ice Cream I hadn't eaten for more than 25 years. I like to serve this and most other Ice Dreams over sliced fresh fruit, fruit salad, or topped with one of my cooked fruit sauces. Of course, you could go all out and add Caramel Sauce (see index for recipes).

1 SERVING (REGULAR):
343 calories
3.8 grams protein
29.6 grams carbohydrate
23 grams fat
123 milligrams sodium

1 SERVING (HALF LITE):
281 calories
2.9 grams protein
27 grams carbohydrate
17.7 grams fat
107 milligrams sodium

Shopping Tip:

If you don't want to make your own brownies (or cookies), look for the brand that is lowest in sugar in natural foods stores or the health foods section of supermarkets.

It should not contain any vegetable oils (corn, safflower, sunflower, canola, or soy oil), hydrogenated oil, fructose, or high fructose corn syrup. The best fats for baked goods include butter, palm shortening, palm oil, and coconut oil. If you follow a gluten-free diet, the cookies should not contain wheat, barley, unbleached flour, cake flour, or all-purpose flour. Pamela's gluten-free baked goods win high praise.

~Continued next page~

Vanilla Brownie Crumble Ice Dream ~ continued

VARIATIONS

* **Vanilla Cookie Crumble Ice Dream:** Replace the gluten-free brownies with Gluten-Free Graham Crackers (Page 230) or commercial gluten-free honey graham crackers. Chocolate chip cookies also taste great folded into Vanilla Ice Dream. (See Page 219 for Chocolate Chip Ice Dream Sandwich Cookies.)

* **Vanilla Ginger Cookie Crumble Ice Dream:** Replace the gluten-free brownies with soft Gingerbread Spice Cookies (Page 226), Pumpkin Spice Cookies (Page 224), or commercial gluten-free gingersnaps.

* **Lite Vanilla Cookie Crumble Ice Dream:** Replace half of the coconut milk with lite (reduced fat) coconut milk. Alternatively, use 100% lite coconut milk, but plan to use the batch immediately or within 24 hours before it becomes hard and icy.

Vanilla Fruit Ripple Ice Dream

ASSEMBLY: 20 MINUTES • **CHURNING:** 20 TO 25 MINUTES • **YIELD:** 6 TO 7 CUPS; 8 TO 10 SERVINGS

INGREDIENTS

1 recipe Vanilla **or** Maple Vanilla Ice Dream (Page 78)

1 to 1 1/2 cups Blueberry, Cherry, Apricot, Peach, **or** Nectarine Sauce, (Page 178 to 183), chilled

DIRECTIONS

1. Prepare the base for Vanilla Ice Dream as directed.

2. Prepare the fruit sauce as directed. Allow sauce to cool to room temperature, then refrigerate until cold to the touch before you churn the Ice Dream. Cover and refrigerate the remaining sauce for another use; it tastes great served over sliced fresh melon or other fruit of a contrasting color.

3. Prepare Vanilla or Maple Vanilla Ice Dream as directed. Spoon about one-fourth of the frozen dessert into 2 or 3 (16-ounce) freezer-safe containers. Spoon a layer of fruit sauce evenly over the Ice Dream. Top with another layer of Ice Dream. Continue to layer Ice Dream and fruit sauce in the same way, ending with a layer of Ice Dream.

4. Cover and freeze for 3 or more hours, until firm, before serving.

5. Soften solidly frozen dessert in the refrigerator for 30 to 45 minutes or on the counter for 15 to 30 minutes before serving.

During the summer and early fall, when fresh fruits reach their peak in ripeness, is the time to make the most delicious whole fruit sauces. They can be served over, or rippled into, ice cream. Alternate layers of Ice Dream and fruit sauce in pint-size containers, and return the mixture to the freezer to harden. When you remove scoops of the frozen dessert, you'll see ripples of fruit.

1 SERVING (REGULAR):
251 calories
2.4 grams protein
21.2 grams carbohydrate
17.6 grams fat
80 milligrams sodium

1 SERVING (HALF LITE):
199 calories
1.5 grams protein
18.6 grams carbohydrate
12.4 grams fat
64 milligrams sodium

VARIATIONS

* **Lite Vanilla Fruit Ripple Ice Dream:** Replace half of the coconut milk with lite (reduced fat) coconut milk. Alternatively, use 100% lite coconut milk, but plan to use the batch immediately or within 24 hours before it becomes hard and icy.

* **Chocolate Fruit Ripple Ice Dream:** Replace Vanilla Ice Dream with Cocoa, Dark Chocolate, or Chocolate Hazelnut Ice Dream (see index for recipes).

~Continued next page~

Vanilla Fruit Ripple Ice Dream ~ continued

* **Cinnamon Fruit Ripple Ice Dream:** Replace Vanilla Ice Dream with Cinnamon Ice Dream (Page 82).

* **Macaroon Fruit Ripple Ice Dream:** Replace Vanilla Ice Dream with Macaroon Madness Ice Dream (Page 106) and replace fudge sauce with fruit sauce.

* **Chestnut Cherry Ripple Ice Dream:** Replace Vanilla Ice Dream with Chestnut Ice Dream (Page 136).

Note: You can make the fruit sauce several days or even a week in advance. If you're removing fruit sauce from the freezer, give it 12 to 24 hours to defrost in the refrigerator, and stir well before using.

Vanilla Fudge Ripple Ice Dream

ASSEMBLY: 20 MINUTES • **CHURNING:** 20 TO 25 MINUTES • **YIELD:** 6 TO 7 CUPS; 8 TO 10 SERVINGS

Will it be chocolate or vanilla? Who says you have to choose? This recipe combines two popular flavors into one tasty treat. You may want to top it off with Strawberry, Blueberry, or Cherry Sauce (see index for recipes).

INGREDIENTS

1 recipe Vanilla or Maple Vanilla Ice Dream (Page 78)

1 1/2 cups Hot Chocolate Sauce (Page 168), Hot Fudge Sauce (Page 166), **or** Peanut Buttery Hot Chocolate Sauce (Page 170)

DIRECTIONS

1. Prepare the base for the Vanilla Ice Dream as directed.

2. Prepare the fudge sauce as directed. Set aside and let cool to room temperature. When cool, remove 1 cup of sauce and let it sit at room temperature. Cover and refrigerate the remaining sauce for another use. It tastes great served over sliced fresh strawberries, peaches, pineapple, or a mixed fruit salad.

1 SERVING (REGULAR):
362 calories
3.6 grams protein
29.2 grams carbohydrate
25.4 grams fat
105 milligrams sodium

1 SERVING (HALF LITE):
309 calories
2.8 grams protein
26.6 grams carbohydrate
20.1 grams fat
89 milligrams sodium

3. Prepare Vanilla or Maple Vanilla Ice Dream as directed. Spoon about one-fourth of the frozen dessert into 2 or 3 (16-ounce) freezer-safe containers. Spoon a layer of chocolate or fudge sauce evenly over the Ice Dream. Top with another layer of Ice Dream. Continue to layer Ice Dream and fudge sauce in the same way, ending with a layer of Ice Dream.

4. Cover and freeze for at least 3 hours, until firm, before serving.

5. Soften solidly frozen dessert by placing it in the refrigerator for 30 to 45 minutes or on the counter for 15 to 30 minutes before serving.

VARIATIONS

* **Almond Buttery Fudge Ripple Ice Dream:** Replace Vanilla Ice Dream with Almond Butter Ice Dream (Page 127).

* **Roasted Banana Fudge Ripple Ice Dream:** Replace Vanilla Ice Dream with Roasted Banana Ice Dream (Page 146).

* **Chai Fudge Ripple Ice Dream:** Replace Vanilla Ice Dream with Chai Ice Dream (Page 118).

~Continued next page~

Vanilla Fudge Ripple Ice Dream ~ continued

* **Cherry Vanilla Fudge Ripple Ice Dream:** Replace Vanilla Ice Dream with Cherry Vanilla Ice Dream (Page 152).

* **Chestnut Fudge Ripple Ice Dream:** Replace Vanilla Ice Dream with Chestnut Ice Dream (Page 136).

* **Cinnamon Fudge Ripple Ice Dream:** Replace Vanilla Ice Dream with Cinnamon Ice Dream (Page 82).

* **Coffee or Espresso Fudge Ripple Ice Dream:** Replace Vanilla Ice Dream with Coffee or Espresso Ice Dream (Page 122).

* **Peanut Butter Fudge Ripple Ice Dream:** Replace Vanilla Ice Dream with Peanut Butter Ice Dream (Page 126).

* **Pumpkin Fudge Ripple Ice Dream:** Replace Vanilla Ice Dream with Pumpkin Ice Dream (Page 92). Pumpkin Ice Dream also tastes great rippled with Caramel Sauce (Page 176).

* **Chocolate Caramel Ripple Ice Dream:** Replace Vanilla Ice Dream with Dark Chocolate or Cocoa Ice Dream, and replace Fudge Sauce with Caramel Sauce.

* **Vanilla Caramel Ripple Ice Dream:** Replace Fudge Sauce with Caramel Sauce (Page 176).

* **Lite Fudge Ripple Ice Dream:** Replace half of the coconut milk with lite (reduced fat) coconut milk. Alternatively, use 100% lite coconut milk, but plan to use the batch immediately or within 24 hours before it becomes hard and icy.

You can make the fudge sauce
several days ahead, and then gently
warm it in a saucepan over very
low heat or in a heatproof bowl in a
toaster oven. Allow it to cool to room
temperature before you layer it with
freshly churned Ice Dream.

Coffee, Tea & Nut Flavors

Best Bites

Chai Tea Ice Dream

HANDS-ON: 30 MINUTES • **CHURNING:** 20 TO 25 MINUTES • **YIELD:** 5 TO 6 CUPS; 8 SERVINGS

INGREDIENTS

1 cup filtered water

2 tablespoons loose (masala) chai (black) tea

2 teaspoons unflavored gelatin **or** 3/4 teaspoon agar agar powder (not the flakes)

1/4 cup honey **or** agave nectar; additional 1 to 2 tablespoons as needed

1/8 to 1/4 teaspoon finely ground, unrefined sea salt

3 1/2 cups (two 14-ounce cans) unsweetened, preservative-free coconut milk (regular, not lite)

1/4 to 1/2 teaspoon *pure* stevia extract powder **or** 1/2 to 1 teaspoon *clear* stevia extract liquid (start with less; add more only if needed)

1 1/2 teaspoon pure vanilla extract **or** alcohol-free vanilla flavoring

2 teaspoons peeled and finely grated fresh ginger root **or** 1 teaspoon ground ginger

1/2 teaspoon ground cardamom

1/4 teaspoon ground cinnamon

1/8 teaspoon ground cloves

1/8 teaspoon ground allspice

2 ounces bittersweet chocolate, coarsely chopped, optional

The word "chai" (say "ch" as in chocolate and "eye," as in sky) originally meant tea in many parts of the world. In the U.S. "chai," has come to mean "Masala Chai" —a mixture of spices, tea, milk, and sugar or honey—a beverage widely consumed in India, Nepal, Pakistan, and Tibet. Food historians trace the drink's history to Ayurvedic medicine, which combines herbs, spices, and sweeteners to cure many health disorders.

1 SERVING (REGULAR):
232 calories
2.2 grams protein
16.2 grams carbohydrate
17.5 grams fat
77 milligrams sodium

1 SERVING (HALF LITE):
171 calories
1.4 grams protein
13.6 grams carbohydrate
12.3 grams fat
61 milligrams sodium

DIRECTIONS

1. Boil 1 cup of water in a medium saucepan. Place the loose tea in a small cheesecloth or muslin bag, a large tea ball, or wrap it in a square of cheesecloth. Secure with twine. Alternatively, add the tea directly to the water. Bring to boil, cover, reduce heat, and simmer for 5 minutes. Remove from heat and allow the tea to steep for 10 minutes.

2. Squeeze the cheesecloth/muslin bag to extract the tea, remove the tea ball, or pour the tea through a fine mesh strainer into a heatproof measuring container. You should have 1/2 cup of tea. If you have more, simmer the tea to reduce it.

3. Return the tea to the saucepan. Slowly sprinkle with gelatin or agar agar

~Continued next page~

Traditionally, cooks created "Masala Chai," by combining and boiling ground spices, adding black tea, steeping and straining the mixture, then adding milk and honey. Recipes can vary in the amounts and proportions of ingredients. Most blends contain cardamom, ginger, cloves, cinnamon, and allspice; some include star anise, nutmeg, peppercorns, fennel seed, saffron, cocoa, or some combination.

Chai Ice Dream ~ continued

powder. Let stand for 2 to 5 minutes to soften. Warm over medium-low heat, without stirring, until gelatin or agar agar dissolves. Scrape the mixture into a blender, Vita-Mix, or food processor. Cover and process until smooth.

4. Add honey, stevia, and sea salt. Blend. Add coconut milk, stevia, vanilla, and spices (ginger through allspice). Blend until smooth, stopping to scrape the sides with a spatula. For a sweeter taste, add 1/8 teaspoon additional stevia and/or 1 tablespoon honey. Blend, taste, and repeat if needed.

5. Pour into one or more wide-mouth jars. Cover and refrigerate for at least 6 hours before churning.

6. Scrape the chilled custard into the canister of your ice cream maker. Churn according to the manufacturer's instructions. When the mixture reaches the soft-serve stage, add the optional chocolate bits to the machine. Run the machine for 1 or 2 more minutes.

7. Serve immediately or spoon into several 8- to 16-ounce freezer-safe containers. Cover and freeze for 3 or more hours for a firmer texture.

8. Soften solidly frozen dessert by placing it in the refrigerator for 30 to 45 minutes or on the counter for 15 to 30 minutes before serving.

VARIATIONS

* **Lite Chai Ice Dream:** Replace half of the coconut milk with lite (reduced fat) coconut milk. Alternatively, use 100% lite coconut milk, but plan to use the batch immediately or within 24 hours before it becomes hard and icy.

* **Decaf Chai Ice Dream:** Use loose (decaf) chai black tea in the master recipe.

* **Chai Fudge Ripple Ice Dream:** Use the Ice Dream from the master recipe above in the Fudge Ripple Ice Dream recipe on Page 114.

Although you can buy chai tea bags, I don't recommend them for this recipe. Loose tea is more flavorful.

Green Tea Ice Dream

HANDS-ON: 20 MINUTES • **CHURNING:** 20 TO 25 MINUTES • **YIELD:** 5 TO 6 CUPS; 8 SERVINGS

Green tea powder adds a crisp flavor and a powerful dose of antioxidants to this creamy, dairy-free frozen dessert. Look for powdered green tea (also called *matcha*) in Asian grocery stores and natural foods markets. Green tea leaves will not work here.

INGREDIENTS

1/3 cup cool or cold filtered water

2 teaspoons unflavored gelatin **or** 3/4 teaspoon agar agar powder (not the flakes)

1/4 cup + 2 tablespoons honey **or** agave nectar; additional 1 to 2 tablespoons as needed

1/4 to 1/2 teaspoon *pure* stevia extract powder **or** 1/2 to 1 teaspoon *clear* stevia extract liquid (start with less; add more only if needed)

1/8 to 1/4 teaspoon finely ground, unrefined sea salt

3 1/2 cups (two 14-ounce cans) unsweetened coconut milk (regular, not lite)

1/4 cup green tea powder (also called *matcha*)

1 SERVING (REGULAR):
230 calories
2.2 grams protein
15.7 grams carbohydrate
17.6 grams fat
77 milligrams sodium

1 SERVING (HALF LITE):
169 calories
1.4 grams protein
13.1 grams carbohydrate
12.3 grams fat
61 milligrams sodium

DIRECTIONS

1. Add 1/3 cup water to a small saucepan. Slowly sprinkle with gelatin or agar agar powder. Let stand for 2 to 5 minutes to soften. Warm over medium-low heat, without stirring, until gelatin or agar agar dissolves. Scrape the mixture into a blender, Vita-Mix, or food processor. Cover and process until smooth.

2. Add the honey, stevia, and sea salt. Blend. Add the coconut milk and green tea powder. Blend until smooth, stopping to scrape the sides with a spatula. For a sweeter taste, add an additional 1/8 teaspoon stevia and/ or 1 tablespoon honey. Blend, taste, and repeat if needed.

3. Pour into one or more wide-mouth jars. Cover and refrigerate for at least 6 hours before churning.

For a striking presentation, serve over a fresh fruit salad, or top it with a Cherry, Peach, Apricot, Blueberry, Chocolate, or Fudge Sauce (see index for recipes).

~Continued next page~

Green Tea Ice Dream ~ continued

4. Scrape the chilled custard into the canister of your ice cream maker. Churn according to the manufacturer's instructions.

5. Serve immediately or spoon into several 8- to 16-ounce freezer-safe containers. Cover and freeze for 3 or more hours for a firmer texture.

6. Soften solidly frozen dessert by placing it in the refrigerator for 30 to 45 minutes or on the counter for 15 to 30 minutes before serving.

VARIATIONS

* **Lite Green Tea Ice Dream:** Replace honey or agave nectar with 1/2 cup pure maple syrup. Use a total of 1/2 teaspoon stevia extract powder and replace vanilla with 1 to 1 1/2 teaspoons maple extract or alcohol-free maple flavoring. Use darker maple syrup for a stronger maple flavor.

* **Green Tea Ice Dream with Sake:** Add 2 tablespoons sake (Japanese rice wine) to the base before churning. This will keep the mixture from getting icy hard even after several weeks in the freezer.

Coffee Ice Dream

HANDS-ON: 30 MINUTES • **CHURNING:** 20 TO 25 MINUTES • **YIELD:** 4 TO 5 CUPS; 8 SERVINGS

INGREDIENTS

1 cup brewed dark roast coffee (double strength), chilled

2 teaspoons unflavored gelatin **or** 3/4 teaspoon agar agar powder (not the flakes)

3 cups unsweetened coconut milk (regular, not lite)

1/3 cup honey **or** agave nectar; additional 1 to 3 tablespoons as needed

1/2 teaspoon *pure* stevia extract powder **or** 1 teaspoon *clear* stevia extract liquid added to the wet ingredients

1/8 teaspoon finely ground unrefined sea salt

1 teaspoon pure vanilla extract **or** alcohol-free vanilla flavoring

2 tablespoons light rum, brandy, **or** cognac, optional

DIRECTIONS

1. Simmer the coffee in a saucepan until it reduces to 1/2 cup. Slowly sprinkle with gelatin or agar agar powder. Let stand for 2 to 5 minutes to soften. Warm over medium-low heat, without stirring, until gelatin or agar agar dissolves. Scrape the mixture into a blender, Vita-Mix, or food processor. Cover and blend until smooth. Add the honey, sea salt, and stevia. Blend.

2. Add the coconut milk, vanilla, and optional liqueur. Blend. For a sweeter taste, add an additional 1/8 teaspoon stevia and/or 1 tablespoon maple syrup or honey. Blend, taste, and repeat if needed.

3. Pour into one or more wide-mouth jars. Cover and chill for at least 6 hours before churning.

4. Scrape the chilled custard into the canister of your ice cream maker. Churn according to the manufacturer's instructions.

Eat this dessert early in the day if caffeine keeps you awake at night. Try it with Caramel, Chocolate, or Fudge Sauce, or with a fresh fruit salad. Chocolate chips, chunks of bittersweet chocolate, or cocoa nibs can be added during the last few minutes of churning.

Note: Use dark-roasted coffee beans to make the coffee for this recipe. Medium-roasted beans won't provide the same intensity of flavor. One of my recipe testers used Millstone Organic Mayan Black Onyx Blend coffee. Even though I rarely drink coffee, I found this flavor to be out of this world, especially in the Ice Dream Pie with cookie crust and Caramel Sauce (Page 176).

1 SERVING (REGULAR):
215 calories
2.0 grams protein
18.1 grams carbohydrate
15.1 grams fat
75 milligrams sodium

1 SERVING (HALF LITE):
163 calories
1.2 grams protein
15.5 grams carbohydrate
10.6 grams fat
61 milligrams sodium

~Continued next page~

FYI: The addition of liqueur will help make the Ice Dream softer and easier to scoop even after weeks in the freezer; it will also make it easier to slice when used to make Ice Dream Pie.

Coffee Ice Dream ~ continued

5. Serve immediately or spoon into several 8- to 16-ounce freezer-safe containers. Cover and freeze for 3 or more hours for a firmer texture.

6. Soften solidly frozen dessert by placing it in the refrigerator for 30 to 45 minutes or on the counter for 15 to 30 minutes before serving.

VARIATIONS

* In step #1, replace brewed coffee with 1/2 cup filtered water and 2 to 4 teaspoons instant coffee or espresso powder according to desired strength. Sprinkle with gelatin or agar agar powder and proceed as directed.

* **Mexican Coffee Ice Dream:** In step #3, add 1/2 teaspoon ground cinnamon and 1/4 teaspoon ground nutmeg.

* **Mocha Ice Dream:** In step #3, add 1 tablespoon unsweetened cocoa powder. If desired, replace the light rum, brandy, or cognac, with chocolate liqueur or Kahlúa (coffee liqueur).

* **Coffee Chocolate Chip Ice Dream:** Coarsely chop 1 cup malt-sweetened, fruit-sweetened, dairy-free, or bittersweet chocolate chips **or** a 4-ounce bar of bittersweet dark chocolate (70 to 73%). When Ice Dream reaches the soft-serve stage, add the chocolate bits and churn for 1 or 2 more minutes or fold them into the frozen Ice Dream as you remove it from the machine.

* **Lite Coffee Ice Dream:** Replace half of the coconut milk with lite (reduced fat) coconut milk. Alternatively, use 100% lite coconut milk, but plan to use the batch immediately or within 24 hours before it becomes hard and icy.

* **Coffee Raspberry Ripple Ice Dream:** Stir 3 tablespoons of water into 1/2 cup fruit-sweetened raspberry preserves to thin. Refrigerate. Churn Coffee Ice Dream as directed. Alternate layers of Coffee Ice Dream and fruit preserves when layering the mixture into storage containers. When you scoop it out, ripples will form.

* **Cookies-N-Coffee Ice Dream:** As you remove the frozen Ice Dream from the machine, fold in 1 1/2 cups of crumbled gluten-free graham crackers, ginger snaps, or brownies (try the Better Brownies on Page 216), cut into 1/4-inch pieces.

* See Page 114 for Fudge Ripple Ice Dream, then make a **Coffee Fudge Ripple** variation or try **Coffee Caramel Ripple**.

Date Rum Pecan Ice Dream

HANDS-ON: 30 MINUTES • **CHURNING:** 20 TO 25 MINUTES • **YIELD:** 4 TO 5 CUPS; 8 SERVINGS

INGREDIENTS

4 ounces (by weight) dried, soft, pitted dates, about 1/2 cup

1/3 cup dark rum

1/3 cup cool or cold filtered water

2 teaspoons unflavored gelatin **or** 3/4 teaspoon agar agar powder (not the flakes)

1/4 cup honey, agave nectar **or** 1/4 cup + 2 tablespoons maple syrup

1/4 to 1/2 teaspoon *pure* stevia extract powder **or** 1/2 to 1 teaspoon *clear* stevia extract liquid (start with less; add more only if needed)

1/8 teaspoon finely ground, unrefined sea salt

1 3/4 cups (one 14-ounce can) unsweetened, preservative-free coconut milk (regular, not lite)

1 teaspoon pure vanilla extract **or** alcohol-free vanilla flavoring

1 cup shelled pecan halves, toasted and coarsely chopped (Page 75)

DIRECTIONS

1. Chop dates into 1/2-inch pieces. Combine with the rum in a small saucepan. Bring to a low boil over medium heat. Stir, cover, and remove from heat. Let stand for at least 4 hours. You may do this up to 1 day in advance, refrigerating the mixture in a glass bowl or jar after it has cooled.

2. Add 1/3 cup water to a small saucepan. Slowly sprinkle with gelatin or agar agar powder. Let stand for 2 to 5 minutes to soften. Warm over medium-low heat, without stirring, until gelatin or agar agar dissolves. Scrape the mixture into a blender, Vita-Mix, or food processor. Cover and process until smooth.

Dates add a thick and creamy texture and sublime sweetness to this dairy-free ice cream alternative. Rum adds a kick in the taste buds; nuts add crunch. Serve this over fruit salad, a brownie, or along with a scoop of Peach, Strawberry, or Cherry Vanilla Ice Dream.

FYI: Botanists have identified 1500 varieties of dates worldwide. Most people are familiar only with Medjools and Degletnoors. You can use other varieties— Honey Dates, Halawy, Khadrawy, Zahadi, or Black Sphinx Dates. All of these are grown in Arizona and California. Coconut date rolls, made from soft, pitted, pulverized dates rolled in shredded unsweetened coconut, also work well.

1 SERVING (REGULAR):
284 calories
2.9 grams protein
25.4 grams carbohydrate
19 grams fat
51 milligrams sodium

1 SERVING (HALF LITE):
245 calories
2.4 grams protein
23.8 grams carbohydrate
15.4 grams fat
40 milligrams sodium

~Continued next page~

Note: Look for whole, unpitted dates—they'll be fresher, more moist, and they'll last longer. (You can easily pit them yourself.) They should feel soft and look plump. Their slightly shiny, smooth (only slightly wrinkled) skin should be free of dry, cracked, or shriveled sections and crystallization. They should not have a fermented smell. Dates can be stored at room temperature in a jar. You can substitute coconut date rolls made from soft, pitted, pulverized dates formed into logs and sold in the produce or bulk foods section of most natural foods stores.

When heating the rum, use a pan that is larger than what the contents would indicate, and use moderate heat to keep it from flaming up. If you don't keep alcohol in the house, replace the rum with water in step #1, then add 1 teaspoon natural rum flavoring in step #3, then allow more time to soften before serving.

Date Rum Pecan Ice Dream ~ continued

3. Add honey, stevia, and sea salt. Blend. Add the date mixture, coconut milk, and vanilla. Blend until smooth, stopping to scrape the sides with a spatula. For a sweeter taste, add an additional 1/8 teaspoon stevia and/or 1 tablespoon honey. Blend, taste, and repeat if needed.

4. Pour into one or more wide-mouth jars. Cover and refrigerate for at least 6 hours before churning.

5. Scrape the chilled custard into the canister of your ice cream maker. Churn according to the manufacturer's instructions. When the mixture reaches the soft-serve stage, add the nuts. Run the machine for 1 or 2 more minutes.

6. Serve immediately or spoon into several 8- to 16-ounce freezer-safe containers. Cover and freeze for 3 or more hours for a firmer texture.

7. Soften briefly in the refrigerator or on the counter before serving if desired.

VARIATIONS

*   **Date Rum Walnut Ice Dream:** Replace pecans with lightly toasted walnuts. After toasting, and before chopping the walnuts, wrap them in a clean kitchen towel; rub back and forth to loosen the bitter skins. Remove the nuts and leave the skins behind. Do the same thing if you substitute hazelnuts.

*   **Date Rum Chocolate Chunk Ice Dream:** In step #5, replace pecans with 4 ounces bittersweet dark chocolate (70 to 73% cocoa content), coarsely chopped into pieces one-quarter to one-half the size of chocolate chips.

*   **Maple Date Rum Ice Dream:** Replace honey or agave nectar with 1/4 cup + 2 tablespoons pure maple syrup. Use a total of 1/2 teaspoon *pure* stevia extract powder or 1 teaspoon *clear* stevia extract liquid. Replace the vanilla with 1 to 1 1/2 teaspoons maple extract or alcohol-free maple flavoring. Use darker maple syrup for a stronger maple flavor.

Peanut Butter & Jelly Ice Dream

HANDS-ON: 30 MINUTES • **CHURNING:** 20 TO 25 MINUTES • **YIELD:** 5 TO 6 CUPS; 8 SERVINGS

INGREDIENTS

1 cup cool or cold filtered water, divided

2 teaspoons unflavored gelatin **or** 3/4 teaspoon agar agar powder (not the flakes)

1/4 cup honey **or** agave nectar; additional 1 to 3 tablespoons as needed

1/4 to 1/2 teaspoon *pure* stevia extract powder **or** 1/2 to 1 teaspoon *clear* stevia extract liquid (start with less; add more only if needed)

1/4 teaspoon finely ground, unrefined sea salt (omit if using salted peanut butter)

3/4 cup unsweetened, salted or unsalted, organic peanut butter; mixed thoroughly in a bowl before measuring

2 1/2 cups unsweetened, preservative-free lite coconut milk

1 cup Blueberry, Cherry, Peach, Nectarine, or Apricot Sauce (Page 180 to 183) **or** 2/3 cup fruit-sweetened preserves thinned with 1/3 cup water.

DIRECTIONS

1. Add 1/3 cup water to a small saucepan. Slowly sprinkle with gelatin or agar agar powder. Let stand for 2 to 5 minutes to soften. Warm over medium-low heat, without stirring, until gelatin or agar agar dissolves. Scrape the mixture into a blender, Vita-Mix, or food processor. Process until smooth.

2. Meanwhile heat the remaining 2/3 cup reserved water until hot but not boiling; add this to the blender or food processor with the honey, stevia, optional sea salt, and peanut butter. Blend. Add coconut milk and blend until smooth, stopping to scrape the sides with a spatula. For a sweeter taste, add 1/8 teaspoon additional stevia and/or 1 tablespoon honey. Blend, taste, and repeat

Even people who don't ordinarily care for peanut butter and jelly sandwiches commented that this tasted just like a PBJ.

Note: I prefer to make this with one of the thick fruit sauces in Chapter 8. If you substitute fruit preserves, look for a fruit-sweetened brand. Fruit (not juice) should appear as the first ingredient on the list with fruit juice concentrate as the sweetener rather than sugar, sucanat, or fructose. I prefer St. Dalfours brand; you can find it in natural foods stores and many chain supermarkets. Unfortunately, most of the small, locally made preserves contain sugar, which doesn't provide any antioxidants.

1 SERVING (LITE):
231 calories
6.7 grams protein
11.8 grams carbohydrate
17.4 grams fat
70 milligrams sodium

1 SERVING (LITE, NO JELLY):
208 calories
6.6 grams protein
6.5 grams carbohydrate
17.3 grams fat
69 milligrams sodium

~Continued next page~

Look for preservative-free creamy, natural peanut butter free of hydrogenated oil, sugar, fructose, and corn syrup in natural foods stores or the health foods or peanut butter section of supermarkets. Buy organic because conventional peanuts are usually grown in rotation with cotton, one of the most heavily sprayed crops.

Peanut Butter & Jelly Ice Dream ~ continued

if needed. Take care not to make the mixture too sweet as the fruit sauce or preserves will add additional sweetness.

3. Pour into one or more wide-mouth jars. Cover and refrigerate for at least 6 hours before churning. Meanwhile, stir 2 to 3 tablespoons of water into 1/2 cup of fruit-sweetened preserves to loosen them up. Cover and refrigerate.

4. Pour the chilled custard into the canister of your ice cream maker. Churn according to the manufacturer's instructions.

5. When done, spoon 1/4 of the frozen dessert into 2 or 3 pint-sized freezer-safe containers. Spoon a layer of diluted fruit preserves evenly over the Ice Dream. Top with another layer of Ice Dream. Continue layering Ice Dream and fruit sauce in the same way, ending with a layer of Ice Dream.

6. Cover and freeze for at least 3 hours, until firm, before serving.

7. Soften solidly frozen dessert by placing it in the refrigerator for 30 to 45 minutes or on the counter for 15 to 30 minutes before serving.

VARIATIONS

* **If you don't have lite coconut milk:** Substitute 1/2 cup unsweetened premium (full fat) coconut milk plus 1/2 cup water.

* **Peanut Butter Ice Dream:** Omit the fruit preserves above.

* **Peanut Butter Cookie Crunch Ice Dream:** Omit the fruit preserves. Add 1 cup crumbled gluten-free oatmeal cookies or graham crackers to the machine when the mixture reaches the soft-serve stage. Run the machine for 1 or 2 more minutes. Or, fold the cookies in as you remove the frozen dessert from the machine

* **Almond Butter & Jelly Ice Dream:** Replace peanut butter with roasted almond butter in the master recipe. Prepare as above.

* **Cashew Butter & Jelly Ice Dream:** Replace peanut butter with raw or roasted cashew butter in the master recipe. Prepare as above.

Cocoa Macadamia Ice Dream

HANDS-ON: 30 MINUTES • **CHURNING:** 20 TO 25 MINUTES • **YIELD:** 5 TO 6 CUPS; 8 SERVINGS

INGREDIENTS

2 1/2 cups cold filtered water, divided

2 teaspoons unflavored gelatin **or** 3/4 teaspoon agar agar powder (not the flakes)

1/3 cup honey **or** agave nectar; additional 1 to 2 tablespoons as needed

1/4 to 1/2 teaspoon *pure* stevia extract powder **or** 1/2 to 1 teaspoon *clear* stevia extract liquid (start with less; add more only if needed)

1/8 to 1/4 teaspoon finely ground, unrefined sea salt

1/2 cup unsalted, unsweetened macadamia nut butter, stirred well before measuring

1/2 cup unsweetened cocoa powder

1 cup unsweetened, preservative-free lite coconut milk

2 teaspoons pure vanilla extract **or** alcohol-free vanilla flavoring

2 tablespoons crème de cacao **or** other chocolate liqueur or rum, optional

Coconut milk and macadamia nut butter create a rich flavor and silky-textured ice dream. The monounsaturated fats in macadamia nut butter make it easy to scoop even after a month in the freezer. Don't tell your family it's healthy. Just serve it topped with sliced fresh fruit, fruit salad, or a homemade fruit sauce and watch it disappear (see index for sauce recipes).

1 SERVING (MACADAMIA):
155 calories
2.2 grams protein
16.3 grams carbohydrate
8.9 grams fat
33 milligrams sodium

**1 SERVING
(ALMOND BUTTER):**
198 calories
3.9 grams protein
18.5 grams carbohydrate
11.9 grams fat
35 milligrams sodium

**1 SERVING
(PEANUT BUTTER):**
195 calories
5.6 grams protein
18.3 grams carbohydrate
10.9 grams fat
36 milligrams sodium

DIRECTIONS

1. Add 1/2 cup water to a small saucepan. Slowly sprinkle with gelatin or agar agar powder. Let stand for 2 to 5 minutes to soften. Warm over medium-low heat, without stirring, until gelatin or agar agar dissolves. Scrape the mixture into a blender, Vita-Mix, or food processor. Cover and process until smooth.

2. Add honey, stevia, and sea salt. Blend. Add macadamia nut butter, unsweetened cocoa powder, coconut milk, remaining 2 cups water, vanilla, and optional chocolate liqueur. Blend until smooth, stopping to scrape the sides with a spatula. For a sweeter taste, add an additional 1/8 teaspoon stevia and/or 1 tablespoon honey. Blend, taste, and repeat if needed.

3. Pour into one or more wide-mouth jars. Cover and refrigerate for at least 6 hours before churning.

~Continued next page~

> **FYI:** When you open a new jar of nut butter, don't try to stir it in the jar. Transfer the entire contents of the jar to a bowl or food processor. Stir with a sturdy spoon (or process) until smooth. Measure out what you need and return the rest to the jar. Cover and refrigerate. You'll have a more even consistency and avoid making an oily mess, and the nut butter will never separate again.

Cocoa Macadamia Ice Dream ~ continued

4. Scrape the chilled custard into the canister of your ice cream maker. Churn according to the manufacturer's instructions.

5. Serve immediately or spoon into several 8- to 16-ounce freezer-safe containers. Cover and freeze for 3 or more hours for a firmer texture.

6. Soften solidly frozen dessert by placing it in the refrigerator for 30 to 45 minutes or on the counter for 15 to 30 minutes before serving.

VARIATIONS

*   **If you don't have lite coconut milk:** Substitute 1/2 cup unsweetened premium (full fat) coconut milk mixed with 1/2 cup water.

*   **Cocoa Almond Butter Ice Dream:** Replace macadamia nut butter with roasted, unsweetened almond butter. Add 1/2 teaspoon pure almond extract in step #2.

*   **Cocoa Peanut Butter Ice Dream:** Replace macadamia nut butter with roasted, unsweetened salted or unsalted natural peanut butter.

*   **Cocoa Cashew Butter Ice Dream:** Replace macadamia nut butter with roasted, unsweetened cashew butter.

Chocolate Hazelnut Ice Dream

HANDS-ON: 30 MINUTES • **CHURNING:** 20 TO 25 MINUTES • **YIELD:** 4 1/2 TO 5 CUPS; 8 SERVINGS

INGREDIENTS

1/3 cup cool or cold filtered water

2 teaspoons unflavored gelatin **or** 3/4 teaspoon agar agar powder (not the flakes)

3/4 cup raw hazelnuts (filberts), toasted and skinned (as described on next page), plus extra, coarsely chopped, for optional garnish

1/8 to 1/4 teaspoon finely ground unrefined sea salt

1/4 cup honey **or** agave nectar; additional 1 to 3 tablespoons as needed

1/4 to 1/2 teaspoon *pure* stevia extract powder **or** 1/2 to 1 teaspoon *clear* stevia extract liquid (start with less; add more only if needed)

2 1/4 cups unsweetened, preservative-free lite (not full fat) coconut milk, divided

4 to 4 1/2 ounces bittersweet dark chocolate bar (70 to 73%), coarsely chopped into 1/4-inch pieces

1 teaspoon pure vanilla extract **or** alcohol-free vanilla flavoring

Toasted hazelnuts add a rich taste and nutty crunch to Ice Dream. If you think you don't like hazelnuts, this Ice Dream might change your mind. This recipe makes use of a technique that removes their bitter skins. Look for shelled raw hazelnuts. If possible, buy them from a store that keeps them refrigerated to prevent spoilage.

1 SERVING (LITE):
248 calories
3.4 grams protein
15.5 grams carbohydrate
19.1 grams fat
41 milligrams sodium

DIRECTIONS

1. Add 1/3 cup water to a small saucepan. Slowly sprinkle with gelatin or agar agar powder. Let stand for 2 to 5 minutes to soften. Warm over medium-low heat, without stirring, until gelatin or agar agar dissolves. Add honey and stevia. Stir and pour into a blender, Vita-Mix, or food processor. Cover and process until smooth. Add the hazelnuts and sea salt. Blend until smooth.

2. Add 1 cup coconut milk to a small saucepan and bring to a low boil. Remove from heat. Add chocolate. Whisk until smooth, and then add to the gelatin mixture. Blend until smooth. Add the remaining coconut milk and vanilla. Blend. For a sweeter taste, add an additional 1/8 teaspoon stevia and/or 1 tablespoon honey. Blend, taste, and repeat if needed.

3. Pour into one or more wide-mouth jars. Cover and refrigerate for at least 6 hours before churning.

4. Scrape the chilled custard into the canister of your ice cream maker. Churn according to the manufacturer's instructions.

~Continued next page~

To toast and skin hazelnuts: Position an oven rack in the center of the oven and preheat to 350° F. Spread the nuts in a single layer in a shallow, rimmed baking pan and toast them until they turn golden beneath the skins (which will slip off some of the nuts) for 10 to 15 minutes, shaking the pan 2 or 3 times during cooking. To check for doneness, remove a nut from the oven after about 10 minutes and cut it open. Check every few minutes until the nuts look golden brown all the way through. Wrap them in a clean kitchen towel and let cool completely. Rub them in the towel to loosen the skins, then remove the nuts and discard the skins.

Chocolate Hazelnut Ice Dream ~ continued

5. Serve immediately or spoon into several 8- to 16-ounce freezer-safe containers. Cover and freeze for 3 or more hours for a firmer texture.

6. Soften solidly frozen dessert by placing it in the refrigerator for 30 to 45 minutes or on the counter for 15 to 30 minutes before serving.

VARIATIONS

* **If you don't have lite coconut milk:** Substitute 1-1/4 cup unsweetened premium (full fat) coconut milk mixed with 1 cup water.

* **Hazelnut Raspberry Swirl Ice Dream:** Stir 3 tablespoons of water into 1/2 cup fruit-sweetened raspberry preserves to thin. Alternate layers of Hazelnut Ice Dream and fruit preserves when layering the mixture into storage containers. Freeze for at least 3 hours. Swirls will form when you scoop it out.

* **Hazelnut Cherry Swirl Ice Dream:** Use Hazelnut Ice Dream and Cherry Sauce (Page 182) in the Vanilla Fruit Ripple Recipe on Page 112.

* **Chocolate Almond Ice Dream:** Replace hazelnuts with almonds in the recipe above. Toast as directed (you don't need to rub to remove the skins), and then chop before adding. Add 1/2 teaspoon pure almond extract with the vanilla.

* **Chocolate Pecan Ice Dream:** Replace hazelnuts with pecans in the recipe above.

Sensuous Vanilla Nut Delight Ice Dream

ASSEMBLY: 30 MINUTES • **CHURNING:** 20 TO 25 MINUTES • **YIELD:** 5-1/2 TO 6-1/2 CUPS; 10 TO 12 SERVINGS

INGREDIENTS

1/2 to 3/4 cup lightly toasted nuts (Page 75):
Almonds, pecans, cashews, **or** pistachios

1 1/2 teaspoons Sensuous Spice Mix (see FYI on next page) **or** 1 teaspoon ground cardamom

1 cup ripe fruit, washed, drained, and patted dry:
pitted sweet cherries, sliced peaches, blueberries, **or** *halved seedless grapes*

1 recipe (4 to 5 cups) Vanilla or Maple Vanilla Ice Dream (Page 78)

DIRECTIONS

1. Have ready the toasted nuts, ground spice, and washed, drained fruit.

2. Prepare Vanilla Ice Dream as directed in the master recipe. Before removing it from the machine, sprinkle with the nuts, spice, and fresh fruit. Swiftly fold these ingredients into the Ice Dream with a wide wooden spoon or rice paddle. Alternatively, transfer the Ice Dream to a 3- to 4-quart bowl, then add the mix-ins.

3. Serve immediately or spoon into several 8- to 16-ounce freezer-safe containers. Cover and freeze for 3 or more hours for a firmer texture.

4. Soften solidly frozen dessert in the refrigerator for 30 to 45 minutes or on the counter for 20 to 30 minutes before serving.

I got the idea for this recipe from a former French pen pal and chef named Julien many years ago. I stashed it away, then unearthed it along with other notes as I began working wholeheartedly on this book. Julien's version called for regular ice cream, fresh mint leaves, ground coriander, and a dash of cayenne. However, I found those flavors too strong against the coconut Ice Dream base, so I changed the spices.

1 SERVING (REGULAR):
297 calories
3.8 grams protein
20.6 grams carbohydrate
22.1 grams fat
78 milligrams sodium

1 SERVING (HALF LITE):
236 calories
2.9 grams protein
18 grams carbohydrate
16.8 grams fat
65 milligrams sodium

··Dressed for Company·····

This makes an impressive dessert for company. For a festive presentation during the summer and fall, Julien suggested serving the ice cream, fruit, and nut mixture in melon halves. It would also look pretty served in ice cream dishes, parfait glasses, or wine goblets. It needs no accompaniments, but, of course, you won't be disappointed with a drizzle of one of the chocolate or fudge sauces in Chapter 8.

~Continued next page~

FYI: Sensuous Spice Mix contains an enticing blend of cinnamon, damiana, shatavari, maca root, Korean Ginseng, cardamom, dark sweet chili, ginger, turmeric, cumin, and coriander. Besides its use in this recipe, it happens to be very good added to chocolate sauces. If you don't live in Phoenix, Arizona, you can mail order Sensuous Spice Mix from Chakra 4 Herb & Tea House (see Appendix for contact information).

Sensuous Vanilla Nut Delight Ice Dream ~ continued

VARIATIONS

* Replace cardamom or Sensuous Spice Mix with apple pie spice or pumpkin pie spice. It won't taste the same, but will still be delicious.

* **Lite Sensuous Vanilla Nut Delight Ice Dream:** Replace half of the coconut milk with lite (reduced fat) coconut milk. Alternatively, use 100% lite coconut milk, but plan to use the batch immediately or within 24 hours before it becomes hard and icy.

* **For a fancier presentation:** Have ready 2 fresh honeydew, Crenshaw, cantaloupe, Tuscan, or Canary melons (about 5-inch diameter, 2 1/2 pounds each). Cut each in half and remove the seeds. With a paring knife in hand, score the melon by cutting lines across in one direction, then in the opposite direction, cutting 3/4 of the way through, leaving the bottom portion attached. This will make it easier to remove the melon slices when serving. Alternatively, scoop the flesh out with a melon baller, then return the melon balls to the hollowed-out halves. Chill the melons if you're not ready to serve. To serve, scoop the Ice Dream into the melon halves and serve immediately with large spoons or ice cream paddles.

* Replace the toasted nuts with Pecan Pralines **or** Almond Pralines (Page 214).

Chocolate Date Nut Truffle Ice Dream

ASSEMBLY: 30 MINUTES • **CHURNING:** 20 TO 25 MINUTES • **YIELD:** 6 TO 7 CUPS; 9 TO 12 SERVINGS

INGREDIENTS

2 cups chilled Dark Chocolate-Dipped Date Nut Truffles (Page 208), cut into 1/2-inch pieces, then frozen

1 recipe Vanilla or Maple Vanilla Ice Dream (Page 78)

DIRECTIONS

1. Prepare Vanilla Ice Dream as directed in the master recipe. Fold the chopped Date Nut Truffles into the frozen dessert as you remove it from the machine.

2. Serve soft, or spoon into several 8- to 16-ounce freezer-safe containers. Cover and freeze for 3 or more hours for a firmer texture.

3. Soften solidly frozen dessert in the refrigerator for 30 to 45 minutes or on the counter for 20 to 30 minutes before serving.

VARIATIONS

* Replace homemade Chocolate-Dipped Date Nut Truffles with a commercial honey-sweetened truffle.

* **Lite Date Nut Truffle Ice Dream:** Replace half of the coconut milk with lite (reduced fat) coconut milk. Alternatively, use 100% lite coconut milk, but plan to use the batch immediately or within 24 hours before it becomes hard and icy.

You can use the Date Nut Truffles shaped into balls or squares in this recipe. You'll get a slightly different texture either way.

My cooking students have voted my Dark Chocolate-Dipped Date Nut Truffles their favorite dessert. They're easy to assemble, and they look impressive—at least as good as chocolates you'd buy in a store or a candy shop. They're completely free of refined sugar and dairy products; the sweetness comes from the coconut date rolls that form the base and filling. Best of all, you can make them days or weeks in advance. Chopped and added to Vanilla Ice Dream, they make an extra special treat.

Note: This recipe needs no accompaniments, but if you serve it over fruit salad or with a homemade fruit sauce, you'll add antioxidants and likely eat less Ice Dream (probably a good thing).

1 SERVING (REGULAR):
386 calories
4.2 grams protein
34.7 grams carbohydrate
25.3 grams fat
77 milligrams sodium

1 SERVING (HALF LITE):
331 calories
3.4 grams protein
32.4 grams carbohydrate
20.6 grams fat
62 milligrams sodium

All About Chestnuts

About Chestnuts: Most nuts provide about 700 to 800 calories per cup, with 70 to 80 percent of those calories from fat. In contrast, chestnuts contain only 350 calories per cup, with 80 percent of the calories in the form of sweet-tasting complex carbohydrates. Only 9 percent of the calories are from fat and 5 to 10 percent are from protein. Chestnuts are native to North America, but also grow widely in Europe and Asia. You'll find more recipes for chestnuts in French and Italian cookbooks.

To cook fresh chestnuts in the shell: To prepare fresh chestnuts, start with heavy, glossy nuts with firm, smooth shells. With a paring knife, cut a small cross on one side of each shell to let steam escape as the nuts roast and to make them easier to peel afterward. Place chestnuts in a shallow roasting pan and sprinkle with water. Roast in a 400° F oven for 20 to 30 minutes, shaking the pan or rolling the chestnuts over at about half-way through. The shells will start to peel back. Pour them into a paper bag; fold the top down and allow to steam for 15 minutes. Or, wrap the hot chestnuts in a towel and squeeze to crush the shells, keeping the nuts wrapped for 10 to 15 minutes. Remove the hard outer shell and the pellicle (brown skin inside), being careful not to burn your fingers. One pound of fresh chestnuts will yield about two cups when shelled.

To cook dried, peeled chestnuts: Dried, peeled chestnuts cost more than fresh, but they are more convenient. You don't have to soak them, cut "Xs" in each nut, or roast and peel them one by one. Look for dried, American-grown chestnuts over the Internet or in Italian and Oriental markets. Dried chestnuts are *not* ready to eat. Like dried beans, they require soaking to reconstitute and cooking to make them tender. Don't discard the sweet soaking liquid; it will be used to cook the chestnuts.

Place 1 cup dried chestnuts in a medium-size bowl or saucepan. Add 2 cups boiling water. Soak at room temperature for 6 to 8 hours or overnight uncovered, or covered loosely with a bamboo mat or clean kitchen towel. Refrigerate in extremely hot weather. Do not pour off soak water. Boil or pressure cook the chestnuts in their soaking liquid which contains a lot of the flavor and sweetness.

To pressure cook: Pour chestnuts and soaking water into a small- or medium-size pressure cooker. Seal cooker and bring to pressure over medium heat. When the pot comes to pressure, reduce heat to medium-low and cook for 30 minutes. Allow the pressure to come down naturally, or, to reduce the pressure faster, immerse the cooker in several inches of cold water in the sink or a large bowl.

To boil: Pour chestnuts and their soak water into a 2- to 3-quart pot. Add 3 more cups of water. Cover and bring to boil over medium-high heat. Reduce heat to medium-low and simmer until tender, 2 to 3 hours, depending upon the batch of chestnuts. Check often, adding more water as needed to cover and prevent burning. When tender, remove the lid and simmer away the liquid. Refrigerate cooked chestnuts in a covered, preferably glass, container. Use within 5 days.

Bottled or frozen precoooked chestnuts: If you buy precooked, bottled chestnuts, they will require additional cooking time to make them soft enough to purée. Cover them with water and bring to a boil. Reduce heat to medium-low and simmer for 20 to 40 minutes. Remove the lid and cook away any excess liquid.

To make a purée of chestnuts: Combine 1 cup of tender, cooked chestnuts with 3/4 cup hot water in a Vita-Mix, blender, or food processor. Blend until smooth, stopping to scrape the sides with a spatula.

Convenient canned chestnut purée: If you really want it easy, you can buy canned or bottled, unsweetened chestnut purée from France. Look for it in specialty foods stores or over the Internet. Read labels carefully to avoid products sweetened with sugar.

Chunky Chestnut Ice Dream

HANDS-ON: 60 MINUTES • **CHURNING:** 20 TO 25 MINUTES • **YIELD:** 5 1/2 CUPS; 8 SERVINGS

INGREDIENTS

2 3/4 cups unsweetened, preservative-free coconut milk (regular, not lite), divided

2 teaspoons unflavored gelatin **or** 3/4 teaspoon agar agar powder (not the flakes)

1/4 cup honey **or** agave nectar; additional 1 to 2 tablespoons as needed

1/4 to 1/2 teaspoon *pure* stevia extract powder **or** 1/2 to 1 teaspoon *clear* stevia extract liquid (start with less; add more only if needed)

1/8 teaspoon finely ground unrefined sea salt

1/2 teaspoon cinnamon, optional

1 cup unsweetened chestnut purée (Page 135), homemade or store bought

2 tablespoons rum

1 cup cooked, peeled chestnuts, coarsely chopped (Page 135)

DIRECTIONS

1. Add 1/3 cup coconut milk to a small saucepan. Slowly sprinkle with gelatin or agar agar powder. Let stand for 2 to 5 minutes to soften. Warm over medium-low heat, without stirring, until gelatin or agar agar dissolves. Add the honey, stevia, sea salt, and optional cinnamon. Scrape the mixture into a blender, Vita-Mix, or food processor. Cover and blend until smooth.

2. Add the chestnut purée and reserved coconut milk. Blend. For a sweeter taste, add an additional 1/8 teaspoon stevia and/or 1 tablespoon honey. Blend, taste, and repeat if needed.

3. Pour into one or more wide-mouth jars. Cover and refrigerate for at least 6 hours before churning.

You can make this Ice Dream using whole chestnuts in the shell or dried, peeled chestnuts that require soaking and cooking, or you can buy unsweetened chestnut purée, which costs more but saves time.

Don't confuse chestnuts with Chinese water chestnuts, a different species altogether, nor with poisonous look-alike horse chestnuts. Look for chestnuts in supermarkets, farmers' markets, specialty foods stores, or over the Internet. See Page 135 to learn more about chestnuts and the various forms you can buy.

Note: The Resource section in the back of the book lists sources for various kinds of chestnuts. To save time, buy bottled, precooked chestnuts or unsweetened chestnut purée.

1 SERVING (REGULAR):
246 calories
2.8 grams protein
26.8 grams carbohydrate
14.2 grams fat
68 milligrams sodium

1 SERVING (HALF LITE):
198 calories
2.1 grams protein
24.7 grams carbohydrate
10.1 grams fat
56 milligrams sodium

~Continued next page~

Chunky Chestnut Ice Dream ~ continued

4. Scrape the chilled custard into the canister of your ice cream maker along with the optional rum. Churn according to the manufacturer's instructions. When the mixture reaches the soft-serve stage, add the chestnuts and churn for 1 or 2 more minutes, or fold the chestnuts into the frozen dessert as you remove it from the machine.

5. Serve immediately or spoon into several 8- to 16-ounce freezer-safe containers. Cover and freeze for 3 or more hours for a firmer texture.

6. Soften solidly frozen dessert by placing it in the refrigerator for 30 to 45 minutes or on the counter for 15 to 30 minutes before serving.

VARIATIONS

* **Chunky Chestnut Caramel Ice Dream:** When you remove the Ice Dream from the machine, layer it with Caramel Sauce (Page 176) in storage containers.

* **Chunky Chocolate Chestnut Ice Dream:** In step #2, add 1/3 cup unsweetened cocoa powder. If desired, replace rum with chocolate liqueur.

* **Chunky Chocolate Chestnut Caramel Ice Dream:** When you remove the Chocolate Chestnut Ice Dream from the machine, layer it with Caramel Sauce (Page 176) in storage containers.

* **Chestnut Almond Praline Ice Dream:** In step #4, replace 1 cup of chopped, cooked chestnuts with 1 cup of coarsely chopped Almond Pralines (Page 214), or use a combination of the chopped, cooked chestnuts and almonds.

* **Chestnut Pecan Praline Ice Dream:** In the variation above, replace Almond Pralines with Pecan Pralines.

* **Lite Chunky Chestnut Ice Dream:** Replace half of the coconut milk with lite (reduced fat) coconut milk. Alternatively, use 100% lite coconut milk, but plan to use the batch immediately or within 24 hours before it becomes hard and icy

chapter 7

Fruity Favorites

Best Bites

Dried Apricot Pistachio Ice Dream

HANDS-ON: 30 MINUTES • **CHURNING:** 20 TO 25 MINUTES • **YIELD:** 4 TO 5 CUPS; 8 SERVINGS

INGREDIENTS

1 cup dried apricots (see notes on right), quartered (5 ounces by weight)

3/4 cup dry or sweet white wine:
Chardonnay, Fume Blanc, Sauvignon Blanc, Pinot Grigio, Moscato, Riesling, or dry *Riesling*

1/2 cup shelled, unsalted, raw pistachio nuts (without pink dyes or salt)

1/3 cup cool or cold filtered water

2 teaspoons unflavored gelatin **or** 3/4 teaspoon agar agar powder (not the flakes)

1/4 cup honey **or** agave nectar; additional 1 to 2 tablespoons as needed

1/4 to 1/2 teaspoon *pure* stevia extract powder **or** 1/2 to 1 teaspoon *clear* stevia extract liquid (start with less; add more only if needed)

1/8 teaspoon finely ground, unrefined sea salt

2 1/2 cups unsweetened, preservative-free coconut milk (regular, not lite)

Dried apricots add a silky texture and tangy flavor to this dairy-free ice cream alternative. Look for sulfite-free dried apricots in natural foods stores, gourmet shops, the health foods section of supermarkets, or over the Internet. Use American-grown dried apricots for a tart and tangy flavor, or try the sweeter Turkish or Chinese variety. The sweet varieties are my favorites.

For a colorful contrast, serve this flavor with a scoop of Chocolate, Blueberry, Cherry, Date, or Avocado Ice Dream, or add a drizzle of Hot Fudge or Chocolate Sauce (see index for recipes).

DIRECTIONS

1. Combine the apricot pieces and wine (or fruit juice) in a small saucepan. Bring to a low boil. Stir, reduce heat, and simmer 5 minutes. Cover and remove from heat. Let stand for 1 hour. You may do this 1 day ahead, refrigerating the mixture in a glass bowl or jar after it has cooled.

2. Coarsely chop the pistachios and set aside.

3. Add 1/3 cup water to a small saucepan. Slowly sprinkle with gelatin or agar agar powder. Let stand for 2 to 5 minutes to soften. Warm over medium-low heat, without stirring, until gelatin or agar agar dissolves. Scrape the mixture into a blender, Vita-Mix, or food processor. Add the honey, stevia, and sea salt. Cover and process until smooth.

4. Add the apricot mixture and coconut milk. Blend until smooth, stopping to scrape the sides with a spatula. For a sweeter taste, add an additional

1 SERVING (REGULAR):
270 calories
4 grams protein
26.6 grams carbohydrate
16.5 grams fat
66 milligrams sodium

1 SERVING (HALF LITE):
226 calories
3.4 grams protein
24.7 grams carbohydrate
12.7 grams fat
55 milligrams sodium

~Continued next page~

Note: Purchase pistachios that have not been salted or dyed red. If possible, buy them in the shells. When pistachios ripen, the shells crack open, making it easy to remove the nuts. Place shelled pistachios on a clean kitchen towel; roll up the towel, and rub back and forth to loosen (and discard) the skins. If you buy pre-shelled pistachios, try to get them from a store that keeps them refrigerated to prevent spoilage.

FYI: If you don't care for pistachios, substitute toasted almonds or pecans. If you prefer not to use wine, replace with white grape juice or apricot nectar, but start with only half the amount of honey listed. Adjust the amount upwards as needed. The alcohol does improve the texture, making this Ice Dream easy to scoop right from the freezer, even after 8 weeks.

Dried Apricot Pistachio Ice Dream ~ continued

1/8 teaspoon stevia and/or 1 tablespoon honey. Blend, taste, and repeat if needed.

5. Pour into one or more wide-mouth jars. Cover and refrigerate for at least 6 hours before churning.

6. Scrape the chilled custard into the canister of your ice cream maker. Churn according to the manufacturer's instructions. When mixture reaches the soft-serve stage, add the nuts. Run the machine for 1 or 2 more minutes.

7. Serve immediately or spoon into several 8- to 16-ounce freezer-safe containers. Cover and freeze for 3 or more hours for a firmer texture.

8. Soften briefly in the refrigerator or on the counter before serving if desired.

VARIATIONS

* **Maple Apricot Pistachio Ice Dream:** Replace honey with 1/4 cup + 2 tablespoons pure (grade A or B) maple syrup.

* **Dried Peach Pistachio Ice Dream:** Replace dried apricots with sulfite-free dried peaches.

* **Dried Banana Pistachio Ice Dream:** Replace dried apricots with dried, unsweetened banana slices (not fried banana chips); they look like strips and have nothing added. Also replace white wine with coconut rum, light rum, or banana liqueur. Use pistachios or substitute toasted, coarsely chopped pecans (see Page 75 for toasting tips). Don't forget to change the name of the recipe.

* **Dried Cherry Pistachio Ice Dream:** This flavor has a lovely magenta color. Replace dried apricots with dried, unsweetened or fruit-sweetened Bing (not sour) cherries. Replace sweet white wine with kirsch, a clear brandy distilled from cherry juice and pits.

* **Lite Dried Apricot/Peach/Cherry/or Banana-Pistachio Ice Dream:** Replace half of the coconut milk with lite (reduced fat) coconut milk. Alternatively, use 100% lite coconut milk, but plan to use the batch immediately or within 24 hours before it becomes hard and icy.

Banana Daiquiri Ice Dream

HANDS-ON: 30 MINUTES • **CHURNING:** 20 TO 25 MINUTES • **YIELD:** 4 TO 5 1/2 CUPS; 8 SERVINGS

INGREDIENTS

1/3 cup fresh lime juice (from 2 to 3 limes)

1/2 to 1 teaspoon lime zest (finely grated lime peel; colored part only)

2 teaspoons unflavored gelatin **or** 3/4 teaspoon agar agar powder (not the flakes)

3 tablespoons honey **or** agave nectar; additional 2 tablespoons as needed

1/8 teaspoon finely ground, unrefined sea salt

1/4 to 1/2 teaspoon *pure* stevia extract powder **or** 1/2 to 1 teaspoon *clear* stevia extract liquid (start with less; add more only if needed)

2 cups unsweetened, preservative-free coconut milk (regular not lite), mixed well before measuring

2 cups packed ripe bananas, sliced (2 large, or 3 to 4 medium)

2 tablespoons coconut rum **or** dark rum **or** 1 teaspoon natural rum flavoring

1/4 cup coarsely chopped macadamia nuts for garnish, optional

Here's a grown up version of banana ice cream that I almost left out of the book. Don and I weren't impressed with it, but we didn't want to toss it. So, I gave it to a few friends. They raved about it. In fact, two little boys wouldn't let their parents have any of it. Banana lovers, judge for yourself. If you don't like alcohol, try the variation with rum flavoring or try the Roasted Banana Ice Dream on Page 146.

Note: If using bottled lime juice, taste it before you use it. If left to sit too long in the refrigerator, lime juice (as well as lemon juice) can develop a strong bitter flavor.

DIRECTIONS

1. Grate the zest from the limes using a microplane or the small holes of a cheese grater. Set aside.

2. Juice the limes and add to a small saucepan. Slowly sprinkle with gelatin or agar agar powder. Let stand for 2 to 5 minutes to soften. Warm over medium-low heat, without stirring, until gelatin or agar agar dissolves. Scrape the mixture into a blender, Vita-Mix, or food processor. Cover and process until smooth.

3. Add the honey or agave, sea salt, and stevia. Blend. Add the coconut milk, banana, lime zest, and rum, or rum flavoring. Blend until smooth, stopping to scrape the sides with a spatula. For a sweeter taste, add an additional 1/8 teaspoon stevia and/or 1 tablespoon honey. Blend, taste, and repeat if needed.

1 SERVING (REGULAR):
234 calories
2.5 grams protein
25.9 grams carbohydrate
13.4 grams fat
56 milligrams sodium

1 SERVING (HALF LITE):
199 calories
2 grams protein
24.4 grams carbohydrate
10.4 grams fat
47 milligrams sodium

~Continued next page~

Banana Daiquiri Ice Dream ~ continued

4. Pour into one or more wide-mouth jars. Cover and refrigerate for at least 6 hours before churning.

5. Scrape the chilled custard into the canister of your ice cream maker. Churn according to the manufacturer's instructions.

6. Serve immediately or spoon into several 8- to 16-ounce freezer-safe containers. Cover and freeze for 3 or more hours for a firmer texture.

7. Soften briefly in the refrigerator or on the counter before serving if desired.

VARIATIONS

* **Lite Banana Daiquiri Ice Dream:** Replace half of the coconut milk with lite (reduced fat) coconut milk. Alternatively, use 100% lite coconut milk, but plan to use the batch immediately or within 24 hours before it becomes hard and icy.

* **Strawberry Daiquiri Ice Dream:** Replace bananas with fresh or frozen (but thawed), unsweetened strawberries and their juices. Adjust the sweetness with 1 or 2 more tablespoons honey or agave nectar as needed.

Garnish with coarsely chopped macadamia nuts
and fresh or frozen (but thawed) sweet cherries
or the Cherry Sauce on Page 182.

Carob Banana Ice Dream

HANDS-ON: 30 MINUTES • **CHURNING:** 20 TO 25 MINUTES • **YIELD:** 4 1/2 TO 5 CUPS; 8 SERVINGS

INGREDIENTS

1/3 cup cool or cold filtered water

2 teaspoons unflavored gelatin **or** 3/4 teaspoon agar agar powder (not the flakes)

1/8 teaspoon finely ground, unrefined sea salt

1/4 cup honey **or** agave nectar; additional 1 to 3 tablespoons as needed

1/4 to 1/2 teaspoon *pure* stevia extract powder **or** 1/2 to 1 teaspoon *clear* stevia extract liquid (start with less; add more only if needed)

2 cups unsweetened, preservative-free coconut milk (regular, not lite)

2 cups very large ripe or slightly overripe bananas (2 large, or 3 or 4 medium)

1/4 cup roasted carob powder

1 1/2 teaspoons pure vanilla extract **or** alcohol-free vanilla flavoring

Bananas add a silky smooth texture and sweetness to this healthy indulgence. The bananas should be ripe or slightly overripe, but not black on the inside. If you buy them green and hard, allow them to ripen on the counter until they are spotty on the outside, fragrant, and they yield to pressure.

1 SERVING (REGULAR):
217 calories
2.3 grams protein
28.9 grams carbohydrate
10.3 grams fat
57 milligrams sodium

1 SERVING (HALF LITE):
182 calories
1.8 grams protein
27.4 grams carbohydrate
7.3 grams fat
48 milligrams sodium

DIRECTIONS

1. Add 1/3 cup water to a small saucepan. Slowly sprinkle with gelatin or agar agar powder. Let stand for 2 to 5 minutes to soften. Warm over medium-low heat, without stirring, until gelatin or agar agar dissolves. Scrape the mixture into a blender, Vita-Mix, or food processor. Cover and process until smooth.

2. Add honey, stevia, and sea salt. Blend. Add coconut milk, banana, carob powder, and vanilla. Blend until smooth, stopping to scrape the sides with a spatula. For a sweeter taste, add an additional 1/8 teaspoon stevia and/or 1 tablespoon honey. Blend, taste, and repeat if needed.

3. Pour into one or more wide-mouth jars. Cover and refrigerate for at least 6 hours before churning.

4. Scrape the chilled custard into the canister of your ice cream maker. Churn according to the manufacturer's instructions.

5. Serve immediately or spoon into several 8- to 16-ounce freezer-safe containers. Cover and freeze for 3 or more hours for a firmer texture.

~Continued next page~

Carob Banana Ice Dream ~ continued

6. Soften solidly frozen dessert by placing it in the refrigerator for 30 to 45 minutes or on the counter for 15 to 30 minutes before serving.

VARIATIONS

* **Lite Cocoa Banana Ice Dream:** Replace half of the coconut milk with lite (reduced fat) coconut milk. Alternatively, use 100% lite coconut milk, but plan to use the batch immediately or within 24 hours before it becomes hard and icy.

* **Carob Banana Nut Ice Dream:** Add 1/2 cup lightly toasted, coarsely chopped almonds, pecans, or skinned hazelnuts (Page 75) when Ice Dream reaches the soft-serve stage. Mix for 1 or 2 more minutes.

Top with Strawberry, Cherry, or Caramel Sauce, or sprinkle with coarsely chopped Pecan or Almond Pralines (see index for recipes).

Roasted Banana Ice Dream

HANDS-ON: 30 MINUTES • **CHURNING:** 20 TO 25 MINUTES • **YIELD:** 4 TO 5 CUPS; 8 SERVINGS

My inspiration for this, and many of the other recipes, came from *The Perfect Scoop* by David Lebovitz. Roasting brings out a rich butterscotch-like flavor and enhances the natural sweetness of bananas. The fiber in bananas renders this recipe silky smooth even after several weeks in the freezer.

Serve this solo, or top it off with Hot Fudge Sauce, Hot Chocolate Sauce, Peanut Butter Fudge Sauce, or Caramel Sauce (see index for recipes).

INGREDIENTS

3 medium-size ripe bananas, peels removed (about 2 1/2 cups when sliced)

2 to 3 tablespoons real maple syrup

1 tablespoon virgin-pressed coconut oil **or** palm shortening

1/3 cup cool or cold filtered water

2 teaspoons unflavored gelatin **or** 3/4 teaspoon agar agar powder (not the flakes)

1 tablespoon honey **or** agave nectar **or** 1 1/2 tablespoons maple syrup; additional 1 tablespoon as needed

1/4 to 1/2 teaspoon *pure* stevia extract powder **or** 1/2 to 1 teaspoon *clear* stevia extract liquid (start with less; add more only if needed)

1/8 teaspoon finely ground, unrefined sea salt

1 teaspoon pure vanilla extract **or** alcohol-free vanilla flavoring

1/2 teaspoon ground cinnamon **or** 1/4 teaspoon ground nutmeg, optional

1 3/4 cups (one 14-ounce can) unsweetened, preservative-free coconut milk (regular, not lite)

1 SERVING (REGULAR):
208 calories
2.1 grams protein
25.6 grams carbohydrate
10.8 grams fat
52 milligrams sodium

1 SERVING (HALF LITE):
177 calories
1.7 grams protein
24.3 grams carbohydrate
8.2 grams fat
45 milligrams sodium

DIRECTIONS

1. Gently melt coconut or palm oil in a small saucepan over low heat. Set aside. Preheat the oven to 450° F. Lightly oil a 2-quart (preferably glass or Pyrex) baking dish. I use an 8x10 or 9x9x2-inch pan or 9-inch Pyrex pie plate. Don't use a larger pan or the syrup will burn.

2. Slice the bananas into 2-inch pieces into a medium bowl. Toss with maple syrup and coconut or palm oil. Scrape into the prepared pan. Reduce the heat to 400° F and bake for 30 to 35 minutes (stir only one time) until bananas look browned and cooked through.

3. Add 1/3 cup water to a small saucepan. Slowly sprinkle with gelatin or agar agar powder. Let stand for 2 to 5 minutes to soften. Warm over medium-low heat, without stirring, until gelatin or agar agar dissolves.

~Continued next page~

Roasted Banana Ice Dream ~ continued

Scrape the mixture into a blender, Vita-Mix, or food processor. Add the honey, sea salt, and stevia. Blend until smooth.

4. Add the roasted banana mixture, coconut milk, vanilla, and optional cinnamon. Blend again until smooth, stopping to scrape the sides with a spatula. For a sweeter taste, add an additional 1/8 teaspoon stevia and/or 1 tablespoon honey. Blend, taste, and repeat if needed.

5. Pour into one or more wide-mouth jars. Cover and refrigerate for at least 6 hours before churning.

6. Scrape the chilled custard into the canister of your ice cream maker. Add the optional liqueur. Churn according to the manufacturer's instructions.

7. Serve immediately or spoon into several 8- to 16-ounce freezer-safe containers. Cover and freeze for 3 or more hours for a firmer texture.

8. Soften solidly frozen dessert by placing it in the refrigerator for 30 to 45 minutes or on the counter for 15 to 30 minutes before serving.

VARIATIONS

* **Lite Roasted Banana Ice Dream:** Replace half of the coconut milk with lite (reduced fat) coconut milk. Alternatively, use 100% lite coconut milk, but plan to use the batch immediately or within 24 hours before it becomes hard and icy.

* **Roasted Banana Rum Ice Dream:** In step #3 add 2 tablespoons banana liqueur or coconut rum. This will make the mixture easier to scoop even after several days or weeks in the freezer.

* **Roasted Banana Nut Ice Dream:** Add 1/2 cup lightly toasted, coarsely chopped walnuts or pecans to the machine when Ice Dream reaches the soft-serve stage. Run the machine for 1 or 2 more minutes. **Note:** See Page 75 for tips for toasting nuts and removing their bitter skins before chopping.

* **Roasted Banana Chocolate Chip Ice Dream:** Add 1/2 to 3/4 cup coarsely chopped, malt-sweetened, fruit-sweetened, dairy-free, or bittersweet chocolate chips or bittersweet dark chocolate (70 to 73%) to the machine when Ice Dream reaches the soft-serve stage. Run the machine for 1 or 2 more minutes.

* **Roasted Banana Carob Chip Ice Dream:** In the variation above, replace chocolate chips with chopped carob chips or a carob candy bar. You may have to try several brands to find one you like. If you follow a gluten-free diet, be sure to read labels as most carob products have warnings that their product may share common packaging machinery with gluten-containing products.

Roasted Pear Ice Dream

HANDS-ON: 30 MINUTES • **CHURNING:** 20 TO 25 MINUTES • **YIELD:** 4 TO 4 1/2 CUPS; 8 SERVINGS

INGREDIENTS

4 medium to large ripe pears (1 1/2 to 2 pounds total)

2 tablespoons honey **or** agave nectar **or** 3 tablespoons maple syrup

1 tablespoon virgin-pressed coconut oil **or** palm shortening

1/3 cup pear juice **or** pear nectar

2 teaspoons unflavored gelatin **or** 3/4 teaspoon agar agar powder (not the flakes)

1/4 cup honey or agave nectar **or** 1/4 cup + 2 tablespoons pure maple syrup

1/4 to 1/2 teaspoon *pure* stevia extract powder **or** 1/2 to 1 teaspoon *clear* stevia extract liquid (start with less; add more only if needed)

1/8 teaspoon finely ground, unrefined sea salt

2 3/4 cups unsweetened, preservative-free coconut milk (regular, not lite), mixed well

1 teaspoon pure vanilla extract **or** alcohol-free vanilla flavoring

1/2 teaspoon ground cinnamon **or** 1 1/2 teaspoons peeled and finely grated fresh gingerroot, optional

1 teaspoon caramel **or** butterscotch flavoring, optional

Roasted pears add a creamy flavor and texture to ice cream. The flavor of sweet juicy pears with a hint of caramel will delight your taste buds as you bite into this Ice Dream. Unlike the Hagen Daaz version, it is not high in fat and sugar. Try it as is, or top with Caramel Sauce, Hot Chocolate Sauce, or Pecan Pralines, or serve it over a gluten-free brownie (see index for recipes).

1 SERVING (REGULAR):
282 calories
2.2 grams protein
32.8 grams carbohydrate
15.8 grams fat
67 milligrams sodium

1 SERVING (HALF LITE):
181 calories
1.2 grams protein
29 grams carbohydrate
6.8 grams fat
41 milligrams sodium

DIRECTIONS

1. Gently melt the coconut or palm oil in a small saucepan over low heat. Set Aside. Preheat oven to 450° F. Lightly oil a 2-quart (preferably glass or Pyrex) baking dish. I use an 8x10 or 9x9x2-inch pan or 9-inch Pyrex pie plate. Don't use a larger pan or the syrup and juices will burn.

2. Peel, core, and cube the pears and add to the prepared pan. Pour on the honey or maple syrup and melted oil; toss to coat.

   Reduce the heat to 400° F and bake for 30 to 35 minutes, stirring just once during baking, until the pears appear browned and cooked through.

3. Add 1/3 cup pear juice to a small saucepan. Slowly sprinkle with gelatin or agar agar powder. Let stand for 2 to 5 minutes to soften.

~Continued next page~

Roasted Pear Ice Dream ~ continued

Warm over medium-low heat, without stirring, until gelatin or agar agar dissolves. Scrape the mixture into a blender, Vita-Mix, or food processor. Add the honey, stevia, and sea salt. Cover and process until smooth.

4. Add the coconut milk, the optional cinnamon or ginger, and the optional caramel or butterscotch flavoring. Blend and set aside.

5. Scrape the roasted pears and any pan juices into a fine mesh strainer or sieve. Mash with the back of a spoon and push the pears through the sieve into a bowl. Use a spatula to scrape the purée from the underside of the sieve. Discard pulp left in the top of the sieve. Add the pear purée to the coconut mixture in the blender. Blend until smooth. For a sweeter taste, add an additional 1/8 teaspoon stevia and/or 1 tablespoon honey. Blend, taste, and repeat if needed.

6. Pour into one or more wide-mouth jars. Cover and refrigerate for at least 6 hours before churning.

7. Scrape the chilled custard into the canister of your ice cream maker. Add the optional liqueur. Churn according to the manufacturer's instructions.

8. Serve immediately or spoon into several 8- to 16-ounce freezer-safe containers. Cover and freeze for 3 or more hours for a firmer texture.

9. Soften solidly frozen dessert by placing it in the refrigerator for 30 to 45 minutes or on the counter for 15 to 30 minutes before serving.

VARIATIONS

* **Lite Roasted Pear Ice Dream:** Replace half of the coconut milk with lite (reduced fat) coconut milk. Alternatively, use 100% lite coconut milk, but plan to use the batch immediately or within 24 hours before it becomes hard and icy.

* **Roasted Pear Ice Dream with Pecan Pralines:** Add 1/2 cup coarsely chopped Pecan Pralines (Page 214) to the machine when Ice Dream reaches the soft-serve stage. Run the machine for 1 or 2 more minutes.

When ripe, pears should yield to gentle pressure and emit a slightly fruity fragrance. You can use Anjou, Comice, Bartlett, Forell, or Bosc pears. If they are hard (unripe), allow them to ripen in a bowl or basket at room temperature. Place a ripe apple or banana next to the pears and they'll ripen faster.

Strawberry Ice Dream

HANDS-ON: 25 MINUTES • **CHURNING:** 20 TO 25 MINUTES • **YIELD:** 4 1/2- 5 1/2 CUPS; 8 SERVINGS

I NGREDIENTS

2 cups unsweetened, preservative-free coconut milk (regular, not lite), divided

2 teaspoons unflavored gelatin **or** 3/4 teaspoon agar agar powder (not flakes)

1/4 cup honey **or** agave nectar; additional 1 to 2 tablespoons as needed

1/4 to 1/2 teaspoon *pure* stevia extract powder **or** 1/2 to 1 teaspoon *clear* stevia extract liquid (start with less; add more only if needed)

1/8 teaspoon finely ground, unrefined sea salt

3 heaping cups fresh strawberries, rinsed, drained, and hulled (see notes above)

1 1/2 teaspoons pure vanilla extract **or** alcohol-free vanilla flavoring

Look for small, organic strawberries that are grown locally. They should have dark red skins with moist green leaves and stems, and should smell sweetly aromatic. Avoid berries with white or green shoulders and wilted leaves; they were picked long ago and far away, before they were fully ripened.

1 SERVING (REGULAR):
166 calories
1.8 grams protein
16.8 grams carbohydrate
10.2 grams fat
56 milligrams sodium

1 SERVING (HALF LITE):
131 calories
1.3 grams protein
15.3 grams carbohydrate
7.2 grams fat
47 milligrams sodium

D IRECTIONS

1. Add 1/3 cup coconut milk to a small saucepan. Slowly sprinkle with gelatin or agar agar powder. Let stand for 2 to 5 minutes to soften. Warm over medium-low heat, without stirring, until gelatin or agar agar dissolves. Scrape the mixture into a blender, Vita-Mix, or food processor. Add the honey, stevia, and sea salt. Cover and process until smooth. Pour into a small bowl and set aside.

2. Purée the strawberries in a blender, food processor, or Vita-Mix. You should have about 2 cups of purée. Combine this with the gelatin mixture, the remaining coconut milk, and vanilla. Blend until smooth, stopping to scrape the sides with a spatula. For a sweeter taste, add an additional 1/8 teaspoon stevia and/or 1 tablespoon honey. Blend, taste, and repeat if needed.

3. Pour into one or more wide-mouth jars. Cover and refrigerate for at least 6 hours before churning.

4. Scrape the chilled custard into the canister of your ice cream maker. Churn according to the manufacturer's instructions.

5. Serve immediately or spoon into several 8- to 16-ounce freezer-safe containers. Cover and freeze for 3 or more hours for a firmer texture.

~Continued next page~

> **FYI:** Did you ever wonder what it means to hull strawberries? Simply cut out the stem with a small, sharp paring knife. Mystery solved.

Strawberry Ice Dream ~ continued

6. Soften solidly frozen dessert by placing it in the refrigerator for 30 to 45 minutes or on the counter for 15 to 30 minutes before serving.

Variations

* **Lite Strawberry Ice Dream:** Replace half of the coconut milk with lite (reduced fat) coconut milk. Alternatively, use 100% lite coconut milk, but plan to use the batch immediately or within 24 hours before it becomes hard and icy.

* **Strawberry Almond Ice Dream:** Add 1/2 teaspoon almond extract or natural almond flavoring or 1 tablespoon amaretto liqueur with the vanilla. Proceed with the recipe as directed. Add 1 cup toasted, coarsely chopped almonds to the machine when the mixture reaches the soft-serve stage. Run the machine for 1 or 2 more minutes. (See Page 75 for nut toasting tips.)

For a special occasion, top this Ice Dream
with Hot Fudge or Chocolate Sauce,
or layer a scoopful over Gluten-Free
Brownies, or arrange it next to a scoop
of Dark Chocolate, Chocolate Hazelnut,
Blueberry, Peach, or Vanilla Ice Dream
(see index for recipes).

151

Cherry Vanilla Ice Dream

HANDS-ON: 30 MINUTES • **CHURNING:** 20 TO 25 MINUTES • **YIELD:** 6 CUPS; 8 SERVINGS

INGREDIENTS

1/2-pound fresh sweet cherries **or** 1 heaping cup frozen, unsweetened Bing cherries, emptied into a bowl while frozen and allowed to thaw (to capture all the juices)

1 tablespoon fresh lemon juice **or** kirsch (cherry liqueur)

1 tablespoon honey **or** agave nectar **or** 1 1/2 tablespoons maple syrup

1 recipe Vanilla or Maple Vanilla Ice Dream (Page 78)

Bite-size pieces of sweet cherries and their juices add a burst of flavor and a sweet pink color to this dairy-free frozen dessert. Serve it solo or top it off with a Hot Fudge Sauce or Chocolate Sauce, or sprinkle with mini malt-sweetened chocolate chips or finely chopped bittersweet dark chocolate.

DIRECTIONS

1. *If using fresh cherries,* remove any stems. Rinse well and pat dry with unbleached paper towels. Working over the bowl of a food processor to catch the juices, cut each cherry in half with a paring knife, then cut out the pit with the tip of the knife and drop the cherry into the bowl. Alternatively, use a cherry pitter, which is much safer. Either way, use one hand to push out the pit, and place the other hand under each cherry and make sure you catch and discard one pit for every cherry.

    If using thawed cherries, pour them into the work bowl of a food processor fitted with a metal blade. If you don't have a food processor, drain the cherries, saving the juices, then chop them on a cutting board. Pour into a bowl with any juices.

2. Add the honey and lemon juice (or kirsch) to the cherries and pulse to chop coarsely. Pour into a small bowl. Cover and refrigerate until needed.

3. Prepare Vanilla Ice Dream. When it reaches the soft-serve stage, add the chopped, sweetened cherries. Run the machine for 2 more minutes.

4. Serve immediately or spoon into several 8- to 16-ounce freezer-safe containers. Cover and freeze for 3 or more hours for a firmer texture.

5. Soften solidly frozen dessert by placing it in the refrigerator for 30 to 45 minutes or on the counter for 15 to 30 minutes before serving

1 SERVING (REGULAR):
262 calories
2.6 grams protein
23 grams carbohydrate
17.8 grams fat
77 milligrams sodium

1 SERVING (HALF LITE):
201 calories
1.7 grams protein
20.4 grams carbohydrate
12.5 grams fat
61 milligrams sodium

~Continued next page~

Cherry Vanilla Ice Dream ~ continued

VARIATIONS

* **Cherry Vanilla Lite Ice Dream:** Replace half of the coconut milk with lite (reduced fat) coconut milk. Alternatively, use 100% lite coconut milk, but plan to use the batch immediately or within 24 hours before it becomes hard and icy.

* **Pineapple Cherry Ice Dream:** Use 1 cup of chopped fresh pineapple and 1 cup of cherries in the master recipe.

* **Cherry Vanilla Chocolate Chunk Ice Dream:** Coarsely chop a 4-ounce bar of bittersweet dark chocolate, then refrigerate. When Ice Dream reaches the soft-serve stage, add the chocolate bits with the cherries. Mix for 1 or 2 more minutes.

* **Chocolate Cherry Ice Dream:** Replace Vanilla Ice Dream with Cocoa Ice Dream or Dark Chocolate Ice Dream (Page 86 or 88).

* **Blueberry Vanilla Ice Dream:** In the master recipe, substitute blueberries for the cherries. Replace lemon juice with orange or lime juice. Replace honey with maple syrup, and then use Maple Vanilla Ice Dream in place of Vanilla Ice Dream.

Dried Cherry Pecan Ice Dream

HANDS-ON: 30 MINUTES • **CHURNING:** 20 TO 25 MINUTES • **YIELD:** 5 TO 5 1/2 CUPS; 8 SERVINGS

INGREDIENTS

- 2 1/2 cups unsweetened, preservative-free coconut milk (regular, not lite), divided

- 3/4 cup dried, fruit-sweetened Bing cherries (not a sour variety), coarsely chopped

- 1/8 teaspoon finely ground, unrefined sea salt

- 1/4 cup black cherry juice concentrate (not sour cherry) + 1 1/2 tablespoons water

- 2 teaspoons unflavored gelatin **or** 3/4 teaspoon agar agar powder (not the flakes)

- 2 tablespoons honey, agave nectar **or** 3 tablespoons pure maple syrup; additional 1 to 2 tablespoons as needed

- 1/2 teaspoon *pure* stevia extract powder **or** 1 teaspoon *clear* stevia extract liquid

- 1 teaspoon pure vanilla extract **or** alcohol-free vanilla

- 2 tablespoons Cointreau, Kirsch, **or** other cherry-flavored liqueur, optional

- 1/2 cup toasted, coarsely chopped, pecans (Page 75)

Toasted pecans add crunch to Vanilla Ice Dream, and dried cherries turn it a pretty pink. If pecans are not available, you can substitute cashews, walnuts, almonds, or pistachios. (The pistachios should be green, not the kind that are dyed pink.) Start with raw nuts and dry toast them yourself (see Page 75 for instructions) for the best flavor.

1 SERVING (REGULAR):
253 calories
2.3 grams protein
21.6 grams carbohydrate
17.5 grams fat
69 milligrams sodium

1 SERVING (HALF LITE):
208 calories
1.6 grams protein
19.7 grams carbohydrate
13.7 grams fat
58 milligrams sodium

DIRECTIONS

1. Bring 1 cup coconut milk to a low boil in a small saucepan. Remove from heat. Add dried cherries. Cover, and let steep at room temperature for 30 to 60 minutes. Scoop out the cherries and set aside in a covered bowl or jar. Reserve the liquid for step #3.

2. Add 1/4 cup black cherry juice concentrate and 1 1/2 tablespoons water to a small saucepan. Slowly sprinkle with gelatin or agar agar powder. Let stand for 2 to 5 minutes to soften. Warm over medium-low heat, without stirring, until gelatin or agar agar dissolves. Scrape the mixture into a blender, Vita-Mix, or food processor. Add the honey, stevia, and vanilla. Blend until smooth.

3. Add the reserved cup of coconut milk from step #1, the remaining 1 1/2 cups coconut milk, and optional cherry liqueur. Blend until smooth. For a sweeter taste, add 1 more tablespoon honey (optional).

~Continued next page~

> **Note:** Look for black cherry juice concentrate in natural foods stores or the health foods section of supermarkets. Whatever you don't use in this recipe, you can add judiciously to fruit smoothies, or reconstitute to make an antioxidant-rich beverage. Research indicates that cherries can help fight inflammation and free radical damage, slow down the aging process, and protect against many diseases.

Dried Cherry Pecan Ice Dream ~ continued

4. Pour into one or more wide-mouth jars. Cover and refrigerate for at least 6 hours before churning. Refrigerate the softened dried cherries.

5. Scrape the chilled custard into the canister of your ice cream maker. Churn according to the manufacturer's instructions. When the mixture reaches the soft-serve stage, add the chopped nuts and reserved dried cherries. Run the machine for 1 or 2 more minutes.

6. Serve immediately or spoon into several 8- to 16-ounce freezer-safe containers. Cover and freeze for 3 or more hours for a firmer texture.

7. Soften solidly frozen dessert by placing it in the refrigerator for 30 to 45 minutes or on the counter for 15 to 30 minutes before serving.

VARIATIONS

* **Lite Dried Cherry Pecan Ice Dream:** Replace half of the coconut milk with lite (reduced fat) coconut milk. Alternatively, use 100% lite coconut milk, but plan to use the batch immediately or within 24 hours before it becomes hard and icy.

* **Dried Cherry Pecan Fudge Ripple Ice Dream:** See Page 114 for instructions for layering freshly made Dried Cherry Pecan Ice Dream with Hot Fudge Sauce or Chocolate Sauce.

If you add the optional cherry liqueur, the Ice Dream will usually remain soft enough to scoop right from the freezer, even after several days or weeks.

Date Delight Ice Dream

HANDS-ON: 30 MINUTES • **CHURNING:** 20 TO 25 MINUTES • **YIELD:** 5 TO 6 CUPS; 8 SERVINGS

INGREDIENTS

1 cup soft pitted dates **or** coconut date rolls

2 teaspoons unflavored gelatin **or** 3/4 teaspoon agar agar powder (not the flakes)

1/3 cup honey **or** agave nectar; additional 1 to 2 tablespoons as needed

1/4 to 1/2 teaspoon *pure* stevia extract powder **or** 1/2 to 1 teaspoon *clear* stevia extract liquid (start with less; add more only if needed)

1/4 teaspoon finely ground unrefined sea salt

3 cups unsweetened, preservative-free coconut milk (regular, not lite)

1 teaspoon ground cinnamon

1/4 teaspoon ground allspice

1/4 teaspoon ground cloves

1 teaspoon pure vanilla extract **or** alcohol-free vanilla flavoring; double if desired

2 teaspoons finely grated orange zest (colored part only; see note above)

1/2 cup chopped, toasted pecans **or** almonds (Page 75), optional

2 tablespoons Triple Sec **or** Cointreau, optional

Dates fill in for sugar while adding a thick and creamy texture to this frozen dessert. Look for unpitted dates—they'll be fresher and you can pit them yourself. Choose whole dates rather than chopped; they'll last longer and will retain more moisture. They should be soft and plump with a slightly shiny and smooth skin free of dry, cracked, or shriveled sections or crystallization. They should not have a fermented smell.

1 SERVING (REGULAR):
284 calories
2.4 grams protein
34.5 grams carbohydrate
15 grams fat
97 milligrams sodium

1 SERVING (HALF LITE):
231 calories
1.6 grams protein
32.2 grams carbohydrate
10.5 grams fat
83 milligrams sodium

DIRECTIONS

1. If dates do not feel soft and squishy, place them in a heatproof bowl on a rack over boiling water. Cover and steam for 5 minutes until soft. Let stand for 10 minutes.

2. Add 1/3 cup water to a small saucepan. Slowly sprinkle with gelatin or agar agar powder. Let stand for 2 to 5 minutes to soften. Warm over medium-low heat, without stirring, until gelatin or agar agar dissolves. Scrape the mixture into a blender, Vita-Mix, or food processor. Cover and process until smooth.

3. Add the honey, stevia, and sea salt. Blend again. Add dates, coconut milk, cinnamon, allspice, cloves, and vanilla. Blend until smooth, stopping to scrape the sides with a spatula. For a sweeter taste, add an

~Continued next page~

FYI: You can store dates at room temperature in glass jars. Try Medjool, Deglet Noor, Honey, Halawy, Khadrawy, Zahadi, and Black Sphinx dates. Each has its own distinct flavor. You may also substitute coconut date rolls made from soft, pitted, pulverized dates formed into cylinders and sold in the produce section of most natural foods stores and over the Internet.

Note: To grate the zest of an orange, first wash and pat it dry, then rub it along the smallest holes of a cheese grater or a microplane grater. Rotate the fruit to grate off only the colored part (the white part tastes bitter). Use a spatula, not your fingers—it's razor sharp—to scrape the zest from the back of the microplane. Store the naked orange in a covered container in the refrigerator to keep it from drying out.

If you add the optional orange liqueur or rum, you'll find that the Ice Dream retains a softer texture, making it easier to scoop even after several weeks in the freezer.

Date Delight Ice Dream ~ continued

additional 1/8 teaspoon stevia and/or 1 tablespoon honey. Blend, taste, and repeat if needed.

4. Pour into one or more wide-mouth jars. Cover and refrigerate for at least 6 hours before churning.

5. Scrape the chilled custard into the canister of your ice cream maker along with the optional liqueur, and churn according to the manufacturer's instructions. When the mixture reaches the soft-serve stage, add optional nuts through the hole in the top of the machine and run the machine for 2 more minutes.

6. Serve immediately or spoon into several 8- to 16-ounce freezer-safe containers. Cover and freeze for 3 or more hours for a firmer texture.

7. Soften solidly frozen dessert by placing it in the refrigerator for 30 to 45 minutes or on the counter for 15 to 30 minutes before serving.

VARIATIONS

* **Lite Date Delight Ice Dream:** Replace half of the coconut milk with lite (reduced fat) coconut milk. Alternatively, use 100% lite coconut milk, but plan to use the batch immediately or within 24 hours before it becomes hard and icy.

* **Date Rum Ice Dream:** Replace the Triple Sec or Cointreau with 2 tablespoons light or dark rum or coconut rum. This will keep the ice dream softer in the freezer, making it easier to scoop.

Blueberry Ice Dream

HANDS-ON: 30 MINUTES • **CHURNING:** 20 TO 25 MINUTES • **YIELD:** 4 1/2 TO 5 CUPS; 8 SERVINGS

INGREDIENTS

1 cup blueberry juice blend **or** white grape juice, divided

1 tablespoon arrowroot starch

2 cups fresh or frozen blueberries (if using frozen, see notes below)

2 teaspoons unflavored gelatin **or** 3/4 teaspoon agar agar powder (not the flakes)

1/4 cup honey **or** agave nectar; additional 1 to 2 tablespoons as needed

1/4 to 1/2 teaspoon *pure* stevia extract powder **or** 1/2 to 1 teaspoon *clear* stevia extract liquid (start with less; add more only if needed)

1/8 teaspoon finely ground, unrefined sea salt

2 cups unsweetened, preservative-free coconut milk (regular, not lite), mixed well

DIRECTIONS

1. Dissolve arrowroot in 3/4 cup juice in a medium saucepan. Bring to a boil over medium-high heat, stirring periodically until the mixture turns clear, about 2 minutes. Add fresh blueberries, reduce heat, and simmer for 1 minute. Remove from heat. Let stand for 30 minutes. **Note:** If using frozen blueberries, place them in a heatproof bowl. Cook the arrowroot-juice mixture as described; pour over berries and allow to cool.

2. Add reserved 1/3 cup blueberry juice or white grape juice to a small saucepan. Slowly sprinkle with gelatin or agar agar powder. Let stand for 2 to 5 minutes to soften. Warm over medium-low heat, without stirring, until gelatin or agar agar dissolves. Scrape the mixture into a blender, Vita-Mix, or food processor. Add honey or agave nectar, stevia, and sea salt. Cover and process until smooth. Pour into a bowl and set aside.

This recipe is best during the height of blueberry season, late spring through early fall. If you substitute frozen blueberries, select smaller, wild blueberries, which will be more intense in flavor than the larger commercial varieties. Bottled blueberry-apple juice can be found in natural foods stores or the health foods section of supermarkets. Buy juice bottled in glass rather than plastic to avoid toxic plasticizers that can migrate from the container into its contents.

This deep blue Ice Dream is a feast for the eyes when served with Avocado, Peach, Cherry, or Vanilla Ice Dream. Top it off with Chocolate or Carob Sauce (see index for recipes).

1 SERVING (REGULAR):
192 calories
1.7 grams protein
23.5 grams carbohydrate
10.1 grams fat
61 milligrams sodium

1 SERVING (HALF LITE):
157 calories
1.2 grams protein
22 grams carbohydrate
7.1 grams fat
52 milligrams sodium

~Continued next page~

Blueberry Ice Dream ~ continued

3. Transfer the cooked blueberry mixture to a Vita-Mix, food processor, or blender. Process until smooth (about 1 minute). Place a fine mesh strainer or sieve over a bowl. Pour the blueberry purée into the strainer, and then gently push with the back of a spoon to extract as much purée as possible. Discard the pulp that remains in the sieve.

4. Combine the strained blueberry mixture with the gelatin mixture, coconut milk, and sea salt in the Vita-Mix, blender, or food processor. Blend until smooth. For a sweeter taste, add an additional 1/8 teaspoon stevia and/or 1 tablespoon honey. Blend, taste, and repeat if needed.

5. Pour the mixture into one or more wide-mouth jars. Cover and refrigerate for at least 6 hours before churning.

6. Scrape the chilled custard into the canister of your ice cream maker. Churn according to the manufacturer's instructions. Serve immediately or spoon into several 8- to 16-ounce freezer-safe containers. Cover and freeze for 3 or more hours for a firmer texture or longer storage.

7. Soften solidly frozen dessert in the refrigerator for 45 minutes or on the counter for 20 to 30 minutes before serving.

VARIATIONS

* **For more blueberry flavor:** Add 3 tablespoons fruit-sweetened blueberry preserves thinned with 1 to 2 tablespoons water. When the mixture reaches the soft-serve stage, add 3 tablespoons fruit-sweetened blueberry preserves thinned with 1 to 2 tablespoons water. Mix for 1 or 2 more minutes.

* **Lite Blueberry Ice Dream:** Replace half of the coconut milk with lite (reduced fat) coconut milk. Alternatively, use 100% lite coconut milk, but plan to use the batch immediately or within 24 hours before it becomes hard and icy.

* **Raspberry Ice Dream:** Replace blueberry juice with white grape juice and blueberries with 3 cups fresh or frozen, unsweetened raspberries. **Note:** Rinse berries gently under cool running water. Discard any that show signs of spoilage. Do not allow berries to soak in water for any amount of time or they will absorb moisture and become mushy. Spread berries in a single layer to dry on a double thickness of unbleached paper towels.

* **Blackberry Ice Dream:** Follow the raspberry Ice Dream variation above, replacing raspberries with 3 cups of fresh or frozen, unsweetened blackberries. **Note:** You may replace blackberries with blackberry hybrids—loganberries or boysenberries—and then change the name of the recipe.

Mango Orange Ice Dream

HANDS-ON: 30 MINUTES • **CHURNING:** 20 TO 25 MINUTES • **YIELD:** 4 TO 5 CUPS; 8 SERVINGS

INGREDIENTS

1/3 cup fresh squeezed orange or tangerine juice (see variations below)

2 teaspoons unflavored gelatin **or** 3/4 teaspoon agar agar powder (not the flakes)

3 tablespoons honey **or** agave nectar; additional 1 to 2 tablespoons as needed

1/4 to 1/2 teaspoon *pure* stevia extract powder **or** 1/2 to 1 teaspoon *clear* stevia extract liquid (start with less; add more only if needed)

1/8 teaspoon finely ground, unrefined sea salt

2 large or 3 medium-size ripe mangoes

2 cups unsweetened, preservative-free coconut milk (regular, not lite)

1 tablespoon coconut rum **or** dark rum, optional

Mangoes give this dessert a sherbert-like texture. Any variety of mango will do; just make sure it's ripe. A ripe mango will give off a fruity fragrance and should yield to gentle pressure. Store hard mangoes at room temperature in an open bowl, a wire basket, or in a paper bag next to a ripe banana or apple. Ripe fruit gives off ethylene gases that will help the mango ripen faster. Once ripe, use within a couple of days or refrigerate to prevent spoilage.

Note: I recommend that you buy an extra mango or two just in case one turns out bad, which you won't discover until you cut it open. You can always peel, seed, slice, and freeze the extra for a future fruit smoothie or fruit sauce.

DIRECTIONS

1. Add 1/3 cup orange or peach juice to a small saucepan. Slowly sprinkle with gelatin or agar agar powder. Let stand for 2 to 5 minutes to soften. Warm over medium-low heat, without stirring, until gelatin or agar agar dissolves. Scrape the mixture into a blender, Vita-Mix, or food processor with the honey, stevia, and sea salt. Cover and process until smooth.

2. Wash the mangoes. Cut each one in half and, while holding the fruit over a bowl, twist to separate the halves. Cut the pulp from the seeds and scoop the flesh from the skin with a spoon. Discard the pits. You should have about 1 1/2 to 2 cups of mango including any juice. Add this to the gelatin mixture with the coconut milk. Blend until smooth, stopping to scrape the sides with a spatula. For a sweeter taste, add an additional 1/8 teaspoon stevia and/or 1 tablespoon honey. Blend, taste, and repeat if needed.

1 SERVING (REGULAR):
173 calories
1.8 grams protein
18.6 grams carbohydrate
10.1 grams fat
56 milligrams sodium

1 SERVING (HALF LITE):
138 calories
1.3 grams protein
17.1 grams carbohydrate
7.1 grams fat
47 milligrams sodium

~Continued next page~

Mango Orange Ice Dream ~ continued

3. Pour into one or more wide-mouth jars. Cover and refrigerate for at least 6 hours before churning.

4. Scrape the chilled custard into the canister of your ice cream maker. Add the optional liqueur, and then churn according to the manufacturer's instructions.

5. Serve immediately or spoon into several 8- to 16-ounce freezer-safe containers. Cover and freeze for 3 or more hours for a firmer texture.

6. Soften solidly frozen dessert by placing it in the refrigerator for 30 to 45 minutes or on the counter for 15 to 30 minutes before serving.

VARIATIONS

* Replace orange or tangerine juice with pineapple juice or apricot, peach, or nectarine juice above.

* **Mango Hazelnut Ice Dream:** Add 1/2 cup chopped, toasted hazelnuts, skins removed (see Page 75), when mixture reaches the soft-serve stage. Run the machine for 1 or 2 more minutes.

* **Mango Ginger Ice Dream:** Add 2 tablespoons peeled and finely chopped or grated fresh gingerroot or ginger juice (Page 33) to the blender or food processor with the mango in step #2. If desired, before removing Ice Dream from the machine, fold in 1 to 1 1/2 cups of crumbled, gluten-free Ginger Snap Cookies.

* **Tropical Mango Ice Dream:** Replace orange/tangerine juice with pineapple juice in step #1. When the mixture reaches the soft-serve stage, add 1/4 cup chopped, unsweetened dried pineapple bits and 1 teaspoon grated fresh lime zest. Run the machine for 1 or 2 more minutes.

* **Lite Mango Ice Dream:** Replace half of the coconut milk with lite (reduced fat) coconut milk. Alternatively, use 100% lite coconut milk, but plan to use the batch immediately or within 24 hours before it becomes hard and icy.

Serve this Ice Dream solo or with Avocado, Chocolate, Blueberry, or Vanilla Ice Dream. Garnish with a Chocolate or Hot Fudge Sauce (see index for recipes).

Peach Ice Dream

HANDS-ON: 30 MINUTES • **CHURNING:** 20 TO 25 MINUTES • **YIELD:** 4 TO 5 CUPS

INGREDIENTS

- 1 1/3 pounds squishy, ripe fresh peaches (about 4 large peaches)

- 1/2 cup bottled peach nectar or juice (to cook with the peaches)

- 1/4 cup honey, agave nectar, **or** 1/4 cup + 2 tablespoons maple syrup; additional 1 or 2 tablespoons if needed

- 1/8 teaspoon finely ground, unrefined sea salt

- 1/3 cup bottled peach nectar or juice (to cook with the gelatin)

- 2 teaspoons unflavored gelatin **or** 3/4 teaspoon agar agar powder (not the flakes)

- 1 1/2 cups unsweetened preservative-free coconut milk, mixed well (regular, not lite)

- 1 1/2 teaspoons pure vanilla extract **or** alcohol-free vanilla flavoring

- 1/4 to 1/2 teaspoon *pure* stevia extract powder **or** 1/2 to 1 teaspoon *clear* stevia extract liquid (start with less; add more only if needed)

- 2 drops almond extract; additional 1 or 2 drops as needed

- 1 teaspoon freshly squeezed lemon juice

- 1 to 2 tablespoons Triple Sec **or** Cointreau liqueur, optional

DIRECTIONS

1. Peel the peaches as described in the notes on the right. Slice them in half, removing the pits; cut into chunks. Cook with 1/2 cup peach juice in a medium-size, non-reactive saucepan over medium heat, covered, stirring once or twice, until soft and cooked through, about 10 minutes.

2. Remove peaches from heat; add honey and sea salt, and set aside.

3. Add 1/3 cup cool or cold peach nectar/ juice to a small saucepan. Slowly sprinkle

Peaches add a sweet, slightly tangy flavor to this dessert. Like other Ice Dreams made with fresh fruit, this one tastes best served right out of the machine. The longer it sits in the freezer, the icier it gets.

Serve it solo or topped with Raspberry, Blueberry or Cherry Sauce, or over a fresh fruit salad during the summer. For a special treat, top it off with Chocolate or Hot Fudge Sauce (see index for recipes).

Note: This recipe works equally well with nectarines or apricots. The easiest way to peel peaches and other stone fruits is to cut an X at the bottom of each fruit, then lower them, one at a time, into a pot of boiling water for about 20 seconds. Use a slotted spoon to transfer the peaches to a bowl of ice water to stop the cooking. Drain in a colander. The fuzzy skins will slip right off.

1 SERVING (REGULAR):
172 calories
1.9 grams protein
23.9 grams carbohydrate
7.5 grams fat
49 milligrams sodium

1 SERVING (HALF LITE):
146 calories
1.5 grams protein
22.8 grams carbohydrate
5.3 grams fat
42 milligrams sodium

~Continued next page~

Peach Ice Dream ~ continued

with gelatin or agar agar. Let stand for 2 to 5 minutes to soften. Warm over medium-low heat, without stirring, until gelatin or agar agar dissolves. Scrape the mixture into a blender, Vita-Mix, or food processor. Cover and blend until smooth.

4. Add the coconut milk, vanilla, stevia, almond extract, lemon juice, reserved peaches and their cooking liquid. Blend until smooth, stopping to scrape the sides with a spatula. Add the optional liqueur. For a sweeter taste, add an additional 1/8 teaspoon stevia and/or 1 tablespoon honey. Blend, taste, and repeat if needed.

5. Pour into one or more wide-mouth jars. Cover and refrigerate for at least 6 hours before churning.

6. Scrape the chilled custard into the canister of your ice cream maker. Churn according to the manufacturer's instructions.

7. Serve immediately or spoon into several 8- to 16-ounce freezer-safe containers. Cover and freeze for 3 or more hours for a firmer texture.

8. Soften solidly frozen dessert by placing it in the refrigerator for 30 to 45 minutes or on the counter for 15 to 30 minutes before serving.

VARIATIONS

* **For a peachier flavor:** When the mixture reaches the soft-serve stage, add 3 tablespoons fruit-sweetened peach preserves thinned with 1 to 2 tablespoons water. Run the machine for 1 or 2 more minutes.

* **Peach Almond Ice Dream:** When the mixture reaches the soft-serve stage, add ¼ cup chopped, toasted almonds. Run the machine for 1 or 2 more minutes.

* **Nectarine Ice Dream:** Replace peaches with 1 pound of squishy, ripe fresh nectarines (3 or 4, depending upon size). See notes above about adding fruit preserves.

* **Apricot Ice Dream:** Replace peaches with 1 pound of squishy, ripe fresh apricots (10 to 16, depending on size). See notes above about adding fruit preserves.

* **Lite Peach, Apricot, or Nectarine Ice Dream:** Replace half of the coconut milk with lite (reduced fat) coconut milk. Alternatively, use 100% lite coconut milk, but plan to use the batch immediately or within 24 hours before it becomes hard and icy.

* **Peaches-N-Cookies Ice Dream:** Before removing Ice Dream from the machine, fold in 1 to 1 1/2 cups crushed gluten-free oatmeal cookies, gingersnaps, or honey graham crackers. Run the machine for 1 or 2 more minutes.

163

chapter

8
Sauces

Best Bites

Hot Fudge Sauce

HANDS-ON: 20 MINUTES • **COOKING:** 5 MINUTES • **YIELD:** 1 1/4 CUPS; 10 SERVINGS

INGREDIENTS

3/4 cup unsweetened premium **or** lite (reduced fat) coconut milk **or** plain almond, cashew, or hazelnut milk; additional 1/4 cup as needed to thin

2 teaspoons arrowroot powder

1/4 cup honey **or** agave nectar; additional 1 to 3 tablespoons as needed

1/8 teaspoon finely ground unrefined sea salt

2 ounces unsweetened baker's chocolate, coarsely chopped or broken into 1/2-inch pieces

1/2 teaspoon *clear* stevia extract liquid

1 teaspoon pure vanilla extract **or** alcohol-free vanilla flavoring

Unlike commercial hot fudge sauces, this one doesn't contain refined vegetable oils, hydrogenated oil, or high fructose corn sweeteners that undermine your health. I use coconut milk or nut milk to replace milk and cream. The combination of honey or agave nectar and stevia adds a sweet taste without a lot of sugar or calories.

Note: Read labels carefully to find *unsweetened* baker's chocolate. You will find many brands to choose from.

DIRECTIONS

1. Combine the coconut milk or nut milk and arrowroot in a small saucepan. Whisk to dissolve. Add the honey or agave nectar and sea salt. Bring to a boil over medium heat, stirring or whisking constantly, until the mixture thickens, 3 to 5 minutes.

2. Remove from heat. Add the chocolate, stevia, and vanilla, stirring until the chocolate melts. For a sweeter taste, add an additional 1 tablespoon honey. Blend, taste, and repeat one or two more times as needed.

2 TABLESPOONS (REGULAR):
100 calories
0.9 gram protein
10.3 grams carbohydrate
6.1 grams fat
28 milligrams sodium

2 TABLESPOONS (LITE):
79 calories
0.7 gram protein
9.3 grams carbohydrate
4.3 grams fat
23 milligrams sodium

3. Let stand for 10 minutes, then serve hot or allow to cool. Refrigerate unused sauce in a covered heatproof bowl, a few custard cups, or a wide-mouth jar.

4. Gently warm leftover sauce in a heatproof bowl in a 250° F oven, or in a double boiler or saucepan over very low heat, stirring periodically, or use the bowl-on-a-rack method (Page 74). If too thick, add 1 or 2 tablespoons additional coconut milk.

~Continued next page~

Hot Fudge Sauce ~ continued

VARIATIONS

* Add 1/2 teaspoon almond extract if desired.

* **Peppermint Hot Fudge Sauce:** Add 1/4 teaspoon peppermint extract or natural peppermint flavoring with the vanilla. Add another 1/8 to 1/4 teaspoon if desired. Or, replace peppermint flavoring with 1 tablespoon crème de menthe.

* **Hot Fudge Sauce à l'Orange:** Add 1 1/2 tablespoons minced or finely grated orange zest (colored part only) and/or 1 1/2 tablespoons orange liqueur, such as Grand Marnier, with the vanilla.

* **Mocha Fudge Sauce:** Add 2 to 3 teaspoons instant coffee granules or espresso powder in step #1.

* **Hot Rum Fudge Sauce:** Add 1 1/2 tablespoons light or dark rum with the vanilla.

* **Brandied Hot Fudge Sauce**: Add 1 1/2 tablespoons brandy with the vanilla.

* **Cherry Fudge Sauce:** Add 1 1/2 tablespoons cherry brandy with the vanilla. Experiment with other liqueurs, such as raspberry, banana, or hazelnut liqueur or amaretto.

This sauce makes the perfect topping for almost any flavor of Ice Dream. You can also layer it in containers with freshly made Ice Dream for a rippled effect (see Page 114). This sauce is divine served over a single fresh fruit or a colorful fruit salad.

Hot Chocolate Sauce

HANDS-ON: 20 MINUTES • **COOKING:** 4 MINUTES • **YIELD:** 1 1/2 CUPS; 12 SERVINGS

INGREDIENTS

2/3 cup plain almond, cashew, or hazelnut milk **or** lite coconut milk

1/4 cup honey **or** agave nectar; additional 1 or 2 tablespoons as needed

1/4 to 1/2 teaspoon *pure* stevia extract powder **or** 1/2 to 1 teaspoon *clear* stevia extract liquid: plain **or** vanilla, chocolate, chocolate raspberry, **or** toffee-flavored (start with less; add more only if needed)

1/4 cup unsweetened cocoa powder (spoon into cup and level top)

2 tablespoons virgin-pressed coconut oil **or** palm shortening

1/8 teaspoon finely ground unrefined sea salt

2 ounces bittersweet chocolate (70 to 73% cocoa content), finely chopped

1 teaspoon pure vanilla extract **or** alcohol-free vanilla flavoring

DIRECTIONS

1. Combine the nut milk, honey, stevia, cocoa powder, coconut oil, and sea salt in a small to medium saucepan. Bring to a very low boil over medium heat, stirring all the while with a wire whisk. Reduce heat to medium and cook for 2 to 3 minutes, stirring frequently. Remove from heat.

2. Add chopped chocolate and vanilla, and stir until chocolate melts. For a sweeter taste, add an additional tablespoon of honey or more stevia. Blend, taste, and repeat if needed. Let cool slightly, and then serve. Transfer leftover sauce to a heatproof Pyrex bowl, custard cups, or a wide-mouth jar. When cool, cover and refrigerate.

3. Gently warm leftover sauce in a heatproof bowl in a 250° F oven, or in a double boiler

Imagine a lower-in-sugar version of a chocolate ice cream topping that blends the taste of hot fudge sauce and chocolate syrup. I started with a recipe from the August 2002 issue of *Cooking Light* magazine. I replaced the cow's milk with nut milk, the butter with coconut oil (light-colored palm oil also works), and the sugar with honey and stevia. This sauce keeps well in the refrigerator. It can turn even a simple sliced banana into a special treat.

Note: Store coconut oil and palm shortening at room temperature. Coconut oil will harden in the winter and liquefy during hot weather. Temperature changes won't harm either oil; their naturally saturated fatty acids render them more heat stable than vegetable oils.

2 TABLESPOONS (ALMOND):
85 calories
1.1 grams protein
8.6 grams carbohydrate
5.2 grams fat
16 milligrams sodium

2 TABLESPOONS (LITE COCONUT):
90 calories
1 gram protein
8.2 grams carbohydrate
6 grams fat
19 milligrams sodium

~Continued next page~

FYI: Commercial dessert sauces almost always contain hazardous hydrogenated or partially hydrogenated vegetable oils, soy, safflower, sunflower, canola, or corn oil, as well as fructose, high fructose corn syrup, or artificial sweeteners that are best avoided.

Hot Chocolate Sauce ~ continued

or saucepan over very low heat, stirring periodically, or use the bowl-on-a-rack method (Page 74). If too thick, add 1 or 2 tablespoons additional coconut milk.

VARIATIONS

* **Hot Chocolate Espresso Sauce:** Use an espresso-flavored chocolate bar in the recipe above, or simply add 2 teaspoons instant coffee granules or instant espresso powder at the end of step #2.

* **Hot Chocolate Rum Sauce:** Add 1 1/2 tablespoons dark rum with the vanilla.

* **Hot Chocolate Ginger Sauce:** Add 1 to 1 1/2 tablespoons juice from finely grated and squeezed gingerroot (Page 33) with the vanilla.

* **Peppermint Hot Chocolate Sauce:** Add 1/4 teaspoon peppermint extract or natural peppermint flavoring with the vanilla. Taste for flavoring, then add more peppermint extract if needed, a few drops at a time.

* **Hot Chocolate Sauce à l'Orange:** Add 1 1/2 tablespoons minced or finely grated orange zest (colored part only) and/or 1 1/2 tablespoons orange liqueur, such as Grand Marnier, with the vanilla.

This sauce also tastes great cold or
at room temperature.

Peanut Buttery Hot Chocolate Sauce

HANDS-ON: 20 MINUTES • **COOKING:** 5 MINUTES • **YIELD:** 2 1/4 CUPS; 18 SERVINGS

INGREDIENTS

1 1/3 cups unsweetened coconut milk (regular or lite)

8 ounces bittersweet chocolate (70 to 73% cocoa content), cut into 1/2-inch pieces

1/4 cup natural peanut butter, salted or unsalted, mixed well before measuring

1/8 teaspoon finely ground unrefined sea salt; omit if using salted peanut butter

1/2 teaspoon *clear* stevia extract liquid (regular or vanilla); additional 1/2 teaspoon if needed

2 tablespoons honey **or** agave nectar; additional 1 to 2 tablespoons as needed

This sauce makes the perfect topping for Chocolate, Vanilla, Coffee, Pumpkin, or Cinnamon Ice Dream. You can also alternate layers of freshly churned Ice Dream and sauce in storage containers, and then freeze the mixture for a rippled effect. But don't stop there—dress up sliced (fresh or frozen) bananas, fresh peaches, pears, or fruit salad. It gets thick in the fridge so you'll need to reheat it gently before serving.

DIRECTIONS

1. Bring the coconut milk to a low boil in a 1- to 1 1/2-quart saucepan over medium heat. Turn off the heat and add the chocolate. Cover the pan and let it sit for 5 minutes. Add the peanut butter and the stevia, and whisk until smooth.

2. Taste, and if you want it sweeter, add an additional 1 tablespoon honey or 1/4 teaspoon stevia. Stir. Repeat as needed.

3. Let cool slightly and then serve. Cover and refrigerate unused sauce in a heatproof bowl, custard cups, or a wide-mouth jar.

4. Gently warm leftover sauce in a heatproof bowl in a 250° F oven, or in a double boiler or saucepan over very low heat, stirring periodically, or use the bowl-on-a-rack method (Page 74). If too thick, add 1 or 2 tablespoons additional coconut milk.

2 TABLESPOONS (REGULAR):
145 calories
2.7 grams protein
7.4 grams carbohydrate
11.6 grams fat
23 milligrams sodium

2 TABLESPOONS (LITE):
125 calories
2.4 grams protein
6.5 grams carbohydrate
10 grams fat
18 milligrams sodium

VARIATIONS

* **Almond Buttery Hot Chocolate Sauce:** Replace peanut butter with unsweetened, roasted almond butter and add 1 teaspoon pure almond extract.

~Continued next page~

> **FYI:** If you don't like peanut butter or you want a change of taste, try the variations for other nut butters listed below. This recipe was inspired by one I found in Emily Luchetti's book, *A Passion for Ice Cream*.

Peanut Buttery Hot Chocolate Sauce ~ continued

* **Cashew Buttery Hot Chocolate Sauce:** Replace peanut butter with unsweetened, roasted cashew butter.

* **Coconut Buttery Hot Chocolate Sauce:** Replace peanut butter with coconut butter (not the same as coconut oil; coconut butter is made from whole coconut, both the meat and the oil). If too hard to scoop, run hot water over the jar to soften the mixture so you can stir it well, and then scoop out what you need. (See Appendix for Resources.)

* **Hazelnut Buttery Hot Chocolate Sauce:** Replace peanut butter with unsweetened, roasted hazelnut butter.

* **Macadamia Buttery Hot Chocolate Sauce:** Replace peanut butter with unsweetened, roasted macadamia nut butter.

* **If you don't have a bittersweet chocolate bar on hand:** In a medium saucepan combine 1 1/4 cups coconut milk, 1 cup unsweetened cocoa powder, 1/3 cup coconut oil or palm shortening, 1/2 cup honey or agave nectar, and 1/2 teaspoon *clear* stevia extract liquid. Bring to a low boil over medium heat, stirring constantly with a wire whisk. Remove from heat; add 1/4 cup peanut butter (or other unsweetened nut butter), and whisk until smooth. For a sweeter taste, add an additional 1/8 to 1/4 teaspoon stevia extract liquid. If too thick, add 1 or 2 tablespoons coconut milk.

2 TABLESPOONS
(w/PALM SHORTENING):
159 calories
2.4 grams protein
13.7 grams carbohydrate
10.6 grams fat
11 milligrams sodium

• **YIELD:** 2 HEAPING CUPS; 16 SERVINGS •

When you open a new jar of nut butter, transfer the entire contents of the jar to a bowl, stir with a large sturdy spoon, return the mixture to the jar, and refrigerate. The nut butter will never separate again and you'll have a smooth and even consistency—guaranteed.

Caffeine-Free Hot Cocoa Mocha Sauce

HANDS-ON: 15 MINUTES • **COOKING:** 4 MINUTES • **YIELD:** 1 1/3 TO 1 1/2 CUPS; 10 SERVINGS

INGREDIENTS

1 to 1 1/4 cups strong brewed Teeccino (Page 249) **or** Roasted Chicory & Dandelion Root Coffee Alternative (Page 248), brewed and allowed to cool

2 teaspoons arrowroot

1/4 cup honey **or** agave nectar; additional 1 tablespoon if needed

1/2 teaspoon *pure* stevia extract powder **or** 1 teaspoon *clear* stevia extract liquid, plain or vanilla-flavored

1/8 teaspoon finely ground unrefined sea salt

1/2 cup unsweetened cocoa powder (spoon into cup and level); additional 1/4 cup if desired

2 tablespoons virgin-pressed coconut oil **or** palm shortening **or** 1/4 cup roasted almond or hazelnut butter, stirred thoroughly before measuring

1 teaspoon pure vanilla extract **or** alcohol-free vanilla flavoring

1/2 to 1 teaspoon natural coffee flavoring, optional

The inspiration for this recipe came from *The Best Ice Cream Maker Cookbook Ever* by Peggy Fallon. As usual, I tweaked her recipe to fit my specifications.

I replaced the coffee with Teeccino or, you could use my Roasted Chicory & Dandelion Root Coffee Alternative. Both are free of caffeine. I replaced the sugar with one-fourth to one-third the amount of honey, then added stevia and vanilla. I substituted coconut oil for the butter (palm shortening or nut butter will work well, too). Peggy's recipe calls for 3/4 cup of cocoa powder. I prefer it with only 1/2 cupful, but you might want to add more. For a stronger coffee flavor, you can add some natural coffee flavoring.

DIRECTIONS

1. In a medium saucepan, whisk the arrowroot into 1 cup brewed Teeccino or Chicory & Dandelion Root Coffee. Add the honey, stevia, and sea salt and bring to a boil over medium heat, stirring to dissolve. Reduce heat to low and whisk in the cocoa powder until smooth. Simmer for 3 minutes.

2. Add the coconut or palm shortening, stirring until melted. If using nut butter, or if adding extra cocoa powder, you may need to stir in an additional 2 to 4 tablespoons Teeccino or Chicory & Dandelion Root Coffee. For a sweeter taste, add an additional tablespoon of honey or an additional 1/8 teaspoon stevia. Blend, taste, and repeat if needed.

2 TABLESPOONS (COCONUT):
75 calories
0.8 gram protein
10.5 grams carbohydrate
3.3 grams fat
22 milligrams sodium

2 TABLESPOONS (ALMOND):
92 calories
1.7 grams protein
11.8 grams carbohydrate
4.3 grams fat
23 milligrams sodium

~Continued next page~

Caffeine-Free Hot Cocoa Mocha Sauce ~ continued

3. Serve immediately or transfer leftover sauce to a heatproof Pyrex bowl, custard cups, or a wide-mouth jar. When cool, cover and refrigerate.

4. Gently warm leftover sauce in a heatproof bowl in a 250° F oven, or in a double boiler or saucepan over very low heat, stirring periodically, or use the bowl-on-a-rack method (Page 74). If too thick, add 1 or 2 tablespoons additional coconut milk.

VARIATIONS

* Use flavored Teeccino––Vanilla Nut, Mocha, Hazelnut, Java, or Almond Amaretto flavor.

* For a full throttle, caffeine-rich coffee sauce, replace the herbal brew in the master recipe with strongly brewed organic coffee or espresso.

This sauce tastes best warm. Try it over Vanilla or Chocolate Ice Dream, strawberries, sliced fresh or frozen bananas, or a colorful fruit salad.

Karly's Carob Sauce

HANDS-ON: 20 MINUTES • **COOKING:** 0 • **YIELD:** 1 3/4 TO 2 CUPS; 14 TO 16 SERVINGS

INGREDIENTS

1 cup pure maple syrup **or** a combination of raw honey and maple syrup

1/3 to 1/2 cup virgin-pressed almond or avocado oil

1/2 cup raw or roasted carob powder, sifted before measuring if lumpy (spoon into cup and level top)

1/8 to 1/4 teaspoon finely ground unrefined sea salt

1 teaspoon pure vanilla extract **or** alcohol-free vanilla flavoring

1/2 teaspoon pure almond extract **or** alcohol-free almond flavoring

DIRECTIONS

1. Combine all ingredients in a blender, Vita-Mix, or food processor or in a medium bowl with a mixer, immersion blender, or large whisk. Mix until smooth.

2. Scrape the mixture into custard cups or wide-mouth jars and refrigerate.

3. If you wish to thin the sauce before serving, heat it briefly using the bowl-on-a-rack method (Page 74), or add a few tablespoons of warm water.

VARIATIONS

* **Karly's Cocoa Sauce:** Replace carob powder with unsweetened cocoa powder.

> **FYI:** Karlene tested this with 6 different oils. Peanut, sesame, walnut, and flax oil added intensely bitter overtones. To avoid rancid oils, look for unrefined, virgin-pressed avocado or almond oil in a dark bottle, preferably in the refrigerator section of natural foods stores. Be sure to keep them refrigerated at home.

One of my cooking students, Karlene Blair, shared this recipe with me, which she got from raw foods chef Becky Johnson. Sometimes Karlene uses carob powder, sometimes unsweetened cocoa powder. She likes to use less oil and a combination of honey and maple syrup, but I find that too sweet, so I increased the oil slightly and decided to use only maple syrup.

Karlene's kids love this sauce served over sliced fruit or ice cream. Some of my recipe testers thought the chocolate version tasted like Hershey's Syrup. It's easy to prepare, and it remains pourable right from the refrigerator, where it will keep for months.

2 TABLESPOONS (CAROB):
122 calories
0.2 gram protein
18.6 grams carbohydrate
5.3 grams fat
18 milligrams sodium

2 TABLESPOONS (COCOA):
121 calories
0.5 gram protein
17 grams carbohydrate
5.7 grams fat
18 milligrams sodium

Use this sauce judiciously—it contains more syrup and oil than the other sauce recipes. Use a delicate hand to drizzle, rather than slather, it over Ice Dream.

Almond Honey Drizzle

PREP: 20 MINUTES • **COOKING:** 0 • **YIELD:** 1 1/4 CUPS + 2 TABLESPOONS; 10 SERVINGS

INGREDIENTS

1/2 cup roasted, unsalted, unsweetened almond butter

1/8 to 1/4 teaspoon finely ground, unrefined sea salt

1/2 cup warm or hot filtered water

2 tablespoons honey or agave nectar; additional tablespoon if desired

1 teaspoon pure vanilla extract **or** alcohol-free vanilla flavoring

1/4 teaspoon *pure* stevia extract powder **or** 1/2 teaspoon *clear* stevia extract liquid

DIRECTIONS

1. Do not discard the oil on top of a new jar of nut butter. Process the contents of the jar in a food processor, Vita-Mix, or in a bowl with a sturdy spoon until smooth. Return the nut butter to the original jar and refrigerate whatever you don't plan to use immediately.

2. Dissolve sea salt in warm water. Add almond butter and mix until smooth. Add the honey, vanilla, and stevia. Blend. For a sweeter taste, add an additional tablespoon of honey.

3. Scrape the sauce into a wide-mouth jar or small bowl. Cover and refrigerate for at least 4 hours or freeze for 1 to 2 hours, until thick, before serving. Use within 1 week or freeze for up to 6 months in a covered glass jar leaving at least 1 inch of space at the top of the jar.

VARIATIONS

* **Cashew Almond Drizzle:** Replace almond butter with lightly roasted cashew butter.

* **Peanut Honey Drizzle:** Replace almond butter with unsalted, unsweetened, unhydrogenated peanut butter. Use organic because peanuts are usually grown in rotation with cotton, one of the most heavily sprayed crops.

To make almond butter and other nut butters more spreadable with fewer calories, I often emulsify them with warm water and a little sea salt. I add a little honey and vanilla to create a delectable sauce for tangy fruit salads or tart fruit compotes. Use this sauce over Apple Apricot Compote or Cranberry Apple compote as a tasty alternative to Ice Dream. It's especially nice for breakfast.

Note: Select a bottled brand of nut butter that doesn't contain added salt, sugar, hydrogenated oil, or soybeans. I prefer to buy it in a bottle rather than from the grinders in stores, which produce a thinner, more airy nut butter. This sauce spoils more quickly than other dessert sauces, so if you make a large batch, freeze what you don't plan to use within a week; otherwise, it will sour in the refrigerator.

2 TABLESPOONS (ALMOND):
100 calories
1.9 grams protein
6.3 grams carbohydrate
7.4 grams fat
21 milligrams sodium

2 TABLESPOONS (CASHEW):
95 calories
2.2 grams protein
7.1 grams carbohydrate
6.3 grams fat
22 milligrams sodium

2 TABLESPOONS (PEANUT):
97 calories
3.3 grams protein
6.1 grams carbohydrate
6.6 grams fat
22 milligrams sodium

Caramel Sauce

HANDS-ON: 20 MINUTES • **COOKING:** 5 TO 6 MINUTES • **YIELD:** 1 1/3 TO 1 1/2 CUPS; 10 TO 12 SERVINGS

INGREDIENTS

1 cup unsweetened premium coconut milk (not lite)

2 teaspoon arrowroot powder

1/4 cup + 2 tablespoons cool or cold filtered water

3/4 cup maple syrup, gluten-free brown rice syrup, honey **or** agave nectar (see notes above)

1/4 teaspoon finely ground unrefined sea salt

1 teaspoon pure vanilla extract **or** alcohol-free vanilla flavoring

1/2 teaspoon natural caramel flavoring, optional; additional 1/4 teaspoon if needed

2 to 3 tablespoons virgin-pressed coconut oil **or** palm shortening, optional

DIRECTIONS

1. In a small saucepan, dissolve the arrowroot into the coconut milk. Bring to a low boil over medium heat, stirring to dissolve. Cook for about 1 minute until the mixture thickens. Cover and remove from heat. Add the optional palm or coconut oil.

2. Combine the water and syrup in a heavy 1 1/2- to 2-quart saucepan. Do not use a pan with a dark, non-stick interior or you will find it difficult to tell when the syrup darkens. Stir over medium-high heat until the syrup dissolves into the water, 1 or 2 minutes. Increase the heat to high. Immediately cover the saucepan tightly, and boil the syrup for 2 minutes without stirring. (Set a timer—don't guess.)

3. Uncover the saucepan and continue to boil the syrup, without stirring, until it begins to darken around the edges. Gently swirl the pan by the handle and continue cooking until it turns deep amber (the color of iced tea) and begins to smoke, about 1 or 2 more minutes. Watch carefully; it can go from perfectly browned to burnt very quickly. Remove from heat.

Caramel is made by cooking sugar to the point that it melts and then begins to burn. Old cookbooks referred to it as burnt sugar. Butterscotch is similar, except that it contains butter. To turn either one of these into a sauce, recipes call for adding butter, cream, water, or some other liquid while the syrup is still hot; otherwise the sauce will turn into hard candy.

I experimented with various sweeteners. I like the maple syrup version best. It contains fewer calories per tablespoon than honey. I find honey makes the sauce too sweet for my taste. Using coconut milk in place of cream cuts the fat and the calories.

2 TABLESPOONS (MAPLE):
110 calories
0.4 gram protein
18.1 grams carbohydrate
4.1 grams fat
34 milligrams sodium

2 TABLESPOONS (RICE SYRUP):
122 calories
0.6 gram protein
21 grams carbohydrate
4 grams fat
35 milligrams sodium

2 TABLESPOONS (HONEY W/COCONUT OIL):
156 calories
0.5 gram protein
23.2 grams carbohydrate
6.7 grams fat
33 milligrams sodium

~Continued next page~

Note: If you decide to use honey, agave nectar, or sorghum syrup, which make a much sweeter sauce, I recommend that you add 2 or 3 tablespoons of coconut oil or palm shortening to the milk before you add it to the hot syrup.

Caramel Sauce ~ continued

4. Whisk in half of the warm coconut milk mixture. It will steam and bubble up furiously; keep stirring. Add the remaining coconut milk, vanilla, and optional caramel flavoring, and whisk until smooth. If sauce seems thin, simmer and stir over medium heat for a few more minutes to thicken.

5. Allow the sauce to cool slightly, and then serve. Refrigerate any unused sauce in a covered heatproof bowl, custard cups, or a wide-mouth jar.

6. Serve leftover sauce at room temperature if pourable, or gently warm in a heatproof bowl in a toaster oven at 250° F, or in a saucepan over very low heat, stirring periodically, or use the bowl-on-a-rack method (Page 74).

VARIATIONS

* **Lemon Caramel Sauce:** This adds a mild citrus flavor and helps keep the sauce from crystallizing. Add a few drops of lemon juice in step #2, then 2 tablespoons freshly squeezed lemon juice at the end of step #4. Taste and add an additional 1 or 2 tablespoons lemon juice if desired.

* **Butterscotch Sauce:** Replace caramel flavoring with butterscotch flavoring.

• •How Do You Know When the Caramel Sauce is Done Cooking? • • • • •

The authors of *The All New All Purpose Joy of Cooking* describe it perfectly:

"As the syrup approaches the caramelization point, the bubbles in the saucepan become smaller and quieter. Then, around the edges of the pan, the first signs of darkening will appear. Begin swirling the pan by the handle to disperse the heated edges of the syrup toward the cooler center. Continue to cook the syrup until it becomes a deep amber color and begins to smoke, but stop before it becomes reddish or mahogany.

"If overcooked, the syrup will taste bitter and salty. [This will be obvious after it cools and you taste it.] Remove the syrup from the heat immediately and add the butter and cream, water, or some other liquid to stop the cooking. Be prepared for the caramel to rear up into a sputtering, foaming mass. If adding water [or coconut milk], as in the making of caramel syrup, stand back to prevent yourself from being spattered. Stir the sauce briskly to amalgamate it..."

Source: Rombauer, Irma S, and Marion Rombauer Becker. *The All New All Purpose Joy of Cooking.* New York: Scribner, 1997.

Caramel sauce gets dangerously hot. To avoid getting burned, use a large enough pot, wear oven mittens, and stand back when stirring in the coconut milk.

Apricot Sauce

HANDS-ON: 20 MINUTES • **COOKING:** 30 MINUTES • **YIELD:** 3 1/2 TO 4 CUPS; 16 SERVINGS

INGREDIENTS

1/2 cup honey, agave nectar, **or** maple syrup; additional 1 tablespoon if needed

1/4 cup filtered water

3 pounds ripe apricots, halved and pitted (about 8 cups)

1/4 to 1/2 teaspoon *pure* stevia extract powder **or** 1/2 to 1 teaspoon *clear* stevia extract liquid (start with less; add more only if needed)

DIRECTIONS

1. Combine the honey, water, and apricots (or quartered peaches) in a heavy 2- to 3-quart saucepan. Cover and bring to boil over high heat and stir for 3 minutes until the syrup dissolves. Reduce heat to medium. Uncover and cook, stirring frequently, for 25 to 30 minutes or until the fruit breaks down and the mixture thickens.

2. Remove from heat and add stevia. Purée the mixture in a blender, Vita-Mix, or food processor. For a sweeter taste, add an additional 1/8 teaspoon stevia extract powder. Repeat if needed.

3. Transfer the sauce to wide-mouth jars or Pyrex bowls with lids. When cool, cover and refrigerate. Freeze what you don't plan to use within 3 to 4 weeks, leaving at least 1 inch of space at the top of the jar.

4. Serve close to room temperature, or warm briefly in a small saucepan over low heat, or use the bowl-on-a-rack method (Page 74).

VARIATIONS

* **Peach Sauce:** Replace apricots with fresh peaches.

* **Nectarine Sauce:** Replace apricots with fresh nectarines.

To make this sauce, wait for fresh apricots grown in your state, region, or bioregion. If you can't find apricots, substitute peaches or nectarines, and cut them into quarters. You can serve this sauce slightly warm, chilled, or at room temperature. Try it over Vanilla, Chocolate, Ginger, Coffee, or Avocado Ice Dream. It also tastes great spooned over fresh blueberries, strawberries, or cubed honeydew melon sprinkled with shredded, unsweetened coconut or chopped toasted almonds or pecans.

Note: If you tolerate yogurt, you can stir this sauce into plain goat or cow milk yogurt to produce naturally-flavored yogurt without all of the sugar used in commercial brands.

FYI: The inspiration for this recipe came from *Cooking Light* magazine. I changed the type of sweetener and simplified the preparation.

1/4 CUP (APRICOT):
81 calories
1.2 grams protein
18.2 grams carbohydrate
0.3 gram fat
1 milligram sodium

1/4 CUP (PEACH):
76 calories
0.6 gram protein
18.1 grams carbohydrate
0.1 gram fat
0 milligrams sodium

Raspberry Sauce

HANDS-ON: 20 MINUTES • **COOKING:** 0 • **YIELD:** 1 CUP; 8 SERVINGS

INGREDIENTS

1 pint (2 cups) fresh raspberries rinsed and drained **or** a 12 ounce package frozen (unsweetened) raspberries transferred to a bowl while frozen and allowed to thaw

2 tablespoons honey **or** agave nectar

2 tablespoons orange juice **or** 1 tablespoon orange liqueur (e.g. Triple Sec) + 1 tablespoon water

1/8 to 1/4 teaspoon *pure* stevia extract powder **or** 1/4 to 1/2 teaspoon *clear* stevia extract liquid (start with less; add more only if needed)

DIRECTIONS

1. In a medium saucepan over medium heat, bring raspberries, honey, stevia, and water to a boil. Reduce heat and simmer for 3 to 5 minutes, stirring a few times.

2. Place a fine mesh strainer or sieve over a medium-size bowl. Pour the fruit mixture into the strainer and, using a flexible rubber spatula, press the pulp through the sieve.

3. Press firmly, and periodically scrape the inside of the sieve clear of seeds, which can otherwise block the holes. Do not waste any of the precious pulp. Continue to press until you are left with just 1 or 2 heaping tablespoons of stiff, clumped-together seeds.

   Scrape the bottom of the strainer to get the pulp that sticks to it. Discard the seeds and skins at the top of the strainer.

4. With a wire whisk or sturdy spoon, stir in the orange juice or liqueur and stevia. For a sweeter taste, add an additional 1/8 teaspoon stevia extract powder or 1/4 teaspoon stevia extract liquid.

5. Refrigerate until ready to serve. Use within 1 week or freeze.

VARIATIONS

* **For a thicker sauce:** Dissolve 1 tablespoon arrowroot in 2 tablespoons cool or cold water. Add this to the sauce, then simmer over medium heat for 2 or 3 minutes, stirring to thicken.

* **Blackberry Sauce:** Replace raspberries with blackberries in the master recipe above.

* **Boysenberry Sauce:** Replace raspberries with boysenberries in the master recipe above.

This recipe yields a colorful, low-calorie topping for Ice Dream. I like it best on Chocolate, Carob, or Vanilla Ice Dream. Dress up your morning melon or peaches with this tasty topping, and add a sprinkle of shredded, unsweetened coconut if you like.

Note: Consider doubling the recipe as this sauce freezes well. Rinse fresh raspberries just before using and don't soak them in water for any length of time, or they'll become soggy and lose flavor.

2 TABLESPOONS:
37 calories
0.3 gram protein
8.2 grams carbohydrate
0.2 gram fat
0 milligrams sodium

Blueberry Sauce

HANDS-ON: 20 MINUTES • **COOKING:** 8 MINUTES • **YIELD:** 4 CUPS; 16 SERVINGS

INGREDIENTS

4 cups fresh blueberries, rinsed and drained **or** 5 cups frozen blueberries

1/4 cup honey, agave nectar, **or** 1/3 cup maple syrup

1 pinch unrefined mineral-rich sea salt

2 tablespoons arrowroot powder

1/4 to 1/2 teaspoon *pure* stevia extract powder **or** 1/2 to 1 teaspoon *clear* stevia extract liquid (start with less; add more only if needed)

2 tablespoons fresh lemon juice **or** orange juice

DIRECTIONS

1. Combine the blueberries and honey in a heavy 2- to 3-quart saucepan. Cook over medium heat until the berries bubble and release their juices, about 5 minutes.

2. Dissolve the arrowroot and stevia in lemon or orange juice and add to the fruit. Bring the mixture to a low boil. Reduce heat to medium-low and cook for 2 to 4 more minutes until the mixture begins to thicken. Remove from heat and allow to cool.

3. For a smoother sauce, mash or purée half the berries with a potato masher or pulse on and off in a Vita-Mix, blender, or food processor fitted with a metal blade. For a sweeter taste, add an additional 1/8 to 1/4 teaspoon stevia and/or 1 tablespoon honey. Repeat if needed.

4. Transfer the mixture to wide-mouth jars or glass bowls. Cover when cool, and refrigerate. When cold to the touch, freeze what you don't plan to use within 3 or 4 weeks, leaving at least 1 inch of space at the top of the jar.

5. Serve close to room temperature, or warm briefly in a small saucepan over low heat, or use the bowl-on-a-rack method (Page 74).

If you like blueberries, you'll like this chunky fruit sauce. It cooks up quickly, and it goes nicely over Vanilla, Cocoa, Dark Chocolate, Avocado, Macaroon, Lemon, or Ginger Ice Dream. It also makes a great stand-in for jelly in Peanut Butter & Jelly Ice Dream.

For a delicious finale to breakfast, lunch, or dinner, spoon leftover sauce over sliced melon, peaches, or nectarines and drizzle with coconut butter (not the oil) or sprinkle with shredded, unsweetened coconut.

2 TABLESPOONS (BLUEBERRY):
44 calories
0.2 gram protein
10.6 grams carbohydrate
0.1 gram fat
2 milligrams sodium

2 TABLESPOONS (STRAWBERRY):
35 calories
0.2 gram protein
8.2 grams carbohydrate
0.1 gram fat
0 milligrams sodium

~Continued next page~

Blueberry Sauce ~ continued

VARIATION

* **Strawberry Sauce:** Replace blueberries with 1 quart of rinsed, hulled, and sliced fresh strawberries or 1 pound of frozen, unsweetened strawberries, transferred to a bowl while frozen and allowed to thaw. Do not slice the frozen berries. The bowl will catch all the juices, which you'll cook with the fruit. In step #1, reduce cooking time to 3 minutes if using frozen strawberries; in step #2 reduce cooking time to 1 to 2 minutes for fresh or frozen strawberries. This sauce does not store as well. It loses its bright color within a few days.

If you tolerate yogurt, you can stir this sauce into plain goat or cow milk yogurt to produce naturally-flavored yogurt without all of the sugar used in commercial brands.

Cherry Sauce

HANDS-ON: 20 MINUTES • **COOKING:** 25 MINUTES • **YIELD:** 3 ½ CUPS; 16 SERVINGS

INGREDIENTS

3 pounds fresh sweet cherries (about 8 cups pitted fresh **or** 9 cups frozen):
Bing, Rainier, or Queen Anne variety

1/4 cup honey **or** agave nectar; additional 1 or 2 tablespoons as needed

1/8 to 1/4 teaspoon unrefined, mineral-rich sea salt

1/4 to 1/2 teaspoon *pure* stevia extract powder **or** ½ to 1 teaspoon *clear* stevia extract liquid (start with less; add more only if needed)

1 tablespoon fresh lemon juice **or** orange juice

3 tablespoons arrowroot powder dissolved in

1/4 cup cool or cold filtered water

For the best flavor, wait until summer when fresh cherries are available from your state, region, or bioregion. If you can't wait, use frozen dark sweet cherries (they're naturally sweet with no added sugar), which are sold in the freezer section of supermarkets and natural foods stores.

Serve this sauce with breakfast or after dinner over cubed melon sprinkled with shredded, unsweetened coconut or chopped, toasted nuts.

**1 SERVING
(3-1/2 TABLESPOONS):**
91 calories
1 gram protein
19.9 gram carbohydrate
0.8 gram fat
12 milligrams sodium

DIRECTIONS

1. *If using fresh cherries,* remove the stems. Rinse cherries and pat dry with paper towels. Working over a large bowl to catch the juices, cut each cherry in half with a paring knife; remove the pit with the tip of the knife and drop the cherries into the bowl. Or (better and safer), use a cherry pitter. Either way, use one hand to push out the pit, and place the other under each cherry, making sure you catch and discard one pit for every cherry.

   If using frozen cherries, pour into a bowl and allow to thaw, and then measure to make sure you have the right amount.

2. Combine cherries, honey, and sea salt in a heavy 3- or 4-quart pot. Cover and bring to boil over high heat. Remove the lid and stir for 3 minutes until the syrup dissolves. Reduce heat to medium, uncover, and cook for 20 minutes or until the fruit breaks down and the mixture becomes slightly thick; stir frequently.

3. Remove from heat. Process the mixture in a blender, Vita-Mix, or food processor fitted with a metal blade until mostly smooth (leave some chunks). Return the mixture to the pot. Add the stevia, lemon or orange

~Continued next page~

Cherry Sauce ~ continued

juice, and arrowroot dissolved in water. For a sweeter taste, add an additional 1/8 teaspoon stevia and/or 1 tablespoon honey. Blend, taste, and repeat if needed. Bring the mixture to a boil, stirring periodically. Reduce heat to medium-low and simmer to thicken, about 2 to 3 minutes.

4. Store in wide-mouth glass jars or bowls with lids. When cool, cover and refrigerate. When cold to the touch, freeze what you don't plan to use within 3 or 4 weeks, leaving at least 1 inch of space at the top of the jar.

5. Serve cold or at room temperature, or warm briefly in a small saucepan over low heat, or use the bowl-on-a-rack method (Page 74).

If you tolerate yogurt, you can stir this sauce into plain goat or cow milk yogurt to produce naturally-flavored yogurt without all of the sugar used in commercial brands.

Mango Sauce

PREP: 30 MINUTES • **COOKING:** 30 MINUTES • **YIELD:** 4 CUPS; 16 SERVINGS

INGREDIENTS

4 cups coarsely chopped, ripe fresh mango from 2 (1-pound) mangoes **or** 1 1/2 pounds frozen mango cubes (a 24-ounce bag)

1/2 cup filtered water

1/8 to 1/4 teaspoon finely ground unrefined sea salt

1 tablespoon arrowroot powder dissolved in

2 tablespoons cool or cold filtered water

2 tablespoons fresh orange juice **or** lime juice, additional 1 or 2 tablespoons as needed

1/4 to 1/2 teaspoon *pure* stevia extract powder **or** 1/2 to 1 teaspoon *clear* stevia extract liquid (start with less; use more only if needed)

1 tablespoon honey **or** agave nectar, optional; additional tablespoon if needed

This sauce makes a great topping for plain Chocolate or Vanilla Ice Dream. You can serve the leftover sauce over cubed honeydew melon, strawberries, or a mixed fruit salad.

How to slice a mango: Wash mangoes, cut in half and, while holding the fruit over a bowl, twist to separate halves. Cut the mango pulp from the seeds and scoop the flesh from the skin with a spoon. Discard the pit.

2 TABLESPOONS:
37 calories
0.2 gram protein
8.7 grams carbohydrate
0.1 gram fat
13 milligrams sodium

DIRECTIONS

1. Combine the mango, water, and sea salt in a 2-quart saucepan. Cover and bring to boil over medium-high heat. Reduce the heat to medium-low, and, stirring periodically, simmer fresh mango for about 10 minutes or frozen mango for about 5 minutes, or until the fruit breaks down and the mixture becomes soft.

2. For a chunky sauce, mash the fruit in the pot with a potato masher. For a creamy sauce, purée the mixture in a blender, Vita-Mix, or food processor until smooth. Return the mixture to the saucepan. Add the stevia.

3. Dissolve the arrowroot in 2 tablespoons water and add this to the pot along with the orange or lime juice. Bring to a low boil over medium heat and stir to thicken, 2 or 3 more minutes. For a more tart taste, add an additional 1 to 2 tablespoons orange or lime juice. For a sweeter taste, add an additional 1/4 teaspoon stevia and/or 1 tablespoon honey. Repeat if needed.

4. Transfer the sauce to wide-mouth jars or glass bowls. Cover when cool, and refrigerate. When cold to the touch, freeze what you don't plan to use within 3 or 4 weeks, leaving at least 1 inch of room at the top of the jar.

~Continued next page~

Shopping for mangoes

Mangoes are ready to use when they yield to pressure and smell slightly fragrant and fruity. I like to buy an extra mango, just in case one turns out bad, which you won't discover until you cut it open. If hard, allow them to ripen at room temperature in an open bowl for several days. Add a ripe apple or banana to the bowl and they'll ripen faster.

Mango Sauce ~ continued

5. Serve close to room temperature, or warm briefly in a small saucepan over low heat, or use the bowl-on-a-rack method (Page 74).

VARIATION

* **Mango Ginger Sauce:** In step #3, add 2 or 3 teaspoons juice from freshly grated and squeezed gingerroot (Page 33). You may add additional ginger juice 1 teaspoon at a time to taste.

If you tolerate yogurt, you can stir this sauce into plain goat or cow milk yogurt to produce naturally-flavored yogurt without all of the sugar used in commercial brands.

Homemade Applesauce

PREP: 30 MINUTES • **COOKING:** 15 TO 45 MINUTES • **YIELD:** ABOUT 6 CUPS; 8 SERVINGS

INGREDIENTS

4 pounds sweet or tart-sweet apples (8 large to 12 medium), washed, cored, peeled, diced, one type: *Gravenstein, Yellow Newton, Pink Lady, Ginger Gold, Early Gold, Braeburn, Gala, Fuji, Cortland, Macoun, Jonathan,* or *Jonagold*

1 cup unsweetened apple juice **or** apple cider

1 teaspoon ground cinnamon, ginger **or** apple pie spice

1/8 to 1/4 teaspoon unrefined sea salt, optional

1/4 to 1/2 teaspoon *pure* stevia extract powder **or** ½ to 1 teaspoon *clear* stevia extract liquid (start with less; add more if needed), optional

Applesauce à la Mode? Not a bad idea if you use Vanilla Ice Dream. I added this recipe to the book because so many of my cookies and bars call for apple sauce to add moisture without extra fat. Why make your own applesauce when you can buy it so readily? Homemade applesauce tastes better than anything from a can or bottle. It also costs less than organic, unsweetened apple sauce. You can sweeten it simply with apple juice and stevia.

3/4 CUP:
157 calories
0.3 gram protein
37.5 grams carbohydrate
0.7 gram fat
6 milligrams sodium

DIRECTIONS

1. If using a pressure cooker, boil the juice down to reduce it to 1/2 cupful. Check it by pouring into a liquid measuring cup.

2. Combine all ingredients except stevia in a 6-quart stainless steel pressure cooker, a wide 3- to 4-quart saucepan, or a non-reactive Dutch oven.

To pressure cook: Add the apple juice to the pressure cooker; bring to boil and cook until reduced to 1/2 cup. Add remaining ingredients (except stevia) to the pressure cooker. Lock the lid in place. Bring to full pressure, then reduce heat to medium-low and cook for 15 minutes.

To boil: Cover and bring to boil over medium heat. Reduce heat to low. Simmer until tender, thick, and jammy, 45 to 60 minutes. If too watery, remove lid and simmer to thicken.

3. **For a coarse texture (best for baking),** mash the apples against the side of the pot with a wide wooden spoon or press and blend with a potato masher.

For a smoother texture, purée the mixture in batches in a blender, Vita-Mix or a food processor fitted with a metal blade.

For either method: For a sweeter taste, add the smallest amount of stevia listed above. Blend, taste, and repeat if needed.

~Continued next page~

FYI: Use the timesaving variation below if you own a non-electric hand food mill (e.g., a Moulinex, Foley, Cuispro, Norpro, or other).

Homemade Applesauce ~ continued

4. Serve hot, warm, or at room temperature. Transfer the sauce to wide-mouth jars or glass bowls that have covers. Cover when cool, and refrigerate. When cold to the touch, freeze what you don't plan to use within 2 or 3 weeks, leaving at least 1 inch of room at the top of the jar.

5. Serve cold or at room temperature, or warm briefly in a heatproof bowl in a toaster oven, or use the bowl the bowl-on-a-rack method (Page 74).

VARIATIONS

*   Wash apples, but don't peel or core. Remove stems and cut fruit into 1 1/2-inch pieces. Combine ingredients and cook as above. Transfer cooked apples and pan juices to a food mill fitted with a medium disk. Purée, leaving skin, seeds, and core behind. Now taste and add the optional sweetener.

*   Omit ground spices. Add **one** of the following: 4 (3-inch) pieces of cinnamon sticks, 2 to 3 pieces of star anise, 4 (1/2-inch thick) slices of fresh gingerroot, or 4 whole cloves. Cook as above. Remove and discard cinnamon, star anise, and ginger or cloves before puréeing the cooked sauce.

*   **Apple Apricot, Apple Peach, or Apple Cherry Sauce:** Replace 1 pound of apples with pitted apricots, peaches, or sweet cherries.

Try to make this during the fall and winter when you can get locally grown apples from an orchard, farmer's market, or a natural foods store that supports local farmers. If you have to buy apples from out of state, select those grown as close to home as possible (from the U.S. if you live here, rather than imports from New Zealand). If you have the freezer space, make large batches and freeze some for the months ahead.

chapter 9

à la Mode

Best Bites

Apple Apricot Compote

HANDS-ON: 30 MINUTES • **COOKING:** 30 MINUTES • **YIELD:** 6 CUPS/8 SERVINGS

INGREDIENTS

1/3 to 1/2 cup dried, unsulphured, unsweetened dried (preferably Turkish) apricots

1/3 to 1/2 cup raisins

3 to 3 1/2 pounds tart-sweet apples (6 large or 8 medium; 1 to 3 varieties):
   Braeburn, Cortland, Cameo, Fuji, Gala, Ginger Gold, Pink Lady, Sundowner, or other

1/2 cup filtered water

1 teaspoon ground cinnamon **or** apple pie spice

1 tablespoon arrowroot powder dissolved in 3 tablespoons cold water, optional

1/8 to 1/4 teaspoon *pure* stevia extract powder **or** 1/4 to 1/2 teaspoon *clear* stevia extract liquid **or** 1 to 2 tablespoons honey, optional (taste before adding)

1 recipe (1- to 1 1/2-quarts) Vanilla or Cinnamon Ice Dream (Page 78 or 82), optional

DIRECTIONS

1. Chop or cut dried apricots into 1/4- to 1/2-inch pieces with kitchen shears or a knife. Add them to a 3- to 4-quart pot with the raisins. Wash and core the apples. (Peel if they've been waxed.) Halve, quarter, and then cut into 1/4-inch to 1/2-inch thick slices. Layer over dried fruit and sprinkle with spices.

2. Add the water. Cover and bring to boil without stirring. Reduce heat. Simmer until tender and saucy, 25 to 35 minutes. Uncover and stir gently. If much liquid remains, remove lid and cook away the juices or add dissolved arrowroot. Simmer and stir until thick. For a sweeter taste, add stevia, 1/8 teaspoon at a time, or honey, 1 tablespoon at a time. Repeat as needed.

3. Serve warm or close to room temperature, topped with freshly churned Ice Dream or solidly frozen Ice Dream that has been softened at room temperature for 20 to 30 minutes.

This sweet, simmered fruit medley makes a great alternative to apple pie during the fall, winter, and spring. It's easier to make and more nutritious because it's sweetened with dried fruit rather than sugar. You can vary the flavor by using different kinds of apples and spices. Serve leftovers at room temperature, or warm in a heatproof bowl in a toaster oven. Top with Ice Dream, or serve it for breakfast topped with chopped, toasted nuts.

Note: If you don't have apple or pumpkin pie spice, substitute 3/4 teaspoon ground cinnamon, 1/2 teaspoon dried ginger (powder), 1/4 teaspoon ground nutmeg, 1/4 teaspoon dried orange zest, and 1/8 teaspoon ground cloves.

1 SERVING WITHOUT TOPPING (ABOUT 3/4 CUP):
152 calories
0.7 gram protein
35.7 grams carbohydrate
0.6 gram fat
2 milligrams sodium

~Continued next page~

> **FYI:** Turkish dried apricots taste much sweeter than other varieties. They usually eliminate the need for added sweeteners. They can be found in natural foods stores and specialty markets. If you use conventional American-grown dried apricots, use the higher volume of dried fruit listed and replace the water with apple, peach, pear, apricot, or white grape juice, or add the optional stevia to produce a sweet flavor.

Apple Apricot Compote ~ continued

4. Refrigerate leftover compote in wide-mouth jars or Pyrex containers with lids. Use within 5 days or freeze. Leave 1 ½ to 2 inches of space in the top of the jar, and chill to refrigerator temperature before freezing to prevent the glass from cracking.

VARIATIONS

* **Apple, Prune & Apricot Compote with 5-Spice:** Replace cinnamon or pie spice with 1 1/2 teaspoons Chinese 5-spice powder and replace the raisins with pitted prunes.

* Replace cinnamon or pie spice with 2 teaspoons ground caraway, anise, or fennel seeds, or 1 tablespoon peeled and grated fresh gingerroot.

Poached Pears with Raisins & Dried Apricots

HANDS-ON: 20 MINUTES • **COOKING:** 25 TO 30 MINUTES • **YIELD:** 12 SERVINGS

INGREDIENTS

1/3 to 1/2 cups raisins, depending upon desired sweetness

1/3 to 1/2 cup dried, pitted, unsulphured (preferably Turkish) apricots, coarsely chopped

1 1/2 teaspoons apple pie spice, pumpkin pie spice, **or** cinnamon (see variations below)

6 medium-size ripe, fragrant, but firm, unblemished pears (2 1/2 to 3 pounds total):

Bosc, Comice, Bartlett, Spartlet, Anjou, or other variety

Coarsely grated zest of 1/2 orange or tangerine, colored part only, optional

1 1/3 cups filtered water, divided

1 tablespoon arrowroot powder

1 recipe (1 to 1 ½ quarts) Vanilla, Cocoa, Dark Chocolate, Chocolate Hazelnut, Cinnamon, **or** Ginger Ice Dream (see index for recipes), optional

DIRECTIONS

1. Chop or cut dried apricots into 1/4- to 1/2-inch pieces with kitchen shears or a knife. Combine them with the raisins and spices in a 3- to 4-quart pot or a shallow 12- to 13-inch sauté pan. Wash and peel pears, then cut in half from end to end. Scoop out and discard the seed center with a teaspoon or melon baller.

2. Arrange the pear halves cut side down over the dried fruit. Add the optional citrus zest and 1 cup of the water. Cover and bring to boil over medium heat without stirring. Reduce heat and simmer until fork tender, 20 to 25 minutes. Meanwhile, dissolve arrowroot in 1/4 cup of cold water. Set aside.

Don created this recipe more than 15 years ago, and I've tweaked it a few times since to arrive at this version. Raisins and dried apricots sweeten this dessert without refined sugar, providing extra antioxidants along with a sweet taste. Serve the pears warm or close to room temperature, unadorned, or topped with chopped, toasted nuts or scoops of Ice Dream.

Note: If possible, use Turkish dried apricots; they taste sweeter than other varieties of dried apricots, eliminating the need for added sweeteners in this dessert. Look for them in natural foods stores and specialty markets. If you must use conventional dried apricots, use the higher volume of dried fruit listed below and replace the water with apple, peach, pear, apricot, or white grape juice to produce a sweet flavor.

1 PEAR HALF WITHOUT TOPPING:
88 calories
0.6 grams protein
20.7 grams carbohydrate
0.4 gram fat
1 milligram sodium

~Continued next page~

Poached Pears with Raisins & Dried Apricots ~ continued

3. With a slotted spoon, transfer the pears to a platter, 12 serving bowls, or 3 to 6 Pyrex containers, leaving the dried fruit and juices in the pan. Stir the arrowroot mixture, then add it to the pan. Simmer over medium-high heat and stir until thick and saucy, then spoon over pears. Serve warm or allow to cool, then cover and refrigerate.

4. Spoon 1 or 2 pear halves onto each serving plate with some of the sauce. Top with a scoop of Ice Dream and serve. Refrigerate the leftovers and use within 4 days.

VARIATIONS

* **To make your own pie spice:** Combine 1 teaspoon ground cinnamon, 1/3 teaspoon dried ginger, 1/8 teaspoon ground nutmeg, and 1/8 teaspoon ground cloves.

* **Poached Pears with Raisins, Dried Apricots & Anise:** Replace pie spice with 2 teaspoons ground cinnamon.

* **Poached Pears with Raisins, Dried Apricots & Anise:** Replace pie spice with 2 teaspoons of whole anise seeds or ground anise powder for a licorice-like flavor.

* **Poached Pears with Dried Apricots, Prunes & 5-Spice:** Replace raisins with thinly sliced, pitted prunes, and pie spice with 1 1/2 to 2 teaspoons Chinese 5-spice powder.

* **Poached Pears with Raisins, Dried Apricots & Ginger:** Replace pie spice with 1 1/2 to 2 tablespoons peeled and finely minced or grated fresh gingerroot.

Apple Crisp

HANDS-ON: 30 MINUTES • **COOKING:** 1 HOUR • **YIELD:** 9 SERVINGS

INGREDIENTS

Filling:

2 to 2 1/2 pounds tart-sweet apples (1 to 3 varieties), cored, peeled if desired, then halved and thinly sliced (6 to 8 packed cups):
Gala, Fuji, Pink Lady, Braeburn, Cameo, Sundowner, Ginger Gold, Melrose, or Cortland

1 tablespoon arrowroot powder

1/4 teaspoon finely ground, unrefined sea salt

1/4 teaspoon *pure* stevia extract powder **or** 1/2 teaspoon *clear* stevia extract liquid

1/3 cup apple juice, apple cider, pear juice **or** freshly squeezed orange juice

Topping:

1 cup rolled oats, regular **or** quick cooking, **or** rolled brown rice flakes **or** quinoa flakes.

1/2 cup mesquite flour, sorghum flour, or brown rice flour

1 teaspoon ground apple pie spice **or** pumpkin pie spice (see notes above)

1/4 to 1/3 cup palm shortening **or** virgin-pressed coconut oil, at room temperature

1/3 cup maple syrup, honey, **or** agave nectar

1/4 cup toasted and finely chopped pecans, almonds, or walnuts (Page 75) **or** unsweetened, sulfite-free, finely shredded coconut

1 recipe (1 to 1 1/2 quarts) Vanilla or Cinnamon Ice Dream (Page 78 or 82), optional

DIRECTIONS

1. Preheat oven to 400° F. Lightly grease a 2-quart baking dish such as a 9x9x2-inch baking pan or 11x7-inch baking dish, a 9-inch deep-dish pie plate, or 12-inch oval gratin dish.

You can make the cookie-like topping for this dish with mesquite flour (also called mesquite powder), which is made by pulverizing the pods of the mesquite tree, which is native to Arizona. You can buy this unusual flour at some farmers' markets or online. Both sorghum flour and brown rice flour work equally well. If you suffer from Celiac Sprue, seek out certified gluten-free rolled oats, or substitute quinoa flakes or rolled brown rice flakes, sold in natural foods stores or online.

Note: I list several sweetener choices. Use maple syrup for a mildly sweet flavor, honey for a sweeter taste, and agave nectar if you're cooking for vegans or anyone who doesn't use honey. Vary this simple recipe with different kinds of apples, pears, or spices. Leftovers are delicious warmed in a heatproof bowl in a toaster oven, served solo or topped with Ice Dream.

1 SERVING
WITHOUT ICE DREAM:
253 calories
2.8 grams protein
39.5 grams carbohydrate
9.4 grams fat
23 milligrams sodium

~Continued next page~

> **FYI:** If you don't have apple pie spice or pumpkin pie spice, substitute 3/4 teaspoon ground cinnamon, 1/2 teaspoon dried ginger (powder), 1/4 teaspoon ground nutmeg, 1/4 teaspoon dried orange zest, and 1/8 teaspoon ground cloves. See variations below for other spice options.

Apple Crisp ~ continued

2. Place the sliced apples in a 3 1/2- to 4-quart mixing bowl. Sprinkle with arrowroot, sea salt, and stevia. Toss to coat. Pour on the apple juice and stir to distribute. Transfer the mixture, including any juices, to the prepared pan. Press down on the apples to compress in the pan. Don't worry if the apples look like they're bursting out of the pan; they'll shrink down as they cook.

3. If coconut oil is semi-solid, melt it over low heat, then set aside to cool. To prepare the topping, mix the dry ingredients. Work in the shortening or oil, then the syrup, using a pastry cutter or large sturdy spoon, and then rub the mixture between your palms. Toss in the nuts. Distribute the topping evenly over the fruit.

4. Tightly cover the baking dish with a glass lid or aluminum foil. If using foil, cut a piece of parchment paper to fit over only the fruit and crisp; place it over the filling, then cover with a larger piece of aluminum foil. Crimp the edges to seal.

5. Bake until fruit is soft when pierced with a fork and juices are bubbling, 35 to 45 minutes. Uncover and return the dish to the oven until the topping is golden, 10 to 20 more minutes.

6. Serve hot or warm, with or without a scoop of Vanilla Ice Dream.

7. When cool, re-cover with parchment and foil or a glass lid, or transfer leftover portions to heatproof containers with lids and refrigerate. Freeze what you don't plan to consume within 5 days.

Variations

*   **Apple & Pear Crisp:** Use a mixture of half apples and half pears in the recipe above.

*   **Pear Crisp:** Replace apples with Red Crimson, Barlett, Spartlett, Anjou or Comice Pears.

*   Replace pie spice with 1/3 teaspoon cinnamon plus 1/8 teaspoon nutmeg, or 1/4 teaspoon ground cinnamon plus 1/4 teaspoon ground ginger (powder), **or** 1 teaspoon Chinese 5-spice powder.

Baked Blueberry Peach Compote

HANDS-ON: 5 MINUTES • **COOKING:** 45 TO 60 MINUTES • **YIELD:** 4 TO 5 CUPS (6 TO 8 SERVINGS)

INGREDIENTS

2 (16 ounce) packages frozen peaches (about 4 cups frozen), partially thawed if desired

2/3 of a (12 ounce) package frozen blueberries (about 2 cups frozen); do not defrost

1/4 teaspoon finely ground unrefined sea salt, optional

1/4 teaspoon *pure* stevia extract powder **or** 1/2 teaspoon *clear* stevia extract liquid, optional

1 teaspoon pure vanilla extract, optional

1 recipe (1 to 1 1/2 quarts) Vanilla Ice Dream **or** Cinnamon Ice Dream (Page 78 or 82), optional

DIRECTIONS

1. Place frozen or semi-frozen peaches in a 9x9x2-inch or 11x7-inch baking dish, a 9 or 10-inch deep-dish pie plate, or 12-inch oval gratin dish. Let thaw at room temperature for 1 hour if time permits. You can skip this step if you like. Add frozen blueberries.

2. Sprinkle fruit with the optional sea salt, stevia, and vanilla. Stir to distribute.

3. Bake uncovered at 350° F until very soft, about 45 minutes for defrosted peaches, 1 to 1 1/2 hours for completely frozen peaches, depending on their density.

4. Serve as is, topped with Honey Almond Drizzle, or topped with Ice Dream for Blueberry Peach Compote à la Mode.

5. Refrigerate leftover compote in wide-mouth jars or heatproof containers with lids. Use within 3 days or freeze.

My long-time friend and editor, Marilyn Glidewell, came up with this quick and delicious recipe. Basically, it's frozen peaches and blueberries, about twice the volume of peaches (in cups) as blueberries. If you buy the peaches frozen in a big block (as opposed to small packages that are quick frozen), you can put them in warm water to soak for 15 minutes to help them bake faster. The blueberries don't require any soaking.

Note: The long baking time is needed because the peaches are frozen. It would be faster if not for that. It's such a nice and incredibly simple dessert. It requires no effort at all, and can be made as a last minute decision. Longer baking brings out the sweetness. It's done whenever the peaches are completely soft.

1 SERVING
WITHOUT TOPPING
(ABOUT 3/4 CUP):
85 calories
1.1 gramps protein
19.4 grams carbohydrate
0.3 gram fat
3 milligrams sodium

~Continued next page~

FYI: We've not tried this with fresh fruit (they're out of season as we write this), but I'm sure it would work; you'd just have to reduce the cooking time.

Serve it hot out of the oven, at room temperature, or cold topped with Ice Dream. For a special occasion, add a drizzle of Caramel Sauce or one of the chocolate sauces in Chapter 8.

Baked Blueberry Peach Compote ~ continued

VARIATIONS

*   Try this recipe with fresh fruit. Cut the peaches (or nectarines) into slightly thick wedges. For a juicier texture, toss the fruit with 1 tablespoon arrowroot and 1/2 cup apple juice.

*   Add 1/2 teaspoon ground cinnamon or pie spice to the fruit.

For breakfast, serve it warm or chilled, and add some coconut butter, Almond Honey Drizzle, or shredded, unsweetened sulfite-free coconut.

Peach Melba

HANDS-ON: 20 TO 30 MINUTES • **COOKING:** 25 MINUTES • **YIELD:** 4 TO 8 SERVINGS

INGREDIENTS

2 cups cool or cold filtered water

1/4 teaspoon *pure* stevia extract powder **or** 1/4 to 1/2 teaspoon *clear* stevia liquid

2 tablespoons honey **or** agave nectar

1 teaspoon pure vanilla extract **or** natural vanilla flavoring

4 large ripe peaches

1 to 1 1/2 quarts **or** 8 scoops Vanilla Ice Dream (Page 78)

1 to 1 1/2 cups Raspberry Sauce (Page 179)

Additional raspberries for garnish

1/4 to 1/2 cup toasted almonds (Page 75) **or** Almond Pralines (Page 214)

The great French Chef, Escoffier, created this dessert in honor of the Australian opera singer, Nellie Melba, at the Hotel Savoy in London in 1892. (Maybe he had a crush on her?). I first learned to make this dish in seventh grade, in French club, in Albuquerque, New Mexico. I'll never forget my French teacher, Chantal Ryland, who helped fuel my joy for cooking.

Note: I've made substitutions to reduce the sugar and omit the milk products.

1 SERVING:
597 calories
6.8 grams protein
71.2 grams carbohydrate
31.6 grams fat
134 milligrams sodium

DIRECTIONS

1. Combine the water, stevia, optional honey, vanilla, and peaches in a 2- to 3-quart pot. Bring to boil over medium-high heat. Reduce heat to medium-low and simmer, uncovered, for 15 minutes, until fork tender. Turn the peaches 3 times, about once every 3 or 4 minutes. (Set them in the pot with their stem ends up, then turn them upside down. This way, you always know which direction they should be facing as opposed to just setting them on their sides.) Exact time will depend upon the size and ripeness of the peaches.

2. Remove peaches and reduce the poaching liquid by slow boiling for about 15 minutes, uncovered, until you have about 1/2 cup. Transfer the peaches to a Pyrex bowl and the juices to another bowl or small jar. Cover and refrigerate until cold. You can do this up to 2 days ahead.

3. To serve, peel, halve and pit the peaches. Divide reserved poaching liquid among 4 dessert dishes or wine glasses. Add a scoop of vanilla Ice Dream, and place a peach half on either side of the Ice Dream. Spoon the raspberry sauce in a wide band overlapping both the peach halves and the Ice Dream. Garnish with nuts and serve immediately.

4. Refrigerate unused peaches and sauce and use within a few days.

~Continued next page~

Peach Melba ~ continued

VARIATIONS

*   Replace water with white grape juice; then omit stevia and honey.

*   Replace peaches with nectarines, or Raspberry Sauce with Strawberry, Blueberry, or Cherry Sauce (see index for recipes).

Cranberry Apple Compote

HANDS-ON: 30 MINUTES • **COOKING:** 25 MINUTES • **YIELD:** 8 CUPS; 12 SERVINGS

INGREDIENTS

1 cup raisins **or** chopped, pitted dates

2 cups cranberries, fresh **or** frozen, rinsed and drained

2 1/2 pounds tart-sweet apples (about 5 large apples), cored and peeled if desired:
    Braeburn, Cortland, Cameo, Fuji, Gala, Ginger Gold, Pink Lady, Sundowner

1 tablespoon finely grated orange zest (colored part only) **or** 1 teaspoon dried orange zest or peel

1/2 cup white grape juice **or** apple juice

1/4 to 1/3 teaspoon *pure* stevia extract powder **or** 1/2 to 2/3 teaspoon *clear* stevia extract liquid, optional (taste before adding)

1 tablespoon arrowroot powder dissolved in 3 tablespoons cold water, optional

1 recipe (1- to 1 1/2-quarts) Vanilla, Cinnamon, Nutmeg, or Ginger Ice Dream (see index for recipes), optional

This tart-sweet fruit compote has been a holiday tradition in our home for more than 15 years. Easy to assemble, it can be made a day or two ahead; extra can go in the freezer. For years, we have enjoyed it topped with chopped toasted nuts or Almond Honey Drizzle. Of course, you can dress it up with some Ice Dream for a special effect. Warm the leftover compote for a nice contrast with the cold Ice Dream.

> **1 SERVING (3/4 CUP):**
> 255 calories
> 2.3 grams protein
> 34.1 grams carbohydrate
> 12.1 grams fat
> 54 milligrams sodium

DIRECTIONS

1. Layer raisins and cranberries in a 4-quart pot. Grate and add 1 apple to the bottom of the pot along with the orange zest. Wash and core the apples. Peel if waxed. Halve, quarter, and then cut each apple into 1/4- to 1/2-inch thick slices. Layer over dried fruit and sprinkle with spices.

2. Add the fruit juice. Cover and bring to a boil over medium-high heat without stirring. Reduce heat to medium-low, and simmer until fork-tender, 20 to 30 minutes.

3. Stir gently with large, wide spoon without mashing. For a sweeter taste, sprinkle and add 1/4 teaspoon stevia or 1 tablespoon honey. Stir, taste, and repeat if needed. For a thicker consistency, add the dissolved arrowroot, then simmer and stir over medium heat until thick, 2 or 3 minutes.

4. Serve warm or chilled, and top each serving with a scoop of Ice Dream. Refrigerate leftover compote in wide-mouth glass jars or covered glass containers. Once chilled, freeze whatever you don't plan to consume within 5 days. Always leave 1 1/2 to 2 inches of space in the top of the jar, and chill to refrigerator temperature before freezing to keep the glass from cracking.

The Basics of Beating Egg Whites

Stiffly beaten egg whites are a must for meringues and macaroons. Because egg whites are far more finicky than whole eggs or yolks, you need to take special care when you select bowls and utensils, and when separating the whites from the yolks.

Secrets for success:

1. Separate the whites from yolks when the eggs are cold (right from the refrigerator), then allow the whites to come to room temperature for 1 or 2 hours before beating. This will allow them to beat into higher peaks. Cover and refrigerate the unused yolks, which you can use in scrambles, omelets, meatloaf, burgers, or to make mayonnaise. Or, you can smear raw egg yolk all over your face, allow it dry, then rinse it off, for a healing, pore-cleansing, vitamin A-rich facial. You'll get two or three facials from each egg yolk.

2. Start with impeccably clean, non-plastic bowls. Slightly dirty or plastic bowls will retain oils from foods previously stored in them, which can prevent the whites from whipping. Copper bowls are ideal, but stainless steel or Pyrex works well. Beaters must be spotless.

3. Separate the eggs into three bowls to avoid letting traces of yolk spoil the whites. After breaking each egg, transfer the yolk back and forth between the halved eggshells, letting the white drop into a small bowl. Gently drop the unbroken yolk into a separate bowl or small jar; if a yolk breaks, set the entire egg aside and wash out the bowl or use a new one for the next egg. Even a tiny trace of yolk can prevent the whites from forming stiff peaks. Transfer the pure egg white to a 1- to 1 1/2-quart glass, stainless steel or copper bowl.

4. Repeat this process with remaining eggs, continuing to add the pure whites to the large bowl until you have 4 pure whites. (Use a larger bowl for a double batch).

5. Beat the whites until frothy. Add the cream of tartar (in the amount specified in the recipe), and beat until stiff peaks form and the tips of the whites stand straight when the beaters are turned off and lifted away.

   Note: A copper bowl will produce the stiffest and most voluminous egg white foam you can imagine, and the whites will rarely deflate after you add the coconut or other ingredients. However, I've made this recipe dozens of times over many years without a copper bowl.

My Favorite Macaroons

HANDS-ON: 30 MINUTES • **COOKING:** 20 TO 25 MINUTES • **YIELD:** 24 MACAROONS

These wheat-free, grain-free, dairy-free treats are easy to assemble. The combination of honey and stevia, a noncaloric herbal swetener, reduces the need for refined sugar. The coconut improves immune function, so bar any guilt about making or eating these.

Note: Test your oven for accuracy with an oven thermometer (the kind that stays in the oven). If your oven runs higher or lower than the temperature it's set at, you can adjust the temperature accordingly, or have a technician recalibrate it for accuracy.

INGREDIENTS

4 egg whites from large or extra-large eggs (about 1/2 to 2/3 cup)

1/4 teaspoon cream of tartar

1/3 cup honey **or** agave nectar

1/4 teaspoon *pure* stevia extract powder (do not substitute stevia extract liquid)

1 1/2 teaspoons pure vanilla extract **or** alcohol-free vanilla flavoring

2 cups unsweetened, sulfite-free, finely shredded coconut; additional 1/4 to 3/4 cup if needed

Unrefined coconut oil **or** palm shortening at room temperature to grease baking sheets

---

1 MACAROON
(24 PER BATCH):
43 calories
0.7 gram protein
5 grams carbohydrate
2.2 grams fat
9 milligrams sodium

DIRECTIONS

1. Start with impeccably clean bowls and utensils. Separate the whites from yolks when the eggs are cold. Crack each egg into a small bowl, then transfer to a 1- to 1 1/2-quart metal, copper, or glass bowl (larger for a double batch). If a yolk breaks, set the entire egg aside for another use, then use a new bowl to crack the remaining eggs. Even a tiny trace of yolk can prevent the whites from forming stiff peaks. Let whites stand at room temperature for 1 to 2 hours. Refrigerate unused yolks and any broken eggs for another use.

2. Preheat oven to 300° F (lower if your oven runs hot). Oil a large cookie sheet, or line with unbleached parchment paper and then oil, or use a Silpat nonstick bake liner.

3. Using an electric mixer or beaters on medium speed, beat the whites until frothy. Add cream of tartar. Beat until stiff peaks form when mixer is turned off and beaters are lifted away.

4. Gradually add honey or agave nectar, then stevia and vanilla. Turn off mixer. Gently fold coconut in with a wide wooden spoon or stiff rubber spatula. Whites may deflate—don't panic. Add additional coconut, a little

~Continued next page~

> **FYI:** Supermarkets rarely sell unsweetened, sulfite-free flaked coconut. Look for it on the baking aisle or in the bulk foods section of natural foods stores, or buy it over the Internet. If you get medium- or large-flaked coconut, pulse it in a blender or food processor to create a fine powder, fluff it up with a fork, then measure out what you need. This recipe can be doubled.

My Favorite Macaroons ~ continued

at a time if batter appears wet and loose. You want it to be stiffer than meringue batter, but not as stiff as cookie dough. To test, place a spoonful of batter on a baking tray. It should stand in a mound 3/4-inch thick. If it threatens to run, add more coconut.

5. Drop batter by level tablespoons onto prepared baking sheet(s), creating an oval shape, or use 2 spoons to make a round shape or an upward chocolate kiss shape. If the last bit of batter looks too thin, add more coconut.

6. Bake in the center of the oven until set and lightly brown around edges, 20 to 25 minutes. Immediately remove the cookies from the tray(s) by slipping a thin metal spatula under the edge of each cookie and sawing back and forth. Cool macaroons on wire racks. Store in airtight containers at room temperature for up to 2 weeks, or in the refrigerator for up to 4 weeks. Freeze for longer storage.

7. Serve as is, or alongside scoops of Ice Dream, or crumble and fold into freshly churned Ice Dream.

VARIATIONS

*   **My Favorite Coconut Orange Macaroons:** In step #4, replace vanilla with 1 to 1 1/4 teaspoons pure orange extract.

*   **My Favorite Cocoa Macaroons:** In step #4, before adding the coconut, sift and add 1/4 cup unsweetened cocoa and increase stevia to 1/2 teaspoon.

*   **My Favorite Carob Macaroons:** In step #4, before adding the coconut, sift and add 1/4 cup carob powder.

*   **Mini Macaroon Cups:** Liberally grease a 24 cup mini muffin pan with palm shortening or coconut oil. In step #5, divide macaroon batter between muffin tins. Bake for 25 to 35 minutes or until lightly golden around the edges and a toothpick inserted into the center comes out clean. For a fancy finish, melt 1 1/2 to 2 ounces unsweetened baker's chocolate, then dip the bottom half of each cooled macaroon into the chocolate and place on a parchment-lined tray. Drizzle more chocolate over the tops and allow to cool.

Why Angel Foods Can Be Devilishly Challenging To Make

Because angel food cake doesn't contain any chemical leaveners, such as baking soda or baking powder, the volume of air beaten into the whites and the way you fold in the ingredients makes the utmost difference between success and failure. It's important to pay special attention to the details.

The Angel Food Cake Baker's Dilemma:

"Angel food cake is a pain because you have to bake it in an ungreased pan. The egg whites need a surface to cling to as they bake, so nonstick pans don't work. As for greasing, fat will deflate the egg whites in your batter, so you can't grease your pan. That's why angel food cake pans usually come apart—you can take the cake pan parts away from the cake without tearing it.

"You can bake mini angel food cakes in a muffin pan lined with regular cupcake liners. [I prefer the unbleached kind to avoid the dioxins and chemical dyes.] Or, you can bake them in single-serving nut cups, sold in cake decorating shops or in craft stores in the cake decorating section; they're basically little paper cups. We like them because you don't need a muffin tin and can bake more servings just by placing as many cups as you need on a cookie sheet and baking them. You can also try lining ramekins with a strip of parchment. That way, the sides won't stick. You can also cut out paper rounds for the bottoms, but that's fussy work."

~Chef Julie Elefante of
http://onewallkitchen.blogspot.com

Do's & Don'ts for Making Angel Food Cake:

1) Don't use egg whites that have been frozen and thawed; they produce a less stable egg white foam. You can purchase liquid egg whites, provided they don't contain additives.

2) Make sure the bowl, beaters, and all utensils are impeccably clean and dry, and completely free of grease (any traces of oil can prevent the whites from foaming).

3) Do not exceed medium speed on the mixer. Over beating the whites is the most common mistake when making angel food cake.

4) Use cold eggs taken straight from the refrigerator to prevent overbeating and to produce sturdier air bubbles. (This is in contrast to tips for making meringues or macaroons.)

5) Unlike egg whites used to make meringues, do not beat the whites until stiff. Stop at soft peaks. The finished batter should be soft enough to pour into the pan, although you still want to scrape every drop of batter into the pan.

6) Take care when folding flour into the egg white foam. Use a rubber spatula, never a mixer, and go slowly.

FYI: How to Fold Flour Into Angel Food Cake Batter:

After sifting the flour over the foamy egg whites, use the edge of a sturdy rubber or silicone spatula to cut through the middle of the whites down to the bottom of the bowl. Draw the spatula toward you, scraping a big scoop of whites up the side of the bowl. Lift and turn the spatula so that the flour falls gently back on top of the egg whites in the center. Rotate the bowl slightly and repeat the steps, always cutting into the center of the biggest mass of egg whites as you proceed.

Mini Angel Food Cakes

HANDS-ON: 20 MINUTES • **COOKING:** 12 TO 14 MINUTES • **YIELD:** 10 CUPCAKES

INGREDIENTS

1/4 cup sifted sweet brown rice flour **or** brown rice flour (spoon into cup and level)

1/4 cup sifted, unmodified potato starch **or** arrowroot powder (spoon into cup and level)

1/8 teaspoon finely ground, unrefined sea salt

2/3 cup (4 to 5) egg whites, cold, taken straight from the refrigerator

1 1/2 teaspoon lemon juice

1/2 teaspoon cream of tartar

1/4 to 1/3 cup honey **or** agave nectar, depending upon desired sweetness (do not grease the measuring cup before measuring this)

1/3 teaspoon *pure* stevia extract powder (do not use stevia extract liquid here)

1 teaspoon pure vanilla extract **or** alcohol-free vanilla flavoring

1/4 teaspoon almond extract **or** alcohol-free almond flavoring, optional

1 recipe (1 to 1 1/2 quarts) Vanilla or Cinnamon Ice Dream (Page 78 or 82), optional

DIRECTIONS

1. Start with impeccably clean bowl and utensils. Preheat oven to 375° F. Line a cookie sheet with 8 to 10 nut cups (see previous page) or fill a muffin pan with 10 to 12 unbleached parchment paper muffin liners.

2. Sift the flour, then measure, then sift 3 more times. Add the salt

3. Using an electric mixer or beaters on medium speed, beat the whites until frothy. Add lemon juice and cream of tartar, and beat until the mixture increases in volume 4 1/2 to 5 times and resembles a bowl of slightly translucent soft foam composed of

An angel food cake is a sponge cake made without egg yolks or butter. This light, airy, delicate, fat-free cake relies on beaten egg whites for its volume and texture. It's usually made in a large tube pan, which many home cooks don't have. I got the idea for making a half batch of angel food cake from a recipe in Bette Hagmen's book, *The Gluten Free Gourmet Makes Dessert*. Then I decided to make cupcakes. My version contains less sugar than other recipes because I used a mix of honey (agave nectar also works) and stevia.

Note: Pay special attention to the instructions for preparing the pans and mixing the ingredients. See tips for separating egg whites from yolks (Page 201).

**1 CUPCAKE
(6 PER BATCH):**
111 calories
3.3 grams protein
24 grams carbohydrate
0.2 gram fat
78 milligrams sodium

**1 CUPCAKE
(10 PER BATCH):**
67 calories
2 grams protein
14.4 grams carbohydrate
0.1 gram fat
47 milligrams sodium

~Continued next 2 pages ~

Note: Don't let the amount of detail scare you off. Just read through the instructions a couple of times before you start, to make sure you understand the steps, and then follow them to the letter. The payoff: enchanting, pristine white, little cupcakes that look dazzling served on pretty plates topped with, or served alongside scoops of Ice Dream and fruit sauce, or sliced fresh fruit and chocolate sauce (see index for recipes).

FYI: If you haven't recently tested your oven for accuracy with an oven thermometer, refer to the instructions for doing this on page 61.

Mini Angel Food Cakes ~ continued

tiny bubbles (about 2 to 4 minutes). The foam should hold a very soft, moist shape when the beaters are lifted.

4. Beat in the honey, 1 tablespoon at a time, taking about 2 to 3 minutes. Beat in the vanilla and optional almond extract. The foam will be creamy white and hold soft, moist, glossy peaks that bend over at the points; do not beat until stiff. If the bowl is nearly full, gently transfer the mixture to a wider and larger bowl for easier folding.

5. Sift about one-quarter of the flour mixture evenly over the surface of the batter. Fold gently with a rubber spatula only until the flour is almost incorporated. (See tips on previous page.) Do not stir or mix. Repeat 3 more times, folding in the last addition until no traces of flour are visible.

6. Spoon about 1/4 to 1/3 cup batter into each standard (2 1/2-inch) muffin liner or similar-sized nut cup to make 10 cupcakes. Evenly divide any remaining batter. If using jumbo (3 1/2-inch) liners figure about 1/3 cup to 1/2 cup batter for 6 larger liners.

7. Bake until a toothpick inserted into the center comes out clean, 15 to 18 minutes for 10 standard-size cupcakes; 20 minutes for 6 larger cupcakes.

8. Cool cupcakes on a rack. Store in a cookie tin, cookie jar, or covered bowl, separating each layer with parchment paper to prevent sticking. Serve as is or topped with Ice Dream for Mini Angel Food Cake à la Mode.

VARIATIONS

* **Mini Lemon or Orange Angel Food Cakes:** Replace almond extract with 1/2 teaspoon lemon or orange extract, or natural lemon or orange flavoring (do not use lemon or orange oil—it can cause egg white foam to deflate). Stir 1/2 teaspoon finely grated lemon zest or 1 tablespoon grated orange zest into the flour mixture.

~Continued next page~

Mini Angel Food Cakes ~ continued

* **Mini Coffee-Flavored Angel Food Cakes:** Crush 1 1/2 tablespoons freeze-dried instant coffee with a rolling pin, or powder in a coffee grinder (do not substitute Teeccino or chicory/dandelion root grinds; they are not instantized). Sprinkle over the batter and fold in with the last addition of flour.

* **Mini Cocoa Angel Food Cakes:** Replace 1/4 cup of the flour with 1/4 cup unsweetened cocoa powder.

* **Extra Chocolate Angel Food Cakes:** Pulverize in a food processor or finely chop 1/2 to 1 ounce bittersweet dark (70 to 73%) or semisweet chocolate. Fold this into the basic batter (or the cocoa variation above) with the last addition of flour.

* **Mini Carob Angel Food Cakes:** Replace 1/4 cup of the flour with 1/4 cup carob powder.

Dark Chocolate–Dipped Date Nut Truffles

HANDS-ON: 30 MINUTES • **COOKING:** 5 MINUTES • **YIELD:** 36 SERVINGS

INGREDIENTS

4 ounces unsweetened baker's chocolate (e.g., Ghirardelli, Valrhona, Callebaut, Scharffen Berger, or Bakers), broken or chopped into 1/4- to 1/2-inch pieces

1 pound coconut date rolls (about 16 long pieces, but varies with brand)

1/2 to 1 cup unsweetened, sulfite-free, finely shredded coconut

3/4 to 1 cup dry toasted, unsalted, pine nuts, walnuts, almonds, pecans, pistachios, or hazelnuts **or** combination of 2 or 3 kinds of nuts (Page 75)

Who would think that a chocolate indulgence, free of refined sugar, and with so few ingredients, could taste so good? Dates stand in for refined sugar and dairy products in these truffle-like creations. They make a fine stand-alone dessert, and they're equally good chopped and added to Chocolate or Vanilla Ice Dream during the last few minutes of churning. Drizzle on some Caramel Sauce or Cherry Sauce for a fancy finish.

1 SERVING (1 PIECE):
91 calories
1.1 grams protein
10.3 grams carbohydrate
4.9 grams fat
5 milligrams sodium

DIRECTIONS

1. Line one or more rimmed baking sheets with parchment paper wrappings from the chocolate, unbleached parchment paper, or a nonstick bake liner.

2. Melt chocolate in a double boiler over hot—but not boiling—water, or in a small saucepan over very low heat. If using a saucepan on a gas range, slip a heat deflector under the pan to keep the heat low. When mostly melted, lower heat to warm.

3. Arrange whole or crushed nuts and coconut in separate small bowls. Cut date rolls in half. Roll each half into a ball, or shape into 2 small squares.

4. Add 4 to 6 date squares or balls to the melted chocolate. Using 2 spoons, turn the pieces in the chocolate one at a time to coat. Drip excess chocolate back into the pan.

   For square pieces: Transfer a chocolate-coated date square to the prepared sheet. Press a half or whole nut on top, or sprinkle with pine nuts.

   For round pieces: Transfer a chocolate-coated date ball to a small bowl of coarsely chopped, toasted nuts or coconut. Using 2 clean spoons, scoop the nut meal or coconut over the ball and turn to coat. Transfer to the prepared sheet. Repeat with remaining coconut date pieces.

~Continued next page~

FYI: Look for coconut date rolls and sulfite-free, unsweetened coconut flakes in natural foods stores or over the Internet. The coconut date rolls are made from dried pitted dates put through a grinder twice, and then rolled in sulfite-free, unsweetened coconut flakes and shaped into logs. Different brands vary in their moisture content, size, and sweetness. Experiment to find your favorite source.

Dark Chocolate~Dipped Date Nut Truffles ~ continued

5. Refrigerate or freeze on one or more plates or trays until firm. Transfer truffles to containers. Cover and store in the refrigerator or freezer. Chill for at least 24 hours, or freeze for 12 hours before adding to Ice Dream. They can be transported in an insulated bag with ice packs.

If you're using walnuts or hazelnuts, toast, and then wrap them in a clean kitchen towel. Roll the towel back and forth to loosen the skins. Remove the nuts and discard the bitter skins.

• To Make Your Own Coconut Date Rolls • • • • •

Pulverize soft pitted dates in a food processor, adding warm water a tablespoon at a time as needed to create a cookie dough texture. Add 1/2 cup unsweetened, sulfite-free coconut per half pound of pitted dates. Coconut can be left out if allergy is a concern. Form into 1 ounce cylinders, then cut each one in half to form two pieces.

Squash/Pumpkin Pudding Pie

HANDS-ON: 30 MINUTES • **COOKING:** 1 HOUR • **YIELD:** 1 (10-INCH) PIE; 8 SERVINGS

Ingredients

3 cups baked or simmered winter squash, scooped from the skin and mashed (Page 211):
butternut, buttercup, sweet dumpling, delicata, kabocha, sweet mama or Hokkaido

3/4 cup blended, preservative-free (full fat, not lite) unsweetened, coconut milk

1/4 cup honey **or** agave nectar; additional 1 or 2 tablespoons as needed

3 whole eggs **or** 6 egg whites

1 1/2 tablespoons arrowroot powder

2 teaspoons apple pie spice **or** pumpkin pie spice

1 1/2 teaspoons pure vanilla extract **or** natural vanilla flavoring **or** maple extract or flavoring

1/4 teaspoon finely ground, unrefined sea salt

¼ to ½ teaspoon *pure* stevia extract powder **or** ½ to 1 teaspoon *clear* stevia extract liquid (start with less; add more only if needed)

1 recipe (1 to 1 1/2 quarts) Vanilla, Cinnamon, Cocoa, Dark Chocolate, Rum Raisin, **or** Basil Ice Dream (see index for recipes), optional

We have been enjoying this recipe for many years. Not just for Thanksgiving, this delicious dairy-free, low-sugar twist on the classic pumpkin pie makes an impressive dessert or snack throughout the fall and winter. It has a taste and texture like pie but contains a fraction of the carbs and fat grams. It also takes less time to assemble than pie with a crust. For a fancy presentation, serve a scoop of Vanilla, Cinnamon, or Ginger Ice Dream on top of or next to each serving of pie. Try Basil Ice Dream if you're feeling adventurous.

1 SERVING (WITH EGGS):
148 calories
4.5 grams protein
18 grams carbohydrate
6.4 grams fat
68 milligrams sodium

1 SERVING (WHITES ONLY):
125 calories
4.1 grams protein
18 grams carbohydrate
4.1 grams fat
76 milligrams sodium

Directions

1. Preheat oven to 350° F.

2. Purée all of the ingredients in a blender, Vita-Mix, food processor, or food mill, or in a bowl with an electric mixer. If using a blender or small processor, blend in 2 batches, then combine in a bowl. Mixture should be thick. If too stiff to blend, add 1/4 cup water and blend again. For a sweeter taste, add 1/4 teaspoon additional stevia and/or 1 tablespoon honey. Blend, taste, and repeat if needed. **Note:** Pie will become sweeter and more concentrated as it bakes.

3. Pour into an oiled 10-inch deep-dish pie plate. Smooth with a spatula. Bake in the center of the oven until firm, slightly golden, and dry around the edges, about 60 minutes. Allow pie to cool for ½ hour. Refrigerate until completely cool and firm, several hours or overnight, before serving

4. Cut into 8 slices and serve. Use within 4 days.

~Continued next page~

Shopping for winter squash: Look for Hokkaido pumpkin, kabocha, buttercup, honey delight, or butternut squash that feels heavy for its size. Kabocha, Hokkaido, and buttercup squash should have dark green skins, and any spots should be bright orange—not pale or yellow. A ripe butternut squash will be orange all over with no hint of green. Store all hard winter squashes at room temperature.

To cut and cook hard winter squash: Cut off the stem. Place a folded dish towel on a cutting board (this will keep the squash from slipping). Lay the squash on the towel. Cut in half from top to bottom, rocking the knife back and forth. Scoop out and discard the seeds. Bake squash halves cut side down on a rimmed baking sheet, uncovered, in a 400° F oven for 35 to 50 minutes until fork tender and juicy. Scoop out the flesh and discard the skin. Purée the flesh in a food processor, or force it through a medium-mesh sieve or the medium disk of a food mill. Freeze what you don't plan to use within 3 days.

Note: If apple or pumpkin pie spice is not available, substitute 3/4 teaspoon ground cinnamon, 1/2 teaspoon dried ginger (powder), 1/4 teaspoon ground nutmeg, 1/4 teaspoon dried orange zest, and 1/8 teaspoon ground cloves.

Squash/Pumpkin Pudding Pie ~ continued

Variation

* Replace 1/4 cup honey or agave nectar with 1/4 cup + 2 tablespoons pure maple syrup. For a sweeter taste, add an additional 1/4 teaspoon stevia and/or 1 tablespoon maple syrup. Blend, taste, and repeat if needed. Add another 2 teaspoons arrowroot in step #2.

* For a gingery flavor, replace pie spice with 1 1/2 tablespoons peeled and finely grated fresh gingerroot plus 1/2 teaspoon dried ground ginger (powder). If desired, add the finely grated zest of 1 fresh orange or tangerine.

I recommend baking fresh winter squash—don't steam, boil, or microwave as it won't have much flavor. Use frozen squash as a second option or canned pumpkin as a last resort. If you use sweet winter squash rather than pumpkin, you'll enjoy a sweeter taste with less added sweetener.

---

chapter 10
Additional Indulgences

Best Bites

Pecan Pralines

HANDS-ON: 20 MINUTES • **COOKING:** 15 TO 20 MINUTES • **YIELD:** 1 1/4 CUPS; 20 SERVINGS

INGREDIENTS

1 cup shelled raw pecan halves (see variations below)

1/4 cup honey, agave nectar, maple syrup, sorghum syrup, **or** brown rice syrup

2 tablespoons unsweetened, preservative-free coconut milk (regular, not lite), optional

1/4 teaspoon finely ground, unrefined sea salt, optional

1 teaspoon ground cinnamon, apple pie spice, **or** pumpkin pie spice, optional

DIRECTIONS

1. Preheat an oven or toaster oven to 350° F.

2. Line a 9-inch cake pan or pie plate, a 9x12- or 8x10-inch baking pan, or a rimmed baking sheet with unbleached parchment paper or a silicone baking mat.

3. Combine all the ingredients in a bowl and stir enough to thoroughly coat the nuts. Scrape the mixture (nuts and all the liquid) onto the prepared pan. With a lightly greased flexible spatula or large spoon, spread the nuts one layer deep.

4. Bake for 10 minutes. Stir, then bake for another 5 minutes until the coating looks dry. Check frequently after the first 10 minutes; nuts burn quickly.

5. Remove the pan from the oven. Let cool for 5 minutes, and then turn the nuts over using one or two heatproof spatulas. Bake 4 to 6 more minutes to crisp the other side. Place the tray on a rack to cool.

6. When cool enough to handle, break the nuts apart or place them on a cutting board and chop into 1/4-inch pieces. Store in a covered glass bowl or jar in the refrigerator. Use within 3 months for best results.

Consider making a double, triple, or quadruple batch of these crunchy candied nuts. They're easy to make, fun to eat, and versatile. After scouring many cookbooks, I settled on baking the pralines—rather than cooking them on the stovetop—to reduce the hands-on time. I got the idea from Debra Lynn Dadd's website, www.sweetsavvy.com. Instead of using sugar or evaporated cane juice, my recipe calls for local honey. Coconut milk is used in place of cream. If you leave out the coconut milk, the nuts will have a more pronounced crunchy, candy-like coating. Sea salt enhances the flavor.

1 TABLESPOON (W/COCONUT MILK):
59 calories
0.5 gram protein
4.7 grams carbohydrate
4.2 grams fat
1 milligram sodium

1 TABLESPOON (W/OUT COCONUT MILK):
56 calories
0.5 gram protein
4.6 grams carbohydrate
3.9 grams fat
0 milligrams sodium

~Continued next page~

> **FYI:** I don't recommend eating these by the handful. Half a cup of nuts packs 300 to 400 calories *before* you add syrup or coconut milk. I recommend that you measure out 1 or 2 tablespoons per person, then coarsely chop and sprinkle them over Ice Dream or fruit salad, or add them to the ice cream maker during the last two minutes of churning.

Pecan Pralines ~ continued

VARIATIONS

* **Almond Pralines:** Replace pecan halves with shelled, raw, whole almonds.

* **Walnut Pralines:** Replace pecan halves with shelled, raw walnut halves. Before mixing the walnuts with the syrup, wrap them in a clean kitchen towel and rub to loosen the skins. Pick out the nuts and discard the bitter skins.

* **Cashew Pralines:** Replace pecan halves with shelled, raw, whole cashews.

* **Pumpkin Seed Pralines:** Replace pecan halves with shelled, raw, green pumpkin seeds, sometimes labeled Pepitas. Do not use the seeds from a fresh pumpkin—they contain a tough outer shell that is difficult to digest.

* **Sesame Seed Pralines:** Replace pecan halves with shelled, raw, unhulled brown or black sesame seeds. For a colorful effect, use a combination of the black and brown sesame seeds. These pralines will clump up more than whole nuts but they'll still taste great and add a delightful crunch when sprinkled over Ice Dream. No need to chop these.

You can substitute different kinds of nuts (see variations) and sweeteners. Use light colored honey for a mild flavor, darker honey for a stronger flavor. The darkest varieties taste similar to molasses. Agave nectar, maple syrup, sorghum syrup, and brown rice syrup work equally well, each having a slightly different flavor. Maple syrup contains less sugar per tablespoon than the other syrups, and is a good choice if you prefer a less sweet taste.

Gluten-Free Better Brownies

HANDS-ON: 30 MINUTES • **COOKING:** 25 TO 30 MINUTES • **YIELD:** 16 BROWNIES

INGREDIENTS

Wet ingredients:

1/2 cup packed soft, pitted dates

1/3 cup virgin-pressed coconut oil **or** palm shortening, at room temperature

2 ounces dark chocolate (70 to 73%), coarsely chopped

1 teaspoon instant coffee **or** espresso powder, optional

1/4 cup honey **or** agave nectar

2 medium to large eggs, at room temperature

2 teaspoons pure vanilla extract **or** alcohol-free vanilla flavoring

Dry ingredients:

1/3 cup sweet brown rice flour, sorghum flour, **or** a combination of the two (lightly spoon into measuring cup and level)

2 tablespoons unmodified potato starch (spoon into measuring cup and level)

1/3 cup unsweetened cocoa powder; sifted if lumpy (spoon into measuring cup and level)

1/2 teaspoon gluten-free, non-aluminum baking powder

1/2 teaspoon xanthan gum **or** guar gum

1/4 teaspoon finely ground unrefined sea salt

1/4 teaspoon *pure* stevia extract powder **or** 1/2 teaspoon *clear* stevia extract liquid added with the wet ingredients.

- -

You will need a food processor, a blender, or a Vita-Mix to purée the dates with the wet ingredients. You want them to blend into the cookies so they're unnoticeable. They'll add moisture and sweetness, but you don't want to see chunky date bits. Allow enough time for soaking the dates before combining the ingredients.

- -

If you're a fan of brownies, but you don't want all the fat and sugar, or you want to avoid wheat, you're in for a treat with this remake of a recipe I found in *The Healthy Oven Baking Book* by Sarah Phillips.

These brownies taste delicious on their own or topped with a cooked fruit sauce. They're even more special when topped with Vanilla, Coffee, Ginger, Chai, Cinnamon, Pumpkin, or Peanut Butter Ice Dream. For a healthy twist on Cookies-n-Cream Ice Cream, chop the brownies and fold them into a freshly churned batch of Vanilla Ice Dream (see index for recipes).

1 CHOCOLATE BROWNIE:
134 calories
1.9 grams protein
14.6 grams carbohydrate
7.4 grams fat
46 milligrams sodium

1 DATE PECAN BLONDIE:
112 calories
1.6 grams protein
12.1 grams carbohydrate
6.2 grams fat
46 milligrams sodium

1 CAROB BROWNIE:
130 calories
1.2 grams protein
15.5 grams carbohydrate
6.9 grams fat
47 milligrams sodium

~Continued next 2 pages~

Gluten~Free Better Brownies ~ continued

DIRECTIONS

1. Place the dates in a bowl. Add water to cover by 1-inch. Let soak for 1 to 2 hours. Drain and save the liquid to drink or sweeten tea.

2. Position the rack in the center of the oven and preheat to 350° F. Generously grease an 8-inch square baking pan or a 9-inch round cake pan (preferably stainless steel). Line with unbleached parchment paper, then lightly oil the top of the parchment to prevent sticking.

3. Combine the coconut oil or shortening, chocolate, and optional coffee or espresso powder in a small saucepan over very low heat. (A double boiler also works well.) Stir occasionally with a wire whisk until smooth. When almost melted, add the honey. Stir and remove from heat. Set aside to cool.

4. In a medium bowl, whisk the dry ingredients until well combined.

5. Combine the dates, eggs and vanilla in a blender, Vita-Mix, food processor, or a medium bowl with an electric hand-held mixer. Blend until creamy and smooth. Add the melted chocolate mixture. If using a blender, Vita-Mix, or food processor, scrape the purée into a medium bowl before proceeding.

6. Add the dry ingredients. Mix only enough to combine. Do not over mix. Batter will be stiff. Scrape into the prepared pan. Smooth the top with a damp spatula.

7. Bake until the edges begin to pull away from the sides of the pan and a toothpick inserted into the center comes out clean, 25 to 30 minutes, depending upon the moisture content of the dates you use. Do not over bake. The center may seem unset, but will firm up as it cools. Place the tray on a rack to cool.

8. Cut into 16 squares. Remove with a metal spatula. Store in a cookie jar or a covered tin for up to 1 week. Refrigerate for longer storage.

~Variations next page~

Gluten-Free Better Brownies ~ continued

VARIATIONS

* Fold in 1/2 cup lightly toasted, coarsely chopped almonds, walnuts, or pecans (Page 75) at the end of step #5.

* **Gluten-Free Date Pecan Blondies:** This batter reminds me of chocolate chip cookie dough without the chips. Omit the dark chocolate and coffee or espresso powder. In step #4, use the sweet rice flour or sorghum flour in the master recipe or replace it with millet flour, and replace the cocoa powder with almond or pecan meal (made from dry roasted or toasted nuts, cooled and powdered in a blender, Vita-Mix, or food processor).

* **Gluten-Free Chocolate Chip Blondies**: Coarsely chop a 4-ounce bittersweet dark chocolate (70 to 73%) bar or measure out 1/2 cup of bittersweet dark chocolate chips. Fold into batter (above) before scraping into pan.

* **Gluten-Free Chestnut Blondies:** Omit the dark chocolate in step #3. Replace cocoa powder with chestnut flour (see Appendix A for mail order sources), then add 1/3 cup pecan meal (dry roasted or toasted pecans cooled and powdered in a food processor or Vita-Mix).

* **Gluten-Free Chestnut Chocolate Chip Blondies**: Coarsely chop a 4-ounce bittersweet dark chocolate (70 to 73%) bar or measure out 1/2 cup of bittersweet dark chocolate chips. Fold into batter (above) before scraping into pan.

* **Gluten-Free Carob Brownies:** Replace unsweetened cocoa powder with 1/2 cup carob powder, and replace dark chocolate with 2 more tablespoons coconut oil or palm shortening. Add the carob powder with the honey in step #3 after melting the oil.

Chocolate Chip Ice Dream Sandwich Cookies

HANDS-ON: 45 TO 60 MINUTES • **COOKING:** 9 TO 12 MINUTES • **YIELD:** 20 COOKIES FOR 10 SANDWICHES

INGREDIENTS

Dry ingredients:

3/4 cup sweet brown rice flour, brown rice flour, **or** a combination of the two

3/4 cup sorghum flour (spoon into measuring cup and level)

3/4 cup unmodified potato starch, arrowroot, **or** sweet white rice flour (spoon into measuring cup and level)

1 teaspoon baking soda

3/4 teaspoon xanthan gum **or** guar gum

1 teaspoon finely ground, unrefined sea salt

1/4 teaspoon *pure* stevia extract powder **or** 1/2 teaspoon *clear* stevia extract liquid added with the wet ingredients

Wet ingredients:

1 cup packed soft, pitted dates

1/4 cup + 2 tablespoons virgin-pressed coconut oil **or** palm shortening, at room temperature

1/3 cup honey **or** agave nectar

1/4 cup + 2 tablespoons applesauce, at room temperature

2 medium to large eggs, at room temperature

1/4 cup plain almond or hazelnut milk, **or** date soaking liquid, at room temperature

1 teaspoon vanilla extract **or** alcohol-free vanilla flavoring

Coconut oil **or** palm shortening to grease baking pans

1 cup malt-sweetened, fruit-sweetened, dairy-free, or bittersweet chocolate chips **or** a bittersweet dark chocolate bar (70 to 73%), coarsely chopped into 1/4-inch pieces

I have fond memories of helping my mother make Toll House Chocolate Chip Cookies when I was in first grade. I've taken liberties with the original.

To achieve a soft texture without a lot of fat, I made the dough very wet. To make the dough easier to work with, refrigerate it for at least 3 hours before baking. After the cookies have cooled, you can fill them with freshly made Ice Dream, or Ice Dream softened at room temperature for 15 to 20 minutes, to make Ice Dream Sandwiches. (See Page 236 for assembly tips and suggestions.) The cookies also taste great with a steaming hot cup of Roasted Chicory & Dandelion Root Coffee Alternative or Teeccino.

1 LARGE COOKIE:
167 calories
1.7 grams protein
26.1 grams carbohydrate
6.4 grams fat
147 milligrams sodium

You will need a food processor, a blender, or a Vita-Mix to purée the dates with the wet ingredients. You want them to blend into the cookies so they're unnoticeable. They'll add moisture and sweetness, but you don't want to see chunky date bits. Allow enough time for soaking the dates before combining the ingredients.

~Continued next 2 pages~

Chocolate Chip Ice Dream Sandwich Cookies ~ continued

DIRECTIONS

1. Place dates in a bowl. Add water to cover by 1 inch. Let soak for 1 to 2 hours. Drain and save the liquid for use later in this recipe

2. Measure the dry ingredients into a medium bowl. Whisk and set aside.

3. If using coconut oil that is solid, melt it in a small saucepan over low heat; measure out what you need and allow it to cool. If using palm shortening, do not melt.

4. In a blender, Vita-Mix, or food processor, mix the shortening or liquefied and cooled coconut oil, honey, dates, and applesauce until smooth and very creamy. Add the eggs, nut milk, and vanilla. Mix until smooth. If using a blender or Vita-Mix, transfer the purée to a medium bowl.

5. Add the dry ingredients and mix until well combined. Do not over mix. Dough will be very sticky. To make it easier to work with, you may wish to cover it with a lid or plate, and refrigerate for at least 3 hours.

6. Preheat oven to 350° F. Liberally oil 2 large or 4 small baking pans, or line with non-stick bake liners or unbleached parchment paper.

7. Form the dough into 10 slightly rounded 1/3-cup portions using a metal 1/3-cup measure. Divide each mound of dough in half to make 20 portions. Dip your hands in ice water and roll the portions into balls.

8. Place the balls of dough on the baking sheets. Then, using your fingertips or the bottom of a metal measuring cup dipped repeatedly into ice water, flatten each ball making it 3 to 3-1/2 inches across. Allow about 1/2 inch between each. They will not spread. **Note:** You can get 12 on a 13x18-inch half sheet pan, with 4 going lengthwise and 3 across, or 8 on a standard 11x17-inch sheet with 3 going lengthwise down the sides and 2 in the center in between. Repeat with remaining dough, leaving 1/2 to 1 inch of space between each cookie.

9. Bake cookies 9 to 12 minutes; rotate the baking sheets (top to bottom and back to front) halfway through. They will be done when the centers feel barely firm when lightly pressed, they are lightly golden on the bottom, and a toothpick inserted into the center comes out clean. Cookies will firm up as they cool.

10. Cool on the baking pan for 2 to 3 minutes, then transfer to wire racks using a spatula.When cool, store in a covered Pyrex bowl, cookie tin, or cookie jar, separating each layer of cookies with unbleached parchment paper. Store at room temperature for up to 1 week. Refrigerate or freeze for longer storage.

~Variations next page~

Chocolate Chip Ice Dream Sandwich Cookies ~ continued

VARIATIONS

* **To use liquid stevia:** Replace 1/4 teaspoon *pure* stevia extract powder with 1/2 teaspoon *clear* stevia extract liquid. Add liquid stevia to the liquid ingredients.

* **For eggless cookies:** Replace each egg with 1 1/2 teaspoons Ener-G Egg Replacer plus 2 tablespoons warm water. Mix thoroughly before adding to the recipe. For additional moisture, add 2 more tablespoons water, nut milk, or applesauce for each egg you replace (1 egg = 1/4 cup volume).

* If you're short on chocolate or chocolate chips, use 1/2 cup raisins and 1/2 cup chocolate chips, or 1/2 cup chopped walnuts, almonds, or pecans plus 1/2 cup chocolate chips.

* For 36 to 40 smaller cookies, shape dough into rounded tablespoons, then into balls. Flatten to make 2- to 2 1/2-inch round disks. Bake for about 5 to 8 minutes.

Chocolate Ice Dream Sandwich Cookies

HANDS-ON: 1 HOUR • **COOKING:** 9 TO 12 MINUTES • **YIELD:** 18 TO 20 COOKIES FOR 9 OR 10 SANDWICHES

INGREDIENTS

Dry ingredients:

1/2 cup unsweetened cocoa powder; sift if lumpy

1/3 cup sweet brown rice flour **or** brown rice flour (spoon into measuring cup and level)

1/3 cup sorghum flour (spoon into measuring cup and level)

1/3 cup unmodified potato starch **or** arrowroot (spoon into measuring cup and level)

1/2 teaspoon baking soda

1/2 teaspoon xanthan gum **or** guar gum

1/2 teaspoon *pure* stevia extract powder **or** 1 teaspoon *clear* stevia extract liquid added with the wet ingredients.

1/8 teaspoon finely ground, unrefined salt

Wet ingredients:

1/2 cup packed soft, pitted dates

2 ounces bittersweet dark chocolate (70 to 73%), chopped or broken into 1/2- to 1-inch pieces **or** semisweet chocolate for a sweeter taste

1/3 cup virgin-pressed coconut oil **or** palm shortening, at room temperature

1/3 cup honey **or** agave nectar

1 medium to large egg **or** 2 small eggs at room temperature

1/2 cup plain almond or hazelnut milk, **or** date soaking liquid, at room temperature

1 teaspoon vanilla extract **or** alcohol-free vanilla flavoring

1/8 to 1/4 teaspoon *pure* stevia extract powder **or** 1/2 to 1 teaspoon *clear* stevia extract liquid (start with less; add more only if needed)

Coconut oil **or** palm shortening to grease baking pans

These soft fudgy cookies contain a fraction of the fat and less sugar than most cookies. To achieve their amazing texture, I created a very wet cookie dough. To make it easier to work with, refrigerate the dough for at least 3 hours before shaping and baking.

After the cookies have cooled, they can be filled with freshly made Ice Dream or Ice Dream that has been softened at room temperature for 15 or 20 minutes to make some incredibly delicious Ice Dream Sandwiches. (See Page 236 for assembly tips and suggestions for flavor combinations.) The cookies also taste great served with a steaming hot cup of Roasted Chicory & Dandelion Root Coffee or Teeccino.

> **1 LARGE COOKIE:**
> 129 calories
> 1.8 grams protein
> 15.5 grams carbohydrate
> 6.6 grams fat
> 50 milligrams sodium

You will need a food processor, a blender, or a Vita-Mix to purée the dates with the wet ingredients. You want them to blend into the cookies so they're unnoticeable. They'll add moisture and sweetness, but you don't want to see chunky date bits. Allow enough time for soaking the dates before combining the ingredients.

~Continued next page~

Chocolate Ice Dream Sandwich Cookies ~ continued

DIRECTIONS

1. Place dates in a bowl. Add water to cover by 1 inch. Let soak for 1 to 2 hours. Drain and save the liquid for use later in this recipe

2. Measure the dry ingredients into a medium bowl. Whisk and set aside.

3. Gently melt the chocolate and coconut oil or palm shortening in a small saucepan over very low heat or in the top of a double boiler. Remove from heat when almost melted. Allow it to cool to the touch before combining with other ingredients.

4. In a blender, Vita-Mix, or food processor, combine the melted chocolate, coconut oil or shortening, honey, and dates. Mix until smooth and very creamy. Add the eggs, milk, vanilla, and stevia. Mix until smooth. Scrape the purée into a medium bowl before proceeding.

5. Gradually add the dry ingredients and blend until well mixed. (Do not over mix.) At this point the dough will be very sticky. To make it easier to work with, cover and refrigerate for at least 3 hours.

6. Preheat oven to 350° F. Liberally oil 2 large or 4 small baking pans, or line with non-stick bake liners or unbleached parchment paper.

7. Form the dough into 9 slightly rounded 1/3-cup portions using a metal 1/3-cup measure. Divide each mound of dough in half to make 18 portions. Dip your hands in ice water and roll the portions into balls.

8. Place the balls of dough on the baking sheets. Then, using your fingertips or the bottom of a metal measuring cup dipped repeatedly into ice water, flatten each ball making it 3 to 3 ½ inches across. Allow about ½ inch between each cookie. They will not spread. **Note:** You can get 12 on a 13x18-inch half sheet pan, with 4 going lengthwise and 3 across, or 8 on a standard 11x17-inch sheet with 3 going lengthwise down the sides and 2 in the center in between. Repeat with remaining dough.

9. Bake cookies for 9 to 12 minutes; rotate the baking sheets (top to bottom and back to front) halfway through. Cookies are done when the centers feel barely firm when lightly pressed, they are lightly golden on the bottom, and a toothpick inserted into the center comes out clean. They will firm up as they cool.

10. Cool on the baking pan for 2 to 3 minutes, then transfer to wire racks using a spatula. When cool, store in a covered Pyrex bowl, cookie tin, or cookie jar, separating each layer of cookies with unbleached parchment paper. Store at room temperature for up to 1 week. Refrigerate or freeze for longer storage.

VARIATIONS

* **For eggless cookies:** Replace each egg with 1 1/2 teaspoons Ener-G Egg Replacer plus 2 tablespoons warm water. Mix thoroughly before adding to the recipes. For additional moisture, add 2 more tablespoons water, nut milk, or applesauce for each egg you replace (1 egg = 1/4 cup volume).

* For 36 to 40 smaller cookies, shape dough into rounded tablespoons, then into balls. Flatten to make 2- to 2 1/2-inch round disks. Bake for about 5 to 8 minutes.

Pumpkin Spice Ice Dream Sandwich Cookies

HANDS-ON: 45 TO 60 MINUTES • **COOKING:** 12 TO 15 MINUTES • **YIELD:** 36 LARGE COOKIES FOR 18 SANDWICHES

INGREDIENTS

Dry ingredients:

1 cup sweet brown rice flour **or** brown rice flour (spoon into measuring cup and level); you may need 1/4 cup more

1 cup sorghum flour (spoon into measuring cup and level)

1 cup unmodified potato starch **or** arrowroot (spoon into measuring cup and level)

4 teaspoons baking soda (1 tablespoon + 1 teaspoon)

1 teaspoon xanthan gum **or** guar gum

1/2 teaspoon finely ground, unrefined sea salt

1/2 teaspoon *pure* stevia extract powder **or** 1 teaspoon *clear* stevia extract liquid added to the wet ingredients

2 teaspoons ground ginger

2 teaspoons ground cinnamon

1/2 teaspoon ground cloves

1/2 teaspoon ground allspice

1/2 teaspoon ground nutmeg

Wet ingredients:

1 cup packed soft, pitted dates

1/2 cup palm shortening **or** virgin-pressed coconut oil, at room temperature

1 cup unsweetened, canned pumpkin **or** baked and puréed winter squash (Page 211)

1/2 cup honey **or** agave nectar

1/2 cup unsulphured molasses (no more than 3 tablespoons as *blackstrap* molasses)

1 large or 2 small eggs, at room temperature

1 teaspoon pure vanilla extract **or** alcohol-free vanilla flavoring; double if desired

1 tablespoon apple cider vinegar **or** unseasoned rice vinegar

Coconut oil **or** palm shortening to grease baking pans

These soft and cakey gingerbread cookies contain a fraction of the fat and sugar found in most cookies.

The dough will look wetter than regular cookie dough; this is the secret for making moist, flat, low-fat cookies for Ice Dream Sandwiches. After you've baked the cookies and allowed them to cool, fill with freshly made Ice Dream or Ice Dream softened at room temperature for 15 to 20 minutes to make wonderfully-moist, cake-like Ice Dream Sandwiches. (See Page 236 for assembly tips.)

> **1 LARGE COOKIE:**
> 108 calories
> 0.8 gram protein
> 18.7 grams carbohydrate
> 3.3 grams fat
> 166 milligrams sodium

You will need a food processor, a blender, or a Vita-Mix to purée the dates with the wet ingredients. You want them to blend into the cookies so they're unnoticeable. They'll add moisture and sweetness, but you don't want to see chunky date bits. Allow enough time for soaking the dates before combining the ingredients.

~Continued next page~

Pumpkin Spice Ice Dream Sandwich Cookies ~ continued

DIRECTIONS

1. Place the dates in a bowl. Add water to cover by 1-inch. Let soak for 1 to 2 hours. Drain and save the liquid to drink or sweeten tea.

2. Measure the dry ingredients into a medium bowl. Whisk and set aside.

3. If using coconut oil that is solid, melt it in a small saucepan over low heat; measure out what you need and allow it to cool. If using palm shortening, do not melt.

4. In a blender, Vita-Mix, or food processor, mix the shortening or liquefied and cooled coconut oil, dates, pumpkin, honey, and molasses until creamy. Add the egg(s) and vinegar. Mix until smooth and very creamy. If using a blender or Vita-Mix, transfer the purée to a medium bowl.

5. Add the dry ingredients and mix until well combined. Do not over mix. Dough will be sticky. To make it easier to work with, cover with a lid or plate, and refrigerate for at least 3 hours.

6. Preheat oven to 350° F. Liberally oil 2 large or 4 small baking pans, or line with non-stick bake liners or unbleached parchment paper.

7. Form the dough into 18 slightly rounded 1/3-cup portions using a metal 1/3-cup measure. Divide each mound of dough in half to make 36 portions. Dip your hands in ice water and roll the portions into balls.

8. Place the balls of dough on the baking sheets. Then, using your fingertips or the bottom of a metal measuring cup dipped repeatedly into ice water, flatten each ball making it 3 to 3 ½ inches across. Allow about ½ inch between each cookie. They will not spread. **Note:** You can get 12 on a 13x18-inch half sheet pan, with 4 going lengthwise and 3 across, or 8 on a standard 11x17-inch sheet with 3 going lengthwise down the sides and 2 in the center in between. Repeat with remaining dough.

9. Bake cookies for 12 to 15 minutes; rotate the baking sheets (top to bottom and back to front) halfway through. Cookies are done when the centers feel barely firm when lightly pressed, they are lightly golden on the bottom, and a toothpick inserted into the center comes out clean. They will firm up as they cool.

10. Cool on the baking pan for 2 to 3 minutes, then transfer to wire racks using a spatula. When cool, store in a covered Pyrex bowl, cookie tin, or cookie jar, separating each layer of cookies with unbleached parchment paper. Store at room temperature for up to 1 week. Refrigerate or freeze for longer storage.

VARIATIONS

* **For eggless cookies:** Replace each egg with 1 1/2 teaspoons Ener-G Egg Replacer plus 2 tablespoons warm water. Mix thoroughly before adding to the recipes. For additional moisture, add 2 more tablespoons water, nut milk, or applesauce for each egg you replace (1 egg = 1/4 cup volume).

* For 36 to 40 smaller cookies, shape dough into rounded tablespoons, then into balls. Flatten to make 2- to 2 1/2-inch round disks. Bake for 7 to 10 minutes.

Gingerbread Ice Dream Sandwich Cookies

Hands-on: 45 to 60 minutes • **Cooking:** 13 to 15 minutes • **Yield:** 24 cookies for 12 Sandwiches

Ingredients

Dry ingredients:

1 cup sweet brown rice flour **or** brown rice flour (spoon into measuring cup and level)

1 cup sorghum flour (spoon into measuring cup and level)

1 cup unmodified potato starch **or** arrowroot (spoon into measuring cup and level)

2 teaspoons baking soda

1 1/2 teaspoons xanthan gum **or** guar gum

3/4 to 1 teaspoon *pure* stevia extract powder **or** 1 1/2 to 2 teaspoons *clear* stevia extract liquid added to the wet ingredients

1 tablespoon ground ginger

2 teaspoons cinnamon

1/2 teaspoon ground cloves

1/2 teaspoon finely ground, unrefined sea salt

Wet ingredients:

3/4 cup packed soft, pitted dates

1/4 cup + 2 tablespoons palm shortening **or** virgin-pressed coconut oil, at room temperature

1/2 cup honey **or** agave nectar (do not substitute maple syrup)

1/2 cup molasses (no more than 1/3 cup as *blackstrap* molasses)

1/4 cup unsweetened applesauce, homemade (Page 186) **or** store-bought

2 medium to large eggs, at room temperature

1/4 cup plain almond or hazelnut milk, **or** date soaking liquid, at room temperature

2 teaspoons pure vanilla extract **or** alcohol-free vanilla flavoring

Coconut oil **or** palm shortening to grease baking pans

These soft and cakey gingerbread cookies contain far less fat than most cookies. Because the dough has a high moisture content, you'll need to chill it for a few hours before you shape and bake the cookies. Once baked, you can transform them into Ice Dream Sandwiches. (See Page 236 for assembly tips and suggestions for flavor combinations.)

1 LARGE COOKIE:
176 calories
1.9 grams protein
32.1 grams carbohydrate
4.3 grams fat
147 milligrams sodium

You will need a food processor, a blender, or a Vita-Mix to purée the dates with the wet ingredients. You want them to blend into the cookies so they're unnoticeable. They'll add moisture and sweetness, but you don't want to see chunky date bits. Allow enough time for soaking the dates before combining the ingredients.

~Continued next page~

Gingerbread Ice Dream Sandwich Cookies ~ continued

DIRECTIONS

1. Place dates in a bowl. Add water to cover by 1 inch. Let soak for 1 to 2 hours. Drain and save the liquid for use later in this recipe

2. Measure the dry ingredients into a medium bowl. Whisk and set aside.

3. If using coconut oil that is solid, melt it in a small saucepan over low heat; measure out what you need and allow it to cool. If using palm shortening, do not melt.

4. In a food processor, a blender, or a Vita-Mix, cream the shortening or oil, honey, molasses, dates, and applesauce. Add the eggs and vanilla. Blend until smooth. Transfer the purée to a medium bowl.

5. Add the dry ingredients. Mix until well blended and smooth. Batter will be sticky and wet. Cover the bowl with a lid or plate and refrigerate for at least 3 hours.

6. Preheat oven to 350° F. Liberally oil 2 large or 4 small baking pans, or line with non-stick bake liners or unbleached parchment paper.

7. Form the dough into 12 slightly rounded 1/3-cup portions using a metal 1/3-cup measure. Divide each mound of dough in half to make 24 portions. Dip your hands in ice water and roll the portions into balls.

8. Place the balls of dough on the baking sheets. Then, using your fingertips or the bottom of a metal measuring cup dipped repeatedly into ice water, flatten each ball making it 3 to 3-1/2 inches across. Allow about 1/2 inch between each. They will not spread. **Note:** You can get 12 on a 13x18-inch half sheet pan, with 4 going lengthwise and 3 across, or 8 on a standard 11x17-inch sheet with 3 going lengthwise down the sides and 2 in the center in between. Repeat with remaining portions of dough.

9. Bake cookies 13 to 15 minutes; rotate the baking sheets (top to bottom and back to front) halfway through. They will be done when the centers feel barely firm when lightly pressed, they are lightly golden on the bottom, and a toothpick inserted into the center comes out clean. Cookies will firm up as they cool.

10. Cool on the baking pan for 2 to 3 minutes, then transfer to wire racks using a spatula. When cool, store in a covered Pyrex bowl, cookie tin, or cookie jar, separating each layer of cookies with unbleached parchment paper. Store at room temperature for up to 1 week. Refrigerate or freeze for longer storage.

VARIATION

* For 36 to 48 smaller cookies, drop batter by rounded tablespoons onto prepared pans. Flatten and bake for 9 to 10 minutes.

Banana Oatmeal Raisin Ice Dream Sandwich Cookies

ASSEMBLY: 30 TO 45 MINUTES • **BAKING:** 16 MINUTES • **YIELD:** 24 COOKIES

INGREDIENTS

Dry ingredients:

3/4 cup sweet brown rice flour, brown rice flour, **or** a combination (spoon into measuring cup and level)

3/4 cup sorghum flour (spoon into measuring cup and level)

1 cup unmodified potato starch, white rice flour, **or** white sweet rice flour

2 cups quick-cooking oats (do not use thick-rolled oats)

1 cup raisins

2 teaspoons baking soda

1 teaspoon xanthan gum **or** guar gum

1/2 teaspoon *pure* stevia extract powder **or** 1 teaspoon *clear* stevia extract liquid added to wet ingredients

1 teaspoon cinnamon, optional

1/4 teaspoon nutmeg, optional

1/2 teaspoon finely ground, unrefined sea salt

Finely grated zest of 1 orange, optional

Wet ingredients:

1/2 cup packed soft, pitted dates

1/2 cup palm shortening **or** virgin-pressed coconut oil, at room temperature

1/2 cup unsweetened applesauce **or** prune purée, store bought or homemade (Page 186)

1/3 cup honey **or** agave nectar

1/3 to 1/2 cup plain almond or hazelnut milk, **or** date soaking liquid, at room temperature

3 ripe medium-size bananas, peeled and mashed

2 medium to large eggs, at room temperature

1 teaspoon pure vanilla extract **or** natural vanilla flavoring

Kelli Meechem, a friend, cooking student, and recipe tester, shared Chef Cary Neff's version of this cookie with me. (Neff works at Miraval Spa.) Kelli and I tweaked the recipe to make it gluten-free and dairy-free. We replaced the sugar with a combination of dates, honey, and stevia, and the chocolate chips with raisins. (The chocolate chip version also tastes fantastic.)

1 LARGE COOKIE:
216 calories
3.1 grams protein
37.6 grams carbohydrate
5.8 grams fat
143 milligrams sodium

You will need a food processor, a blender, or a Vita-Mix to purée the dates with the wet ingredients. You want them to blend into the cookies so they're unnoticeable. They'll add moisture and sweetness, but you don't want to see chunky date bits. Allow enough time for soaking the dates before combining the ingredients

~Continued next page~

> **FYI:** To make fairly flat cookies suitable for Ice Dream sandwiches, you will need to press the dough flat before baking (see instructions). It makes a difference.

Banana Oatmeal Raisin Ice Dream Sandwich Cookies ~ continued

DIRECTIONS

1. Place dates in a bowl. Add water to cover by 1 inch. Let soak for 1 to 2 hours. Drain and save the liquid for use later in this recipe

2. Measure the dry ingredients into a medium bowl. Whisk and set aside.

3. If using coconut oil that is solid, melt it in a small saucepan over low heat; measure out what you need and allow it to cool. If using palm shortening, do not melt.

4. In a blender, Vita-Mix, or food processor fitted with a metal blade, blend the shortening or the liquefied and cooled coconut oil with the applesauce, dates, and honey until creamy and smooth. Add the eggs, banana, nut milk, and vanilla. Mix until smooth. Transfer the purée to a medium bowl.

5. Add the dry ingredients. Stir until incorporated. Batter will be wet and sticky. Cover the bowl with a lid or plate. Refrigerate for at least 3 hours.

6. Preheat oven to 350° F. Liberally oil 2 large or 4 small baking pans, or line with non-stick bake liners or unbleached parchment paper.

7. Form the dough into 12 slightly rounded 1/3-cup portions using a metal 1/3-cup measure. Divide each mound of dough in half to make 24 portions. Dip your hands in ice water and roll the portions into balls.

8. Place the balls of dough on the baking sheets. Then, using your fingertips or the bottom of a metal measuring cup dipped repeatedly into ice water, flatten each ball making it 3 to 3-1/2 inches across. Space them evenly with about 1/2 inch between each. They will not spread. **Note:** You can get 12 on a 13x18-inch half sheet pan, with 4 going lengthwise and 3 across, or 8 on a standard 11x17-inch sheet with 3 going lengthwise down the sides and 2 in the center in between. Repeat with remaining portions of dough.

9. Bake cookies 15 to 16 minutes; rotate the baking sheets (top to bottom and back to front) halfway through. They will be done when the centers feel barely firm when lightly pressed, they are lightly golden on the bottom, and a toothpick inserted into the center comes out clean. Cookies will firm up as they cool.

10. Cool on the baking pan for 2 to 3 minutes, then transfer to wire racks using a spatula. When cool, store in a covered Pyrex bowl, cookie tin, or cookie jar, separating each layer of cookies with unbleached parchment paper. Store at room temperature for up to 1 week. Refrigerate or freeze for longer storage.

VARIATION

* For smaller cookies, drop batter by rounded tablespoons onto prepared pans. Flatten to about 1 1/2 inches in diameter and bake for 10 to 14 minutes.

Gluten-Free Graham Crackers

HANDS-ON: 30 MINUTES • **COOKING:** 30 TO 35 MINUTES • **YIELD:** 30 TO 36 CRACKERS

INGREDIENTS

Dry ingredients:

1 cup brown rice flour **or** combination of brown rice flour and sweet brown rice flour (spoon into measuring cup and level)

1 cup sorghum flour (spoon into measuring cup and level)

1/2 cup white rice flour (spoon into measuring cup and level)

1/2 cup potato starch **or** arrowroot; you may replace 3 tablespoons of this with quinoa flour if available (spoon into measuring cup and level)

2 teaspoons ground cinnamon

1 tablespoon gluten-free, non-aluminum baking powder

1 teaspoon xanthan gum **or** guar gum

1/2 teaspoon baking soda; sift if lumpy

1/2 teaspoon finely ground, unrefined sea salt

1/2 teaspoon *pure* stevia extract powder **or** 1 teaspoon *clear* stevia extract liquid added to the wet ingredients

Wet ingredients:

1/2 cup packed soft, pitted dates

1/2 cup palm shortening **or** virgin-pressed coconut oil

1/3 cup honey **or** agave nectar; additional 1 to 3 tablespoons if desired

1/2 cup date soaking water; additional 1 to 4 tablespoons if needed

1 teaspoon vanilla extract **or** alcohol-free vanilla flavoring

I modified Bette Hagman's recipe for Mock Graham Crackers from her book, *More from the Gluten-Free Gourmet.* I replaced the brown sugar with dates and stevia and the butter with palm shortening. (Coconut oil works equally well.) I reduced the amount of fat and increased the amount of whole grain flour and cinnamon, and then came up with variations.

Graham crackers make a great accompaniment to Ice Dream. You can crumble and add them during the last few minutes of churning or fold them in before removing the Ice Dream from the machine for a Cookies-n-Cream effect. Use them to make a graham cracker crust for Ice Dream Pie, or serve them as a snack or dessert with a steaming hot cup of Roasted Dandelion & Chicory Root Coffee Alternative (Page 246).

1 CRACKER:
94 calories
0.8 gram protein
14 grams carbohydrate
3.8 grams fat
91 milligrams sodium

You will need a food processor, a blender, or a Vita-Mix to purée the dates with the wet ingredients. You want them to blend into the cookies so they're unnoticeable. They'll add moisture and sweetness, but you don't want to see chunky date bits. Allow enough time for soaking the dates before combining the ingredients.

~Continued next 2 pages~

> **FYI:** If you use quinoa flour, you can grind whole grain quinoa (pronounced keen-wa) in a spice-dedicated coffee grinder. You will need a Vita-Mix or grain mill to turn short or medium grain brown rice or white rice into flour. Or, you can buy these flours already ground.

Gluten-Free Graham Crackers ~ continued

DIRECTIONS

1. Place dates in a bowl. Add water to cover by 1 inch. Let soak for 1 to 2 hours. Drain and save the liquid for use later in this recipe

2. Measure the dry ingredients into a medium bowl. Whisk and set aside.

3. If using coconut oil that is solid, melt it in a small saucepan over low heat; measure out what you need and allow it to cool. If using palm shortening, do not melt.

4. In a food processor fitted with a metal blade, a blender, or a Vita-Mix, cream the shortening or liquefied and cooled coconut oil, dates, honey, and 1/2 cup of the date soak liquid, until creamy and smooth. If using a blender or Vita Mix, transfer the purée to a medium bowl.

5. Add the dry ingredients and mix in the food processor or in a bowl using a pastry blender or large, sturdy spoon. The dough should be soft and slightly tacky. If it's too dry to hold together, add more water, 1 tablespoon at a time. For a sweeter taste, add one more tablespoon of honey. Blend. Repeat if needed.

6. Divide dough into 2 balls. Place each ball of dough on a lightly greased sheet of parchment paper approximately 12x15 or 11x17. Press to form the dough into an 8x9-inch or 6x9-inch rectangle, then fold the parchment over to cover. Stack the packages of dough on a plate or oblong pan. Cover tightly and refrigerate for 2 to 3 hours.

7. Preheat oven to 325° F. Cut 2 more pieces of parchment paper to fit the size of each cookie sheet, such as 12x15 1/2- or 11x17-inch, by placing baking sheet over the paper and tracing the outline with a pen. Then grease one side of each piece of paper.

8. One at a time, remove a wrapped rectangle of dough from the refrigerator and place on a cutting board. Unwrap, leaving the dough on the parchment. Place a second piece of parchment, greased side down, over the dough so the pieces of paper match. Evenly roll out the dough lengthwise and widthwise until it nearly covers the size of the pan (marked on the paper with a pen) and is 1/8 inch thick. Trim the edges. Transfer dough and parchment to a cookie sheet and peel off the top piece of parchment.

~Continued next page~

Gluten~Free Graham Crackers ~ continued

9. Cut into 3-inch squares using a pastry wheel, pizza cutter, or sharp chef's knife. Prick each square 5 times with a fork. Repeat with remaining dough and another cookie sheet.

10. Bake for 25 to 35 minutes until lightly browned but not crisp; remove crackers around the edges if they get too brown. Do not over bake. Cookies will crisp as they cool. Let cool for a few minutes, then transfer to a cooling rack. If you do not have 2 cookie sheets, repeat the procedure with the second piece of dough.

11. Store in a cookie jar or tin and use within 2 weeks, or freeze in an airtight container. If crackers soften in storage, briefly crisp them in an oven or toaster oven.

VARIATIONS

* **Chocolate Graham Crackers:** Replace potato starch or arrowroot and quinoa flour with unsweetened cocoa powder.

* **Carob Graham Crackers:** Replace potato starch or arrowroot with carob powder.

* **Lemon Graham Crackers:** Soak the dates in lemon juice instead of water. Add 1 teaspoon lemon extract **or** alcohol-free lemon flavoring and 2 teaspoons of finely grated lemon zest. Zest the lemon before slicing and juicing.

* **Orange Graham Crackers:** Soak the dates in orange juice instead of water. Add 1 teaspoon orange extract **or** alcohol-free orange flavoring and 1 tablespoon of finely grated orange zest. Zest the orange before slicing and juicing.

Help! My Chocolate Just Seized Up!

Seizing is when the chocolate you are melting suddenly becomes grainy and firms up, looking like a dull, thick paste. Chocolate is composed of fine, dry particles (cocoa and sugar) and fat (cocoa butter). When you are melting chocolate, if you inadvertently let a few drops of water, or even steam, contact the chocolate, it will moisten the dry particles and cause them to stick together and form a dull, dry, grainy mass that has seized up.

Once your chocolate seizes, it can no longer be used for tempering, because it is no longer considered pure. Don't throw it out—use it in baking recipes or chocolate sauces.

Seizing can happen for a couple of reasons:

1. A small amount of moisture has been added to the melting chocolate. Chocolate is very finicky about liquids. Even the tiniest amount of liquid, a single drop of water, the moisture clinging to a just-washed strawberry or just washed wooden spoon, or the steam from a double boiler that gets too hot, will cause this kind of damage to your chocolate.

To prevent the chocolate from seizing, you can take a few steps to keep moisture out:

* If using a double boiler, keep the water to a simmer, not a rolling boil, so it won't splash onto the chocolate.

* Don't use a wooden spoon to stir melted chocolate because it could hold moisture.

* Make sure the heatproof glass or metal bowl you are using to melt the chocolate in is *dry*.

* **Do not** place a cover over the bowl or the container of chocolate. Moisture will condense on the inside of the lid and cause seizing.

* Before adding melted chocolate to a recipe, let it cool until it is close to the batter's temperature but still liquid. Then add it a spoonful at a time and quickly stir to raise the temperature of the batter. Once you've incorporated half of the chocolate you can add the rest more quickly, then combine the chocolate mixture with the rest of the batter.

* If a recipe calls for adding warm chocolate to colder eggs, add a tablespoon or two of melted chocolate to the beaten eggs and stir to combine. Repeat a couple of times until you've added at least half of the chocolate,

then combine the chocolate mixture with the rest of the egg mixture.

* If a recipe calls for chocolate and milk, coarsely chop the chocolate and place it in a heatproof bowl; then warm the milk, pour it over the chocolate, and stir. The chocolate will melt without seizing. If recipe calls for semisolid fat or oil, you can melt it with the chocolate (I do that when making brownies). The oil will prevent seizing.

2. Cool liquids have been added to the melting chocolate. Another oddity about chocolate: small amounts of liquid can spoil melted chocolate, but large amounts are okay as long as the liquid is warmed to match the temperature of the melted chocolate. If you add cold cream or milk, for example, the chocolate will begin to solidify and you'll end up with a mess. Instead, properly warm liquids before adding to the chocolate.

3. Chocolate was overheated during melting or tempering. Chocolate is so sensitive to rapid temperature changes, such as melting under high heat.

To fix seized chocolate: As an emergency measure only, stir in 1 level tablespoon solid vegetable shortening for each 6 ounces of chocolate you are melting. (6 ounces is equal to 1 cup baking chips or 6 (1-oz squares) of baking chocolate). **Rachel's note**: Instead of conventional shortening, I recommend palm shortening, a non-hydrogenated product made from unrefined palm oil.

Source: Some of the information above was taken from www.baking911.com, an award-winning, top-ranking baking web site created by Sara Phillips, author of *The Healthy Oven Baking Book* and *Baking 911: Rescue from Recipe Disasters*. You'll find answers to all your baking questions there.

Chocolate-Covered Ice Dream Pops

Hands-on assembly: 30 minutes • **Freezing:** 24 to 30 hours • **Yield:** 6 to 9 servings

Ingredients

About 3 cups Ice Dream, freshly churned or made ahead:

> Vanilla, Ginger, Nutmeg, Cinnamon, Rum Raisin, Avocado, Carob Banana, Cocoa, Dark Chocolate, Chocolate Hazelnut, Cocoa Macadamia, Peppermint Wafer, Peanut Butter, Coffee, Roasted Banana, Chai, **or** Pumpkin flavor (see index for recipes)

4 ounces bittersweet dark chocolate (70 to 73%), cut into pieces

1 cup coarsely chopped toasted almonds, pecans, hazelnuts, or cashews (Page 75), **or** 1 cup cocoa nibs, **or** unsweetened, sulfite-free shredded coconut, or slightly more as needed

Directions

1. Freeze the empty Popsicle molds for at least 6 hours.

2. *If using freshly churned Ice Dream,* prepare it according to the recipe, removing it from the ice cream maker as soon as it's done churning.

   If using solidly frozen Ice Dream, allow it to soften in the refrigerator for 30 to 45 minutes or at room temperature for 15 to 30 minutes, depending upon the flavor, until soft enough to spread. Do not allow it to liquefy.

3. Spoon the soft Ice Dream into the frozen Popsicle molds, filling each mold almost to the top, leaving 1/8 to 1/4 inch of space. Most molds hold between 1/3 and 1/2 cupful. Quickly press in the Popsicle sticks (or tops) and place the molds in the freezer. Keep them standing upright (vertically). Freeze for at least 24 hours.

4. Spread the nuts, cocoa nibs, or shredded coconut onto a large plate. Cover a plate, platter, or shallow baking tray with parchment paper.

When I was a kid, I loved the vanilla ice cream bars with a crisp chocolate coating. Believe it or not, I've not eaten anything like that (not even the health food store version) in 25 years. When I saw this recipe in Avner Laskin's book *The Ice Cream Maker Companion,* I knew it would make a great addition to my book. I upgraded the ingredients and made it dairy-free.

This recipe will take some skillful timing and intuitive decision making to avoid any frustrations. The chocolate can't be too warm, but it also can't be allowed to get too stiff. Filling the molds is somewhat messy.

1 SERVING (6 per batch):
406 calories
6.9 grams protein
21.2 grams carbohydrate
32.8 grams fat
67 milligrams sodium

1 SERVING (9 per batch):
272 calories
4.6 grams protein
14.3 grams carbohydrate
21.8 grams fat
44 milligrams sodium

~Continued next page~

> **Note:** If you use 100% lite variations of Ice Dream, they will freeze harder than the half-lite or full-fat recipes in this book. It's easier to use freshly churned Ice Dream to make pops, but you can use previously-made Ice Dream if you let it soften enough to pack into the molds. It just takes a little more patience.
>
> Plastic Popsicle molds come in various sizes. We tested this recipe using molds that hold 1/3 cup and others that hold between 1/3 and 1/2 cup.

Chocolate-Covered Ice Dream Pops ~ continued

5. Melt the chocolate in a double boiler or in a saucepan over very low heat. When almost melted, remove from heat; stir for a few minutes and let it cool slightly.

6. Remove the pops from the freezer and, one at a time, carefully remove them from the molds. If they don't slide out easily, dip the molds into lukewarm water or wrap with a warm washcloth for a few seconds until they release. Be careful with this—if you get water on the pop and then it drips into the chocolate, the chocolate will seize up and get lumpy, or worse, become unworkable.

7. Use a small ladle to pour some of the melted chocolate onto the pop and allow it to cool for a few seconds. Gently press the chocolate-covered pop into the nuts, cocoa nibs, or coconut, rolling it slowly until completely coated. Lay the pop gently on parchment paper. The first couple of pops might melt as you spoon the chocolate over them. Don't let the Ice Dream Pops drip into the chocolate, which will make it seize. Repeat with the other pops.

   Note: The chocolate will start to stiffen after you've coated the first couple of pops, so warm it again over very low heat for a few minutes to loosen it up.

8. Return the pops to the freezer until the coating sets, at least 10 minutes, but you can leave them longer. Once set, wrap each one in parchment or wax paper, and then slip into zip-locking bags or freezer-safe containers for longer storage.

When my friend Julie tested this recipe with store-bought rice ice cream, the first couple of pops melted as she spooned the chocolate over them, then it dripped into the chocolate, which made it seize up just a little. She had much better success with my homemade Ice Dream.

Ice Dream Sandwiches

HANDS-ON: 20 MINUTES • **COOKING:** 0 • **YIELD:** 8 PORTIONS

Children and adults alike will enjoy eating these sweet treats with their hands. They make a great snack or dessert. Unlike leftover Ice Dream that can take 20 to 30 minutes to soften enough to scoop, these are usually ready to eat right out of the freezer or with only a 5 to 10 minute wait. If you're feeling impatient or you want only a few bites, place an Ice Dream sandwich on the cutting board and cut into 1-inch pieces or wedges with a chef's knife.

INGREDIENTS
Crust:

16 Ice Dream Sandwich Cookies:
Pumpkin Spice, Gingerbread Spice, Chocolate, Chocolate Chip, **or** *Banana Oatmeal Raisin* (see index for recipes)

4 cups Vanilla Ice Dream (Page 78), or other flavor, freshly churned or made in advance

DIRECTIONS

1. If using solidly frozen Ice Dream, allow it to soften in the refrigerator for 30 to 45 minutes or at room temperature for 15 to 30 minutes, depending upon the flavor, until soft enough to scoop and spread over the crust. Do not allow it to liquefy. If using freshly made Ice Dream, have the cookies ready before the Ice Dream is done churning.

2. Arrange 8 cookies flat side up on a baking pan or platter. Using a stainless steel 1/2-cup measure or an ice cream scoop that holds 1/2-cup water, place a 1/2-cup portion of Ice Dream on each cookie. Cover with the remaining 8 cookies, pressing down gently to form a sandwich. Smooth the edges with a spatula if desired.

3. Place the tray of sandwiches in the freezer, uncovered, until firm to the touch, 30 to 60 minutes.

1 SERVING
(W/PUMPKIN SPICE COOKIE):
400 calories
3.4 grams protein
50.1 grams carbohydrate
20.6 grams fat
95 milligrams sodium

1 SERVING
(W/CHOCOLATE COOKIE):
442 calories
7 grams protein
43.7 grams carbohydrate
27.2 grams fat
162 milligrams sodium

4. Wrap the sandwiches individually in unbleached wax paper bags or in parchment paper, folded around the tops and sides. Place the wrapped sandwiches in freezer-safe Pyrex containers with lids or in zip-locking bags. Insert a straw into the bag. Zip the bag all the way to the straw, then suck out as much air as possible and seal the bag.

5. Label with masking tape and return to the freezer. Use within 6 to 8 weeks for best results.

~Continued next page~

> **Note:** Use regular, half-lite or 100% lite versions of Ice Dream to make Ice Dream Sandwiches. Feel free to halve the recipe if needed. See ideas below for filling and cookie combinations.

Ice Dream Sandwiches ~ continued

Variations

* For a fancier treat, at the end of step #2, pat chopped, toasted nuts or unsweetened, sulfite-free, shredded coconut around the edges, or roll the sandwiches in the pieces to coat.

* Fill Gingerbread Spice or Pumpkin Spice Cookies with Vanilla, Dark Chocolate, Cocoa, Almost Chocolate, Rum Raisin, or Peanut Butter Ice Dream.

* Try Chocolate Ice Dream Sandwiches filled with Nutmeg, Maple Pecan, Avocado, Chai, Coffee, Roasted Banana, Dried Cherry Pecan, Pumpkin, or Peanut Butter Ice Dream.

Make them with freshly churned Ice Dream or Ice Dream softened briefly at room temperature. They'll keep well for at least a month in the freezer. Have fun experimenting with different combinations of cookies and Ice Dream. Soft, thin cookies make the best sandwiches. Crunchy cookies are more apt to crumble and fall apart as you bite into them.

237

No~Bake Cookie Pie Crust

HANDS-ON: 20 MINUTES • **COOKING:** 0 • **YIELD:** 1 (9-INCH) PIE

INGREDIENTS

Crust:

6 ounces (by weight) gluten-free store bought
cookies:
*Graham crackers, shortbread, gingersnaps,
carob, chocolate,* **or** *chocolate chip; or slightly
more as needed to make 1 1/2 cups finely
crushed cookie crumbs*

or 6 to 8 ounces (by weight) gluten-free Ice Dream
Sandwich Cookies:
*Chocolate, Chocolate Chip, Gingerbread Spice,
or Pumpkin Spice (see index for recipes), 1 3/4
to 2 1/4 cups finely crushed*

1/4 cup unsweetened, roasted almond, cashew,
macadamia nut, hazelnut **or** peanut butter, stirred
thoroughly before measuring

DIRECTIONS

1. Lightly grease the bottom and sides of a 9- or
   10-inch deep-dish pie plate or an 8- or 10-
   inch springform pan. If using a springform
   pan, trace and cut a piece of unbleached
   parchment paper to fit the bottom of the
   pan. Line bottom of pan with parchment,
   then oil the top of the parchment.

2. Grind the cookies to a powder in a food
   processor, Vita-Mix, or blender. If using
   a blender, break cookies into pieces and
   pulverize; or put the cookies in a sturdy zip-
   locking bag and press out the air. Seal the
   bag, then crush with a rolling pin.

3. Mix cookie crumbs and nut butter until
   well combined using a food processor fitted
   with a metal blade, or in a bowl with a pastry cutter or sturdy spoon.
   Spread the mixture evenly in the prepared pan. Using your fingertips or
   the bottom of a drinking glass, firmly press the mixture over the bottom
   and ½ inch up the sides of the pie plate, or press over the bottom of a
   springform pan and ½ to 1 inch up the sides. Cover with wax paper or
   unbleached parchment. Freeze until firm, at least 1 hour.

4. See Page 244 for recommended fillings, toppings, and tips.

Conventional graham
cracker crusts usually
contain dangerous
refined and/or
hydrogenated oils. You
can make a healthier
version using finely
crushed, gluten-free
homemade or store-
bought cookies and nut
butter.

Once you've made
the crust, you can
follow the recipe for
Ice Dream Pie on
Page 244. I got the
idea for this recipe
from Linda Leszynski,
health educator and
president of Healthy
Young Children
Enterprises, Inc. I met
Linda when we both
gave presentations at
a Health Expo for the
Arthritis Foundation of
Southwest Arizona.

ENTIRE PIE
1373 calories
49.4 grams protein
143.3 grams carbohydrate
66.9 grams fat
707 milligrams sodium

1 SERVING (1/8 PIE):
172 calories
6.2 grams protein
17.9 grams carbohydrate
8.4 grams fat
88 milligrams sodium

~Continued next page~

FYI: If you're buying cookies, look for brands with the simplest and fewest ingredients in natural foods stores or the health foods section of supermarkets. Examples include Pamela's, Mi-Del, Kinnikinnick, and Trader Joe's Gluten-Free Ginger Snaps. Crunchy cookies make the best crust, although soft cookies, such as the Ice Dream Sandwich Cookies found in this book, also work.

No Bake Cookie Pie Crust ~ continued

VARIATIONS

* **If you are allergic to nuts, but tolerate coconut:** Replace almond or cashew butter with unsweetened coconut butter (not coconut oil—coconut butter is much thicker because it's made from coconut flesh and oil in the same way that peanut butter is made from whole peanuts). (See Resources for recommended brands.) **Note:** If the coconut butter is solid, run the jar under hot water to liquefy so you can stir it well and easily spoon it out to measure.

* **For a double thick cookie crust:** Use 3 cups of cookie crumbs and 1/2 cup of nut butter in the recipe above, and use a springform pan.

Avoid products that contain fructose, corn syrup, high fructose corn sweetener, or artificial sweeteners. Avoid corn, soy, safflower, sunflower, and canola oil as well as all hydrogenated and partially-hydrogenated oil, margarine, and shortening (non-hydrogenated palm shortening is safe). If you are gluten-intolerant, avoid barley, wheat, and unbleached, pastry, cake, or enriched flour.

Low~Fat Baked Cookie Pie Crust

HANDS-ON: 20 MINUTES • **COOKING:** 8 TO 10 MINUTES • **YIELD:** 1 (9-INCH) PIE

INGREDIENTS

Crust:

6 ounces (by weight) gluten-free, store-bought cookies:
Graham crackers, shortbread, gingersnaps, carob, chocolate, or chocolate chip; or slightly more as needed to make 1 1/2 cups finely crushed cookie crumbs

or 6 to 8 ounces (by weight) gluten-free Ice Dream Sandwich Cookies:
Chocolate, Chocolate Chip, Gingerbread Spice, or Pumpkin Spice (see index for recipes) to make 1 3/4 to 2 1/4 cups finely crushed cookie crumbs

1 egg white **or** 3 tablespoons liquid egg whites

1 tablespoon virgin-pressed coconut oil **or** palm shortening, melted

1 to 3 teaspoons water (less for moist cookies, more for dry ones)

1 tablespoon unsweetened cocoa powder, optional

1/4 teaspoon ground cinnamon, optional

Most cookie crumb crusts call for a lot of butter, margarine, or vegetable oil to bind them. Most also use cookies that contain hazardous, refined and/or hydrogenated oils. You can make a healthier version using powdered, gluten-free cookies and egg whites. I got the idea for this recipe from Bette Hagman's book, *The Gluten-Free Gourmet Makes Dessert*. Using egg whites greatly reduces the need for fat and still results in a tender crust. Once you've made the crust, you can follow the recipe for Ice Dream Pie on Page 244. If you love crust, consider doubling the crust recipe below.

DIRECTIONS

1. Lightly grease the bottom and sides of a 9- or 10-inch deep-dish pie plate or an 8- or 10-inch springform pan. If using a springform pan, trace and then cut a piece of unbleached parchment paper the same size as the bottom of the pan. Line the bottom of the pan with parchment, then oil the top of the parchment. Preheat oven to 425° F.

ENTIRE PIE
1101 calories
46.4 grams protein
130.6 grams carbohydrate
43.6 grams fat
800 milligrams sodium

1 SERVING (1/8 PIE):
137 calories
5.8 grams protein
16.3 grams carbohydrate
5.4 grams fat
99 milligrams sodium

2. Grind the cookies to a powder in a food processor, Vita-Mix, or blender. If using a blender, break the cookies into pieces and pulverize; or put the cookies in a sturdy zip-locking bag and press out the air. Seal the bag, then crush with a rolling pin.

~Continued next page~

> **FYI:** If you're buying cookies, look for brands with the simplest and fewest ingredients in natural foods stores or the health foods section of supermarkets. Examples include Pamela's, Mi-Del, Kinnikinnick, and Trader Joe's Gluten-Free Ginger Snaps. Crunchy cookies make the best crust, although soft cookies, such as the Ice Dream Sandwich Cookies found in this book, also work.

Low-Fat Baked Cookie Pie Crust ~ continued

3. Beat the egg white in a medium bowl with a fork, whisk, or electric beaters until foamy, 1 or 2 minutes. Add the cookie crumbs, melted coconut or palm oil, and water. For a chocolate crust, add the cocoa powder. For the taste of graham crackers, add the cinnamon. Mix with a fork or spoon, or in the food processor, just long enough to combine.

4. Spread the mixture evenly in the prepared pan. Using your fingertips or the bottom of a drinking glass, firmly press the mixture over the bottom and 1/2 inch up the sides of the pie pan or, similarly, over the bottom of a springform pan.

5. Bake until slightly browned and firm, 8 to 10 minutes if using dry, crunchy cookies, or 10 to 12 minutes if using soft Ice Dream Sandwich Cookies. Do not overbake. Allow crust to cool before filling. See Ice Dream Pie (Page 244) for recommended fillings and toppings as well as tips.

Avoid products that contain fructose, corn syrup, high fructose corn sweetener, or artificial sweeteners. Avoid corn, soy, safflower, sunflower, and canola oil as well as all hydrogenated and partially-hydrogenated oil, margarine, and shortening (non-hydrogenated palm shortening is safe). If you are gluten-intolerant, avoid barley, wheat, and unbleached, pastry, cake, or enriched flour.

No~Bake Date Nut Pie Crust

PREP TIME: 30 MINUTES • **CHILLING TIME:** 8 HOURS • **YIELD:** 1 (10-INCH) PIE CRUST • **SERVES:** 8

INGREDIENTS

2 cups raw walnuts, pecans, **or** hazelnuts (filberts)

12 ounces (3/4-pound) coconut date rolls **or** 2 cups soft, pitted dates

DIRECTIONS

1. **To prepare the pan:** Lightly grease the bottom and sides of a 9- or 10-inch deep-dish pie plate or an 8-, 9-, or 10-inch springform pan. If using a springform pan, trace and then cut a piece of parchment paper the same size as the bottom of the pan. Line the pan with parchment, then oil the top side of the parchment.

2. **To toast the nuts:** Position an oven rack in the center of the oven and preheat to 350° F. Spread the nuts in a single layer in a shallow, rimmed baking pan and toast until the nuts begin to turn lightly golden and aromatic, 10 to 15 minutes. Shake the pan or stir 2 or 3 times during cooking. To check for doneness, remove a nut from the oven after about 10 minutes and cut it open. Check every few minutes until nuts turn a light golden brown all the way through. Watch closely so they don't burn. Wrap walnuts or hazelnuts in a clean kitchen towel; rub to loosen the skins. Remove the nuts and discard the skins. Allow the nuts to cool before grinding.

3. **To grind the nuts:** Place the nuts in a blender, Vita-Mix, or food processor fitted with a metal blade. Pulse the machine on and off until you have a fine meal, but stop before the mixture turns into nut butter. Pour the meal into a medium-size bowl and set aside.

4. **To pulverize the dates:** If the dates feel dry (as opposed to soft and squishy), place them in a heatproof bowl on a rack over boiling water. Cover the pot and steam for 5 minutes until soft. Let stand for 5 to 10 minutes. Tear the coconut date rolls into small pieces, chop the pitted dates into small pieces, or pulverize date rolls or dates in a Vita-Mix or a food processor fitted with a metal blade.

You'll find countless versions of this recipe on raw foods web sites and cookbooks. I came across this one in Anne Louise Gittleman's book, *Get the Sugar Out,* which she got from Carol Nostrand's *Junk Food to Real Food.* The original called for walnuts, but other nuts work just as well. Although most versions of this crust call for raw nuts, I recommend toasting them to make them more digestible. Once chilled, you can fill the crust with almost any flavor of Ice Dream.

ENTIRE PIE
2953 calories
45.6 grams protein
282.1 grams carbohydrate
182.5 grams fat
137 milligrams sodium

1 SERVING (1/8 PIE):
369 calories
5.7 grams protein
35.3 grams carbohydrate
22.8 grams fat
17 milligrams sodium

~Continued next page~

> **Note:** Look for coconut date rolls in the produce or bulk foods section of natural foods stores. They're made from soft, pitted dates that have been put through a grinder twice, then formed into tube shapes and rolled in coconut. To make your own date rolls, see Page 209. If you buy dates with the pit, simply remove the pits and measure out the amount you need.

No Bake Date Nut Pie Crust ~ continued

5. Add the nut meal to the date mixture. Mix in a food processor or in a bowl using your hands. Form the mixture into a smooth ball and place in a 10-inch deep-dish glass pie plate, or on the bottom of an 8-, 9-, or 10-inch springform pan. Using your palms first, and then your fingertips or the bottom of a drinking glass, firmly press the mixture over the bottom and up the sides of the pie pan or over the bottom of a springform pan and 1 inch up the sides. Cover with wax paper or unbleached parchment paper. Refrigerate for at least 6 hours or freeze for at least 2 hours, until firm, before filling.

6. See Page 244 for recommended fillings and toppings and tips.

Variation

* **Date Raisin Nut Crust:** Use 1 cup raisins and 1 cup dates or coconut date rolls in the recipe above. You'll need a food processor to pulverize the raisins and dates so they form a smooth mixture that holds together.

Do not use 100% lite variations of Ice Dream to fill a pie crust because they freeze hard and ice up. However, you can use half-lite versions of Ice Dream that contain a mix of regular and lite coconut milk, or recipes such as Dark Chocolate Ice Dream or Almost Chocolate that contain melted chocolate or nut butter.

Ice Dream Pie

HANDS-ON ASSEMBLY: 15 MINUTES • **FREEZING:** 4 HOURS • **YIELD:** 8 TO 12 SERVINGS

INGREDIENTS

1 recipe No-Bake Cookie Crust (Page 238**),** Low-Fat Baked Cookie Crust (Page 240), **or** Date Nut Crust (Page 242), frozen

1 to 1 1/2 quarts (4 to 6 cups) Ice Dream, freshly churned or made ahead:
Vanilla, Ginger, Nutmeg, Cinnamon, Carob Banana, Cocoa, Dark Chocolate, Chocolate Hazelnut, Cocoa Macadamia, Chocolate Espresso, Coffee, Chai, **or** *Pumpkin flavor* (see index for recipes)

3/4 cup sauce at room temperature, heated briefly to soften if hard, and then cooled:
Hot Fudge, Hot Chocolate, Peanut or Almond Buttery Hot Chocolate, Caramel **or** *Karly's Carob Sauce* (see index for recipes)

½ cup chopped, lightly toasted, unsalted almonds, walnuts, pecans, cashews, **or** macadamia nuts (Page 75), **or** cocoa (aka cacao) nibs

DIRECTIONS

1. If using solidly frozen Ice Dream, allow it to soften in the refrigerator for 30 to 45 minutes or at room temperature for 15 to 30 minutes, depending upon the flavor, until soft enough to scoop and spread over the crust. Do not allow it to liquefy. Remove sauce from the refrigerator to allow it to come to room temperature.

2. Remove the crust from the freezer. Working quickly, spoon and pack the Ice Dream into the cold crust, smoothing the top with a moistened rubber or metal spatula. You will be able to fit 4 cups of Ice Dream into a large pie plate. You can fit more into a springform pan. Freeze until just set, at least 1 to 2 hours.

3. If the sauce is too thick to spread, heat briefly using the bowl-on-a-rack method (Page 74), then allow to cool. Spread sauce over the Ice Dream using a flexible spatula dipped repeatedly in lukewarm water. Sprinkle with nuts or cocoa nibs if desired. Freeze

You won't miss premium ice cream pies if you make this impressive no-bake pie. It's easy to assemble, and perfect for a birthday, anniversary, graduation party, baby shower, Thanksgiving, or any other special event. Use this recipe as a starting point, and then let your creativity run wild. You can vary the Ice Dream flavors, the sauces, the crust, and the sprinkle-on toppings.

Note: Do not use 100% lite variations of Ice Dream to fill a pie crust because they freeze hard and ice up. However, you can use half lite versions of Ice Dream that contain a mix of regular and lite coconut milk, or recipes such as Dark Chocolate Ice Dream or Almost Chocolate that contain melted chocolate or nut butter.

1 SERVING (1/8 PIE):
382 calories
8.5 grams protein
31.9 grams carbohydrate
24.4 grams fat
159 milligrams sodium

1 SERVING (1/12 PIE):
285 calories
6.1 grams protein
23.3 grams carbohydrate
18.6 grams fat
115 milligrams sodium

~Continued next page~

FYI: It works best to make the crust, freeze it, and then churn the Ice Dream. If you make the Ice Dream more than a day ahead, allow enough time for it to soften before you spread it in the crust.

Ice Dream Pie ~ continued

until firm, at least 2 hours, or up to 3 days. **Note:** If left too long, pie will become icy.

4. If you don't plan to serve the pie within 6 hours after it firms up, cover with a piece of unbleached parchment or wax paper cut to exactly cover the pie, then cover with a larger piece of aluminum foil. Crimp the edges to seal.

5. Transfer pie to the refrigerator 60 minutes before serving, or to the counter 30 minutes before serving to soften.

6. If using a springform pan, wrap a warm, damp kitchen towel around it for 1 or 2 minutes to loosen the sides. Repeat as needed. Unclamp and remove the ring. If too hard to slice, leave the cake at room temperature for another 10 to 20 minutes. To slice, dip a long serrated knife or chef's knife into a bowl of hot water. Repeat as needed.

VARIATIONS

*   **Frozen Pumpkin Pie:** Use gingersnaps or graham crackers in the Cookie Crust, and a nut butter other than peanut butter to bind it. Use Pumpkin Ice Dream for the filling. Proceed as directed, garnishing with chopped, toasted nuts.

*   **Chocolate Ice Dream Pie:** Use graham crackers or chocolate cookies for the Cookie Crust or use the Date Nut Crust. Fill with one of the chocolate-flavored Ice Dreams. After the Ice Dream and sauce firm up, add a layer of Strawberry, Cherry, or Mango Sauce. Freeze for 1 to 3 hours, then garnish with nuts or cocoa nibs, or drizzle with one of the chocolate sauces found in Chapter 8.

*   **Coffee Ice Dream Pie:** Wow! You've got to try this one; just make sure to eat it early in the day, right after lunch, if caffeine keeps you up at night. Use gingersnaps, chocolate cookies, or graham crackers in the Cookie Crust and a nut butter other than peanut butter to bind it. Use Coffee or Espresso Chocolate Ice Dream, with Caramel, Hot Chocolate, Almond Buttery Hot Chocolate, Hot Fudge, or Cherry Sauce (see index for recipes). Or, add a fruit sauce, freeze for 1 hour, then lightly drizzle Chocolate or Caramel Sauce in a zig-zag or cross-hatch pattern over the top.

*   **Ginger Spice Ice Dream Pie:** Use gingersnaps or graham crackers in the Cookie Crust, and a nut butter other than peanut butter to bind it. Use Ginger, Cinnamon, Nutmeg, or Chai Ice Dream along with Chocolate, Fudge, or Caramel Sauce. Add nuts or additional crumbled cookies for garnish (see index for recipes).

*   **Carob Ice Dream Pie:** Use gingersnaps or graham crackers in the Cookie Crust, and a nut butter other than peanut butter to bind it. For the filling use Carob Banana or Almost Chocolate Ice Dream. Top with Cherry or Strawberry Sauce, then drizzle with Karly's Carob Sauce, or Caramel Sauce (see index for recipes). Garnish with toasted nuts or unsweetened, sulfite-free, finely shredded coconut.

Coconut Macaroon Ice Dream Cake

HANDS-ON ASSEMBLY: 60 MINUTES • **FREEZING:** 5 HOURS • **YIELD:** 12 SERVINGS

INGREDIENTS

Coconut oil or palm shortening

1 quart (4 cups) chocolate Ice Dream, freshly churned or made ahead:
  Cocoa, Dark Chocolate, Almost Chocolate, Chocolate Hazelnut, or Cocoa Macadamia flavor (see index for recipes)

2 (8-ounce cans) Jennies Coconut Macaroons **or** 4 cups My Favorite Macaroons (Page 202)

1 quart Ice Dream, freshly churned or made ahead:
  Vanilla, Maple Vanilla, Cinnamon, Nutmeg, Ginger, or Pumpkin (see index for recipes)

3/4 cup Sauce:
  Hot Fudge, Hot Chocolate, Almond Buttery Hot Chocolate, or Karly's Carob Sauce (see index for recipes)

1/2 cup chopped, lightly toasted, unsalted almonds, pecans, cashews, **or** macadamia nuts, unsweetened, sulfite-free, finely shredded coconut, **or** cocoa nibs (aka cacao nibs)

I modeled this recipe on one I found online from *Woman's Day* (August 3, 2004). I upgraded the quality of ingredients and tweaked the instructions to my detailed satisfaction. This cake takes more work than the Ice Dream Pie, but for a little extra fuss, you'll have some very delighted guests.

1 SERVING (1/12 CAKE):
571 calories
6.3 grams protein
51.4 grams carbohydrate
37.8 grams fat
120 milligrams sodium

DIRECTIONS

1. If using solidly frozen Chocolate Ice Dream, allow it to soften at room temperature for 15 to 30 minutes, depending upon the flavor, until soft enough to scoop and spread over the crust. Do not allow it to liquefy.

2. Lightly grease the bottom and sides of an 8 1/2- , 9 1/2-, or 10-inch springform pan. Trace and then cut a piece of parchment paper the same size as the bottom of the pan. Line the pan with parchment; oil top of parchment to prevent sticking.

3. Tear half the macaroons into small pieces. Oil your fingers or dip repeatedly into a bowl of cold water as you press about 2 1/2 cupfuls of macaroons over the bottom and 1/2 inch up the sides of the pan. Try not to pack the crust tightly. Spread Chocolate Ice Dream over the crust.

4. Tear another 1 1/2 cups of macaroons into pieces, then sprinkle evenly over the Chocolate Ice Dream. Freeze for 45 to 60 minutes or until almost firm.

5. Soften the Vanilla Ice Dream as directed above. Spread it evenly over the top of the cake. Freeze again for at least 4 hours or until firm.

~Continued next page~

> **Note:** Don't panic if, when you slice the pie, the layers start to come apart a little. Because homemade Ice Dream doesn't contain the stabilizers found in store-bought ice cream, it requires more time to soften before slicing. Once you bite into this heavenly cake, I don't think you will mind how it looks.

Coconut Macaroon Ice Dream Cake ~ continued

6. Remove from freezer and pour chocolate sauce over the middle of the cake and spread with a flexible spatula. Freeze for 1 to 3 hours.

7. Transfer the pie to the refrigerator about 60 minutes before serving, or to the counter 30 minutes before serving to soften.

8. To serve, wrap a warm, damp kitchen towel around the springform pan for 1 or 2 minutes to loosen the sides. Unclamp and remove the ring. Pat the chopped nuts, coconut, or cocoa nibs onto the sides of the cake. If Ice Dream is too hard for the nuts to stick, or too hard to slice, leave the cake at room temperature for another 10 to 20 minutes. To slice, dip a long serrated knife or chef's knife into a bowl of hot water.

VARIATIONS

* **Frozen Gingerbread Ice Dream Cake:** Replace macaroons with soft Gingerbread Ice Dream Sandwich Cookies (Page 226) or Pumpkin Spice Ice Dream Sandwich Cookies (Page 224). Use a chocolate Ice Dream (see list above), the Vanilla Ice Dream, and then add a chocolate sauce or Caramel Sauce (Page 176).

* **Frozen Chocolate Ice Dream Cake:** Replace macaroons with soft Chocolate Ice Dream Sandwich Cookies (Page 222) or Better Brownies (Page 216). Use Vanilla Ice Dream for the first flavor, Cinnamon, Nutmeg, Coffee, or Pumpkin Ice Dream for the second flavor above, and then add Caramel Sauce or one of the chocolate sauces above.

Do not use 100% lite variations of Ice Dream to fill the cake because they freeze hard and ice up. However, you can use half lite versions of Ice Dream that contain a mix of regular and lite coconut milk, or recipes such as Dark Chocolate Ice Dream or Almost Chocolate that contain melted chocolate or nut butter.

Roasted Chicory & Dandelion Root Coffee Alternative

PREP: 5 MINUTES • **COOKING:** 0 TO 15 MINUTES • **YIELD:** 6 CUPS

INGREDIENTS

6 cups filtered water

4 tablespoons roasted chicory root pieces or grinds, roasted dandelion root pieces or grinds, **or** a combination of the 2

DIRECTIONS

1. **In a saucepan:** Boil water in a 3-quart glass, ceramic, or stainless steel pot. Add roasted chicory and/or dandelion root. Reduce heat and simmer for 15 minutes. If too strong, add more water. Strain before serving.

   In a stove-top percolator: Add roasted chicory and/or dandelion root to the basket of a stainless steel stove top percolator (lined with an unbleached paper liner if desired). Bring to boil, reduce heat, and percolate for 15 minutes. If using an electric percolator, follow the manufacturer's directions.

   In a drip coffee maker: Add roasted chicory and/or dandelion root to the basket of a coffee maker (lined with an unbleached paper liner or re-usable liner if desired). Bring to boil, reduce heat and percolate for 15 minutes. If using an electric percolator, follow the manufacturer's directions.

2. Serve hot or warm, black or with milk or sweetener. Reheat leftovers or pour into 1 or more thermos bottles and seal to keep warm for several hours. Refrigerate leftover herbal coffee in glass jars. Reheat in a saucepan and use within 5 days.

I've been making variations on this brew for more than 15 years. Roasted chicory and dandelion roots give this caffeine-free herbal brew a robust coffee-like flavor and fragrance. This beverage doesn't contain any chemical residues or acidic compounds. You can make a pot, refrigerate the leftovers for up to 5 days, and reheat it as needed. If you find the flavor too strong, add more water and make a note to use less of the grinds the next time.

Instead of milk or cream, try unsweetened coconut milk or almond, cashew, hazelnut, or hemp milk. To sweeten a cup, add a few drops of plain, vanilla, or chocolate-flavored stevia extract liquid (start with 1 drop for every 2 ounces of liquid), a stevia tablet, or a teaspoon of honey or agave nectar.

Note: My basic rule of thumb is 2 teaspoons of roasted chicory or dandelion root grinds, or a combination of the two, per cup of water. I always use filtered rather than tap water for the best flavor and health benefits.

VARIATION

* **Roasted Chicory & Dandelion Chai:** Use the basic recipe and add 3 whole cloves, 4 whole green cardamom pods crushed with a knife, 4 whole black peppercorns, and 1/2 cinnamon stick. Cook, strain, and serve with your favorite milk and sweetener.

Brewing Tips for Teeccino Herbal Coffee Alternative

Each can of Teeccino Herbal Coffee comes with complete brewing instructions. For more on Teeccino, refer to the Ingredient Glossary in Chapter 1 or visit
www.Teeccino.com

FYI: Teeccino is made from a variety of ingredients that are individually ground, roasted, and then blended. Unlike coffee beans which are ground to a specific size for each type of brewing method, herbal coffee contains a composite grind that works in all types of coffee brewing equipment, including drip coffee makers, French press pots, and espresso machines. The tips that follow will help you brew a delicious cup:

Adjust quantities of Teeccino to your own preference.
Just as with coffee, some people like it strong while others prefer it weaker. Experiment by making several cups of Teeccino at different strengths to find the amount that you like best. Use a ratio of 2 to 3 teaspoons of this herbal coffee alternative per cup of water.

Drip coffee makers brew Teeccino best with a "gold" or permanent filter.
Paper filters tend to brew slowly because the composite grind in herbal coffee may have some fine particles that can clog the paper. Permanent gold filters save trees and produce a better flavored brew because they don't absorb some of the flavor. They are easy to rinse clean. They are available for both cone and flat bottom coffee makers. If you switch to reusable gold filters, you'll never again run out of coffee filters.

Percolators work for brewing Teeccino.
You can use an electric or stove-top percolator, with or without a coffee filter. I use an old-fashioned stove-top percolator without coffee filters.

Serve Teeccino anyway you enjoy coffee.
Try it black or with milk, non-dairy milk, coconut milk, or half-and-half if that's how you normally like your coffee. Taste the Teeccino before you add any sweetener. It has a naturally slightly sweet flavor from dates and figs, so you may not need additional sweetener. Instead of sugar, try honey or agave nectar, or for a calorie-free herbal sweetener, try a stevia tablet or a few drops of plain or flavored stevia extract liquid.

• Continued next page •

Does Teeccino contain any gluten?

Although Teeccino contains barley, an independent laboratory at the University of Nebraska that specializes in gluten testing found no detectable levels of gluten in Teeccino. Although gluten is present in barley, it most likely does not extract out of the barley using conventional coffee brewing techniques. Gluten is not extracted by boiling water, although it can be extracted using ethanol alcohol, which of course is not present in Teeccino. The company regularly has Teeccino tested at the University of Nebraska's Allergy Testing lab where it has had no detectable levels of gluten found at 10PPM.

To view the lab report visit:
http://www.teeccino.com/FAQs.aspx#gluten

• Brewing Tips continued •

If you want the flavor of a cappuccino

If you don't have a cappuccino machine, consider ordering the Italian Stovetop Espresso Maker and the Nissan Cappuccino Creamer sold on the Teeccino website under Brewing Tools.

RECOMMENDED AMOUNTS OF TEECCINO TO USE

For Drip Coffee Makers & Percolators:

* **Strong:** 1 rounded tablespoon for every 2 cups water with a permanent gold or paper filter.
* **Medium:** 1 level tablespoon for every 2 cups of water.
* **Light:** 1 teaspoon for every 2 cups water.

For a SwissGold One-Cup Brewer:

1. Put 1 rounded tablespoon into the filter chamber for a 10 to 12 ounce cup.
2. Insert the inner chamber and place the brewer on top of cup.
3. Fill the inner chamber with boiling water and allow 30 seconds to drip into the cup.
4. Add milk and/or sweetener as desired.

In a French Press:

1. Add 1 to 2 tablespoons per 3-cup pot; 3 to 4 tablespoons per 8-cup pot; 5 to 6 tablespoons per 12-cup pot.
2. Pour in boiling water. Let steep for 5 minutes before pressing the plunger down.
3. Pour and enjoy!

In an Espresso Machine:

1. Fill the double filter basket with 1 rounded tablespoon of Teeccino.
2. Tamp firmly.
3. **FYI:** For brewing tips for making Teeccino in an Italian Stovetop Espresso Maker & Cappuccino Creamer, refer to www.teeccino.com. Follow the directions for making cappuccino or latte with steamed milk or soy milk; you may also want to try it with coconut or nut milk.

Note: Unlike coffee, which can get bitter if left over, brewed Teeccino can last up to 5 days in the refrigerator, making it easy to drink iced Teeccino in the summer.

Additional Ideas

Ice Dream Platter

For a pretty presentation, scoop out several different flavors of Ice Dream into small (2-ounce) balls. Place on a chilled platter or serving tray and return to the freezer until party time. Before serving, garnish the platter with fresh, washed mint, lemon tree leaves, or edible flowers. Scatter berries over the tray. Drizzle with one or two sauces, or arrange an assortment of sauces and toppings--chopped toasted nuts, Pralines, cocoa nibs, and unsweetened, sulfite-free, finely shredded coconut—for guests to add at the table.

Ice Dream Pizza

Make a dessert pizza using one of the cookie doughs in this chapter. Press the dough onto a round pizza pan. Bake and cool the crust, then top with scoops of Ice Dream, and drizzle with a combination of toppings, nuts, and sauces such as Caramel, Hot Chocolate, Hot Fudge, Peanut Buttery Hot Chocolate, or Karly's Carob Sauce. Sprinkle with unsweetened, sulfite-free, finely shredded coconut or chopped toasted nuts. Cut into wedges and serve.

Ice Dream Brownie Cake

Bake Better Brownies, Blondies, or cookie dough in an 8-inch square pan. Spread softened Ice Dream over the baked, cooled brownies. Cover and freeze. Cut into squares and serve with Caramel, Hot Chocolate, Hot Fudge, Peanut Buttery Hot Chocolate, or Karly's Carob Sauce and a sprinkle of unsweetened, sulfite-free, finely shredded coconut or chopped toasted nuts.

Ice Dream Brownie Sundae

Serve Better Brownies topped with Vanilla Ice Dream (or some other flavor) and Strawberry, Cherry, or Mango Sauce. Drizzle on some Caramel, Hot Chocolate, Hot Fudge, Peanut Buttery Hot Chocolate, or Karly's Carob Sauce.

Ice Dream Sundaes

Slice ripe bananas, and divide between parfait glasses. Top each with 2 or 3 mini scoops of Ice Dream, a layer of fruit sauce, and then another layer of Ice Dream. Drizzle with Caramel, Hot Chocolate, Hot Fudge, Peanut Buttery Hot Chocolate, or Karly's Carob Sauce. Sprinkle with unsweetened, sulfite-free, finely shredded coconut, chopped toasted nuts, or gluten-free cookie crumbs. Fresh blueberries, sliced strawberries, peaches, or kiwifruit can replace fruit sauce.

Appendix A:
Mail Order & Internet Sources
for Foods Used in this Book

Most of the foods listed below can be found in large natural foods markets, health foods co-ops and through co-op buying clubs. If you cannot find a particular ingredient or product in your area, contact one of the companies listed below or ask your local retailer if s/he will order the product for you.

If you do not follow a wheat-free or gluten-free diet, you will have more brands to choose from. Many food products have labels stating that their products are processed on the same machinery used for products that contain wheat, eggs, soybeans, shellfish, fish oil, tree nuts, or peanuts. If you have food allergies or intolerances, read labels carefully, even for products you've used in the past without problems. Companies often change their formulations or procedures.

Disclaimer: The author has done her best to find out about the manufacturing of the products listed below; however, she cannot be responsible for any adverse reactions you may have from eating a particular food product.

GF = Signifies that a product is processed or packaged on machinery that is *not* shared with wheat, barley, rye, or oats.

GMP = Signifies that a product may be processed on machinery shared with wheat, barley, rye, or oats that is cleaned between product runs according to standards for GMP Certification (Good Manufacturing Procedures) set by the Natural Products Association.

Products without any designation are probably processed on gluten-free machinery, but the author was unable to verify this. For example, many companies that sell dried fruits and nuts get them directly from farmers and do not know what machinery was used to bag the products.

AGAVE NECTAR (cactus honey)

Madhava Honey (GF)
4689 Ute Highway
Longmont, CO 80503
Phone: (303) 823-5166
www.madhavahoney.com
Email: info@madhavahoney.com

Sweet Cactus Farms (GF)
10627 Regent Street
Los Angeles, CA 90034
Phone: (310) 733-4343
www.sweetcactusfarms.com
Email:
agave@sweetcactusfarms.com

Volcanic Nectar - Global Goods (GF)
11382 North 5710 West
Highland, Utah 84003
Phone: 801-492-6295
www.volcanicnectar.com

AGAR AGAR POWDER

Barry Farm
20086 Mudsock Rd.
Wapakoneta, Ohio 45895
Phone: (419) 228-4640
www.barryfarm.com
Email: info@barryfarm.com

NOW® Foods corporate office (GMP)
For store listing contact:
395 Glen Ellyn Road
Bloomingdale, IL 60108
Phone: (888) 669-3663
www.nowfoods.com

To mail order contact:
Fruitful Yield (GMP)
154 South Bloomingdale Road
Bloomingdale, IL 60108
Phone: (800) 469-5552
www.fruitfulyield.com

Bulkfoods.com
3040 Hill Avenue
Toledo, OH 43607
Phone: (419) 324-0032
www.bulkfoods.com

APPLE SAUCE

Eden Foods, Inc. (GF)
701 Tecumseh Road
Clinton, Michigan 49236
Phone: (888) 424-EDEN (3336)
International: +1 517 456-7424
www.edenfoods.com
Email: websales@edenfoods.com

Tropical Traditions, Inc. (GF)
P.O. Box 333
Springville, CA 93265
Phone: (866) 311-2626
www.tropicaltraditions.com
Email: help@tropicaltraditions.com

ARROWROOT STARCH

Bob's Red Mill (GF)
Natural Foods Inc.
5209 S.E. International Way
Milwaukee, OR 97222
Phone: (800) 349-2173
www.bobsredmill.com

Frontier Natural Products Co-op (GMP)
P.O. Box 299
3021 78th Street
Norway, IA 52318
Phone: (800)-669-3275
www.frontiercoop.com

Glutenfree.com (GF)
United-States
glutenfree.com
P.O. Box 840
Glastonbury, CT 06033
Phone: 800-291-8386
www.glutenfree.com
Email: pantry@glutenfree.com

Glutenfree.com
2055 Dagenais West
Laval, QC, H7L 5V1
Canada
Phone: (800) 291-8386
www.glutenfree.com

Natural Lifestyle Supplies
16 Lookout Drive
Asheville, NC 28804-3330
Phone: (800)-752-2775
www.natural-lifestyle.com
Email:
autumn@natural-lifestyle.com

ALMOND OIL

Igourmet.com
508 Delaware Ave.
West Pittston, PA 18643
Phone: 1-877-igourmet
   (1-877-446-8763)
www.igourmet.com

Flora Oils
Flora Inc.
Post Office Box 73
805 E. Badger Road
Lynden, Washington 98264
Phone: (877) 792-0882 **or**
   (800) 446-2110
www.florahealth.com

Oils By Nature
30300 Solon Industrial Parkway,
Suite E
Solon, Ohio 44139
Phone: (440) 498-1180
oilsbynature.com

AVOCADO OIL

Earthy Delights
1161 E. Clark Road, Suite 260
DeWitt, Michigan 48820
Phone: (800) 367-4709
Email: info@earthy.comarthy.com

Olivado Natural Nutrition
Sandys Road, Waipapa (off State Highway 10)
RD2, Kerikeri 0470
Bay of Islands, New Zealand
Phone: (+64) 9 407 3080
www.olivado.com
Email: sales@olivado.com

BAKING POWDER, GLUTEN-FREE

Allergy Grocer (GF)
91 Western Maryland Parkway,
Unit #7
Hagerstown, MD 21740 USA
Phone: (800) 891-0083
   (240) 329-2717 if outside
   the USA.
www.allergygrocer.com
Email: Orders@AllergyGrocer.com
Comments, questions:
CustomerService@AllergyGrocer.com

Frontier Natural Products Co-op (GF)
P.O. Box 299
3021 78th Street
Norway, IA 52318
Phone: (800) 669-3275
www.frontiercoop.com

Gluten-Free Mall (GF)
4927 Sonoma Hwy., Ste C1
Santa Rosa, CA 95409
Phone: (866) 575-3720 **or**
   (707) 509-4528
www.glutenfreemall.com

CAROB CHIPS

Barry Farm*
20086 Mudsock Rd.
Wapakoneta, Ohio 45895
Phone: (419) 228-4640
www.barryfarm.com
Email: info@barryfarm.com

Chattfield's*
American Natural Snacks
405 Golfway West Drive
St. Augustine, FL 32095-8837
Phone: (800) 238-3947
Fax: (904) 940-2234
www.ans-natural.com
Email:
anscustsrv@ansbrands.com

*Note: These products are processed on machinery that may be used for wheat, nuts, eggs, or other common allergens. The author has not found any carob chips made on equipment not shared with wheat.

CAROB POWDER

Barry Farm*
20086 Mudsock Rd.
Wapakoneta, Ohio 45895
Phone: (419) 228-4640
www.barryfarm.com
Email: info@barryfarm.com

Chattfield's*
American Natural Snacks
405 Golfway West Drive
St. Augustine, FL 32095-8837
Phone: (800) 238-3947
Fax: (904) 940-2234
www.ans-natural.com
Email:
anscustsrv@ansbrands.com

*Note: These products are processed on machinery that may also be used for wheat, nuts, eggs, or other common allergens. The author has been unable to find a brand of carob powder processed on equipment that is not shared with wheat.

CHESTNUT FLOUR

Allen Creek Farm (GF)
29112 NW 41st Ave.,
Ridgefield, WA 98642
Mail address:
PO Box 841
Ridgefield, WA 98642
Phone: 360-887-3669
www.chestnutsonline.com
Email:
Info@ChestnutsOnLine.com

Barry Farm*
20086 Mudsock Rd.
Wapakoneta, Ohio 45895
Phone: (419) 228-4640
www.barryfarm.com
Email: info@barryfarm.com

*Note: This product may be processed on machinery used for gluten grains, although it is unlikely, as chestnuts are normally processed on machinery that is dedicated to that purpose only.

Empire Chestnut Company (GF)
3276 Empire Road SW
Carrollton, OH 44615-9515
Phone: (330) 627-3181
www.empirechestnut.com
Email:
empirechestnut@gotsky.com

Gluten-Free Mall (GF)
4927 Sonoma Hwy., Ste C1
Santa Rosa, CA 95409
Phone: (866) 575-3720 **or**
(707) 509-4528
www.glutenfreemall.com

Gluten Solutions, Inc. (GF)
8750 Concourse Court
San Diego, CA 92123
Phone: (858) 292-4564
www.glutensolutions.com
Email: info@glutensolutions.com

Ladd Hill Orchards (GF)
15500 Southwest Roberts Road
Sherwood, Oregon 97140
Phone: (503) 625-1248
www.laddhillchestnuts.com
Email: Laddhill1@aol.com

CHESTNUTS, FRESH OR DRIED

Allen Creek Farm (GF)
29112 NW 41st Ave.,
Ridgefield, WA 98642
Mail address:
P.O. Box 841
Ridgefield, WA 98642
Phone: (360) 887-3669
www.chestnutsonline.com
Email: Info@ChestnutsOnLine.com

Diamond Organics*
The Organic Food Catalog
P.O. Box 2159
Freedom, CA 95019
Phone: (888) ORGANIC or
(888) 674-2642
www.diamondorganics.com
Email: info@diamondorganics.com

Empire Chestnut Company (GF)
3276 Empire Road SW
Carrollton, OH 44615-9515
Phone: (330) 627-3181
www.empirechestnut.com
Email:
empirechestnut@gotsky.com

Gold Mine Natural Foods*
7805 Arjons Drive
San Diego, CA 92126
Phone: (800) 475-FOOD or
(800) 475-3663
www.goldminenaturalfood.com

Ladd Hill Orchards (GF)
15500 Southwest Roberts Road
Sherwood, Oregon 97140
Phone: (503) 625-1248
www.laddhillchestnuts.com
Email: Laddhill1@aol.com

Natural Lifestyle Supplies*
16 Lookout Drive
Asheville, NC 28804-3330
Phone: (800)-752-2775
www.natural-lifestyle.com
Email:
autumn@natural-lifestyle.com

*Note: This product may be processed on machinery used for gluten grains, although it is unlikely, as chestnuts are normally processed on machinery that is dedicated to that purpose only.

COCOA NIBS (AKA CACAO NIBS)

Dagoba Chocolate (GF)
1105 Benson Way
Asland, OR 97520
Phone: (800) 393-6075 ext. 26
www.dagobachocolate.com

Endangered Species Chocolate (GF)
5846 W. 73rd. St.
Indianapolis, IN 46278
Phone: (800) 293-0160 **or**
(317) 387-4372
Email: info@chocolatebar.com

Rapunzel Bittersweet Chocolate (GF)
Tropical Traditions, Inc.
P.O. Box 333
Springville, CA 93265
Phone: (866) 311-2626
www.tropicaltraditions.com
Email: help@tropicaltraditions.com

COCOA POWDER, UNSWEETENED

Allergy Grocer (GF)
91 Western Maryland Parkway,
Unit #7
Hagerstown, MD 21740 USA
Phone: (800) 891-0083 or
(240) 329-2717 if outside
the USA.
www.allergygrocer.com
Email: Orders@AllergyGrocer.com
Comments, questions:
CustomerService@AllergyGrocer.com

Dagoba Chocolate (GF)
1105 Benson Way
Asland, OR 97520
Phone: (800) 393-6075
www.dagobachocolate.com

Equal Exchange Fairly Traded Products*
50 United Drive,
West Bridgewater, MA 02379
Phone: (774) 776-7400
www.equalexchange.com
Email:
orders@equalexchange.coop
*Note: This product is processed on machinery that is shared with wheat; however, Equal Exchange chocolate bars are processed on gluten-free equipment.

*Note: This product may be processed on machinery used for gluten grains, although it is unlikely, as chestnuts are normally processed on machinery that is dedicated to that purpose only.

Gluten-Free Mall (GF)
4927 Sonoma Hwy., Ste C1
Santa Rosa, CA 95409
Phone: (866) 575-3720 **or**
  (707) 509-4528
www.glutenfreemall.com

Ghirardelli Chocolate Company (GF)
1111 - 139th Avenue
San Leandro, CA 94578
Phone: (800) 877-9338
www.ghirardelli.com

Green & Black's Organic Chocolate*
Green and Black's, USA
PO Box 259011
Plano, Texas 75025
Phone: (877) 299 1254
www.greenandblacksdirect.com
Email:
greenandblacks@cohnwolfe.com

Green & Black's
9 Barugh Close,
Barker Business Park
Melmerby, Ripon HG4 5NB UK
Phone: (870) 242-2597
www.greenandblacksdirect.com
Email:
greenandblacks@cohnwolfe.com

*Note: Green & Black's uses cereal ingredients in some of their products. All products are made in a factory that handles cereal ingredients (oat, wheat, barley, and rye flours). There is, therefore, a risk of gluten cross contamination. Please check the ingredients declaration for clarification. The organic Mint and Caramel bars contain glucose syrup, which is derived from wheat, but they do not contain wheat gluten.

Rapunzel Organic Cocoa Powder from
Tropical Traditions, Inc. (GF)
P.O. Box 333
Springville, CA 93265
Phone: (866) 311-2626
www.tropicaltraditions.com
Email:
help@tropicaltraditions.com

CHOCOLATE CHIPS & CHOCOLATE DROPS

Allergy Grocer (GF)
91 Western Maryland Parkway, Unit #7
Hagerstown, MD 21740 USA
Phone: (800) 891-0083 or
  (240) 329-2717 if outside the USA.
www.allergygrocer.com
Email: Orders@AllergyGrocer.com
Comments, questions:
CustomerService@AllergyGrocer.com

Dagoba Chocolate (GF)
1105 Benson Way
Asland, OR 97520
Phone: (800) 393-6075
www.dagobachocolate.com

Enjoy Life Foods Gluten-Free Chocolate Chips (GF)
3810 River Road
Schiller Park, IL 60176
Phone: (847) 260-0300
www.enjoylifefoods.com

Ghirardelli Chocolate Company (GF)
1111 - 139th Avenue
San Leandro, CA 94578
Phone: (800) 877-9338
www.ghirardelli.com

Gluten-Free Mall (GF)
4927 Sonoma Hwy., Ste C1
Santa Rosa, CA 95409
Phone: (866) 575-3720 **or**
  (707) 509-4528
www.glutenfreemall.com

Gluten-Free Trading Company (GF)
3116 South Chase Ave.,
Milwaukee, WI
Phone: (888) 993-9933 **or**
  (414) 747-8700
www.food4celiacs.com
www.gluten-free.net
Email: info@gluten-free.net

Toll House Semi-Sweet Morsels & Chocolate Chunks
Nestlé Chocolate (GF)*
VeryBestBaking.com
PO Box 2178
Wilkes-Barre, PA 18703
Phone: (800) 851-0512

CHOCOLATE, UNSWEETENED & SWEETENED BARS

Angeline's Bakery (GF)
121 W. Main St
Sisters, OR
Phone: 541-549-9122
http://www.angelinesbakery.com/

Artisan Confections (Some GF)*
2000 Folsom Street
San Francisco, CA 94110
Phone: (866) 237-0152
Email:
customercare@artisanconfection.com

Dagoba Chocolate (GF)
1105 Benson Way
Asland, OR 97520
Phone: (800) 393-6075
www.dagobachocolate.com

Equal Exchange Fairly Traded Products (GF)
50 United Drive
West Bridgewater, MA 02379
Phone: (774) 776-7400
Fax: (508) 587-0088
www.equalexchange.com

Ghirardelli Chocolate Company (GF)
1111 - 139th Avenue
San Leandro, CA 94578
Phone: (800) 877-9338
www.ghirardelli.com

Green & Black's
9 Barugh Close,
Barker Business Park
Melmerby, Ripon HG4 5NB UK
Phone: (870) 242-2597
www.greenandblacksdirect.com
Email:
greenandblacks@cohnwolfe.com

*Note: Green & Black's uses cereal ingredients in some of their products. All products are made in a factory that handles cereal ingredients (oat, wheat, barley, and rye flours). There is, therefore, a risk of gluten cross contamination. Please check the ingredients declaration for clarification. The organic Mint and Caramel bars contain glucose syrup, which is derived from wheat, but they do not contain wheat gluten.

Nestlé Chocolatier Baking Bars (GF)*
VeryBestBaking.com
PO Box 2178
Wilkes-Barre, PA 18703
Phone: (800) 851-0512

*Note: Nestlé follows a strict labeling policy with regard to any of the "Big Eight" allergens in their foods and incoming ingredients. They insist that their suppliers notify them if gluten is used in any of their ingredients. Nestlé products will be fully labeled for any presence of gluten or gluten-containing ingredients.

CHICORY ROOT, ROASTED PIECES & GRINDS

Frontier Natural Products Co-op (GMP)
P.O. Box 299
3021 78th Street
Norway, IA 52318
Phone: (800) 669-3275
www.frontiercoop.com

COFFEE ALTERNATIVE

Teeccino Caffé, Inc. (GF)
P. O. Box 42259
Santa Barbara, CA 93140
Phone: 800-498-3434
Customers outside of the USA & Canada, please call:
805-966-0999
www.teeccino.com
Email: info@teeccino.com

COCONUT BUTTER, RAW

Artisana Organic Coconut Butter (GF)*
Premier Organics
2342 Shattuck Ave., #342
Berkeley, CA 94704
Phone: (510) 632-1913
www.premierorganics.org

COCONUT OIL, UNREFINED, VIRGIN PRESSED

Coconutoil-online.com†
Mid-American Marketing Corporation
P.O. Box 295
1531 East Main Street
Eaton, OH 45320
Phone: (800) 922-1744
www.coconutoil-online.com
Email:
gmw@coconutoil-online.com

Garden of Life Inc.†
5500 Village Blvd., Suite 202
West Palm Beach FL, 33407
Phone: (866) 465-0051
www.gardenoflife.com
Email:
In4mation@gardenoflife.com

Nutiva†
P.O. Box 1716
Sebastopol, CA 95473
Phone: (800) 993-4367
www.nutiva.com
Email: help1@nutiva.com

Omega Nutrition, Mail Order Distribution†
6515 Aldrich Road
Bellingham, WA 98226
Phone: (360) 384-1238
Toll-free order line only:
1-800-661-3529
www.omeganutrition.com

Omega Nutrition Canada†
1695 Franklin Street,
Vancouver, BC V5L 1P5
Phone: (604) 253-4677

Tropical Traditions, Inc.†
P.O. Box 333
Springville, CA 93265
Phone: (866) 311-2626
www.tropicaltraditions.com
Email:
help@tropicaltraditions.com

†**Note:** Coconut oil is processed on dedicated machinery not used to process other foods or oils.

COCONUT, UNSWEETENED, SULFITE-FREE, SHREDDED

Barry Farm*
20086 Mudsock Rd.
Wapakoneta, Ohio 45895
Phone: (419) 228-4640
www.barryfarm.com
Email: info@barryfarm.com

* This company cannot guarantee that the coconut is not processed on machinery also used for wheat, barley, rye, or oats.

Let's Do Organic Coconut (GF)
Edward & Sons Trading Company, Inc.
P.O Box 1326
Carpinteria, CA 93014
Phone: (805) 684-8500
www.edwardsons.com
Email: edwardssons@aol.com

Bob's Red Mill*
Natural Foods Inc.
5209 S.E. International Way
Milwaukee, OR 97222
Phone: (800) 349-2173
www.bobsredmill.com
*Note: Processed on machinery shared with wheat.

Bulkfoods.com
3040 Hill Avenue
Toledo, OH 43607
Phone: (419) 324-0032
www.bulkfoods.com

Coconutoil-online.com (GF)
Mid-American Marketing Corporation
P.O. Box 295
1531 East Main Street
Eaton, OH 45320
Phone: (800) 922-1744
www.coconutoil-online.com

Edward & Sons Trading Company, Inc. (GF)
P.O. Box 1326
Carpinteria, CA 93014
Phone: (805) 684-8500
www.edwardandsons.com

Gold Mine Natural Foods
7805 Arjon's Drive
San Diego, CA 92126
Phone: (800) 475-FOOD or
(800) 475-3663
www.goldminenaturalfood.com

Tropical Traditions, Inc. (GF)
P.O. Box 333
Springville, CA 93265
Phone: (866) 311-2626
www.tropicaltraditions.com
Email:
help@tropicaltraditions.com

COCONUT MILK, UNSWEETENED, SULFITE FREE

Native Forest Coconut Milk (GF)
Edward & Sons Trading Company, Inc.
P.O. Box 1326
Carpinteria, CA 93014
Phone: (805) 684-8500
www.edwardandsons.com
Email: edwardssons@aol.com

Thai Kitchen (GF)
Simply Asia Foods, Inc.
P.O. Box 13242
Berkely, CA 94712-4242
Phone: (800) 967-8424
www.thaikitchen.com
Email: info@thaikitchen.com

COOKIES, GLUTEN FREE

Allergy Grocer (Many Certified GF)
91 Western Maryland Parkway, Unit #7
Hagerstown, MD 21740 USA
Phone: (800) 891-0083 or
(240) 329-2717 if outside the USA.
www.allergygrocer.com
Email: Orders@AllergyGrocer.com
Comments, questions:
CustomerService@AllergyGrocer.com

Angeline's Bakery (GF)
121 W. Main St.
Sisters, OR
Phone: 541-549-9122
http://www.angelinesbakery.com/

Good Day Gluten-Free (GF)
514B North Western Avenue
Lake Forest, IL 60045
Phone: orders (847) 615-1208 **or**
customer service (877) 395-2527
www.gooddayglutenfree.com

Jennies Macaroons (GF)
Red Mill Farms, Inc.
209 South 5th Street
Brooklyn, NY 11211
Phone: (888) 294-1164
www.macaroonking.com
Email: info@macaroonking.com

Gluten-Free Mall (GF)
4927 Sonoma Hwy., Ste C1
Santa Rosa, CA 95409
Phone: (866) 575-3720 **or**
        (707) 509-4528
www.glutenfreemall.com

Gluten Solutions, Inc. (GF)
8750 Concourse Court
San Diego, CA 92123
Phone: (858) 292-4564
www.glutenfreesolutions.com
Email: info@glutensolutions.com

Pamela's Products (GF)
200 Clara Ave.
Ukiah, CA 95482
Phone: (707) 462-6605
www.pamelasproducts.com/
Email: info@pamelasproducts.com

MI-DEL Cookies (GF)
c/o Panos Brands
400 Lyster Avenue
Saddle Brook, NJ 07663
www.midelcookies.com
Email:
Customer.services@panosbrands.com

Kinnikinnick Foods (GF)
10940-120 Street
Edmonton, AB, Canada T5H 3P7
Phone: (877) 503-4466 **or**
        (780) 424-2900
www.Kinnikinnick.com

**Trader Joe's Gluten-Free
Ginger Snaps (GF)***
Trader Joe's (Main office)
538 Mission St.
South Pasadena, CA 91031
For a state-by-state listing of
locations visit:
www.traderjoes.com
  ***Note:** Not all Trader Joe's
  cookies are gluten-free. Read all
  package labels.

**DANDELION ROOT, ROASTED
PIECES OR GRINDS**

Alvita Herbal Teas
A Division of TWINLAB Division
American Fork, UT 84003

**Available online from the
following companies:**
www.vitaminlife.com
www.frontierherbs.com
www.loaves-n-fishes.com
www.enknatural.com
www.herbsmd.com
www.betterhealthstore.com
www.cdnf.com

**Frontier Natural Products
Co-op (GMP)**
P.O. Box 299
3021 78th Street
Norway, IA 52318
Phone: (800) 669-3275
www.frontiercoop.com

**DATES & COCONUT DATE
ROLLS**

Barry Farm*
20086 Mudsock Rd.
Wapakoneta, Ohio 45895
Phone: (419) 228-4640
www.barryfarm.com
Email: info@barryfarm.com

* This company cannot guarantee
that the coconut is not processed
on machinery also used for wheat,
barley, rye, or oats.

Bulkfoods.com
3040 Hill Avenue
Toledo, OH 43607
Phone: (419) 324-0032
www.bulkfoods.com

Diamond Organics
The Organic Food Catalog
P.O. Box 2159
Freedom, CA 95019
Phone: (888) ORGANIC or
        (888) 674-2642
www.diamondorganics.com

Jewel Date Co. (GF)
84675 Avenue 60
Thermal, CA 92274
Phone: (760) 399-4474
www.jeweldate.com
Email: jeweldate@aol.com

Oh! Nuts
1305 50th Street
Brooklyn, New York 11219
Phone: (888) 664-6887
www.ohnuts.com
Email: info@ohnuts.com

Sun Organic Farm
P.O. Box 409
San Marcos, CA 92079
Phone: (888) 269-9888
www.sunorganic.com

DRIED FRUITS & NUTS

Barry Farm*
20086 Mudsock Rd.
Wapakoneta, Ohio 45895
Phone: (419) 228-4640
www.barryfarm.com
Email: info@barryfarm.com

Gold Mine Natural Foods*
7805 Arjon's Drive
San Diego, CA 92126
Phone: (800) 475-FOOD or
        (800) 475-3663
www.goldminenaturalfood.com

Natural Lifestyle Supplies*
16 Lookout Drive
Asheville, NC 28804-3330
Phone: (800)-752-2775
www.natural-lifestyle.com
Email:
autumn@natural-lifestyle.com

Oh! Nuts
1305 50th Street
Brooklyn, New York 11219
Phone: (888) 664.6887 or
www.ohnuts.com
Email: info@ohnuts.com

* These companies are unable to
determine whether the products
above are packaged on machinery
used only for gluten-free products.

EGG REPLACER

Ener-G Foods, Inc. (GF)
5960 First Avenue South
P.O. Box 84487
Seattle, WA 98124-5787
Phone: (800) 331-5222 or
  Local to Seattle (206) 767-6660
http://www.ener-g.com/
Email:
customerservice@ener-g.com

Gluten Solutions, Inc. (GF)
8750 Concourse Court
San Diego, CA 92123
Phone: (858) 292-4564
www.glutenfreesolutions.com
Email: info@glutensolutions.com

Gluten-Free Supermarket (GF)
1850 W. 169th St. Suite B
Gardena, California 90247
Phone: (310) 366-7612 or
www.glutenfree-supermarket.com/
Email: sales@authenticfoods.com

FOOD COLORING, NATURAL

Allergy Grocer (GF)
91 Western Maryland Parkway,
Unit #7
Hagerstown, MD 21740 USA
Phone: (800) 891-0083 or
(240) 329-2717 if outside
the USA.
www.allergygrocer.com
Email: Orders@AllergyGrocer.com
Comments, questions:
CustomerService@AllergyGrocer.com

Seelect Herb Tea Company
1145 W. Shelly Court
Orange, CA 92868
Phone: (714) 771-3317
http://www.seelecttea.com/

FLAVORINGS, NATURAL

These include almond, vanilla,
coffee, lemon, orange,
peppermint, vanilla, caramel,
butterscotch, and others. Look
for products in a non-alcoholic
glycerine base if you are sensitive
to grain alcohols, which are used
as a base for many flavorings. You
may also use powdered vanilla
extract; however the amount used
may vary from brand to brand.

Allergy Grocer (GF)
91 Western Maryland Parkway,
Unit #7
Hagerstown, MD 21740 USA
Phone: (800) 891-0083 or
(240) 329-2717 if outside
the USA
www.allergygrocer.com
Email: Orders@AllergyGrocer.com
Comments, questions:
CustomerService@AllergyGrocer.com

Barry Farm (GF)
20086 Mudsock Rd.
Wapakoneta, Ohio 45895
Phone: (419) 228-4640
www.barryfarm.com
Email: info@barryfarm.com

Flavorganics (GF)
268 Doremus Ave.
Newark, NJ 07105
Phone: (973) 344-8014 ext 109
www.flavorganics.com
Email: julie@flavorganics.com

**Frontier Natural Products
Co-op (GF)**
P.O. Box 299
3021 78th Street
Norway, IA 52318
Phone: (800) 669-3275
www.frontiercoop.com

**Gluten-Free Trading Company
(GF)**
3116 South Chase Ave.
Milwaukee, WI
Phone: (888) 993-9933 **or**
(414) 747-8700
www.food4celiacs.com
www.gluten-free.net
Email: info@gluten-free.net

Good Day Gluten-Free (GF)
514B North Western Avenue
Lake Forest, IL 60045
Phone: orders (847) 615-1208 **or**
customer service (877) 395-2527
www.gooddayglutenfree.com

McCormick & Co., Inc (GF)
211 Schilling Circle
Hunt Valley, MD 21031
Phone: (800) 632-5847
www.mccormick.com

**Simply Organics (GF)
Frontier Natural Products
Co-op**
P.O. Box 299
3021 78th Street
Norway, IA 52318
Phone: (800) 437-3301
www.frontiercoop.com
Email:
customercare@frontiercoop.com

Tropical Traditions, Inc. (GF)
P.O. Box 333
Springville, CA 93265
Phone: (866) 311-2626
www.tropicaltraditions.com
Email:
help@tropicaltraditions.com

FRUIT SWEETENED PRESERVES

**Gluten-Free Trading Company
(GF)**
3116 South Chase Ave.,
Milwaukee, WI
Phone: (888) 993-9933 **or**
(414) 747-8700
www.food4celiacs.com
www.gluten-free.net
Email: info@gluten-free.net

Tropical Traditions, Inc. (GF)
P.O. Box 333
Springville, CA 93265
Phone: (866) 311-2626
www.tropicaltraditions.com
Email:
help@tropicaltraditions.com

GELATIN, UNFLAVORED GRANULES

Bulkfoods.com
3040 Hill Avenue
Toledo, OH 43607
Phone: (419) 324-0032
www.bulkfoods.com

Great Lakes (GF)
PO Box 917
Grayslake, IL 60030
Phone: (847) 223-8141
www.greatlakesgelatin.com
Email:
sales@greatlakesgelatin.com

**NOW® Foods corporate office
(GMP)**
For store listing contact:
395 Glen Ellyn Road
Bloomingdale, IL 60108
Phone: (800) 999-8069
www.nowfoods.com

To mail order contact:
Fruitful Yield (GMP)
154 South Bloomingdale Road
Bloomingdale, IL 60108
Phone: (800) 469-5552
www.fruitfulyield.com

GLUTEN-FREE FLOURS & GRAINS

These include brown rice, sweet
rice, sweet brown rice, sorghum,
quinoa flour, and potato starch.

*A ◊ indicates that the company
listed sells quinoa flakes.*

Ancient Harvest Quinoa◊
Quinoa Corporation
P.O. Box 279
Gardena, CA 90248
Phone: (310) 217-8125
www.quinoa.net/
Email: quinoacorp@aol.com

Allergy Grocer (GF)
91 Western Maryland Parkway,
Unit #7
Hagerstown, MD 21740 USA
Phone: (800) 891-0083 or
(240) 329-2717 if outside
the USA.
www.allergygrocer.com
Email: Orders@AllergyGrocer.com
Comments, questions:
CustomerService@AllergyGrocer.com

Barry Farm (GF)
20086 Mudsock Rd.
Wapakoneta, Ohio 45895
Phone: (419) 228-4640
www.barryfarm.com
Email: info@barryfarm.com

**Bob's Red Mill
(Many Certified GF)**
Natural Foods Inc.
5209 S.E. International Way
Milwaukee, OR 97222
Phone: (800) 349-2173
www.bobsredmill.com

Brown Rice Flakes
Eden Foods*
701 Tecumseh Road
Clinton, MI 49236
Phone: (517) 456-7424
www.edenfoods.com

Good Day Gluten-Free (GF)◊
514B North Western Avenue
Lake Forest, IL 60045
Phone: orders (847) 615-1208 **or**
customer service (877) 395-2527
www.gooddayglutenfree.com

Glutenfree.com (GF)◊
P.O. Box 840
Glastonbury, CT 06033
U.S.A.
Phone: (800) 291-8386
www.glutenfree.com
Email: pantry@glutenfree.com

Glutenfree.com (GF)
2055 Dagenais West
Laval, QC, H7L 5V1
Canada
Phone: (800) 291-8386
www.glutenfree.com

Gluten-Free Mall (GF)◊
4927 Sonoma Hwy., Ste. C1
Santa Rosa, CA 95409
Phone: (866) 575-3720 **or**
(707) 509-4528
Fax: (707) 324-6060
www.glutenfreemall.com

Gluten-Free Trading Company
(GF)◊
3116 South Chase Ave.,
Milwaukee, WI
Phone: (888) 993-9933 **or**
(414) 747-8700
www.food4celiacs.com
www.gluten-free.net
Email: info@gluten-free.net

Gluten Solutions, Inc. (GF)◊
8750 Concourse Court
San Diego, CA 92123
Phone: (858) 292-4564
www.glutensolutions.com
Email: info@glutensolutions.com
Gluten-Free Supermarket (GF)
1850 W. 169th St., Suite B
Gardena, California 90247
Phone: 310-366-7612 **or**
800-806-4737
Email: pantry@glutenfree.com

Gluten Free Oats (GF)
578 Lane 9
Powell, WY 82435
Phone: (307) 754-2058
www.glutenfreeoats.com
Email: sales@glutenfreeoats.com

Gluten-Free Trading Company
(GF)
3116 South Chase Ave.,
Milwaukee, WI
Phone: (888) 993-9933 **or**
(414) 747-8700
www.food4celiacs.com
www.gluten-free.net
Email: info@gluten-free.net

GUAR GUM & XANTHAN GUM

Allergy Grocer (GF)
91 Western Maryland Parkway,
Unit #7
Hagerstown, MD 21740 USA
Phone: (800) 891-0083 or
(240) 329-2717 if outside
the USA.
www.allergygrocer.com
Email: Orders@AllergyGrocer.com
Comments, questions:
CustomerService@AllergyGrocer.com

Glutenfree.com (GF)
P.O. Box 840
Glastonbury, CT 06033
U.S.A.
Phone: 800-291-8386
www.glutenfree.com
Email: pantry@glutenfree.com

Glutenfree.com (GF)
2055 Dagenais West
Laval, QC, H7L 5V1
Canada
Phone: (800) 291-8386
www.glutenfree.com

Gluten-Free Mall (GF)
4927 Sonoma Hwy., Ste C1
Santa Rosa, CA 95409
Phone: (866) 575-3720 **or**
(707) 509-4528
www.glutenfreemall.com

Gluten Solutions, Inc. (GF)
8750 Concourse Court
San Diego, CA 92123
Phone: (858) 292-4564
www.glutensolutions.com
Email: info@glutensolutions.com

Gluten-Free Supermarket (GF)
1850 W. 169th St., Suite B
Gardena, California 90247
Phone: (310) 366-7612 or
(800) 806-4737
http://www.glutenfree-
supermarket.com/
Email: sales@authenticfoods.com

NOW® Foods, corporate office
(Many GF Products)
For store listing contact:
395 Glen Ellyn Road
Bloomingdale, IL 60108
Phone: (888) 669-3663
www.nowfoods.com
*To mail order NOW® Foods
products contact:*

Fruitful Yield
(Many GF Products)
154 South Bloomingdale Road
Bloomingdale, IL 60108
Phone: (800) 469-55552
www.fruitfulyield.com

HERBS & SPICES,
NON-IRRADIATED & ORGANIC

Barry Farm (Many GF)
20086 Mudsock Rd.
Wapakoneta, OH 45895
Phone: (419) 228-4640
www.barryfarm.com
Email: info@barryfarm.com

Chakra 4 (GMP)
4773 N. 20th St.
Phoenix AZ 85016
Phone: 602-283-1210
Email: info@chakra4herbs.com

Frontier Natural Products
Co-op (GMP)
P.O. Box 299
3021 78th Street
Norway, IA 52318
Phone: (800) 669-3275
www.frontiercoop.com

Gold Mine Natural Foods
(Some GMP)
7805 Arjon's Drive
San Diego, CA 92126
Phone: (800) 475-FOOD or
(800) 475-3663
www.goldminenaturalfood.com

McCormick & Co., Inc (GF)
211 Schilling Circle
Hunt Valley, MD 21031
Phone: (800) 632-5847
www.mccormick.com

Natural Lifestyle Supplies
(GMP)
16 Lookout Drive
Asheville, NC 28804-3330
Phone: (800)-752-2775
www.natural-lifestyle.com
Email:
autumn@natural-lifestyle.com

Spice Hunter (GMP)
184 Suburban Road
San Luis Obispo, CA 93401
Phone: (800) 444-3061
www.spicehunter.com

MESQUITE FLOUR

Barry Farm*
20086 Mudsock Rd.
Wapakoneta, OH 45895
Phone: (419) 228-4640
www.barryfarm.com
Email: info@barryfarm.com
* This company cannot guarantee
that the mesquite flour is not
processed on machinery also

used for wheat, barley, rye, or oats.

Gluten-Free Mall (GF)
4927 Sonoma Hwy., Ste C1
Santa Rosa, CA 95409
Phone: (866) 575-3720 **or**
(707) 509-4528
www.glutenfreemall.com

San Pedro Mesquite Company (GF)
PO Box 338
Bowie, AZ 85605
Phone: (520) 847-1015
www.shop.spmesquite.com
Email: info@spmesquite.com

**MATCHA
(GREEN TEA POWDER)**

Amazon.com
www.amazon.com

EnjoyingTea.com
1661 Tennessee St. Ste 3L
San Francisco, CA 94107
www.enjoyingtea.com/
Email: sales@enjoyingtea.com

www.greenteapowder.net
3415 Lebon Drive #132
San Diego, CA 92122
Phone: (562) 412-9894
Email: huangdi1122@hotmail.com

NUT BUTTERS

Arrowhead Mills (GF)
The Hain Celestial Group
4600 Sleepytime Dr.
Boulder, CO 80301
Phone: (800) 434-4246
www.arrowheadmills.com

Futters Nut Butters (GF)
P.O. Box 4934
Buffalo Grove, Illinois 60089
Phone: 847-634-6976 (in Illinois)
or 1-877-772-2155 (toll free outside Illinois)
www.futtersnutbutters.com

**Maranatha Nut Butters (GF)
nSpired Natural Foods, Inc.**
1850 Fairway Drive
San Leandro, CA 94577
Phone: (510) 686-0116 **or**
(866) 972-6879 (toll-free)
Email:
info@maranathanutbutters.com

PALM SHORTENING

Glutenfree.com (GF)
United-States
glutenfree.com
P.O. Box 840
Glastonbury, CT 06033
Phone: 800-291-8386
www.glutenfree.com
Email: pantry@glutenfree.com

Spectrum Organic Products, Inc. (GF)
5341 Old Redwood Hwy., Suite 400
Petaluma, CA 94954
Subsidiary of Hain-Celestial Group
www.hain-celestial.com
www.spectrumorganics.com/

Tropical Traditions, Inc. (GF)
P.O. Box 333
Springville, CA 93265
Phone: (866) 311-2626 ext. 2
www.tropicaltraditions.com
Email: help@tropicaltraditions.com

RICE SYRUP

Lundberg Family Farms (GF)
5370 Church Street
P.O. Box 369
Richvale, CA 95974
Phone: (530) 882-4551
www.lundberg.com
Email: info@lundberg.com

**Lundberg Rice Syrup (GF)
Natural Lifestyle Supplies**
16 Lookout Drive
Asheville, NC 28804-3330
Phone:(800)-752-2775
www.natural-lifestyle.com
Email:
autumn@natural-lifestyle.com

Tropical Traditions, Inc. (GF)
P.O. Box 333
Springville, CA 93265
Phone: (866) 311-2626
www.tropicaltraditions.com
Email:
help@tropicaltraditions.com

SEA SALT, UNREFINED, MINERAL RICH

Diamond Organics
The Organic Food Catalog
P.O. Box 2159
Freedom, CA 95019
Phone: (888) ORGANIC or
(888) 674-2642
www.diamondorganics.com

Gold Mine Natural Foods
7805 Arjon's Drive
San Diego, CA 92126
Phone: (800) 475-FOOD or
(800) 475-3663
www.goldminenaturalfood.com

Natural Lifestyle Supplies
16 Lookout Drive
Asheville, NC 28804-3330
Phone: (800)-752-2775
www.natural-lifestyle.com
Email:
autumn@natural-lifestyle.com

**Real Salt
Redmond Trading Company, L.C.**
475 West 910 South
Heber City, Utah 84032
Phone: (800) 367-7258
www.realsalt.com
Email: mail@realsalt.com

The Grain and Salt Society
273 Fairway Drive
Asheville, NC 28805
Phone: (800)-TOP-SALT **or**
(800) 867-7258
www.celtic-seasalt.com

STEVIA EXTRACT POWDER & LIQUID

**NOW® Foods corporate office (GMP)
For store listing contact:**
395 Glen Ellyn Road
Bloomingdale, IL 60108
Phone: (888) 669-3663
www.nowfoods.com

To mail order contact:
Fruitful Yield (GMP)
154 South Bloomingdale Road
Bloomingdale, IL 60108
Phone: (800) 469-5552
www.fruitfulyield.com

Nu Naturals Inc.
2220 West 2nd Avenue #1
Eugene, OR 97402
Phone: (541) 344-9785 **or**
(800) 753-4372(HERB)
www.nunaturals.com

Wisdom Natural Herbs/Wisdom Natural Brands
2546 West Birchwood Avenue,
Suite #104
Mesa, AZ 85202
Phone: (800) 899-9908
www.wisdomnaturalbrands.com
Email:
info@wisdomnaturalbrands.com

Appendix B:
Recommending Reading

Cooking References

Baking 9-1-1: Rescue from Recipe Disasters; Answers to Your Most Frequently Asked Baking Questions; 40 Recipes for Every Baker by Sarah Phillips. New York: Fireside, 2003.

The Coconut Oil Miracle by Bruce Fife, C.N., N.D., Ph.D., New York: Avery Publishing, 2004.

Dangerous Grains: Why Gluten Cereal Grains May Be Hazardous to Your Health by James Braly, M.D., and Ron Hoggan, M.A. New York: Penguin Putman, 2002.

The Food Lover's Tiptionary: More Than 6,000 Food & Drink Tips, Secrets, Shortcuts, and Things Cookbooks Never Tell You by Sharon Tyler Herbst. New York: Harper Collins 2002.

In the Hands of a Chef: The Professional Chef's Guide to Essential Kitchen Tools by The Culinary Institute of America. New York: John Wiley & Sons, 2008.

The Gluten-Free Bible: The Thoroughly Indispensable Guide to Negotiating Life Without Wheat by Jax Peters Lowell. New York: Henry Holt & Company, 2005.

Gluten-Free Diet: A Comprehensive Resource Guide by Shelley Case. Canada: Case Nutrition Consulting, 2006.

Gluten-Free Girl: How I Found the Food That Loves Me Back...And How You Can Too by Shauna James Ahern. New York: J. Wiley & Sons, 2007.

What? No Wheat? A Lighthearted Primer to Living the Gluten-Free Wheat-Free Life by LynnRae Reis. Arizona: What No Wheat Publishing Company, 2003.

Wheat-Free, Worry Free: The Art of Happy, Healthy, Gluten-Free Living by Dana Korn. California: Hay House, Inc., 2002.

Cookbooks

A Passion for Ice Cream by Emily Luchetti. California: Chronicle Books, 2006.

The Best Ice Cream Maker Cookbook Ever by Peggy Fallon. New York: William Morrow Cookbooks, 1998

From Your Ice Cream Maker: Ice Creams, Frozen Yogurts, Sorbets, Sherbets, Shakes, Sodas by Coleen Simmons and Bob Simmons. California: Nitty Gritty Cookbook, 1994

The Healthy Oven Baking Book: Delicious Bake-from-Scratch Desserts with Less Fat and Lots of Flavor by Sarah Phillips. New York: Doubleday, 1999.

Perfect Scoop: Ice Creams, Sorbets, Granitas, and Sweet Accompaniments by David Lebovitz and Lara Hata. California: Ten Speed Press, 2007.

Sweet and Natural: More than 120 Sugar-Free and Dairy-Free Desserts by Meredith McCarty. New York: St. Martins Griffin, 1998.

The Ultimate Ice Cream Book: Over 500 Ice Creams, Sorbets, Granitas, Drinks, And More by Bruce Weinstein. New York: William Morrow Cookbooks, 1999.

Williams-Sonoma Collection: Ice Cream (Williams-Sonoma Collection) by Mary Goodbody and Chuck Williams. New York: Free Press, 2003.

Appendix C:
National Celiac Associations

The following associations and support groups provide information about the gluten-free diet. Many of these groups have local and regional support groups. Check their web sites for additional information.

American Celiac Society
P.O. Box 23455
New Orleans, LA 70183
Phone: (504) 737-3293
Email: info@americanceliacsociety.org
www.americanceliacsociety.org

Celiac Disease Foundation
13251 Ventura Blvd. Ste. 1
Studio City, CA 91604-1838
Phone: (818) 990-2354
Email: cdf@celiac.org
www.celiacdisease.org

Celiac Sprue Association (CSA/USA)
P.O. Box 31700
Omaha, NE 68131-0700
Phone: (877) CSA-4CSA or (402) 558-0600
Email: celiacs@csaceliacs.org
www.csaceliacs.org

Group: Gluten Intolerance Group
31214 124th Ave SE
Auburn, WA 98092-3667
Phone: (253) 833-6655
Email: info@gluten.net
www.gluten.net

ROCK (Raising Our Celiac Kids)
Phone: (858) 756-5313
Email: danna@celiackids.com
www.glutenfreedom.net
www.celiackids.com

Canadian Celiac Association
5170 Dixie Road, Suite 204
Mississauga, ON L4W 1ES
Phone: (800) 363-7296 or (905) 507-6208
www.celiac.ca

Appendix D:
Liquid/Dry Measure Equivalents

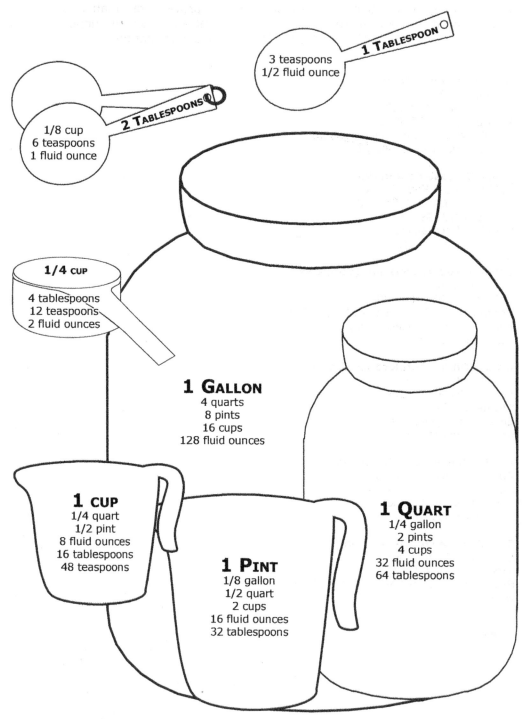

1 TABLESPOON
3 teaspoons
1/2 fluid ounce

2 TABLESPOONS
1/8 cup
6 teaspoons
1 fluid ounce

1/4 CUP
4 tablespoons
12 teaspoons
2 fluid ounces

1 GALLON
4 quarts
8 pints
16 cups
128 fluid ounces

1 CUP
1/4 quart
1/2 pint
8 fluid ounces
16 tablespoons
48 teaspoons

1 PINT
1/8 gallon
1/2 quart
2 cups
16 fluid ounces
32 tablespoons

1 QUART
1/4 gallon
2 pints
4 cups
32 fluid ounces
64 tablespoons

Index

About the Author

Rachel Albert-Matesz graduated from the University of Washington in Seattle in 1985 with a bachelor's degree in sociology and communications. She earned a certificate in macrobiotic studies from the Kushi Institute of Great Britain later the same year. From 1988 to 1989, she operated Rachel's Natural Foods Cafe in Seattle.

Rachel has been a natural foods chef, cooking instructor, freelance food and health writer, and cooking coach and speaker for more than 20 years. She has led more than 800 cooking classes in five states, and published more than 225 articles in national magazines and regional papers, including *Natural Home, Living Without, The Herb Companion, Herbs for Health, Yoga Journal, Let's Live, Oxygen Women's Fitness, Muscle & Fitness, Muscle & Fitness Hers, Conscious Choice, Well Being Journal, Veggie Life, Vegetarian Times, Vegetarian Journal,* and *Macrobiotics Today.* Her articles also appeared in *Fit, New Body,* and *Vegetarian Gourmet,* which are no longer in print.

Rachel's earlier works include *Gourmet Wholefoods, Cooking with Rachel,* and *The Nourishment for Life Cookbook.* Only *Cooking with Rachel* is still in print. Rachel developed 130 recipes for two books by best-selling author Barry Sears, including 90 recipes for *Zone Meals in Seconds* (Harper-Collins, 2004). She co-authored *The Garden of Eating: A Produce-Dominated Diet and Cookbook* (Planetary Press, 2004) with Don Matesz, which won the USA Book News Best Cookbook 2004, and a Glyph Award for Best Cookbook in May 2005.

Rachel lives in Phoenix, Arizona. She is a faculty member of the nutrition department at the Southwest Institute of Healing Arts in Tempe. She leads group and private cooking classes, cooking parties, dinner parties, and healthy shopping tours, coaches people in their kitchens, and speaks about healthy eating. She is the Healthy Chef for Channel 3, Your Life A to Z, in Phoenix.

Known for her passion and expertise, Rachel is dedicated to inspiring healthy choices and demonstrating that great taste and good nutrition go hand in hand. Her mission is to awaken your inner chef and to enhance your appreciation for the nourishing power of natural foods. If you don't like "healthy" foods, you haven't tried Rachel's recipes.

Quick Order Form

Please do not tear out this form. Xerox and use it or share it with a friend.

Telephone Orders: Planetary Press (602) 840-4556
Have your Visa, Mastercard, American Express, or Discover card ready.
Postal Orders: Checks payable to & send to Planetary Press, P.O. Box 97040, Phoenix, AZ 85060-7040
On-line orders: www.IceDreamCookbook.com **or** www.PlanetaryPress.net
Info about orders: Planetarypress@earthlink.net

Please send the following books. I understand that I may return any of them in their original condition for a full refund—for any reason— if I am not completely satisfied

Qty.	Title	Price U.S.	Price CN	Total
____	The Ice Dream Cookbook	$25.00	$25.00	____

Shipping within the U.S.
Add $5.50 *per book* for Media Mail/$7.50 for U.S. Priority — Shipping ____

Shipping to Canada:
Add $10 *per book* for Surface Rate/$20 for International Priority
All other international orders, e-mail: PlanetaryPress@Earthlink.net — Shipping ____

Quantity discounts available to qualified individuals and groups. Call Planetary Press for more information: (602) 840-4556.	Sales Tax, add 8.3% (AZ residents only) ____

TOTAL ENCLOSED ____

Please send me FREE information on the author's services:

- ❑ Cooking class & cooking parties
- ❑ One-on-one phone coaching
- ❑ Consulting
- ❑ Healthy shopping tours
- ❑ Speaking/seminars
- ❑ In-person kitchen coaching
- ❑ Corporate lunch & learn sessions
- ❑ Coporate team building

PLEASE PRINT

Name: _____

Address:_____ City_____

State_____ Zip_____ Telephone: (____)_____

Fax_____Email address: _____

Method of Payment

❑Check ❑Money Order ❑Credit Card: Visa, MasterCard, American Express, Discover

Card number_____ Expiration Date_____

Name on card_____ CV2 (3-digit code):_____

Signature_____

How or where did you hear about *The Ice Dream Cookbook?*_____

We appreciate your business and thank you for telling your friends about us.